Reviewers' Praise for
Why Americans Hate Politics

"Splendid and thoughtful . . . Dionne makes a closely reasoned argument that the majority of Americans are fed-up-to-here with politics because their politicians quit on them."

—George V. Higgins, *The Washington Post*

"[A] broad and detailed intellectual history of liberalism and conservatism since the 1960s . . . An incisive book . . . A very fine guide to how liberals and conservatives ended up so rudderless in a world without Ronald Reagan, the Cold War, and the New Deal."

—*The Wall Street Journal*

"A book destined to become a classic in American political history."

—Elaine Ciulla Kamarck, *Newsday*

"Dionne is seductive, and his intelligent and well-written book should be consulted. . . . Dionne has sharp insights, and every civic-minded person would be better off for heeding them."

—William F. Buckley, Jr., *The Houston Chronicle*

"Dionne has done a fine job describing the frustrations of the public and the paralysis of government in what he calls the politics of false choices."

—Ellen Goodman, *The Boston Globe*

"An astute, entertaining analysis of the reasons that contemporary political debates and divisions misrepresent American issues."

—*The New Yorker*

E. J. DIONNE, JR.

WHY AMERICANS HATE POLITICS

A TOUCHSTONE BOOK
Published by
Simon & Schuster
New York • London • Toronto
Sydney • Tokyo • Singapore

TOUCHSTONE

Rockefeller Center
1230 Avenue of the Americas
New York, New York 10020

14 15 16 17 18 19 20

Library of Congress Cataloging-in-Publication Data is
available

ISBN: 0-671-68255-5
ISBN: 0-671-77877-3 (pbk)

TO MY MOTHER AND FATHER,
WITH LOVE

"As long as people are people, democracy, in the full sense of the word, will always be no more than an ideal. One may approach it as one would the horizon in ways that may be better or worse, but it can never be fully attained. In this sense, you, too, are merely approaching democracy."

—VACLAV HAVEL
To the United States Congress

CONTENTS

INTRODUCTION

Living in the Past: How Liberals and Conservatives Are Failing America

AT THE VERY MOMENT when democracy is blossoming in Eastern Europe, it is decaying in the United States. Over the last three decades, the faith of the American people in their democratic institutions has declined, and Americans have begun to doubt their ability to improve the world through politics. After two centuries in which the United States stood proudly as an example of what an engaged citizenry could accomplish through public life, Americans view politics with boredom and detachment. For most of us, politics is increasingly abstract, a spectator sport barely worth watching. Election campaigns generate less excitement than ever and are dominated by television commercials, direct mail, polling, and other approaches that treat individual voters not as citizens deciding their nation's fate, but as mere collections of impulses to be stroked and soothed.

True, we still praise democracy incessantly and recommend democracy to the world. But at home, we do little to promote the virtues that self-government requires or to encourage citizens to believe that public engagement is worth the time. Our system has become one long-running advertisement against self-government. For many years, we have been running down the public sector and public life. Voters doubt that elections give them any real control over what the government does, and half of them don't bother to cast ballots.

Because of our flight from public life, our common citizenship no longer fosters a sense of community or common purpose. Social gaps, notably the divide between blacks and whites, grow wider. The very language and music heard in the inner city is increasingly estranged from the words and melodies of the affluent suburbs. We have less and less to do with each other, meaning that we feel few obligations to each other and are less and less inclined to vindicate each other's rights.

The abandonment of public life has created a political void that is increasingly filled by the politics of attack and by issues that seem unimportant or contrived. In 1988, George Bush made the pollution of Boston Harbor and the furloughing of a convicted murderer central issues in his campaign for the presidency. Neither Boston Harbor nor prison furloughs mattered once Bush took office. The issues that will matter most in the nineties—the challenges to America's standard of living from global competition, the dangers in the Middle East, the impending collapse of Communist power—were hardly discussed at all in 1988.

The 1988 campaign was just a sign of things to come. In the 1990s, politicians themselves seem as fed up with the process as even their angriest constituents. "We're getting better at symbolism," Sen. Pete Domenici, a New Mexico Republican, told *Washington Post* reporter Helen Dewar in late 1991. "You need more symbols when you don't have much substance." Sen. Joseph R. Biden, Jr., a Delaware Democrat, spoke with equal candor about the tyranny of symbolic politics. "You have to answer symbols," Biden said, "with symbols." Thus did politicians claim that a federal crime bill was battling street violence by subjecting murderers of federal egg inspectors, meat inspectors, and horse inspectors to the death penalty. Did the egg inspectors, let alone anyone else in the country, suddenly feel safer? The 1991 confrontation between Justice Clarence Thomas and Prof. Anita Hill transfixed the nation. It also left partisans on both sides of the battle lines furious and frustrated, and average citizens aghast.

We are even uncertain about the meaning of America's triumph in the Cold War. We worry that the end of the Cold War will mean a diminished role for the United States in world history. Economic power is passing not only to Japan but also to a new Europe, which is finally recovering from the self-inflicted wounds of two world wars. The categories that have dominated our thinking for so long are utterly irrelevant to the new world we face. The international alliance that President Bush assembled against Iraq would have been inconceivable just two years earlier. Indeed, the very weapons we used against Saddam's forces were built for a different conflict in a different place against a different enemy—a conflict we happily avoided. And much of the debate over Iraq was shaped by the Vietnam conflict, as if the use of American force always means the same thing in every part of the world and against every adversary.

Most of the problems of our political life can be traced to the failure of the dominant ideologies of American politics, liberalism and conservatism. The central argument of this book is that liberalism and conservatism are framing political issues as a series of false choices. Wracked by contradiction and responsive mainly to the needs of their various constituencies, liberalism and conservatism prevent the nation from settling the questions that most trouble it. On issue after issue, there is consensus on where the country should move or at least on what we should be arguing about; liberalism and conservatism make it impossible for that consensus to express itself.

To blame our problems on the failure of "ideologies" would seem a convenient way to avoid attaching responsibility to individuals. But to hold ideologies responsible for our troubles is, in fact, to place a burden on those who live by them and formulate them. It is also a way of saying that ideas matter, and that ideas, badly formulated, interpreted, and used, can lead us astray. We are suffering from a false polarization in our politics, in which liberals and conservatives keep arguing about the same things when the country wants to move on.

The cause of this false polarization is the cultural civil war that broke out in the 1960s. Just as the Civil War dominated American political life for decades after it ended, so is the cultural civil war of the 1960s, with all its tensions and contradictions, shaping our politics today. We are still trapped in the 1960s.

The country still faces three major sets of questions left over from the old cultural battles: Civil rights and the full integration of blacks into the country's political and economic life; the revolution in values involving feminism and changed attitudes toward child-rearing and sexuality; and the ongoing debate over the meaning of the Vietnam War, which is less a fight over whether it was right to do battle in that Southeast Asian country than an argument over how Americans see their nation, its leaders, and its role in the world.

It is easy to understand why conservatives would like the cultural civil war to continue. It was the *Kulturkampf* of the 1960s that made them so powerful in our political life. Conservatives were able to destroy the dominant New Deal coalition by using cultural and social issues—race, the family, "permissiveness," crime—to split New Deal constituencies. The cultural issues, especially race, allowed the conservatives who took control of the Republican Party to win over what had been the most loyally Democratic group in the nation, white Southerners, and to peel off millions of votes among industrial workers and other whites of modest incomes.

The new conservative majority that has dominated presidential politics since 1968 is inherently unstable, since it unites upper-income groups whose main interest is in smaller government and lower taxes, and middle-to-lower-income groups, who are culturally conservative but still support most of the New Deal and a lot of the Great Society. The lower-income wing of the conservative coalition has tended to vote Republican for President, to express its cultural values, but Democratic for Congress, to protect its economic interests. Conservative politicians are uneasy about settling the cultural civil war because they fear that doing so would push their newfound supporters among the less well-to-do back toward the Democrats in presidential contests.

The broad political interests of liberals lie in settling the cultural civil war, but many liberals have an interest in seeing it continue. The politics of the 1960s shifted the balance of power within the liberal coalition away from working-class and lower-middle-class voters, whose main concerns were economic, and toward upper-middle-class reformers mainly interested in cultural issues and foreign policy. Increasingly, liberalism is defined not by its support for energetic government intervention in the economy, but by its openness to cultural change and its opposition to American intervention abroad. The rise of the cultural issues made the upper-middle-class reformers the dominant voices within American liberalism. The reformers, no less than the conservatives, have a continuing interest in seeing the cultural civil war continue.

Indeed, what is striking about political events of the 1960s is that they allowed both of the nation's dominant ideologies, and both parties, to become vehicles for upper-middle-class interests. Both the Goldwater campaign and the antiwar forces associated with George McGovern's candidacy were movements of the upper middle class imbued with a moral (or in the eyes of their critics, moralistic) vision. These constituencies were *not* primarily concerned with the political issues that matter to less well-to-do voters—notably the performance of the nation's economy, the distribution of economic benefits, the availability of health care, and the efficacy of the most basic institutions of government, including schools, roads, and the criminal justice system. While upper-middle-class reformers, left and right, argued about morality, anticommunism, imperialism, and abstract rights, a large chunk of the electorate was confined to the sidelines, wondering why the nation's political discussion had become so distant from their concerns. And as the 1980s became the 1990s, many who had become accustomed to middle-class living standards suddenly found their own well-being threatened and worried about how their children would manage to make their way in an increasingly competitive world economy.

By continuing to live in the 1960s, conservatives and liberals have distorted their own doctrines and refused to face up to the contradictions within their creeds. Both sides constantly invoke individual "rights," then criticize each other for evading issues involving individual and collective responsibility. Each side claims to have a communitarian vision but backs away from community whenever its demands come into conflict with one of its cherished doctrines.

Conservatives claim to be the true communitarians because of their support for the values of "family, work, and neighborhood." Unlike liberals, conservatives are willing to assert that "community norms" should prevail on such matters as sex, pornography, and the education of children. Yet the typical conservative is unwilling to defend the interests of traditional community whenever its needs come into conflict with those of the free market. If shutting down a plant throws thousands in a particular community out of work, conservatives usually defend this assault on "family, work, and neighborhood" in the name of efficiency. Many of the things conservatives bemoan about modern society—a preference for short-term gratification over long-term commitment, the love of things instead of values, a flight from responsibility toward selfishness—result at least in part from the workings of the very economic system that conservatives feel so bound to defend. For conservatives, it is much easier to ignore this dilemma and blame "permissiveness" on "big government" or "the liberals."

The liberals often make that easy. Liberals tout themselves as the real defenders of community. They speak constantly about having us share each other's burdens. Yet when the talk moves from economic issues to culture or personal morality, liberals fall strangely mute.

Liberals are uncomfortable with the idea that a virtuous community depends on virtuous individuals. Liberals defend the welfare state, but are uneasy when asked what moral values the welfare state should promote—as if billions of federal dollars can be spent in a "value-free" way. Liberals rightly defend the interests of children who are born into poverty through no choice of their own. Yet when conservatives suggest that society has a vital interest in how the parents of these poor children behave, many liberals accuse the conservatives of "blaming the victim." When conservatives suggest that changing teenage attitudes toward premarital sex might reduce teen pregnancy, many liberals end the conversation by accusing the conservatives of being "prudes" or "out of touch."

Not all conservatives and liberals fall into the neat categories I have just described, and the questions each side raises about the other's proposals are often legitimate. It often *is* more efficient and socially beneficial to shut down a loss-making plant. It *is* unfair to condemn the poor for sexual practices that we celebrate when those engaging in them live in Hollywood or make millions in business.

Still, the way in which liberals and conservatives approach the problem of community is a good example of what I mean by false choices. In truth, America's cultural values are a rich and not necessarily contradictory mix of liberal instincts and conservative values. Polls (and our own intuitions) suggest that Americans believe in helping those who fall on hard times, in fostering equal opportunity and equal rights, in providing broad access to education, housing, health care, and child care. Polls (and our intuitions) also suggest that Americans believe that intact families do the best job at bringing up children, that hard work should be rewarded, that people who behave destructively toward others should be punished, that small institutions close to home tend to do better than big institutions run from far away, that private moral choices usually have social consequences. Put another way, Americans believe in social concern and self-reliance; they want to match rights and responsibilities; they think public moral standards should exist but are skeptical of too much meddling in the private affairs of others.

One fair reaction to the above is to call it a catalogue of the obvious. But that is precisely the point: The false choices posed by liberalism and conservatism make it extremely difficult for the perfectly obvious preferences of the American people to express themselves in our politics. We are encouraging an "either/or" politics based on ideological preconceptions rather than a "both/and" politics based on ideas that broadly unite us.

To be sure, free elections in a two-party system inevitably encourage polarization; voters who like some things about liberals or Democrats and some things about conservatives or Republicans end up having to choose one package or the other. In free elections, each side will always try to polarize the electorate in a way that will leave a majority standing on its side. But if free elections leave so many in the electorate dissatisfied with where they have to stand, and push large numbers out of the electorate entirely, then it is fair to conclude that the political process is badly defective.

Moreover, after the election is over, parties have to govern. But putting such a premium on false choices and artificial polarization, our electoral process is making it harder and harder for electoral winners to produce what they were elected for: good government. The false polarization that may be inevitable at election time is carrying over into the policy debates that take place afterward. Political "positioning" may be necessary in an electoral campaign; when it becomes part of the intellectual debate, the talk becomes dishonest. Our intellectual life, which is supposed to clear matters up, produces only more false choices.

In recent years, much has been written about the rise of "negative campaigning" and of the "killer" television spots that instantly bury a political candidate's chances. Much has also been said about the rise of the "character issue" and the seemingly incessant interest of the press in the private lives of politicians. A candidate's sex life or his draft record dominate the public discussion. What were once called "issues" are cast to one side. Taken together, these developments suggest that politics is destined to become ever more seamy. Democracy takes on all the dignity of mud-wrestling. When American political consultants descended upon Eastern Europe to help "guide" newcomers to democracy in the ways of modern politics, there was much alarm. Why should newly founded democracies be "guided" toward the dismal stuff that we Americans call politics?

In explaining these sorry developments, we have tended, I believe, to focus too narrowly on the political *process* and not enough on the *content* of politics.

The focus on process is perfectly sensible as far as it goes. By allowing the paid, thirty-second television spot to become our dominant means of political communication, we have shaped our political life in certain directions. In a thirty-second spot, candidates and parties can only give impressions, appeal to feelings, arouse emotions. Wedged in the midst of ads for all manner of products, the political spot needs to grab its audience. This tends to rule out even thirty seconds of sober discussion of the issues. Sobriety rarely grabs anyone. Most democracies offer political parties and candidates significant blocks of time in which they can tell their stories. And most provide the time free. The fact that our spots must be paid for raises the cost of American campaigns far above the levels in most other democracies. Raising the cost of campaigns has heightened the importance of fund-raising. This forces politicians to spend an untoward amount of time raising money. It also gives lobbyists and political action committees undo influence on our politics and gives average voters much less. The strong and the wealthy tend to have the most money to give away.

Reformers have many good ideas on how the system can be improved. Allocating free or cheap television time to candidates and parties would help. Offering the time in blocks larger than thirty seconds would help, too. There is no shortage of ideas on how to reduce the influence of money on politics, including a variety of limitations on the size and kind of contributions that can be made, and various schemes for total or partial public financing of campaigns. All these things would improve our politics.

But they would not, finally, cure our underlying political problems. The real problem is not the spots themselves but what is said in them. Why is it that they focus so insistently on either character assassination or divisive social issues that leave the electorate so angry and dissatisfied? This is not a technical question, but a political issue. Once upon a time, most of the thirty-second spots that ran on television were *positive*. They sought to mobilize voters behind causes and candidates they could believe in, not in opposition to ideas and constituencies they loathed. The content of political advertising suggested that, on balance, politicians were more concerned with getting things done then with foiling the nasty designs of others.

At its best, democratic politics is about what Arthur Schlesinger, Jr., calls "the search for remedy." The purpose of democratic politics is to solve problems and resolve disputes. But since the 1960s, the key to winning elections has been to reopen the same divisive issues over and over again. The issues themselves are not reargued. No new light is shed. Rather, old resentments and angers are stirred up in an effort to get voters to cast yet one more ballot of angry protest. Political consultants have been truly ingenious in figuring out endless creative ways of tapping into popular anger about crime. Yet their spots do not solve the problem. Endless arguments about whether the death penalty is a good idea do not put more cops on the street, streamline the criminal justice system, or resolve some of the underlying causes of violence.

The decline of a "politics of remedy" creates a vicious cycle. Campaigns have become negative in large part because of a sharp decline in popular faith in government. To appeal to an increasingly alienated electorate, candidates and their political consultants have adopted a cynical stance that, they believe with good reason, plays into popular cynicism about politics and thus wins them votes. But cynical campaigns do not resolve issues. They do not lead to "remedies." Therefore, problems get worse, the electorate becomes more cynical—and so does the advertising. At the end of it all, the governing process, which is supposed to be about real things, becomes little more than a war over symbols.

Politicians engage in symbolic rather than substantive politics for another reason: Liberals and conservatives alike are uncertain about what remedies they can offer without blowing their constituencies apart. The two broad coalitions in American political life—liberal and Democratic, conservative and Republican—have become so unstable that neither side can afford to risk very much. That is because the ties that bind Americans to each other, to their communities, and thus to their political parties have grown ever weaker.

The party system of the New Deal era was relatively stable because definable groups voted together and largely held together, even in bad times. Now, almost everything else conspires against group solidarity. Unions are in trouble—and conservatives have done everything they could to weaken them. The new jobs in the service industries promote individualism. The decline of the small town and the old urban ethnic enclaves and the rise of new suburbs, exurbs, and condominium developments further weakens social solidarity. Old urban neighborhoods feel abandoned by the liberal politicians whom they once counted on for support.

In the new politics, each voter is studied and appealed to as an *individual*. This is both the cause and effect of the rise of polling and television advertising. It also explains the increasing harshness of political attack and counterattack. In the old politics, voters felt real loyalties, which could be appealed to in a positive way. Political loyalties were reinforced by other forms of group solidarity. Now, insofar as voters identify with groups, it is often with abstract national groups rather than concrete local ones. An Italian machinist in a Detroit suburb may identify himself more with his fellow gun owners than with his ethnic group, his neighborhood, or his fellow workers. Since he believes that politics will do little to improve his life or that of his community, he votes defensively. If the government won't do anything *for* him, he damn well won't let it do anything *against* him, such as tax him more heavily or take away his gun. It is not an irrational response, given the current state of our politics.

It does no good to yearn for an America that no longer exists, especially since pluralism and geographical and social mobility have created much that we love about the United States. But if our politics is to get better, it is crucial that we recognize that the fragmentation of American society has made our public life much more difficult. We need to find ways to tie citizens back into public life, not to turn them off even more. Above all, we need to end the phony polarization around the issues of the 1960s that serves only to carry us ever further from a deliberative, democratic public life.

II

To argue that the polarization around the issues of the 1960s is irrelevant to most Americans is to defy many of our political assumptions. Is not race a real and central issue in American life? Why did Willie Horton play such an important role in the 1988 campaign and how can a David Duke haunt the nation? If we are approaching a consensus on moral issues, why does the abortion issue seem to divide us into such passionate factions? Before taking on these questions directly, it is worth examining briefly how much we already hold in common on "the sixties issues" of gender, race, and Vietnam.

Overwhelmingly, the country accepts the entry of women into the work force. The vast majority of Americans see their presence as, at least, an economic necessity and at best, a positive good. Americans know that for all the conservatives' talk about the "traditional" family, the world of the 1950s is gone forever. Trying to re-create it would be counterproductive. Indeed, as I shall be arguing later, the new array of attitudes toward women's rights and roles did not develop, out of nowhere, in the 1960s. The country has been debating the issues at stake since before the turn of the century. The new consensus is thus not the product of some sixties fad, but of a long, considered argument.

Yet if Americans, on balance, agree with liberals that women are in the work force to stay, they agree with conservatives that not all the effects of this revolution are positive. They worry especially about what will happen to children in the new world we have created. They are concerned that in women's rush to the work force, the children are being left behind, since men do not seem eager to take up the slack. The debate the country wants to hear is not one involving false choices between an ideal "feminism" and an idealized "traditional family." The problem with such labels and the false polarization they promote is easily illustrated by example: Women who take time off from their careers to care for young children are routinely "punished" by having their opportunities for promotion reduced. Is it "feminist" or is it "profamily" to suggest that this practice is unfair? Is it "feminist" or "profamily" to contend that this practice shows how little value society really places on the work that parents do? Most Americans wouldn't care much about whether one label or the other was used. What they do care about is figuring out how to make the new balance of work and family work.

Abortion is a more morally complex and personally wrenching issue. It is a difficult issue to straddle or compromise. Yet the evidence from polls is that even on this question, Americans resist yes/no answers. The polls show that Americans overwhelmingly believe that abortion should be available in the "hard" cases, involving rape, incest, or when a mother's life is in danger. The polls show that Americans are uneasy with government restrictions on abortion in other cases, too, believing it is a "private" matter. Yet the same surveys show that Americans are uncomfortable with how many abortions are being performed and feel that women often resort to abortion in circumstances where they should avoid it. Americans oppose outright bans on abortion but favor a series of restrictions, including requirements that minor girls get the permission of their parents before getting abortions. Such a nuanced view has few champions, and it is almost inevitable that the public debate over abortion will be dominated by those who feel most strongly on either side of the question. Yet the public's ambivalence suggests how deep is its thirst for compromise on the issues raised by the cultural civil war that began in the 1960s.

In dealing with America's racial dilemma, the public, black and white, accepts that the last thirty years are not all good news or bad news but a mixture of both. The civil rights revolution was, first, a revolution in *attitudes*, and this revolution was largely successful. Racist views that were routinely expressed by white Americans and their leaders just three decades ago are now beyond the pale. By overwhelming margins, whites support integrated neighborhoods and integrated schools and oppose racial discrimination in jobs, housing, or public accommodations. Even David Duke, a former Nazi and Ku

Klux Klan leader, had to recast his rhetoric and speak piously about "equal rights." This change is too easily dismissed as mere politeness, the result of whites saying certain things simply because they believe the polltakers want to hear them. Over time, when people stop saying things publicly, they stop *believing* them privately. And when they stop believing them, they will, over time, stop *acting* on them.

Tearing down the barriers of segregation has had a series of highly positive results. A substantial share of the black community has seen its incomes and its opportunities grow. The black middle class, which was once hemmed in by racial prejudice, now enjoys something approaching equality with whites. In black families headed by a married couple, 89 percent are above the poverty line. That is still below the 95 percent rate among comparable white couples, but the gap has been closing. In families where both husbands and wives work, black and white incomes are virtually equal.

But this relatively good news is counterbalanced by a great deal of bad news. Overall, the black median family income is roughly 55 percent of white family income. Nearly a third of all blacks, as against only 10 percent of whites, live below the poverty line. Among black children, 45 percent live in poverty, as against only 15 percent of white children. These grim figures are closely related to another statistic: Half of all black children, as against only 16 percent of white children, live in families where the father is not present. Perhaps the grimmest statistic of all is this one: Black men account for 3.5 percent of America's college students but for 40 percent of its prison inmates.

These figures anger blacks and scare whites. Willie Horton's image as a rapist and convicted murderer on the loose played into the deepest white fears about young black men. No doubt the white reaction to Willie Horton is based in part on deeply ingrained racial stereotypes. But it also reflects fears based in the reality of crime in the nation's ghettos and on statistics like the ones just presented. Willie Horton is a figure who strikes terror in the hearts of many blacks, too, since blacks are more likely than whites to be the victims of violent crime—and young black men are the most likely victims of all.

The tragedy of our politics is that the concerns aroused by a Willie Horton are divisive rather than unifying. Blacks and whites agree that the condition of the black poor is a national crisis that needs attention. They agree that the public schools, which in the big cities are increasingly black schools, need to be improved. They agree that life in black neighborhoods needs to be enhanced, in particular by cutting the crime rate. They agree that young blacks should have better job opportunities and job training. They agree that teen pregnancy needs to be reduced. Blacks and whites also agree that the problems require spending money.

But blacks and whites also know that money alone will not suffice. They agree that the problems of the poorest people in urban areas have to do not just with economics, but also with a moral crisis. They agree that whatever money is spent should be directed not only at improving opportunities but at changing values. Fathers need to be required to care for their children, and where feasible, work should be required from those who receive social benefits. Young women need to be encouraged to avoid pregnancy and stay in school, and criminal behavior needs to be sanctioned severely. Both blacks and whites agree that the broader society, has an obligation to lift up those trapped in poverty; both blacks and whites agree that the poor have obligations to society, and to themselves.

It is a sign of how our political culture encourages us to run away from solutions that talk of "spending more money" and "improving values" almost instantly invites disapproval from partisans on one side of the debate or the other. Our national discussion of race is so polarized that we do nothing at all—and thus our problems get worse and many among the poor sink further into hopelessness. We are in desperate need of a new politics that will create alliances across racial lines that will allow us to act.

Among other things, we need to reassert that our goal as a nation is the *integration* of the races. This does *not* mean denying the distinct riches of black, Native American, Asian, or Hispanic cultures. It is not a quest for artificial homogeneity. It *does* mean asserting that Americans, black and white, Hispanic and Asian, in fact share goals and values and are willing to work together to promote them. Separatism, with its implication that "white values" and "black values" are fundamentally different, has proven an abysmal failure.

As for the foreign policy debates fostered by the Vietnam War, events have at last forced us to engage in some new thinking. They have also showed us how flawed our old thinking was.

On the one side, liberals would never have believed that at the end of Ronald Reagan's defense buildup, the Cold War would end. Liberals and conservatives can debate how much Reagan's policies had to do with what happened and how much of the change was "inevitable," given the Soviet Union's internal difficulties. What is clear is that in 1980, few people thought that what has happened in Eastern Europe was at all "inevitable."

Here, conservatives, no less than liberals, proved themselves to be poor prophets. In the late 1980s, many conservatives were convinced that the world would succumb to "the totalitarian temptation." They saw the victory of freedom not as inevitable, but as highly problematic. Most conservatives believed that internal transformations within the Communist block were impossible. "Totalitarian" governments controlled by Communists could never change their stripes.

But they did. First, Soviet hegemony over Eastern Europe collapsed, and then the Soviet Union itself died. As a result, the central worries of the United States about the world changed abruptly. Suddenly, Germany and Japan loomed as much larger competitors—not, this time, as militaristic powers, but as economic giants. The Persian Gulf War demonstrated that military power remained important in the calculus of world influence. But the war did not change the economic fundamentals: The budget deficit, the trade deficit, the troubles facing so many sectors of the economy, notably the banking and finance sectors. Americans welcome the United States' military strength, but they do not see it as a substitute for prosperity. Few expected the phrase American know-how to be confined to the workings of brilliantly designed missile systems. The challenge of the 1990s remains how to extend the country's obvious inventiveness to broader sectors of the economy.

In this new atmosphere, talk about the past needs to give way to talk about the future. Arguments about the morality or immorality of our Vietnam policy have little to do with the most important of the new problems that face us. In foreign policy, more than in any other area, we truly must call a halt to the 1960s political civil war, since its categories are almost entirely irrelevant to the nation's current interests.

The debate over the Persian Gulf War offered some promising signs. The weekend before the war began offered Americans something they hadn't seen in some time: The Congress of the United States debated the issues at stake with seriousness, conviction, and moments of eloquence. America's politicians demonstrated that they were, indeed, capable of coming to grips with each other's arguments. It was possible to debate an issue without name-calling, without questioning the motives of an adversary, and without hopelessly dividing the country. It was even possible to agree on a fundamental issue—in this case, the need to reverse Saddam Hussein's aggression and contain his power—and then to argue thoughtfully over the best means to reaching the shared end.

Saddam Hussein was no Daniel Ortega or Ho Chi Minh: He won almost no defenders on American shores, even among most on the far left who deplored any American role in the Gulf. The old ideological divides showed signs of breaking up. Initially, the strongest criticisms of the president's approach came from a small but resurgent isolationalist right led by conservative columnist Patrick J. Buchanan; though ultimately, most of the opposition came from the left and liberals, many of whom continued to invoke the specter of Vietnam.

Yet the Gulf War ended up meaning far less for the future of American politics than either Bush or the war's most fervent supporters had hoped. The war certainly proved America's military mastery. It may, as Bush claimed, have at least partially broken "the Vietnam syndrome" by showing that American power could be used successfully on a large scale. Still, a war so short and so free of American casualties proved little about the will or desire of Americans to bear large military burdens abroad.

Morever, the collapse of Bush's popularity within nine months of the war's end over the state of the economy made clear that the roots of America's discontent are planted firmly in domestic soil. Ultimately, the debate Americans were seeking in the 1992 campaign and beyond was over maintaining the nation's standard of living, reducing the economic pressures on the nation's middle class, and restoring hope to the poor.

III

This book, an interpretative history of thirty years of political ideas, is an attempt to trace how we got here and why liberalism and conservatism have become obstacles to a healthy political life. The book is divided into three parts. The first part examines how liberalism got into trouble. The second part analyzes the growing problems facing conservatism. The third suggests ways of thinking about politics that might help us surmount our current difficulties.

The sections on liberalism and conservatism are not a matched pair, and this is by design. We already have many good books analyzing liberalism's difficulties, and I do not offer yet another detailed recounting of how liberalism went off track. Rather, the section on liberalism tries to bring its troubles into focus by examining the two great intellectual challenges liberalism confronted in the 1960s and 1970s—from the New Left and from neoconservatism—and what I believe are two of the most important issues that divided liberalism after 1960, race and the array of moral and cultural issues around feminism and the family.

The New Left played an immensely important and, I believe,

widely underestimated role in shaping and transforming both liberalism and our political culture. The New Left, it should be recalled, arose in reaction not to conservatism but to liberalism—what it called "establishment liberalism." The New Left did not direct its anger at conservatism, because it did not take conservatism seriously. I argue that in its earliest days, the New Left offered a well-grounded critique of the inadequacies of American democracy and a noble, if incomplete, program to expand democratic participation. But in later years, the New Left became antidemocratic and highly destructive. It polarized American life around false issues and false choices. In ways it did not intend, the New Left also played a decisive role in undermining liberalism's influence on American life.

The power of the neoconservative challenge to liberalism is widely accepted. The neoconservatives fundamentally changed the tenor of our intellectual discussions. My assessment of the impact of the neoconservatives, like my view of the New Left, is mixed. I believe in their earliest incarnation, in the mid-1960s, the neoconservatives offered an immensely valuable critique of liberal shortcomings. They were largely right to warn us of the dangers of ideology and to urge us to be concerned with whether government programs were promoting socially beneficial virtues in the citizenry. But neoconservatism went off track in response to the polarization bred by the late 1960s. In many cases, the opponents of ideology became ideologues themselves. In the end, neoconservatives, who had once believed deeply in the public sector, fueled a wholesale revolt against it.

I then turn to the issues of race and the family to show how antidemocratic impulses among upper-middle-class liberals greatly impaired their generally desirable efforts at social reform. In the case of both race and feminism, liberals—in ways that I believe were unnecessary—undermined the very political coalitions that were necessary to the quest for greater equality.

The final chapter of the first section is an examination of this electoral unraveling of liberalism. I pay particular attention to Jimmy Carter's term of office and to what I believe were the tragic misunderstandings between Carter and the liberals. I argue that they very much needed each other, and in the end destroyed each other.

If the section on liberalism highlights a particular set of issues, the section on conservatism gives a more detailed treatment of the rise of the right after World War II. One of my purposes is to suggest that the intellectual sources of postwar conservatism are far richer and much more complex than is usually allowed.

Much of the discussion of contemporary conservatism wrongly suggests that it became intellectually serious only in the 1970s, when liberalism supposedly "ran out of ideas." In fact, most of the conservative intellectual work of the 1970s had its roots in the period immediately after World War II, when an able (if at the time, marginal) group of right-wing thinkers began the task of rescuing the conservative creed from its collapse during the New Deal and World War II. What changed in the 1970s is not that conservatives suddenly started thinking great thoughts, but that liberals were finally forced to pay attention to what conservatives were thinking.

By going back to the origins of the postwar conservative revolt against liberalism, I try to show how deeply rooted are the divisions within conservatism. The battles between the "traditionalists" and the "libertarians" that began to plague conservatism in the late 1980s go back to the immediate postwar period. I pay particular attention to the role of William F. Buckley, Jr., and his allies around *National Review* magazine because I believe that conservatism's first political breakthrough was actually an intellectual breakthrough: The success of Buckley and his colleagues in brokering a theoretical compromise between conservatives who revered tradition and religion, and those who valued free market economics above everything else. Appropriately labeled "fusionism," the compromise was rickety, and conservatives are now suffering from its internal inconsistencies. But the new doctrine was strong enough to rout the only alternative "conservatism" that America had, the "Modern Republicanism" associated with Dwight D. Eisenhower. I argue that one of the paradoxes of American politics is that conservatives were helped, not hurt, by Watergate and Richard Nixon's fall precisely because Nixon was the only politician in America who might have made Modern Republicanism work. By routing Modern Republicanism, the conservatives associated with Barry Goldwater's 1964 campaign captured the Republican Party for an upper-middle-class conservatism that, in its political base if not in its content, rather closely resembled "McGovernism."

Conservatism is now being hurt by the paradoxes associated with success. As long as it was a minority opposition movement, conservatism found it easy to hold itself together around *National Review*'s fusionist doctrine, which became conservatism's "vital center." But with the rise of Ronald Reagan, conservatism's two wings, libertarian and traditionalist, became increasingly powerful, challenging both fusionism and each other. I highlight the growing strength of three distinct movements within the right, the religious right, supply-side economics, and libertarianism, each of which brought doctrines long regarded as marginal to American life back to a central position in our public debate. The rise of conservative religiosity came as a particular surprise to a country that had long seen "progress," urbanization, and secularization as the trinity representing the wave of the future. Yet like so many other aspects of modern conservatism, conservative religion had been thriving for a long time. What changed in the 1970s and 1980s is that the interpreters of the culture were forced to notice it.

The widening splits within conservatism and the growing power of its two wings account for the conservatives' difficulties in coming up with a coherent program of government. As a result, conservatives have a powerful interest in fueling the fires of division around the social issues, notably race, the family, and crime. Conservatives need a politics of false choices. As long as conservatives can continue to run against the discredited liberalism of the past, they will not have to provide a road map for the future. Conservatism badly needs the failed old liberalism; without such an enemy, conservatism could fall apart.

This conservative malaise explains why George Bush ran such a persistently negative campaign in 1988. In the absence of a vision of the future, Bush ran against the past. He re-created, once more with feeling, the cultural civil war. It was Michael Dukakis's tactical failure that he allowed George Bush to wage such a campaign. But it is liberalism's more fundamental problems that permitted such a campaign to be so successful.

Bush's presidency grew out of his campaign and also reflected the limits of the conservative vision. The persistent criticism that Bush lacked a domestic policy owed in part to the president's lack of interest in the subject. But it also resulted from the increasing instability of the conservative coalition and its lack of a coherent program. Tax-cutting reached its limits and progressive taxation began winning new friends in the middle class. Communism was defeated. Racially linked appeals were compromised by David Duke. Social issues such as abortion began to work at least as much in favor of liberals as of the right. When the economy turned down, Americans, despite their mistrust of "big government," again looked to government for help. Even conservatives sensed that their revolution was over. And when Patrick J. Buchanan, the conservative columnist, decided to challenge President Bush's 1992 renomination, it was a further sign that the end of the Soviet Union was destined to cause yet more fissures within the right.

While I have attempted throughout this book to demonstrate my great respect for postwar conservatism's intellectual achievements, it is my view that conservatism has reached a stage of intellectual and political exhaustion. What is required to end the popular hatred of politics, I believe, is the creation of a new political center.

What I have in mind is not a bland centrism, but a coalition for progressive social reform that could command broad support among the poor and the middle class. Lasting reform in a democratic society cannot take place in the absence of a broadly based consensus, and the new political center I have in mind is a descendant of the popular politics that helped create the Progressive Era, the New Deal, and the Fair Deal. Such a center would be willing to admit past failures and understand that in their respective critiques of American life over the last thirty years, neither liberals nor conservatives hold the monopoly on wisdom. The new center I have in mind would prefer problem-solving to symbolism. It would rather govern than polarize the country around contrived themes and empty slogans. It would take the economic challenges the United States faces entering the twenty-first century as seriously as the country took the challenge of totalitarianism in the twentieth century.

Some conservatives associated with Jack Kemp's ideas on poverty and with the young White House aides pushing for what they call a "new paradigm" in social policy understand the need for new departures. They clearly have a role to play in creating a new politics. Such conservatives are willing to acknowledge a role for government. They see their own nonbureaucratic and market-oriented approaches to public policy as speaking to the public's obvious anger and impatience with the way government has done business in the past. These conservatives want to promote racial harmony rather than aggravate racial feelings, and they see the benefits of the social tolerance created by the 1960s.

One can only wish this new conservatism well. Indeed, some of its best ideas have already influenced many liberals and Democrats. At a conference on convergences between left and right held in Washington in late 1991, Sen. Joseph Lieberman, a Connecticut Democrat, offered the delightful thought that "sometimes, strange bedfellows fall in love."

Nonetheless, it is my view that if a new center is created, it will be created by liberals. Liberals are in a better position to make peace with the 1960s. Liberals are not tied to the highly ideological approach to regulation, taxation, government spending, and income distribution that characterizes so much of contemporary conservatism. Liberals do not claim to believe, as so many conservatives do, that politics, public life, and government ought to arouse more suspicion than hope.

To create this center and deserve a chance at governing the nation, liberalism must rediscover its commitment to the interests and values of the broad middle class and recall its oldest principle: That while government cannot replace the market, its obligation is to bring equity to market outcomes, which are often unfair. Paradoxically, such a liberalism will be born only if liberals are also willing to profit from the many lessons that conservatism has to teach about the value of tradition, virtue, and community.

My hope is that this book will contribute to convincing liberals that they can learn from conservatives without abandoning their most important principles. And with luck, I hope I can also encourage more conservatives to accept that not all of the changes wrought in the 1960s were decadent or dangerous. For if liberals and conservatives spend all of their time refighting the meaning of the liberal 1960s and conservative 1980s, we will waste the 1990s. And Americans will continue to hate politics.]

PART ONE

The Failures of Liberalism

1

FREEDOM NOW:

The New Left
and the
Assault on Liberalism

T HE NEW LEFT and the counterculture prepared
the way for Ronald Reagan. They did so not only because they created
a backlash against "permissiveness," but also because they embodied
some of the very ideas that came to be represented by the right. In
their 1971 protest song against the late Mayor Richard J. Daley,
Crosby, Stills, Nash and Young declared: "Rules and regulations, who
needs them?" Thus spoke these unlikely prophets of the Reagan Revolution. The New Left saw its enemy as "corporate liberalism" and it
routed that enemy. But the results were not quite what the New Left
had expected—or hoped for.

Discussions of the sixties often get mired in nostalgia and confusion. The confusion is endemic because "the sixties" represent so
many things to so many people. Too many ideas get lumped together,
arbitrarily, under the headline "The New Left," and the New Left is
often confused with the counterculture. The reality is that there were,
in the New Left's own phrase, "one, two, many" New Lefts, and just
as many strains within the counterculture.

The era is also subjected to much parody, in part because different political tendencies see much they can use from the sixties. The left often seeks advantage by contrasting a heroic and generous spirit ascribed to that time with a "culture of selfishness" that is said to have taken root afterward. The right often casts the sixties as a time of disorder, degeneracy, and cultural collapse, contrasting that period with a healthier era of work and "entrepreneurship" that followed. Both parodies are revealing for what they tell us about the current state of American politics.

In the heroic account, the young radicals are pictured as people who took the liberal creed at its word and found the injustices of modern America, notably racial discrimination, intolerable. Freed by prosperity to contemplate life more thoughtfully than their economically pressed parents, these young rebels sought to throw off personal constraints having to do with monogamy, gender roles, and prejudice. Unconstrained by reflexive anticommunism, they saw what others refused to see: that American power in the world could as easily be put to bad use as good, and often was. Inspired by a democratic spirit redolent with the poetry of Walt Whitman and the thought of Emerson, the young left sought a more perfect democracy, "participatory democracy," in which "individuals would control the decisions that affected their own lives."

In the less heroic account, the young rebels are portrayed as spoiled children, the sorry products of Dr. Spock's theories of childrearing. They were restless souls who rejected the necessary constraints of "bourgeois" society. They abandoned the very rules that created prosperity, a prosperity that allowed them to enjoy so many good things in life. They took all these good things for granted. In casting the rules aside, the young created a counterculture that was indifferent to how children were raised. They were blind to the damage that a drug culture could do to a society. They had no idea how dangerous a world lacking an agreed-upon moral code could be. Yes, the New Left threw off reflexive anticommunism, said its critics. But they embraced instead what might be called reflexive procommunism, a tendency to support almost any regime, no matter how dictatorial, that made the United States its adversary. And in the end, the brigades of the New Left and the counterculture proved no less prone to the seductions of American materialism than their elders. Nothing makes a critic of the New Left happier than to run into an old militant now hard at work at a corporate law firm or an investment bank.

These two views embody certain truths, yet each misses the other's truth and each fails to grasp how painfully complicated the 1960s were. Those who would understand the 1960s need to make some crucial distinctions: between the New Left and the counterculture; between the New Left's positive program and its critique of liberalism; and between the movement's origins and what it became.

Of all these distinctions, the most important is between the New Left and the counterculture.

At the beginning, the New Left was consciously a *political* movement. It was not primarily about culture. Its first battles included the protests against the bomb and nuclear testing, the demonstrations against the House Un-American Activities Committee, the free speech movement at Berkeley. In his book, *If I Had a Hammer*, New Left scholar Maurice Isserman showed how many of the currents that fed the New Left had their origins in the old left's quest for new directions in the 1950s. Seen in this light, the New Left was little more than an extension of the old, which led Carl Oglesby, one of the movement's early leaders, to pose the right question. "Why not simply the *current* left?" Oglesby asked. "What makes it new?"

Above all else, the New Left was new because it grew up after the disestablishment of Soviet Communism as the guide to world socialism. By the late 1950s, almost every vestige of left-wing sympathy for the Soviet model was destroyed by Khrushchev's revelations about Stalin—and then by Khrushchev's invasion of Hungary. The Communist Party was in shambles and, for most of the left, no longer defined what was "left." Much has rightly been made of the role of red-diaper babies, the children of Communists and ex-Communists, in organizing the New Left. But even the red-diaper babies, as Todd Gitlin makes clear in his superb account, *The Sixties*, sought a break from the errors of the pro-Soviet past. And many of the leaders of the early New Left, notably Tom Hayden, represented an indigenous form of American radicalism that owed nothing to the Soviet Union and far more to C. Wright Mills, the rebel American sociologist, than to Karl Marx.

But if the New Left rejected the sectarianism of American Communism, so, too, did it reject the sectarianism of the *anticommunist* left. This meant, for example, that Students for a Democratic Society (SDS), the quintessential New Left group, saw banning Communists from membership as a form of "McCarthyism." They decided that there should be no barriers to joining. Ultimately, this led to the destruction of SDS when the dour militants of the Progressive Labor Party were allowed inside to create chaos. But at the time of SDS's founding, the rejection of all kinds of sectarianism, including anti-anticommunism, seemed exciting indeed. It fed the notion that this new radicalism represented a genuine break with the past. "SDSers believe the savage struggles between Stalinists and Social Democrats contributed heavily to the failure of the Old Left," Jack Newfield wrote in his 1966 account of the New Left, "and they are determined not to repeat that chapter of history." Newfield himself defended anticommunism as "one way of affirming one's positive belief in democracy." But he had sympathy for the leaders of SDS, whom he described as "emotionally more antagonistic to red-baiters than reds, but without any real attraction to any of the varieties of Communist experience as a model for social change."

The early New Left was about the unkept promises of liberals, especially on civil rights, an issue on which the left was consistently ahead of the Kennedy and Johnson administrations. Kennedy and Johnson sometimes made use of their left-wing opposition. In alliance with the black civil rights leadership, the young militants made it easier for liberals to act by creating pressure on the left to counter the strength of segregationist Southern Democrats on the right. But often, the militants went away disappointed and angry. By 1965, the young left was in an almost permanent state of discontent over the failure of liberal leaders to bring their actions into line with their words.

At its heart, the politics of the early New Left was profoundly democratic, growing more from America's civic republican tradition than from anything that might be called socialist. This, too, had the feel of something new. Both the language and the style of the New Left embodied the politics of an engaged middle class whose members saw freedom as meaningless if the citizenry was detached from politics. "We seek the establishment of a democracy of individual participation governed by two central aims," declared The Port Huron Statement, SDS's 1962 defining statement of principles, which was largely written by Tom Hayden. The aims were "that the individual share in those social decisions determining the quality and direction of his life" and "that society be organized to encourage independence in men and provide the media for their common participation."

The New Left's key concept was "participatory democracy." Its goal was a democracy in which citizens did more than just cast ballots for one politician or another. Hayden got the idea from Arnold Kaufman, a political philosopher at the University of Michigan who was one of Hayden's teachers. The purpose of participatory democracy, Kaufman wrote, "is and always has been, not the extent to which it protects and stabilizes a community, but the contribution it can make

to human powers of thought, feeling and action." Participatory democracy, Kaufman added, was a much broader and more exciting
concept than representative democracy, which was hemmed in by "all
sorts of institutional features designed to safeguard human rights and
insure social order." The goal of the New Left, then, was not order,
but improving human beings.

The New Left saw the American brand of the human species as
in need of a great deal of improvement. For the New Left, the United
States of the early 1960s was a nation of alienated conformists. "Feeling the press of complexity upon the emptiness of life," The Port
Huron Statement declared, "people are fearful of the thought that at
any moment, things may be thrust out of control. They fear change
itself, since change might smash whatever invisible framework seems
to hold back chaos for them now. For most Americans, all crusades
are suspect, threatening. The fact that each individual sees apathy in
his fellows perpetuates the common reluctance to organize for
change."

A grim picture indeed. "Loneliness, estrangement, isolation describe the vast distance between man and man today," the statement
went on. "Doubt has replaced hopefulness—and men act out of a
defeatism that is labeled realistic."

To understand the New Left, one must remember that The Port
Huron Statement was issued not during the "conformist" Eisenhower
years, but at the high tide of John F. Kennedy's presidency, a time
now remembered as relentlessly hopeful. The New Left always had a
paradoxical relationship to the Kennedy presidency. On the one hand,
it was inspired by Kennedy's call for idealism and self-sacrifice, and
many New Left cadres got their political starts in the Peace Corps. Yet
the New Left saw Kennedy's famous "pragmatism," his disdain for
"ideology," as part of the problem—part of what they called the "defeatism that is labeled realistic." The authors of The Port Huron Statement held Kennedy-style "pragmatism" in low esteem, since they saw
it as undermining utopian thinking and emphasizing technique over
purpose. "To be idealistic is to be considered apocalyptic, deluded,"
The Port Huron Statement declared. "To have no serious aspirations,
on the contrary, is to be tough-minded." So much for the New Frontier.

What is striking in retrospect is that many of the things the New
Left said about liberal pragmatism had important echoes on the right
—among those who gathered around William F. Buckley, Jr.'s National Review, joined Young Americans for Freedom, and campaigned for Barry Goldwater. Like the New Left, these new

conservatives also sensed a moral void in American life. Like the New
Left, the rising right spoke of the limits of "pragmatism." Like the New
Left, the Buckleyites saw the politics of "consensus" as a cover for the
liberal power structure.

The New Left also echoed one important school of conservative
thought in its concern for creating an active citizenry and in its view
that improving the individual citizen was one of the imperatives of
politics. "Man is by nature not an individual with inalienable rights,
but a political being who can achieve his nature, his end, only in the
polis, if at all," Walter Berns, a conservative disciple of Leo Strauss,
wrote in 1957. There is no evidence that Berns influenced the New
Left, but one conservative who did was Robert A. Nisbet. Nisbet's first
major work, *The Quest for Community*, was first published in 1953. It
went out of print and was reissued in the 1960s, according to the
author, because it became so popular with the new radicals. Like the
New Left, Nisbet was in rebellion against liberal conformity and
spoke, as The Port Huron Statement put it, of the need to move "out
of isolation and into community." Declaring that community thrives
on self-help and "also a little disorder," Nisbet scored individual "isolation" and asserted that "everything that removes a group from the
performance of or involvement in its own government can hardly help
but weaken the sense of community." Nisbet proceeded, in good New
Left fashion, to criticize "the intellectual's dread of utopianism" and
also "his pious desire to be 'realistic.' " And he echoed a theme that
was to become central to the New Left's doctrine: that large, inacces-
sible institutions were inherently "alienating." Nisbet, who became
one of the New Left's harshest critics, was in many ways—inadvertently and, he would argue, through certain misunderstandings—one
of its early prophets.

What is important here is that the New Left saw itself in revolt
not primarily against conservatism, since conservative thought
seemed so marginal in the early sixties, but against "establishment
liberalism." Unlike its communist and socialist forerunners, the New
Left declared itself against bureaucracy, centralization, and experts.
Its socialism, insofar as it was socialism, owed more to anarchists and
utopians such as Proudhon than to Marx or Lenin.

Thus the New Left's skepticism about Kennedy-style liberalism.
Richard Flacks, one of the New Left's most influential thinkers, was
explicit in seeing who the enemy was. "The real threat to the left is
not the right wing, but a strengthened liberal center," he said. "We
used to talk about how, if the Kennedys fulfilled their program, it
would be the end of democracy, because the whole thrust was toward

technocratic, top-down control. And that was really what we were against." And so, in its own way, was the emerging right.

As the decade went on, other similarities between the right and the New Left became clear. New Left scholars, for example, took a much more favorable view of the old isolationists such as Robert A. Taft than liberal scholarship ever had. In an important New Left book called *Containment and Change*, Carl Oglesby, an early president of SDS, gave sympathetic notice to the words of Congressman Howard Buffett, the Midwestern campaign manager for Senator Taft's 1952 run for the presidency. "Our Christian ideals cannot be exported to other lands by dollars and guns," Buffett is quoted by Oglesby as declaring. "We cannot practice might and force abroad and retain freedom at home. We cannot talk world cooperation and practice power politics." As opposition to the Vietnam War became ever more central to New Left politics, the warnings of the isolationists that a globally interventionist United States would become less democratic seemed nothing short of prophetic.

One should not, of course, carry the left-right analogies too far. The right and the New Left divided on that most fundamental of political questions, equality. Conservatives such as Nisbet were insistent that viable communities could be built only with clear lines of authority—the word *authority* is central to all of Nisbet's thinking. The antiauthoritarian New Left could hardly have disagreed more. Moreover, the emerging right abandoned the isolationism of its forebears in the 1950s and became thoroughly globalist in its foreign policy. And the New Left's attack on large corporations was not a cause to which conservatives repaired—even though members of Young Americans for Freedom sometimes sounded like New Leftists when they attacked corporations that did business with the Russians.

Still, the New Left's attacks on liberalism were telling and called into question the legitimacy of the liberal state. If liberal ideology began to crumble intellectually in the 1960s, it did so in part because the New Left represented a highly articulate and able wrecking crew. If the New Left took certain conservative ideas more seriously than liberals did, conservatives sometimes returned the favor by using favorite New Left concepts—decentralization, alienation, community control—for their own purposes.

II

Among the many notable aspects of The Port Huron Statement was its attention to issues that were not at the time widely recognized as "political." Words such as *loneliness, isolation,* and *estrangement* reflected the spiritual concerns of the document's principle author, Tom Hayden, who was raised Catholic and was deeply influenced by existentialist thought. At moments, the document sounded like a papal declaration, insisting, for example, that society's fundamental difficulties "cannot be overcome by better personnel management, nor by improved gadgets, but only when a love of man overcomes the idolatrous worship of things by man." Hayden said later that some of the language of the statement was, in fact, drawn verbatim from Pope John XXIII's encyclical *Pacem in Terris.* But such spiritual concerns were not merely Hayden's idiosyncrasies. They were central to how the new movement saw itself, to what made it new. In Morris Dickstein's telling phrase, the New Left "aimed not to appropriate the means of production but to change the character of human relations." And it is because the New Left's concerns were cultural and moral that it became increasingly difficult over time to disentangle the New Left from the counterculture.

If one can date the beginnings of a countercultural sensibility, its origins probably lie in the 1950s with the rise of rock 'n' roll and the appearance of the beats.

Like so many cultural developments, the rise of rock owed much to technological change. With television replacing radio as the primary medium for comedy and drama, radio was forced to search for new formats and new audiences. It carried out this search at precisely the time when rock was born. To survive, radio stations all over the country embraced rock music. Todd Gitlin makes a convincing case that AM radio was one of the most important forces in creating within a generation the sense that it *was* a generation. Disc jockeys, Gitlin wrote, "played an important part in extending the peer group, certifying rock lovers as members of a huge subsociety of knowing." Gitlin went on: "Even as I sat doing my homework to the top forty countdown, I felt plugged in. For those of us who were ten or twelve when Elvis Presley came along, it was rock 'n' roll that named us a generation."

The beats were well off to the society's margins and never won the audience that rock did. But the beat sensibility set the tone for much of what would come next. Jack Kerouac's *On the Road,* published in September 1957, foreshadowed many of the counterculture's themes, including its rebellion against conformity and boredom, its emphasis on sensual gratification, its admiration for black people as society's hip outlaws. "The only people for me are the mad ones," declares Kerouac's narrator and alter ego, Sal Paradise, "the ones who are mad to live, mad to talk, mad to be saved, delirious of everything at the same time, the ones who never yawn or say a commonplace thing but burn, burn, burn like fabulous yellow roman candles exploding like spiders across the stars." —

If one wonders when the neoconservative reaction against the counterculture was born, one could do worse than examine Norman Podhoretz's outburst against Kerouac, written in 1958. Almost all the criticisms Podhoretz levels against Kerouac are criticisms that surfaced later against the counterculture. Podhoretz saw the beat bohemianism of the 1950s as "hostile to civilization," a movement that "worships primitivism, instinct, energy, 'blood,' " and whose intellectual interests ran to "mystical doctrines, irrationalist philosophies." The Beat Generation's "worship of primitivism and spontaneity is more than a cover for hostility to intelligence," Podhoretz went on, "it arises from a pathetic poverty of feeling as well." The beat revolt, Podhoretz declared, was "the revolt of the spiritually underprivileged and the crippled of the soul." Long before anyone had discovered the "me decade," Podhoretz saw the beats as "young men who can't get outside the morass of self and so construct definitions of feeling that exclude all human beings who manage to live, even miserably, in a world of objects."

Podhoretz said the beats were incapable of rebelling against something so specific as "the middle class" or "capitalism," but it was precisely the "free form" nature of the beat rebellion that made it so broadly attractive. If the New Left rejected the sectarianism of the older left, the rebels of the beat generation and their inheritors in the counterculture felt no need to be prissy or precise in defining what they were against. They were against inhibition, including the inhibitions of language. Podhoretz noted that one of Kerouac's favorite responses to all situations was "Wow!" That, of course, became an expression of choice right through the 1980s as beat-speak became Val-speak. Gitlin noted the same skeptical view of language in rock 'n' roll, which linked "distrust of language, distrust of the correct, distrust of practicality itself." The sense, Gitlin said, was that "[w]hat we're feeling is so deep, so difficult, so amazing, it can only be expressed if we leave behind middle class manners, undo the lessons of school, stop *trying* to sound correct." As the historian Fred Siegel put it in another context, "rules of language came to be seen as the thin edge of totalitarianism."

Both Gitlin and Charles Kaiser argue that the culture of rock played a decisive role in shaping the attitudes of young whites toward black people and civil rights. They noted that rock integrated black music into the lives of white people as it had never been before—first, when white musicians picked up on the black sound and then when blacks themselves were finally allowed onto the airwaves of white-oriented stations. This cultural integration, they argue, eased the way toward civil rights and helped explain why so many middle-class white youth were drawn to the black struggle. Gitlin also traces the growing legitimacy of left-wing ideas to the entry of left-wing folk music into the political mainstream. Pete Seeger and Woody Guthrie, once Communist Party heroes, became *national* folk heroes. Bob Dylan, who acknowledged Guthrie as a forebear, integrated the folk tradition into rock and gave it even wider currency. But Dylan was very much a man of his times and not of the Guthrie-Seeger generation. No political group could ever expect to "discipline" him. Some of Dylan's early work was decidedly political, about racial injustice and war. But Dylan was also an individualist, almost Emersonian. Thus, Dylan's "Mr. Tambourine Man" is described accurately by Gitlin as "the transcendentalist fantasy of the wholly free individual." The song struck some of Gitlin's friends as "an ode to a dope dealer."

Drugs became important to the counterculture in part *because* they were illegal. Taking drugs was an adventure, a way for individuals to cast themselves as outlaws, a means of escaping the normalcy and boredom of everyday middle-class life. Drugs were simultaneously an expression of individualism and a way of declaring allegiance to a beloved community. And of course many simply found them fun, in a way earlier and later generations found alcohol fun. A gentle hedonism was one of the most powerful elements of the counterculture, and drugs were part of that hedonism.

To say that an individualistic, apolitical counterculture was at odds with a communitarian and political New Left is to oversimplify the complex relationship that existed between the two. Insofar as the New Leftists were launching a cultural and moral rebellion cast as a political revolt, they had much in common with their comrades in the counterculture who were battling for new "lifestyles." The counterculture offered a kind of answer to the "alienation" that the New Left condemned. And for all its celebration of individualism, the counterculture asserted, if sometimes incoherently, its own sense of community. Hedonism, of the "if it feels good, do it" variety, is often best practiced in groups and can become a principle of group action, even if it can't hold a society together. The counterculture paralleled the left in asserting the value of gentleness over competition, "peace" over "war," living by a code of authenticity today over making "opportunistic" calculations aimed at tomorrow. In his fascinating essay on the 1960s and 1970s, *America's Quest for the Ideal Self*, Peter Clecak argued that what the 1960s produced was "the democratization of personhood." By this he meant that "the expanding idea of personal fulfillment was diversified and extended to include significant numbers of citizens within every social category." Introspection and the pursuit of happiness, and a blissful happiness at that, became the right of every citizen. Black and Native American, gay and lesbian—everyone was "beautiful."

The convergence of the counterculture and the New Left launched one of the most subversive slogans of the era: "The personal is the political." This slogan demanded a kind of moral accountability that is rare to those involved in politics. It declared that individuals should live their private lives in ways that accorded entirely with their publicly stated principles. A gentle and egalitarian politics demanded gentle and egalitarian behavior in private. Ultimately, this helped create the women's movement. It also helps explain one of the ironies of the time: that the counterculture, no less than the antiwar protests, helped give new vigor to the Catholic left. Although the morality of the Catholic left was, at least in theory, opposed to cultural or sexual permissiveness—the Catholic left was critical of all manner of acts between consenting adults, including capitalist ones—the Catholic left, especially the Catholic Worker movement, offered a kind of integral morality designed precisely to square the personal and the political. As Vietnam became the era's central political concern, the Catholic left's pacifism became an increasingly popular expression of moral wholeness.

But the contradictions between the New Left and countercultural worldviews were glaring. Insofar as the New Left was about "the left" as traditionally defined, meaning socialism, it demanded strong government, if only to enforce redistribution. Insofar as the counterculture thought about government at all, it didn't like it. The "rules and regulations" condemned by Crosby, Stills, Nash and Young were seen by the counterculture as rules against drugs, abortion, sexual experimentation, loud rock concerts, controversial books, and alternative newspapers. Only a few critics of the counterculture saw at the time how easily its worldview could elide into right-wing doctrine. One who did was Michael Walzer, who wrote in 1971 that the philosophy of "Do it!" was "the mirror image of political (and why not economic?) laissez-faire."

The New Left also demanded a kind of personal discipline that was alien to the counterculture. Organizing poor communities, the New Left's central project in the midsixties, was hard work that required immense discipline and forbearance. It was work that often defied the counterculture's moral imperative, "If it feels good, do it." As the sixties went on, a gulf opened between the counterculture and elements of the New Left. To the more political New Leftists, it was no surprise that American capitalism adapted so easily to countercultural values—or that the counterculture's adherents adapted so easily to American capitalism.

But the counterculture and the New Left were united when it came to opposing the Vietnam War. And here, too, the young militants saw their enemy, and it was liberalism.

III

Paul Kirk, the former chairman of the Democratic National Committee and a close friend of the Kennedy family, described John Kennedy's presidency as "a call to greatness, it was the country feeling young and good about itself." Being young meant, above all, being active. It meant, in the famous passage of Kennedy's inaugural address, that the country would "pay any price, bear any burden, meet any hardship, support any friend, oppose any foe to assure the survival and the success of liberty." Kennedy's whole approach, embodied in one of his favorite words, *vigor*, was premised on the idea that bold and daring applications of pure will could solve problems. There was nothing "gentle" about Kennedy's approach. Kennedy cast problems as "challenges," called constantly for "sacrifice," told everyone that he would ask much of them and promise nothing in return.

Kennedy was most interested in asserting vigor in the military sphere and in pursuit of America's interests abroad. In the 1960 campaign, Kennedy declared that the Eisenhower-Nixon administration had cut defense spending far too much and charged (wrongly) that the nation faced a "missile gap" with the Soviet Union. In pursuit of global victory, Kennedy called for a much stronger presidency—a view that was "liberal" at the time, since a strong presidency was associated with Franklin D. Roosevelt.

One of Kennedy's major innovations was his emphasis on turning back the challenge of communist wars of "national liberation." Viewed in retrospect, the Eisenhower administration, despite John Foster Dulles's bold talk about rolling back communism, was quite cautious in its application of American power. When it did so, it often preferred covert action (as in Guatemala in 1954) as against overt action. The Eisenhower administration's main commitment was to preserving the postwar balance of power. For Kennedy, in another word now permanently linked to his memory, that was "unacceptable." The revolutionary challenge needed to be met with revolutionary means. "Paying any price" meant innovations such as the Green Berets. It meant a firm commitment to keeping the communists out of South Vietnam.

It is an interesting but fruitless exercise to speculate on whether Kennedy would have expanded the Vietnam War as Lyndon Johnson did. Kennedy gave mixed signals before he died. His pursuit of a testban treaty with the Soviet Union and his 1963 speech at American University—"Let us reexamine our attitude toward the Cold War," Kennedy said—are often interpreted as signaling a "turn left." Kennedy showed some sympathy for the young radicals. In a gesture that was at once patronizing and supportive, Kennedy sent a White House butler out with coffee to a group of young people demonstrating outside the White House for nuclear disarmament in February 1962. Many of the young demonstrators later emerged as leaders of the New Left.

Nonetheless, it is clear that for most of his presidency, Kennedy identified liberalism with an anticommunist policy that was bolder and more vigorous than Eisenhower's. The New Left had ample cause to consider Vietnam liberalism's war. As a result, the New Left turned ferociously on the liberals and nearly all their works. The Great Society was condemned as "the Great Barbecue." Liberal tolerance was called "repressive tolerance." Liberalism became "corporate liberalism." New Left scholar and editor James Weinstein argued that modern liberalism "was the product, consciously created, of the leaders of the giant corporations and financial institutions that emerged astride American society in the last years of the nineteenth century and the early years of the twentieth." Weinstein argued that war was the obvious "fulfillment" of modern liberalism, and it became a central assertion of the New Left that the postwar prosperity had been possible only because a "militarized economy" kept employment high. "Liberal Keynesianism" became "military Keynesianism." Kennedy's price-paying and burden-bearing were, in the eyes of the New Left, the costs of "the Free World empire." Over time, the New Left's critique of America's Vietnam policy became an attack on "American imperialism."

Viewed purely as a matter of fact and history, it was neither irrational nor necessarily anti-American to view the United States as embarking on some sort of "imperial" role after World War II. Nonetheless, the New Left's root-and-branch critique of American policy almost certainly diminished the appeal of the antiwar movement. By 1968, the country was clearly turning against the Vietnam War. But many Americans who opposed the war were not prepared to declare their nation "immoral" or "imperialistic." The more the New Left's critique of American "imperialism" came to be seen as the central ideology of the antiwar movement, the easier it became for supporters of intervention in Vietnam to cast their foes as anti-American. As a young government professor at Harvard, William Schneider interviewed voters door-to-door in working-class Somerville, Massachusetts. An older woman roundly condemned the Vietnam War, charging that it was the creation of the Harvard professors down the road. Schneider then asked if that meant she had sympathy for the student protestors against the war. "Oh, no," she replied, "they're worse." Americans disliked both the war-making professoriat and their increasingly anti-American progeny.

Over the long run, the New Left critique of American foreign policy had a substantial influence on mainstream liberalism. But the war itself turned a movement of utopian hopefulness toward bitterness and violence. In the peculiar setting of media politics, as Gitlin has argued, violence and extremism begat more violence and extremism, because the movement's prime recruiter was not its own cadres, but the television screen. Gitlin contends that the mass media were so fascinated with the violent minority of the New Left they played up extremist views within the movement to the exclusion of virtually all others. As a result, a disproportionate number of new recruits to SDS were so far outside the political mainstream that they ultimately condemned the organization to the path of violence and political irrelevance. But whether or not the New Left's problems were primarily the media's fault, it is clear that bitterness over the war drove the movement further and further away from what most Americans took to be political reality. Increasingly, the New Left's main connection to mainstream politics was as a scapegoat for conservative politicians.

A popular symbol of the New Left's failure was the explosion at a town-house-turned-bomb-factory on West Eleventh Street in New York City on March 6, 1970. The explosion killed three would-be revolutionaries. But it is far too easy to use the town house explosion as the ultimate symbol of the New Left. For one thing, the bombmakers were only a tiny fringe of a much broader movement. And at the very moment when most of the "formal" institutions of the New

Left, including SDS, drifted off into irrelevancy, the movement's ideas were beginning to have a real impact on mainstream liberalism.

IV

If the New Left came to hate liberalism, liberals were by no means unanimous in hating the New Left. Many liberals responded to its challenge not by moving to the right, but by heading left, accepting much of what the New Left said about liberal failure.

The movement of a large number of liberals to the left was in some ways a natural development, a restoration of the political status quo that prevailed before the Cold War. The New Deal coalition had always contained a healthy share of leftists, and they were driven from the Democratic Party only in the anticommunist push after World War II. In fact, many had taken themselves out of the party, supporting Henry Wallace's anti–Cold War insurgency against Harry Truman in 1948. For such "progressives," the New Left was a godsend, a sign that a new generation was prepared to rebuild the left from the ashes of the 1950s.

But at least as important to the transformation of Democratic politics was the rise of a middle-class reform movement inside the party during the 1950s. The Democratic reformers were usually liberals, but they were anything but leftists. Most drew their inspiration from Adlai Stevenson's presidential campaigns. What they admired about Stevenson as much as his views was his *style*—quiet, urbane, and intellectual, exactly in keeping with what the upper middle class sought in a candidate.

The reformers believed that the purposes of politics had to do with policy, not patronage. Thus, they detested those they condemned as "party hacks." The "hacks" often returned the favor by keeping the middle-class reformers out of their organizations. The newcomers responded by establishing independent "reform Democratic" organizations of their own. James Q. Wilson, a political scientist who chronicled their efforts in *The Amateur Democrat*, published in 1962, noted the sharp class cleavages between the supporters of the reformers and those of "the regulars." The reform Democrats were usually much better-off than the regulars. In big cities, notably New York, the reformers were disproportionately white Protestant and Jewish, the regulars disproportionately Catholic. Thus, the class war inside the Democratic Party began not, as is often thought, in the struggles of the late 1960s, but in the skirmishes of the 1950s.

The antiwar insurgency created a new set of allies for the middle-

class reformers. Like the reformers, the generally young activists of
the antiwar movement disliked the party regulars, who tended to stay
loyal to Lyndon Johnson and the Vietnam War. In New York, the
umbrella group pushing for a challenge to Johnson on the war in the
1968 primaries, the Coalition for a Democratic Alternative, was dominated by the old reformers. It was appropriate that the candidate of
the antiwar reformers turned out to be Eugene McCarthy. Before his
presidential campaign, McCarthy's most notable act in national politics was his eloquent nominating speech for Adlai Stevenson at the
1960 Democratic National Convention. The reformers, as a rule, preferred McCarthy's cool, cerebral style to Robert F. Kennedy's fervent
anger. The reformers were also suspicious of Kennedy's willingness to
ally with party regulars wherever he could find some who were prepared to oppose Johnson.

The intellectual link between the New Left and the "New Politics" reformers inside the Democratic Party was Arnold Kaufman, the
political philosopher who had given Tom Hayden the idea of "participatory democracy." Kaufman's goal was to move liberalism leftward,
and his 1970 manifesto was appropriately titled *The Radical Liberal*.
But the new politics as seen by Kaufman was in many respects not so
much radical as a new version of the old reform politics of the Stevenson partisans. "The new politics is principally a politics of issues, not
candidates, Kaufman wrote. Loyalty to party, loyalty to candidates
and winning elections are important only as they contribute to the
fulfillment of the radical liberal's program and values. Those who
practice the new politics are thereby ready to exercise an electoral
veto on Democratic candidates when doing so serves their concern
for issues." One can see instantly why the political professionals, who
attach a good deal of importance to winning elections, looked un-
kindly on the "New Politics." Their view could not have been more
different from Kaufman's. He asserted that "the new politics implies
predominant concern with the overall dynamic of the political process, not with the grubby ambitions of lesser-evil politicians." The
"grubby" political regulars got the message and fought the reformers
and the antiwar activists almost everywhere.

It would go much too far to say that the "New Left" took over the
Democratic Party through the antiwar insurgency. Indeed, the formal
institutions of the New Left, notably SDS, regularly assailed the Democratic Party. But the antiwar movement did allow the left and its
ideas back into the Democratic Party. If the Cold War political order
began domestically with Henry Wallace's split from Harry Truman

and the expulsion of the Communist-linked trade unions from the CIO, then the Cold War ended in the Democratic Party with Eugene McCarthy's declaration of candidacy in November of 1967. Suddenly, a critique of American foreign policy that had been off-limits was very much part of the party's normal discourse. Seen another way: In 1964, only two Democratic senators, Wayne Morse and Ernest Gruening, voted against the Gulf of Tonkin resolution. In 1965, only seven House Democrats voted against the military budget to protest the Vietnam War. By 1970, the antiwar forces held a majority among congressional Democrats. And in the 1980s, clear majorities among the Democrats in both houses opposed American military aid to the Nicaraguan contras. Cold War liberalism, in short, moved from being the Democratic Party's overwhelmingly dominant tendency to representing the view of an influential but embattled minority.

Nowhere was this transformation clearer than in a state that is often seen as modern liberalism's heartland, Massachusetts.

In 1962, Edward M. Kennedy was elected to the United States Senate, defeating Republican George Cabot Lodge. The campaign attracted much national interest, since the President's brother was seeking the President's old Senate seat and suggesting to voters that his familial link with the White House might do the state some good. Kennedy's slogan was: "He can do more for Massachusetts." The voters agreed and Kennedy won.

But the contest was also important because of the candidacy of H. Stuart Hughes, a Harvard professor and a respected intellectual historian who ran as an independent peace candidate. Hughes advocated steps toward unilateral nuclear disarmament as an alternative to Kennedy's Cold War liberalism. By normal electoral measures, Hughes's candidacy failed miserably—he won just 50,000 votes out of about 2 million cast. But the Hughes campaign was astonishingly successful in another respect. Not since Henry Wallace's Progressive candidacy in 1948 had a critic of Cold War liberalism won anything like a respectful hearing. Although his candidacy drew the support of the remnants of the old left, including people who had been in or close to the Communist Party, Hughes himself was decidedly a noncommunist and his candidacy was seen as an expression of liberal idealism more than as a tool of a dangerous radicalism. His campaign drew the support of many of the young Harvard leftists who later became leaders of SDS.

The Hughes campaign proved to be a trial run for the antiwar movement, and it spawned an organization called Massachusetts Po-

litical Action for Peace (Mass Pax). Five years later, in 1967, many of
the leaders of Eugene McCarthy's presidential campaign were veterans of the Hughes campaign and Mass Pax. The seed money for the
Vietnam Moratorium demonstrations of October 1969 came in significant part from two businessmen who were leaders in Mass Pax, Je-
rome Grossman and Bertram A. Yaffe. Grossman, Yaffe, and other
Mass Pax leaders were also heavily involved in the Massachusetts
McGovern campaign in 1972, and Grossman was elected to the Democratic National Committee. Subsequently, Mass Pax merged with
the successor group to the 1968 McCarthy campaign, Citizens for
Participation Politics. (Note the emphasis, drawn from the New Left
and Kaufman, on "participatory democracy.") The New Politics forces
played decisive roles in electing antiwar figures to top jobs in Massachusetts politics—Michael Harrington, Father Robert F. Drinan, Jim
Shannon, Gerry Studds, and Barney Frank to Congress, John Kerry
to the Senate. Although Michael Dukakis's roots lay in the earlier
tradition of Stevensonian reform and not in antiwar politics, he
needed to court and win over the antiwar wing of his party to win the
governorship in 1974.

Today, in short, those who were seen as "radicals" in the time of
Stuart Hughes's campaign are now very much part of the Massachusetts mainstream and help define liberalism. The definitive symbol is
Ted Kennedy himself, the man whom Hughes opposed and who is
now seen as representing left-liberalism, Massachusetts style, to the
nation. The Massachusetts experience had parallels in state Democratic parties throughout the nation, notably in New York, California,
Colorado, Wisconsin, Oregon, and Iowa.

The antiwar insurgency in the party brought other changes with
it. In 1968, Robert Kennedy and McCarthy won virtually all of the
Democratic primaries, but the party's presidential nomination was
awarded to Hubert Humphrey, who won not a single primary victory.
This affront led to a clamor for new party rules, and the reformers
took control of the party's rule-making process through a commission
headed by Sen. George McGovern.

The McGovern Commission created a revolution in the process
of picking presidential nominees. In keeping with a theory of "participatory democracy," the new rules insisted that primaries and open
caucuses, not the wishes of party leaders, should dominate the nominating process. Just as the New Left had attacked distant bureaucrats,
so the new Democratic reformers attacked the "party bosses." The
reform spirit in the Democratic Party had a direct impact on the

Republican Party. Most state legislatures were controlled by Democrats and had to enact new primary laws to keep their states in line with the national rules. The laws usually covered both parties, so the Republicans got "reform" rules, often despite themselves.

The McGovern rules also saw the introduction of affirmative action for convention delegates, to increase the representation of blacks, Hispanics, Asians, women, and "youth" on the convention floor. These rules were yet another instance in which protest movements outside the party made their voices heard within. One of the most celebrated battles spawned by the new rules had symbolic and real consequences for years to come. Antiwar forces tied to George McGovern's campaign challenged Mayor Richard J. Daley's Chicago delegation to the 1972 convention. The challengers charged that the Daley delegation, freely elected by the voters of Illinois, inadequately represented blacks and women (and by numerical standards, it did fall short of the rules). The challengers won and threw the Daley delegation out. The new delegation was seated. One of its leaders was a young minister named Jesse Jackson.

The Daley battle illustrated one major result of the rise of a reform faction in the Democratic Party: the declining power of the party's white, working-class base, which preferred Richard Daley to middle-class reformers (and also to Jesse Jackson). Over the long run, the new party rules that emphasized participation led to an increasing role for the well-to-do and a declining role for the working and lower-middle classes. Thomas Byrne Edsall, a reporter at *The Washington Post*, put matters starkly in a 1988 essay: "The turnout in primaries and in caucuses is skewed in favor of the affluent and upper middle class. . . . These delegate selection processes have been contributing factors in the acceleration of the decline of political organizations in working class communities." That was hardly the result that the egalitarians of the early New Left had in mind when they first broached the idea of "participatory democracy."

But in another sense, the result is not surprising, for the New Left was always primarily a movement of *middle-class* and even upper-middle-class radicalism. Its roots in the working class were precarious or nonexistent. Even at its most democratic moment, at the time of The Port Huron Statement, the New Left displayed a certain contempt for the rest of America. "We are a minority," they declared proudly in the statement. "The vast majority of our people regard the temporary equilibriums of our society and world as eternally functioning parts."

Over time, the ordinary elitism of the well-off and well-educated was linked to Leninist elitism in which the student radicals viewed themselves as a revolutionary vanguard in alliance with the people of the Third World. Herbert Marcuse helped the New Left develop theories that cast the working class, Marx's motive force of history, right into history's dustbin. In Marcuse's view, the white American working class had been bought off by the forces of capital with television sets, washing machines, and other supposedly unsavory products of consumerism. With the young left writing off the working class, the working class wrote off the young left. The cops and construction workers felt they had good reason to swing fists and billy clubs at these children of affluence. The political right, represented in the late 1960s by Richard Nixon and George Wallace, was only too happy to rescue the working class from Marcuse's dustbin and harvest its ballots.

V

If the New Left and the counterculture have been subjected to such wildly diverse treatment by analysts across the political spectrum, that is because the story of the New Left's influence on politics—and particularly on American liberalism—is so filled with irony and paradox. The New Left began its short life asking many of the right questions. In the end, it contributed decisively to a politics of false choices.

The New Left's call for participatory democracy was an admirable effort to put life into an American political system that seemed to foster a passive citizenry. Here, both the New Left and the conservatives were right to be skeptical of liberal "consensus" politics. John F. Kennedy himself, though a master of consensus politics, also sensed the void in American politics and shaped both his campaign and his administration around the ideas of sacrifice and public service. Kennedy, too, knew that American public life was somehow falling away from its republican ideals.

The New Left's early organizing efforts around participatory democracy had some decidedly salutary effects. To a degree, participatory politics will always tilt toward the elites, since the better-off and better-educated will always have more time, money, and resources to devote to politics than those below them on the class ladder. The organizers of the civil rights movement and the New Left sought to remedy that bias and won some important victories. The battle to register black voters in the South and to secure passage of the 1965 Voting Rights Act led to the single largest democratizing step the country had taken since women's suffrage. The spirit of the New Left, which extended beyond any of its organizations, gave thousands of affluent white students the motivation—and the courage—to join with blacks in the hard and dangerous work of securing this change. New Left organizing efforts in the Northern cities had less heroic results, but some of its work helped create political organizations for the impoverished that endure to this day.

The New Left also lives on in the universities and in Democratic politics. The idea of participatory democracy is alive and well in groups such as Citizen Action, which organizes poor and working-class neighborhoods around the country and has contributed significantly to the victories of liberal Senate and gubernatorial candidates in many states. Citizen Action's leading organizers were leaders in the early New Left. New Left veterans can also be found in unions, in public interest law firms, in Ralph Nader's organizations, in state governments, even in Congress.

Yet as the 1960s went on and the political energies of the New Left focused more and more on cultural issues and the war, the movement began defeating its own purposes. Anger at the American government was transformed into hatred of American society. Avantgarde culture and morality created a gulf between the left and the mass of Americans who favored social reform but lived by a traditional moral code. Thus, when the theory of "participatory democracy" was applied, in an admittedly imperfect way, to the Democratic Party, it ended up concentrating power into the hands of a culturally "advanced" upper middle class. This hardly advanced the cause of democracy, since the upper middle class already had much power in both parties.

The paradox of the New Left can be seen most clearly in the antiwar movement, which was at once a great success and an enormous failure. On the one hand, the growing and increasingly well-organized domestic opposition to the war made it increasingly difficult for the government to prosecute it. After the war was over, the antiwar movement's skepticism of intervention abroad was shared by a majority of Americans. "No more Vietnams" was not a leftist view but a mainstream desire, as even President Bush's statements on the Persian Gulf crisis showed.

Yet the Vietnam War and its aftermath created monumental problems for American liberals and their allies on the left. In a sense, liberal and left-of-center Democrats got the worst of all worlds: On the one hand, they were blamed for a conflict that became "liberalism's war," and the New Left played no small part in establishing that Vietnam could fairly be seen as the product of liberalism. On the other hand, the Democratic Party's subsequent close association with the antiwar movement tarred it in the eyes of moderate and conservative voters as the party of military weakness, flag burning, and draft dodging.

Critics of American foreign policy have nearly always been labeled "anti-American" by their foes; being cast into the political darkness is one of the risks of dissent. But rarely have dissenters cooperated so willingly to validate the claims of their enemies. By embracing anti-Americanism as a noble cause, the farther fringes of the New Left divided and set back the antiwar movement. They opened the way for a contentless politics of symbolism that made the care and treatment of the American flag a more important political question than what the flag stood for. Those who despised George Bush's relentless use of the American flag as a partisan symbol can blame the flag burners of the 1960s for making such a tactic possible. Even the Communist Party had the good sense to drape its meetings with American flags and to declare that communism was "twentieth-century Americanism." The New Left thus committed the cardinal political sin: It let itself be defeated more by its own actions than by those of its foes.

A deeper paradox lies in the New Left's relationship with liberalism. From the beginning, it was clear to New Left leaders that their enemy was the liberal state—in part because they never took conservatism seriously. Yet it turned out that in America, radicals who could not live with liberals could not live without them, either. Only after a series of conservative victories did some of the remaining young radicals rediscover the virtues of the liberal establishment they upended. Thus, William Connolly, one of the New Left's most thoughtful theorists, argued shortly after Ronald Reagan's election in 1980 that the left had good reason to lament the passing of liberalism. Connolly argued that "protest politics flourishes best when it faces a healthy liberal establishment that believes that justice and the good life can be fostered by the welfare state." Radicals could hope to gain ground "only if liberal doctrine retained a powerful presence in our politics" and opened up political space in which radicals could operate. But, Connolly lamented, neither the New Left nor liberalism ever fully appreciated their "cozy relationship of mutuality and interdependence" until it was too late. The New Left helped to destroy a liberal establishment that it badly needed.

Conservatives themselves shrewdly used the New Left's ideas for different ends. The notion that "small is beautiful," which grew out of the New Left's fascination with small communities, was used by conservatives to defend "entrepreneurship" and the creativity of small business. Decentralization of power, long a conservative theme, was lent new legitimacy when cast in the language of the left. The New Left's attack on bureaucracy was conveniently used to attack "big government." All of this made it easier for people who supported the antiwar movement and listened to the Jefferson Airplane when they were twenty to vote for Ronald Reagan when they turned thirty—and continue to enjoy rock 'n' roll.

The doctrines of the New Left and the counterculture helped to feed the conservative revival in a more fundamental way. The passage from "yippie" to "yuppie," from the "we generation" to the "me generation," is frequently seen as a sharp break, a change in mood caused by the aging of the baby boom, which got more "serious" (and some said, "selfish") as the years went by. There is little doubt that the aging process seems to make many people increasingly open to conservative ideas. But the rise of the right owed much to the political contradictions between the New Left and the counterculture. The shift to the "me generation" was not so much a break with the past as a shift in emphasis.

Jeff Riggenbach, a libertarian writer, saw this more clearly than most. In Riggenbach's analysis, what mattered about the New Left was its antiauthoritarianism, its individualism, and its skepticism of the state. The Vietnam War bred a mistrust of the military, of the draft, of entangling foreign alliances. The young opposed the Vietnam War for many reasons, Riggenbach argued, but one of them surely was that the war interfered with their own lives—and for no apparently good purpose. The drug culture, in the meantime, had a clear and unmistakably libertarian demand: Repeal drug laws, *"leave us alone."*

And so it went through other issues: Gays wanted an end to laws against sodomy ("leave us alone"); feminists wanted an end to laws against abortion ("leave us alone"); blacks wanted an end to laws enforcing segregation ("leave us alone"); there were many battles against the censorship of music, books, and alternative papers ("leave us alone"); dictatorships everywhere were called upon to lift barriers against emigration and to end torture and the imprisonment of political dissidents ("leave *them* alone").

Riggenbach's analysis overlooks the ways in which the new individualists of the 1960s were willing to use government to advance their cause. Blacks, feminists, and gays, for example, wanted *new* laws to protect them from discrimination. Still, Riggenbach's insight is crucial to understanding the rise of Reaganism. Far from being inconsistent with the antiauthoritarian thrust of the 1960s, much that passed for conservative politics in the 1980s was really *libertarian*. Many young voters who had been drawn to the New Left and the counterculture because they attacked authority were drawn to conservatism because it attacked the state. Thus did the New Left wage war against the paternalistic liberal state and defeat it. The right picked up the pieces.

2

THE VIRTUES OF VIRTUE: The Neoconservative Revolt

WHILE THE NEW LEFT was rebelling at liberalism's left flank, a group of intellectuals who shared some of the New Left's skepticism began a revolt on liberalism's right. The revolt of the neoconservatives was far more successful, and they continue to have a powerful impact on American politics.

Neoconservatives initially rebelled against the label *neoconservative*. They didn't even invent it; the late Michael Harrington, a democratic socialist, did. Harrington's intent was to make clear that a group including many who called themselves liberal was in fact a movement of newly conservative *ex*-liberals. The label eventually stuck because it was so apt—and because over time, so many of the neoconservatives came to accept that they were conservatives after all. By the 1980s, in any event, the term *conservative* was anything but an insult. Irving Kristol, often described as the movement's "godfather," was one of the first to accept the label. He described himself as "the only living and self-confessed neoconservative, at large or in captivity." Conceding that political labeling was more a leftist than a conservative craft, Kristol said that conservatives sometimes had to live with the handiwork of their foes. "The sensible course, therefore, is to take your label, claim it as your own, and run with it," Kristol declared. He and his comrades did just that.

Neoconservatism has received so much attention because it was one of the clearest signs of a realignment in American politics. Neoconservatism represented the defection of an important and highly articulate group of liberals to the other side. Precisely because they knew liberalism from the inside, the neoconservatives were often more effective than the old conservatives at explaining what was wrong with the liberal creed. And on many issues, the neoconservatives were right or partly right—and usually interesting even when they were wrong.

The first accomplishment of neoconservatism was to make criticisms of liberalism from the right acceptable in the intellectual, artistic, and journalistic circles where conservatives had long been regarded with suspicion. The classic view among these elites was expressed definitively by Lionel Trilling in 1954. "In the United States at this time liberalism is not only the dominant, but even the sole intellectual tradition," Trilling wrote. "For it is the plain fact that nowadays there are no conservative or reactionary ideas in general circulation." Certainly, Trilling conceded, there were conservative impulses. But such impulses, he said, rarely expressed themselves "in ideas, but only in action or in irritable mental gestures which seek to resemble ideas." As we shall see, this view was unfair to a powerful conservative intellectual tradition that lived underground at midcentury. But it is because Trilling's view accurately reflected the dominant bias among intellectual elites that the neoconservatives' missionary work was of such importance in dethroning liberalism.

Trilling was right in another respect: that liberalism was such a broad and all-encompassing creed, so central to America's understanding of itself, that it harbored within its ranks an extraordinary range of individuals and ideas. If the intellectual world was a one-party state dominated by liberalism, then virtually all political combat was carried out within the single party. Thus, through the fellow travelers, communists played a part in what passed for liberalism. So did the Wall Street foreign-policy establishment, whose sensibilities and commitments could hardly have been farther removed from Bolshevism. So, too, did the many splinters of the anticommunist left that later bred so many neoconservatives. The sheer sweep of liberalism was such that internal conflict was inevitable, as conflict would later be inexorable within the broad Reagan coalition.

The roots of neoconservatism lie in these internecine liberal conflicts. Most of those who would later create neoconservatism were among the most militant members of the coalition of "Cold War liberals" who saw halting Soviet expansion in the late 1940s as America's first priority. Arrayed against them were those who called themselves "progressives" and saw the Cold War as an obstacle to a new round of New Deal reform at home. The progressives stood with former vice president Henry Wallace in taking a more benign view of the Soviet Union and a more critical view of the United States. That the Communist Party openly supported the Wallace movement was about all the Cold War liberals needed to know about it—much as George McGovern's presence at Wallace's Progressive Party Convention in 1948 was all the neoconservatives needed to know about him twenty-four years later. (McGovern, like the Cold War liberals, eventually rejected Wallace and supported Harry Truman's reelection.)

The importance of neoconservatism's roots in Cold War liberalism cannot be exaggerated. Nothing appalled neoconservatives in the 1960s more than the willingness of so many liberals to abandon the hard-line anticommunism of Truman and Acheson. And the neoconservatives' argument that vigorous anticommunism was very much part of postwar American liberalism cannot be disputed—this was one area in which the New Left and the neoconservatives agreed, though they drew different political conclusions. Thus, though some neoconservatives including Daniel Patrick Moynihan and Nathan Glazer opposed the Vietnam War as imprudent, many others in their ranks supported the war. More important, virtually all of the neoconservatives viewed the antiwar movement with suspicion and mistrust. In this way, as in many others, the rise of the New Left played a central role in the growth of neoconservatism. The very kind of "establishment" anticommunist liberalism that the New Left attacked was the kind of liberalism the future neoconservatives believed in.

II

But if the earliest expressions of the neoconservative impulse were around foreign-policy issues, it first became visible as a movement in domestic politics. The neoconservatives made their first distinct mark as critics of liberal programs that they saw as based in ideological rigidity.

In his excellent critical study of the neoconservatives, Peter Steinfels identifies several key words that became central to the future neoconservatives during the 1950s, when the neoconservatives still thought of themselves as liberals. They feared the growth of *mass society* and the resulting *mass politics*, which they saw as descending into the rule of the mob. They saw mass politics as reaching its logical form in totalitarianism—in Hitlerism and Stalinism. The answer to mass politics lay in *pluralism*, the idea of a politics based on negotiation among the leaders of key social groups. For the neoconservatives, pluralism was America's answer to the dangers of mass politics, modern political sociology's version of Madison's system of checks and balances. Elections, the neoconservative pluralists argued, should be about concrete economic *interests*. Elections in the West, said Seymour Martin Lipset, were an expression of "the democratic class struggle." In the eyes of the neoconservatives, elections dominated by passion and moralism—the kind of elections the New Politics liberals seemed to like—were dangerous. It is one of the many ironies of liberalism's collapse that some of the very people who praised "interest-group pluralism" in the 1950s became sharp critics of the Democratic Party for giving voice and power to too many "special-interest groups." Neoconservatives (and most other conservatives) became increasingly uncomfortable with interest-group politics when more and varied interest groups found seats at the bargaining table.

The crowning concept in this period of intellectual ferment was *the end of ideology*. The end-of-ideology thesis was first floated at conferences of the Congress for Cultural Freedom, an international group of anticommunist intellectuals that was financed by the CIA (though few of its members knew that at the time). The end of ideology was a powerful weapon against communist dogmatism and for democratic tolerance. "For the radical intelligentsia, the old ideologies have lost their 'truth' and their power to persuade," wrote Daniel Bell in *The End of Ideology*. "Few serious minds believe any longer that one can set down 'blueprints' and through 'social engineering' bring about a new utopia of social harmony." Bell was acutely aware that the "end of ideology" thesis would have little attraction for the young New Left, whose rise he noticed long before other political commentators started paying attention. "The young intellectual is unhappy because 'the middle way' is for the middle-aged, not for him; it is without passion and it is deadening." The New Left, Bell wrote, "cannot define the content of the 'cause' they seek, but the yearning is clear." The "end of ideology" had many uses, not the least of which was to celebrate the United States, a nation that seemed allergic to ideologies of all kinds. In Lipset's formulation, the end of ideology was also about the decline of violent class struggle in societies where economic growth had satisfied the working class's needs and where the welfare state had curbed capitalism's excesses.

Viewed from the perspective of the 1990s, the end of ideology thesis looks far better than it did, say, in 1970 or 1980. Bell's misfortune was that the publication of *The End of Ideology* was followed almost immediately by an intensely ideological period, especially in America. First came the New Left, then the New Right. The new era seemed to mark the beginning, not the end, of ideology. Bell's critics rarely noted that even as he was predicting the end of ideology, he had noticed the rise of the New Left; in light of subsequent events, it was easy to dismiss Bell's analysis entirely.

Yet it is now clear that Bell, Lipset, and others among the end-of-ideologists were prescient in seeing the weaknesses that were undermining socialist ideology. Especially in the current era, when the concepts of "left" and "right" seem less useful than ever, Bell's talk of "the exhaustion of political ideas" seems more relevant than ever. The decline of the traditional working class has badly hurt the parties of the left throughout the West. In response, many socialist and social democratic parties in Western Europe—notably those in France, Italy, Spain, and increasingly, in Britain—have jettisoned most of the old socialism. The democratic socialists now cast themselves as modernizers, not Marxists. In Eastern Europe, the spectrum seems to run from those who merely mistrust socialism to those who detest it. The one kind of socialism that has genuine support in the East is the highly moderate brand of social democracy that Bell himself supports. With even the Soviet Union embracing some market mechanisms, Bell and his colleagues look prophetic—even if those who would now proclaim "the end of history" are going too far. And in the last two decades, the most dynamic forces in the world, the forces that have spurred revolution, are not ideological, certainly not class based, but rather ethnic and religious. (Oddly, only the revolution against Communist rule in Poland can be viewed as a working-class revolution in the Marxist sense.) The newspaper headlines these days are mainly about the resurgence of militant Islam and the growth of nationalism within the republics and former satellites of the Soviet Union. These developments, too, were foreseen by neoconservatives. Nathan Glazer, one of their number, long ago predicted what he called "the universalization of ethnicity" and argued that ethnicity often told us much more about modern politics than class.

But whatever the merits of the end of ideology as a prediction, it proved to be a decisive political move by the soon-to-be neoconservatives. Initially a reaction against Marxist dogmatism, it became the animating force behind a critique of liberal optimism—and liberal programs. It was the spirit behind the first neoconservative journal, *The Public Interest*.

The founding of *The Public Interest* in 1965 can be seen as a key event in a pivotal decade. In the first issue, its editors declared that the main obstacle to effective public policy was the blindness caused by "a prior commitment to ideology, whether it be liberal, conservative or radical."

"For it is the nature of ideology," the editors went on, "to *preconceive* reality; and that it is exactly such preconceptions that are the worst hindrances to knowing-what-one-is-talking-about."

Seen from the perspective of the early 1990s, such a view might be read as a liberal response to the dominance of conservative ideology in the Washington shaped by Ronald Reagan. Some of the neoconservatives who drifted back to liberalism and the Democrats—notably Moynihan and Bell—deployed exactly that critique against what they saw as conservative excesses. But when the editors of *The Public Interest* wrote that sentence, the Great Society was dominant in Washington, a young New Left was raising the banner of radicalism, and conservatism seemed routed.

Under the rubric of realism, the neoconservatives were to develop several themes that proved devastating to liberals. The most important was *the law of unintended consequences*. One of the core beliefs of American liberalism going back to the progressive era was its faith in the ability of politicians and planners to analyze social problems rationally and to formulate quasi-scientific solutions. Ironically, it was an article of *The Public Interest*'s own faith that social problems *should* be analyzed rationally. In the first issue, Moynihan spoke of "the professionalization of reform." Yet the journal's editors and writers were perpetually skeptical of the ability of reformers to see things clearly enough. They doubted that imperfect and unpredictable human beings could be organized socially on the basis of "scientific" knowledge alone. This sense was captured by the title of one of Glazer's major essays, "The Limits of Social Policy."

Thus, in article after article, *The Public Interest* chronicled the way in which one well-intended program after another had failed, often by solving one problem only to create a new one. The magazine became the leading exponent of what might be called the bump-in-the-carpet theory of social policy. Pushing down one bump only yields another, and often larger, bump elsewhere. The logic of this view led to a sense that perhaps the first bump should have been left alone. George H. Nash, the able historian of modern conservatism, cites the influence of a "law" discovered by Jay W. Forrester of MIT that "in complicated situations efforts to improve things often tend to make them worse, sometimes much worse, on occasion calamitous."

The notion that liberalism no longer knew what it was talking about became central to the neoconservative worldview. Liberals, said Daniel Patrick Moynihan, had to accept that there were certain problems that "we do not fully understand and certainly do not know how to solve." In his critique of the War on Poverty's community action program, *Maximum Feasible Misunderstanding*, Moynihan scored liberalism's blindness, with the heavy use of italics. "*A program was launched that was not understood, and not explained, and this brought about social losses that need not have occurred. . . . The government did not know what it was doing.* It had a theory. Or, rather, a set of theories. Nothing more."

The catalogue of failure was large and varied. Forced busing often drove so many whites from the public schools that racial segregation grew worse, not better. In any event, busing didn't really do much to help the students being bused. "Maximum feasible participation" in antipoverty programs created Moynihan's "maximum feasible misunderstanding," and the goal of fighting poverty was often lost in the acrimony of political dispute. High welfare payments might encourage the poor not to work at all. The burdens of affirmative action fell most heavily on poorer white males, not on those already well-off, and so in some ways increased social and economic inequality. Bilingual education programs left Spanish-speaking children *less* able to compete in a predominantly English-speaking country.

The neoconservative criticisms of liberal programs were powerful because they nearly always contained at least some truth, unintended consequences being a law of life in social policy. The neoconservatives were also more credible as critics of liberalism than the old-time conservatives. The neoconservatives, after all, were urbane intellectuals, not racists or penny-pinching businessmen. In principle, the neoconservatives really *did* believe in government programs. It was only this program and that one and the other that had failed.

But over time, the neoconservatives were calling nearly all efforts at social reform into question—the bump-in-the-carpet syndrome— and were increasingly skeptical of the reformers themselves. Soon, it seemed that the main consequences of government programs were always the unintended ones. At one level, the message of the neocon-

servatives to would-be reformers was undoubtedly valuable: Be humble, don't pretend to know what you don't know, be aware that you
may cause more harm than good. But the message that came to per-
meate the political culture and was seized upon by harder-line conservatives was quite different: Why bother? If you change things, you'll
probably only make them worse. Many of *The Public Interest*'s editors
were willing to acknowledge that their ideas had, indeed, drifted right,
under the influence of their own analyses. As a result, wrote Mark
Lilla, *The Public Interest*'s associate editor, "a new, more aggressive
line of argument was put forward." The new wisdom? "Whether well-
intentioned or not, the attempt to expand government activity simultaneously in many social spheres has been a counterproductive
mistake." Lilla offered this view in 1985. In two decades, the
neoconservatives attitude toward social reform had moved from skeptical support to principled opposition.

In fact, neoconservatives were gradually moving toward accepting the heart of the conservative faith: That human beings were deeply
flawed and in need of the restraints of *tradition* to keep them from
misbehaving. "The breakdown of traditional modes of behavior is the
chief cause of our social problems," Glazer wrote. The key to solving
many social problems, he said, was the restoration of "traditional restraints." The growing attraction of mainstream conservatism for the
neoconservatives could be seen most clearly in the growing influence
of Leo Strauss, a political theorist who sought to restore the influence
of the "ancients" (Plato and Aristotle) over modern political philosophers. Strauss, and over time most of the neoconservatives, emphasized the state's role in promoting a virtuous citizenry. Implicit in this
view was the contention that some forms of democracy could be held
to be inferior to some forms of authoritarian rule, if the authoritarians
produced "better" citizens. Such an idea was heretical in democratic
America, though neoconservative historians engaged in mighty labor
to show that such a view was exactly the one held by our founding
fathers. The Straussian disposition did much to create the neoconservatives' animosity toward the New Left and the counterculture. Kristol, heavily influenced by Strauss, was scornful of those who departed
from the principle of "self-discipline" in favor of "a 'liberation' of personal and collective selves." The liberationists, Kristol said, took far
too benign a view of human nature and failed to understand that a
democratic polity's destiny "is finally determined by the capacity of its
citizens to govern its passions and thereby rightly understand its enduring common interests." So much for "if it feels good, do it."

In later years, the neoconservatives, ever worried that liberal welfare programs were discouraging self-discipline and "virtue" among the poor, gave serious attention to Charles Murray's radically antistatist argument that since all welfare programs promoted dependency, nearly all of them should be abolished—for the benefit of the poor.

From the discussions of unintended consequences, it was just a short step to another neoconservative theme: that the gravest threat to democracy was *the crisis of authority*. The neoconservatives argued that too many people were demanding too much of government, creating "overload." Samuel P. Huntington warned that an "excess of democracy" would destroy democracy itself, turning on its head Al Smith's famous notion that there was nothing wrong with democracy that more democracy wouldn't cure. The message seemed to be that the disinherited were simply asking too much of government.

But with a few exceptions, the neoconservatives did not blame the poor for the nation's troubles. Rather, they assailed "the new class," the reform-minded intellectuals and bureaucrats whose lust for power, so it was said, knew no limits. Members of the new class were accused of wanting to expand the power of the state not to help the poor, but to help themselves. A large war on poverty, wrote Michael Novak, would generate "hundreds of thousands of jobs and opportunities" for those "whose hearts itch to do good and who long for 'meaningful' use of their talents, skills and years." The "new class" as a category came to include all manner of liberal and leftist enemies—Marxist professors, high school teachers, social workers, and an infinite variety of lawyers who worked for the regulatory commissions, Legal Aid, or Ralph Nader.

"The simple truth is that the professional classes of our modern bureaucratized societies are engaged in a class struggle with the business community for status and power," wrote Kristol in 1972, on the eve of Nixon's reelection. "Inevitably, this struggle is conducted under the banner of 'equality'—a banner also raised by the bourgeoisie in its revolutions." But while the new class expressed its animus toward the business community "in large ideological terms," Kristol wrote, its basic motivation was its belief that it "can do a better job of running our society and feels entitled to have the opportunity." He added: "This is what *they* mean by 'equality.' "

The attack on "the new class" gave neoconservatism real political bite. If the battle for equality was not a fight for the underdog but simply a way for pushy intellectuals and reformers to seize power, it could be dismissed. Nowhere is mistrust of elites more widespread than it is in the United States, so having an elite as an enemy is an enormous political asset. At the very point when mainstream conservatism was realizing its need to become "populist," the decidedly unpopulist neoconservatives gave the right the gift of a perfect elite enemy. In fact, the Goldwater conservatives had long suspected the intellectual classes. William F. Buckley, Jr., a leading defender of Sen. Joseph R. McCarthy, wrote in 1951 that the nation was divided into the " 'university' crowd and the 'nonuniversity' crowd." McCarthy, he said, appealed to the nonuniversity crowd—which Buckley most assuredly did *not* intend as a compliment to the well-educated. The typical view of the New Left among mainstream conservatives came from Jeffrey Hart, a literature professor at Dartmouth, who wrote in the *National Review* in 1970 of "the habitually antagonistic, and sometimes even treasonous, relationship" of intellectuals "to their surrounding society." The neoconservatives, with their gift for class analysis bequeathed them by their Marxist roots, legitimated this conservative mistrust. Right-wing ideas that were once condemned as "anti-intellectual" thus won a highly respectable intellectual pedigree, thanks to the neoconservatives.

The drift of neoconservative thinking would have led many of them to full-hearted conservatism eventually. What speeded the process up substantially was the rise of the New Left and its gradual embrace of the cause of the international revolutionary left. All those chants on behalf of Ho Chi Minh alarmed not only neoconservatives, but also democratic socialists such as Michael Harrington, Irving Howe, and Michael Walzer. Harrington, Howe, and Walzer shared the neoconservatives' background in anti-Stalinist politics and were no less fearful of the rise of a new form of dictator worship on the left. If Ho, Fidel, Chairman Mao, and sometimes even Kim Il Sung could be the proper objects of veneration on the left, then something must surely be wrong on the left. But unlike democratic socialists such as Harrington, the neoconservatives were already drifting right on a broad range of other issues. The more radical elements of the antiwar movement ensured that the conversion to conservatism would be total. One might propose an arithmetic rule: For every Viet Cong flag that sprouted at an antiwar rally, ten new neoconservative sympathizers were born, and ten already committed neoconservatives moved further to the right. Since many of the neoconservatives were Jewish, their horror was increased further by the tendency of many in the New Left to add the Palestine Liberation Organization to the canon of revolutionary organizations worthy of leftist homage.

And when the New Left turned on the universities, it was simply too much for the neoconservatives to bear. However much the neoconservatives mistrusted members of the new class, they believed deeply in the universities that spawned them. Many neoconservatives, sons and daughters of the poor, had found their opportunity for advancement in the academy. But the university was far more to the neoconservatives than a route to status and power. It was a model for the good society itself. The university was simultaneously a place where authority was strong and where freedom ruled. For many of the neoconservatives, it did not seem at all out of place to equate New Leftists who occupied college administration buildings with the young Nazis who had burned books.

Neoconservatism's steady march to the right was thus the result both of its own logic and of events that seemed to confirm it. What is often ignored is how closely neoconservatives were tracing the same path as that taken by less intellectual ex-liberals and ex-Democrats in the old big-city neighborhoods. If neoconservatives were angry at the behavior of privileged college students, so, too, were construction workers and policemen. If neoconservatives said that curbing the crime rates in big cities might be more important to urban survival than curbing poverty, so did many white ethnics, and not a few blacks. If neoconservatives worried that too much social spending went to programs that didn't really work, that sentiment had a wide audience among (not very rich) middle-class taxpayers. Irving Kristol thus had a point when he declared: "It is the self-imposed assignment of neoconservatism to explain to the American people why they are right, and to the intellectuals why they are wrong."

Among the major figures of neoconservatism, James Q. Wilson may have been closest to the feelings of angry whites in the cities. In "The Urban Unease," an important essay published in *The Public Interest* in the summer of 1968, Wilson vigorously defended inner-city whites against charges of racism. Their anger at the black poor, he argued, was based less on racism than on a sense that the black poor refused to live by standards that average whites saw as reasonable and decent. Wilson insisted that such whites had no objections to members of the black working class who shared those standards. In an argument that was to become more popular over the years with liberals such as Mario Cuomo, Wilson declared: "Much of what passes as 'race prejudice' may be little more than class prejudice, with race used as a rough indicator of social class." Blacks would have reason to reject such an argument, since using race as a "rough indicator of social class" sounds suspiciously like racism. Such "rough indicators" are often used as a basis for racial discrimination. But Wilson's analysis was truer to the real sentiments of most rebellious urban whites than the contention of some liberals that such whites were racists, pure and simple. Reality, as the neoconservatives liked to point out, was complicated.

Conservative politicians paid attention to these views and actively courted both the white working class and its intellectual defenders among the neoconservatives. "In a time when the national focus is on the unemployed, the impoverished, and the dispossessed, the working Americans have become the forgotten Americans," Richard M. Nixon declared in 1968. These forgotten Americans, Nixon said, "have a legitimate grievance that should be rectified and a just cause that should prevail." Nixon's speech could easily have been written by Wilson or a half dozen other neoconservatives. In 1968, most of the neoconservatives clung to their liberalism, rejecting Nixon and supporting Hubert Humphrey. By 1972, a large number went over to the other side. They came to see Nixon's as the just cause that deserved to prevail, especially over an opponent such as George McGovern.

The neoconservatives' last hurrah inside the Democratic Party was Henry Jackson's 1976 presidential candidacy. When Jackson lost the nomination to Jimmy Carter, some neoconservatives signed on with the highly moderate Democratic nominee who seemed to have learned many of the lessons the neoconservatives had to teach. But they were bitterly disappointed with Carter's appointments—too many, they thought, went to liberals—and even more disappointed with what they saw as Carter's weak and "Third Worldist" foreign policy. By 1980, most members of this, one of the most sophisticated groups of intellectuals in the country, were ready for a former baseball announcer and actor named Ronald Reagan.

III

So many Democrats of neoconservative orientation shifted so easily from Scoop Jackson in 1976 to Ronald Reagan in 1980 that it now seems to us as the most natural of political conversions. The political language we use is designed to make the shift seem normal. Henry Jackson becomes a "conservative" Democrat and all who followed him logically shifted to the "conservative" Republican after the "McGovernite" takeover of the Democratic Party, presumably reflected in the policies of Jimmy Carter. But there is something wrong here. For most of his career, Scoop Jackson was regarded as a *liberal*. Jimmy Carter was many things, but he bore little resemblance to George McGovern. And Ronald Reagan was by no means a "natural" choice for neoconservatives.

Few developments better illustrate the profound shift in our politics than the embrace of Ronald Reagan by so many neoconservatives. To see why this represents such a far-reaching change, one need only look back to 1964, to the response of the future neoconservatives to Barry M. Goldwater, Ronald Reagan's political avatar. To most of the neoconservatives, Barry Goldwater was a menace, and the movement he represented was little more than a collection of paranoids. Several of the future neoconservatives gave evidence of their view in an important book published in 1955, *The New American Right*, edited by Daniel Bell, and in an expanded edition of the book, *The Radical Right*, published on the eve of the Goldwater campaign in 1963. Their attitude was also captured well by Richard Hofstadter in *The Paranoid Style in American Politics*. Though Hofstadter cannot be neatly pigeonholed as a neoconservative (or as anything else), he is a central contributor to both of the Daniel Bell volumes, and his views on the Goldwater campaign can fairly be seen as a reflection of the sensibilities within the group that came to be the neoconservatives.

The contributors to the Bell volumes worried that the radical right drawn to Goldwater was not conservative at all, but "pseudoconservative" and populist. "The psychological stock-in-trade of the radical right rests on a threefold appeal," Bell wrote, "the breakdown of moral fiber in the United States; a conspiracy theory in the 'control apparatus' in the government which is selling out the country; and a detailed forecast of the Communist 'takeover' of the country." For the critics of the radical right, Joseph McCarthy's anticommunist crusade was not the reaction of traditional Republican elites to years of political failure during the New Deal but a kind of populist revolt against State Department and Wall Street elites. The "radical right" was defined at times just to include the kooky fringe, but at other times seemed to include most of what passed for modern conservatism. In the eyes of *The Radical Right*'s authors, the radical right was motivated less by politics than by a variety of personality disorders—notably "status anxiety" and the inability of the right's followers to adjust to the modern world. George Nash, the conservative historian, said the writers in the Bell volumes tended "to perceive conservatism as a problem of abnormal psychology rather than rational politics."

Goldwater himself was tarred with this brush. Hofstadter saw his candidacy as representing a dangerous departure from the healthiest aspects of the American politics, "the venerable tradition of appealing separately to a variety of special interests in the course of a campaign and then trying to act as a broker among them in the actual process of governing." Goldwater, Hofstadter wrote, saw this as "an ignoble kind of politics, vastly inferior to a politics that would address itself to realizing the religious and moral values of the public and to dealing with 'the moral crisis of our time.' He wanted, in short, to drive the politics out of politics." That is not, in fact, a bad description of what Ronald Reagan believed, or said, in 1980. Yet so many of the neoconservatives who had preached against Goldwaterism when Goldwater was its champion embraced the Goldwaterism of Ronald Reagan. What happened to transform conservatism from a personality disorder into a rational political response that the neoconservatives could endorse?

As we shall see in subsequent chapters, some of the change occurred not among the neoconservatives at all, but within the American right. In particular, by the time of Reagan's candidacy, most of the old conservatives had finally come to accept—as a political necessity, at least—that many aspects of the welfare state could simply not be repealed. George Nash notes that by the early 1970s, the old conservatives had also moved toward the center in their foreign policy views, notably by eschewing bold talk about burying Soviet Communism in the near future. "There was little serious discussion of 'liberation' or 'rollback' anymore," he wrote.

And then there was Ronald Reagan himself. His overall approach, suffused in a splendid optimism, seemed to have little in common with the dour predictions of imminent catastrophe that characterized those elements of the right wing that the neoconservatives had found so distasteful. Irving Kristol accurately captured this difference when he wrote of Reagan in 1983: "His posture was forward-looking, his accent was on economic growth rather than sobriety. All those Republicans with the hearts and souls of accountants—the traditional ideological core of the party—were nervous, even dismayed."

Yet Reagan was not that different from Goldwater. Like Goldwater, he saw the progressive income tax as the product of communist theory and spoke with occasional flippancy over the dangers of nuclear war. Reagan, too, denounced interest-group politics. And Reagan harvested millions of votes by speaking just as clearly as Goldwater did about the "moral crisis of our times." In the process, he helped spawn organizations with names such as the "Moral Majority" to press the gospel in the precincts.

What made the neoconservatives embrace Reagan's latter-day Goldwaterism was a shift in their own thinking and a shift in priorities caused by changing circumstances. As we have seen, the neoconservative critique of specific liberal programs gradually became so all-encompassing as to call into question the liberal project itself. In particular, the neoconservatives became increasingly skeptical of government. Daniel P. Moynihan, who paradoxically maintained more faith in the liberal project than many of his fellow neoconservatives, spoke plainly about the limits of government. "Liberals," he declared in 1967, "must divest themselves of the notion that the nation—and especially the cities of the nation—can be run from agencies in Washington." In an essay published in 1968, Moynihan pressed the theme. "Somehow liberals have been unable to acquire from life," he said, "what conservatives seem to be endowed with at birth, namely, a healthy skepticism of the powers of government agencies to do good."

In addition, the neoconservatives became increasingly skeptical of interest-group pluralism, which they had once hailed as a stabilizing force in politics. When the number of interest groups increased to include blacks, feminists, gays, Native Americans, Hispanics, and others, interest-group bargaining suddenly seemed not stabilizing but disruptive. Neoconservatives argued that liberalism's response to this new array of interest groups was to shift from advocating "equality of opportunity" to trying to achieve "equality of results" through affirmative action. Moynihan accurately captured the fears of the neoconservatives that "the equality revolution" and the expansion of interest-group politics was getting out of hand. "Once this process gets legitimated there is no stopping it," Moynihan wrote in 1968, "and without intending anything of the sort, I fear it will be contributing significantly to the already well-developed tendency to politicize (and racialize) more and more aspects of modern life."

There is some irony to Moynihan's argument, since he had been the proud coauthor of what Lyndon Johnson regarded as his best civil rights speech. In the speech, given at Howard University in June 1965, Johnson declared bluntly: "We seek not just freedom but opportunity —not just legal equity but human ability—not just equality as a right and a theory, but equality *as a fact and as a result*." (Emphasis added.) Affirmative action was especially disturbing to neoconservatives because it disrupted a reward structure that they considered largely just. While the neoconservatives accepted that market outcomes were not always fair and that some redistribution of income through the welfare state was desirable, they believed that such benefits as admission to universities and the professions were largely based on *merit*. It was not lost on the neoconservatives' critics that they were most conservative about the institutions in which they had themselves been successful. For rising groups, especially blacks, challenging old meritocracies through affirmative action was no less reasonable than redistributing income through welfare. But what was, in one sense, a straightforward conflict of interest was inflated into an angry debate about values. To blacks seeking affirmative action, the neoconservatives were no less racist about their own institutions than segregationist restaurateurs were about theirs. To the neoconservatives, such a comparison was libelous. They opposed segregation and believed in equality of opportunity. They drew the line at quotas. But as affirmative action rather than an end to segregation became central to the civil rights debate, this put the neoconservatives on the conservative side of the argument.

The drift right was also noticeable on morality and tradition. Many of the neoconservatives who had scoffed at Goldwater's talk about a "moral crisis" came to believe that the country faced just that. In 1964, talk of "permissiveness" seemed to be the staple of cultural yahoos and prudes who despised modernity and sophistication. But the neoconservatives became so alarmed by the counterculture that they felt compelled to defend what they consciously called "bourgeois morality." They did not do so without qualms. "The attitude of neoconservatives to bourgeois society and the bourgeois ethos is one of detached attachment," Kristol wrote in 1979. "This *modest* enthusiasm distinguishes neoconservatism from the Old Right and the New Right—both of which are exceedingly suspicious of it." But the neoconservatives agreed entirely with both wings of the right that the country needed a lot more bourgeois morality than it was getting. One did not even have to be a conservative to agree with Daniel Bell that "modern capitalism has been transformed by a widespread hedonism that has made mundane concerns, rather than transcendental ties, the center of people's lives." Bell feared that capitalism might be destroyed by its "cultural contradictions." The consumerism and "permissiveness" that capitalism promoted could undermine the very virtues—hard work, discipline, postponement of gratification—that capitalism depended on for its survival. The old conservatives had suspected this for a long time.

Yet if a Daniel Bell (who in any event rejected the neoconservative label) could be skeptical of the workings of capitalism, neoconservatives as a group became increasingly impressed with the system as the years went on. A collection of thinkers that included many ex-Trotskyists, social democrats, and other critics of capitalism spoke with increasing admiration for the modern business system. Asked in 1988 by the conservative journal *Policy Review* how her views on domestic policy had changed, Jeane Kirkpatrick spoke for many in her movement when she replied: "I would say that the single most important change in my views in the last decade has been a much greater appreciation of market economics. I have learned some things about economic questions that I did not know." The new received wisdom of the neoconservatives on economics was summarized by Kristol in the concluding essay of a 1980 special issue of *The Public Interest* on "The Crisis in Economic Theory." Kristol listed five "bedrock truths" about economics:

> (1) the overwhelming majority of men and women are naturally and incorrigibly interested in improving their material conditions; (2) efforts to repress this natural desire lead only to coercive and impoverished polities; (3) when this natural desire is given sufficient latitude so that commercial transactions are not discouraged, economic growth does take place; (4) as a result of such growth, everyone does eventually indeed improve his condition, however unequally in extent or time; (5) such economic growth results in a huge expansion of the property-owning middle class—a necessary (though not sufficient) condition for a liberal society in which human rights are respected.

William F. Buckley, Jr., or Milton Friedman could hardly have offered a more succinct summary of what Goldwater-Reagan conservatism had always preached.

Finally, neoconservatives were pushed rightward by the politics of foreign policy in the 1970s. Many of the neoconservatives were social democrats whose history of combat with communists already made them more anticommunist than the average conservative. And with not only Jimmy Carter but also Richard Nixon and Gerald Ford embracing a policy of détente with the Soviet Union, the neoconservatives were forced to look ever farther to the right for a champion. In 1960, cold warriors who thought the Eisenhower administration was spending too little on defense could repair to John F. Kennedy's campaign and be called "liberal." By 1980, that position in presidential politics was the exclusive province of the Republican right. It was no wonder that conservatives such as Ronald Reagan and Jack Kemp were so eager to invoke John Kennedy's words on behalf of their own foreign policies.

Jimmy Carter posed a particular problem for the neoconservatives. Carter could hardly be viewed as a liberal—most ardent liberals certainly did not see him that way. In fact, it was Carter who began the military buildup that Ronald Reagan took credit for. The neoconservatives could not have asked for a closer friend in the White House than Carter's national security adviser, Zbigniew Brzezinski.

But to the neoconservatives, Carter's policies were based ultimately on an incoherent moralism, and they could not abide his human rights policy. This was ironic, since neoconservatives had originally raised the "human rights" banner themselves in attacking the mistreatment of dissidents and minorities within the Soviet empire. Speaking about human rights gave neoconservatives a way of criticizing the "amorality" of the Nixon-Kissinger policies of détente. But when Jimmy Carter made human rights the cornerstone of his policy, he weakened American support for right-wing dictators who had been America's allies. This was not what the neoconservatives had in mind. Thus, Irving Kristol assailed Carter for holding a "double standard, whereby left-wing governments are given the benefit of every doubt as concerns human rights while right-wing regimes are continually indicted." Jeane Kirkpatrick's famous distinction between "authoritarianism" and "totalitarianism" was aimed at providing neoconservatives with a standard of their own. In Kirkpatrick's view, the United States *should* treat anticommunist "authoritarian" regimes more gently not only because they were America's allies, but also because they were more capable than communist states of transforming themselves in a libertarian direction. To Kirkpatrick's critics, hers was the double standard, which, in any event, has been proven wrong by the recent events in the East Bloc. But whatever the merits, casting Carter as a moralist who had weakened America in the world had the virtue of clarifying the political choices the neoconservatives had to make. It made Ronald Reagan much more attractive.

Thus did most of the neoconservatives give up the fight against Michael Harrington's label and embrace the reality of their conservatism. Although some in their number continued to insist on their liberalism (and were thus, as in the case of Moynihan, abandoned by some of their old neoconservative comrades) many neoconservatives headed right, often finding themselves on the far wing of the Reagan camp. For Norman Podhoretz, one of the pioneer neoconservatives, Reagan's early opening to the Soviets was a betrayal of the principles he had once espoused and represented a form of "appeasement." Jeane Kirkpatrick became a hero within Republican circles not among moderates, who might once have been drawn to her defenses of the welfare state, but among hard-liners, who saw much common ground between their foreign policy vision and hers. William Bennett may have been the most successful case of a neoconservative who became a right-wing hero. The right could only cheer at his attacks on the education establishment (a "new class" stronghold if ever there was one) and on 1960s permissiveness.

The most striking indicator of change within the neoconservative family was the role of William Kristol, Irving Kristol's son, who became one of the most able advocates of the conservative cause within the Reagan and Bush administrations. There was nothing at all faint-hearted about Bill Kristol's embrace of the right; his conservatism needed no prefix. He was even willing to take on a task that the most ardent Republicans and conservatives warned him against: He signed on as Vice President Dan Quayle's top policy adviser and chief of staff. Thus did Midwestern conservatism at last make peace with the intellectuals of the East Coast.

IV

The practical ways in which neoconservatism undermined liberalism are numerous and well-known. The most widely discussed have to do with the sheer number of institutions the neoconservatives helped the right to create. Irving Kristol, who understood better than most the intellectual influence that money could buy, appealed to businessmen to finance their friends in the new class, not their enemies. "You can only beat an idea with another idea, and the war of ideas and ideologies will be won or lost within the 'new class,' not against it," Kristol wrote. "Business certainly has a stake in this war, but for the most part seems blithely unaware of it." The businessmen suddenly became aware and helped create literally scores of conservative research institutes, law centers, and journals. Not all of these were specifically neoconservative in orientation, but the neoconservatives (and especially Irving Kristol) were present at the creation of many of them.

But the intellectual damage that the neoconservatives did to liberalism was much more profound than anything they did organizationally. Put simply, they legitimized the conservative war on the state. In a book defending liberal programs, John E. Schwartz, a political scientist, accurately captured the popular sense that neoconservatism had done so much to create. "Dazed and dispirited, Americans entered the 1980s disturbed by the sensation that the nation's last twenty years had been largely misspent," he wrote, "that during all those years, bit by bit, we had traveled down the wrong road." Ronald Reagan summarized matters in one of the pithy phrases that made him so successful. "In the war on poverty," Reagan said, "poverty won."

There was much irony in what the neoconservatives accomplished. Initially, after all, their project had been to purify policy from the irrationality of ideology. In the end, they lent legitimacy to one of the most ideological administrations in American history. The neoconservatives had been specialists in *public* policy. They had believed in government and in what it could accomplish, provided that government allowed itself to be guided by the evidence. In the end, their project was increasingly guided not by evidence but by anger—at the new class, at advocates of affirmative action, at the counterculture, at foreign-policy moralists.

And at government. In their search for an answer to "the crisis of authority" that so worried them, the neoconservatives, like their enemies in the New Left, were moving toward an antistatist libertarianism. The position certainly had a logic. "The abolition of politics is the libertarians' solution to the crisis of public authority," wrote Stephen L. Newman, a critical but sensitive student of libertarian thought. "Their idea is to replace the government with the market wherever possible." That, increasingly, was the neoconservative solution of choice.

Yet the neoconservatives knew better than to believe that markets —or any other cure-all—could, of themselves, solve intractable social problems. The false rhetoric of our current politics is based on a thoroughly misleading view of what actually happened during the 1960s. It vastly exaggerates what the Great Society did and what it actually spent. At the same time, it ignores what it actually accomplished. No one has been more eloquent on these subjects than the man who had once claimed that government in the Great Society era didn't know what it was doing: Daniel Patrick Moynihan. It is simply preposterous, Moynihan argues, to assert that the government spent huge sums on the Great Society. Moynihan noted that in its best years, the budget of the Office of Economic Opportunity was $1.7 billion. If all that money had been distributed directly to the poor, Moynihan noted, each poor person would have received the munificent sum of $50 to $70. The biggest increases in spending in that period were for social security and the Medicare/Medicaid health programs. The increases in social security did just what they were supposed to do: They virtually wiped out poverty among the elderly. The medical-care programs provided health coverage for millions who had none. One can argue the merits of these programs. But if any programs "threw" huge sums of money at problems, it was these, and they are popular enough that few conservatives would abolish them. As for the "experimental" Great Society programs that were supposed to be such failures, Head Start was so successful that it has become the conservatives' favorite program—George Bush himself wants to spend far more on it. As Moynihan summarized: "There have been more successes than we seem to want to know."

The point here is not that the efforts made at social reform in the 1960s were all smashing successes. Rather, it is that the very approach to social policy that the neoconservatives rightly valued—a sober willingness to examine evidence—suggests that the Great Society was a complicated mixture of successes and failures. The other great neoconservative lesson is that solving complicated social problems is hard. That some Great Society programs were miserable failures should thus hardly be a surprise. Yet by boiling down the debate on social policy to the formula that "liberal programs failed," a view that the neoconservatives inadvertently encouraged, we have simply legitimized doing nothing at all. That doesn't solve social problems, either.

One of neoconservatism's strengths was the delight it took in the ironies of politics and other human endeavors. Neoconservatives might thus delight in the irony that they effectively ganged up with the New Left in defeating liberalism. If the New Leftists opposed the liberal state because they were antiauthoritarians, the neoconservatives documented how the liberal state undermined authority. The neoconservatives were, in theory, defenders of sober, "professionalized" reform, while the New Left made such reform its enemy. But both ended up undermining and defeating the professional reformers.

The tragedy for liberals is that they had much to learn from the neoconservatives, even as they could have learned a few things about democracy and participation from the New Left. In particular, the neoconservatives were right in seeing virtue as a legitimate goal of government policy—even if they were wrong in using virtue as a battering ram against democracy, which they sometimes did. The neoconservatives were right in insisting that a democratic system depended on citizens capable of exercising discipline and self-restraint —even if their fears about the assaults of the New Left and the counterculture on such values were exaggerated.

By the late 1960s, it was clear that liberals needed to pay heed to some of the neoconservatives' warnings. By then, liberals no longer had enough self-confidence to know which, if any, values they wanted the state to encourage. Liberals increasingly forgot that there is a distinction between using the state to *enforce* a rigid moral code—an effort as impractical as it is unappealing—and insisting that programs *promote* certain values that are beneficial to both society and the individuals who practiced them. Over time, liberals were no longer certain what kind of family was worth encouraging; they feared welfare programs that required recipients to work; they nearly always saw understandable worries about law and order as covert forms of racism; and they came to believe that almost all doctrines emphasizing the value of local community were indistinguishable from the phony "states' rights" arguments used by segregationists.

As we shall see in the next two chapters, the liberals' failure to learn such lessons cost them a great deal.

3

NOT
BLACK AND
WHITE:
Race, "Values,"
and Willie Horton

IN THE 1988 PRESIDENTIAL CAMPAIGN, Willie Horton became almost as famous as George Bush or Michael Dukakis. Horton was the convicted murderer who raped a woman in Maryland while on furlough from a Massachusetts prison. Horton was black. The woman was white. Willie Horton became the central figure of the Bush campaign's efforts to discredit Governor Michael Dukakis for being both soft on crime and incompetent. Enraged Democrats said Willie Horton's real purpose was to provide the Republicans with a way of appealing to white racism.

"The symbolism was very powerful," Susan Estrich, Dukakis's campaign manager, said after the election. "You can't find a stronger metaphor, intended or not, for racial hatred in this country than a black man raping a white woman. And that's what the Willie Horton story was." The leaders of the Bush campaign insisted that Dukakis's furlough program, not Horton's race, was the issue. "It defied common sense," Lee Atwater, Bush's campaign manager, said of the furlough program. "Why should you let a guy like that, who has no chance for parole, out for a weekend with no supervision?"

The Atwater-Estrich exchange, at a conference on the 1988 campaign at Harvard University, embodied more than three decades of political argument and posturing around the race issue. On the one side were Democrats and liberals who contended that Republicans had used racial divisions to their advantage for twenty-five years. On the other side were Republicans and conservatives who insisted that when they talked about law and order, busing and quotas, they were really talking about law and order, busing and quotas—and not race.

Both sides are right. As the Republicans saw clearly, many of the grievances that whites expressed in the language of racial politics were still legitimate grievances. To pick the most obvious example: In the 1960s, crime rates did soar, especially in big cities. Because many whites linked rising crime rates with blacks in the underclass, liberals were uneasy with the crime issue and saw the very words *law and order* as a racist code. Over time, liberals gradually accepted that law-abiding citizens of all races were right to expect their politicians to talk about, perhaps even do something about, the upsurge in crime. Still the liberals saw protecting the rights of the accused as an honored value, and many of their number continued to oppose the death penalty. Yet as crime rates soared, the public worried increasingly less about how the accused were treated and a great deal more about crime's victims. The death penalty became a popular symbol of the public's frustration with the workings of the criminal justice system. In a situation where nothing seemed to stem the rate of violent crime, the death penalty had the virtue of seeming *decisive*. Thus, many voters who cited crime as their reason for moving away from liberalism meant precisely what they said. Crime was not simply a code word for race.

Yet liberals were also right: Racial politics has been a driving force in the nation's political life since its inception, and it has been central to the Republican and conservative resurgence since 1968. It is a simple and undeniable truth of American politics that the Republicans gained a great deal both in the South and in white enclaves of Northern big cities because of the reaction against the Democratic Party's stand in favor of civil rights. The race issue also helped Republicans and conservatives indirectly, by providing them with yet another way of casting liberals as "elitists" who were indifferent to the concerns of average (white) Americans. Indeed, racial politics allowed the Republicans to take advantage of the very class inequalities that their laissez-faire economic philosophy defended. The whites who bore the brunt of racial change tended to be the less affluent. In cities, they lived closer to black neighborhoods than better-off whites. In the occupational structure, they were at the lower rungs and were more likely to come into direct competition with blacks. Republicans and conservatives profited from the anger of less well-off whites at wealthier liberals who preached racial tolerance but proposed to pay little price themselves for achieving it. The invention of the term *limousine liberal* by Mario Proccacino, the right-wing Democrat who lost to New York City's Mayor John V. Lindsay in 1969, was thus one of conservatism's most brilliant strokes. The term *new class* had a distant, academic ring. Everyone knew who the "limousine liberals" were.

Racial politics were only part of the much broader attack on liberalism that conservatives mounted in the name of "traditional values." Michael Dukakis spoke contemptuously of the Republicans' campaign of "flags and furloughs." But flags and furloughs spoke precisely to the doubts that many Americans developed about liberalism from 1968 onward. In the eyes of many of their traditional supporters, liberal Democrats seemed to oppose the personal disciplines—of family and tough law enforcement, of community values and patriotism —that average citizens, no less than neoconservative intellectuals, saw as essential to holding a society together. These "middle Americans," as they were labeled in the Nixon years, lived in the modern world but were deeply skeptical of modernity. As Jonathan Rieder, a sensitive student of middle America, put it: "The struggle over patriotism represented a broader cultural struggle between the forces of moral tradition and modernist liberation."

As we have seen, the cultural changes of the 1960s turned liberals into allies—even if they were often reluctant recruits—of a "modernist liberation" associated with the well-off, the well-educated, and the young. This helped foster the perception that most damaged liberals in the sixties and seventies: the sense that liberalism no longer represented the values and aspirations of society's hardworking underdogs. Michael Dukakis's aides instinctively sensed the problem and moved to combat the idea that liberals were out of touch via the slogan "He's on your side." The slogan seemed like a patented Democratic idea. Repeated proclamations of liberal solicitude for the common people had been the key to Democratic triumphs under Franklin Roosevelt. Thus the New Deal slogan "If you want to live like a Republican, vote Democratic." By the 1970s, liberalism had come to be seen as a set of abstract, even exotic commitments felt most strongly by the well-educated members of the upper middle class. This transformation helped create "conservative populism" and gave Republicans their best opportunity in decades to bid on an even basis for the ballots of the less well-off. For Democrats, the most chilling statistic of the 1988 election is this: If only the votes of those earning less than $50,000 a year had been counted, George Bush would still have won. In the end, the old-family, Andover- and Yale-educated millionaire-turned-populist was more successful than Michael Dukakis, the son of immigrants, in persuading the middle class that he was on their side.

Democrats and liberals were complicit in this transformation of American politics. Above all, they failed to understand that the burdens of achieving racial justice were being borne disproportionately by their traditional supporters among the less affluent whites. In explaining his loss in Connecticut's United States Senate election in 1970, Joseph Duffey, a liberal Democrat, saw the nexus of class and race far more clearly than most liberals did. "For a decade now, most liberals and reformers have acted as if there were only two major problems in America, race and poverty," he said. "Many of our policies have been formulated as if there were only two major groups—the affluent and the welfare poor. But somewhere between affluence and grinding poverty stand the majority of American families." The liberals had failed on the issues of race and poverty, Duffey said, because their "policies and the way they were presented have served to further divide the people who should stand together if ever there is to be a majority constituency for change in America."

Liberalism's failures in dealing sympathetically with the legitimate resentments of the white working class should not be allowed to obscure the major achievement that civil rights represented. Civil rights was more than just a series of legal and legislative victories, important though they were. It was a cultural revolution. In concrete terms, a substantial black middle class stands as a monument to the successes of the civil rights movement, even as the growth of the underclass suggests its limits. And the vast change in how people talk, write, and think about race has been breathtaking. It is difficult to remember how fundamental the transformation has been without recalling how pervasive, public, and politically popular racism was in our very recent history. No United States senator would now write a book, as Mississippi's Theodore G. Bilbo did in the late 1940s, called *Separation or Mongrelization: Take Your Choice.* No president now would give credence to such views, as Dwight D. Eisenhower did at a presidential news conference in 1957 when he spoke with at least some sympathy about the fears of Southern whites whom he said "see a picture of the mongrelization of the race." Without the liberal reforms of the 1960s, moreover, two of the most heartening political developments of recent years—L. Douglas Wilder's victory in Virginia as the first elected black governor in the nation's history and David Dinkins's election as the first black mayor of New York City—would have been impossible. And not all of liberalism's defeats on the race issue were self-inflicted. Given the intensity of resistance to desegregation in the South, some of the electoral defeats suffered by liberal Democrats because of civil rights were unavoidable, something Lyndon Johnson saw clearly. Hours after he signed the Civil Rights Act of 1964, he told Bill Moyers, his press secretary: "I think we just delivered the South to the Republican Party for a long time to come."

Nonetheless, liberals made a difficult political situation a great deal worse by fundamentally misunderstanding the dilemmas that the civil rights revolution posed to members of the white working and lower middle classes. For this reason, liberals bear nearly as much responsibility for the growth in white backlash as do the conservatives who profited from it politically.

The task of providing eloquent accounts of that struggle has already ably been carried out by such writers as John Hope Franklin, Taylor Branch, and David Garrow, among many others. Since I am writing not about liberalism's successes but its *failures*, I shall concentrate in what follows on the wrong turns liberalism took in the sixties and seventies. My goal is to try to answer this question: How did one of liberalism's most noble achievements, the civil rights push of the 1960s, turn on the liberal cause with such a vengeance?

II

The thirteen months between the signing of the Civil Rights Act on July 2, 1964, and the signing of the Voting Rights Act on August 6, 1965, represented the high tide of the civil rights movement. In that period, opposition to civil rights seemed to be isolated to a handful of states in the Deep South. True, George Wallace had run strongly in white working-class areas in Wisconsin, Indiana, and Maryland, where he had entered primaries in the spring of 1964 to oppose Lyndon Johnson's civil rights policies. But by November, all these states were safely in the Democratic column. Lyndon Johnson overwhelmed Barry Goldwater in all but five states in the Deep South and in Goldwater's home state of Arizona. White backlash was proclaimed a dying force by politicians, journalists, and academics alike.

How quickly the world changed. Martin Luther King captured

the change in mood well in his aptly titled book *Where Do We Go From Here? Chaos or Community*. King noted that on August 6, 1965, when Lyndon Johnson signed the Voting Rights Act, his office was crowded with black and white leaders who witnessed an event they "confidently felt to be historic." Yet just one year later, some of the very same people "were leading marchers in the suburbs of Chicago amid a rain of rocks and bottles, among burning automobiles, to the thunder of jeering thousands, many of them waving Nazi flags."

The summer of 1966 was a period of deep discontent within the civil rights movement. Having posted so many gains in the first half of the decade, civil rights leaders perceived that the pace of change was slowing down and worried that liberals were growing weary of the political burdens of their cause. The frustration was greatest among younger blacks, who grew suspicious of coalition politics with whites and angry at being dependent on the actions of white politicians. For them, the key event was what came widely to be called "the sellout at Atlantic City."

At the 1964 Democratic National Convention, an integrated delegation organized by the Mississippi Freedom Democratic Party sought to replace the official delegation of the segregationist Democrats—Democrats who felt no loyalty whatsoever to the national party. The Freedom Democrats were led by men and women who had been arrested and beaten in their pursuit of the right to vote. The official delegation was dominated by conservatives committed to the defeat of both civil rights and Lyndon Johnson. But having signed the civil rights bill, Johnson's mind was focused on the pursuit of moderate and conservative votes, and he did not want to offend the South further by unseating the regulars. Instead, Johnson offered a compromise that would permit only two members of the Freedom Democrats' delegation to sit on the floor—and merely as delegates at large. The compromise also pledged full integration of delegations at the *next* convention, which would be held after Johnson was safely reelected.

The compromise infuriated the Freedom Democrats, who felt they had more than just a legal right to be seated. "What entitled the sharecroppers to seats was not their claim to justice alone," wrote Todd Gitlin much later, "but the quality of their suffering, the intensity of their bond, the witness that their entire lives bore forth." A young leader of the Student Nonviolent Coordinating Committee named Stokely Carmichael expressed his rage: "This proves that the liberal Democrats are just as racist as Goldwater."

Carmichael's anger deepened, and it was he who gave the black struggle a new slogan two years later. On June 16, 1966, after a bitter day of demonstrations and police provocations, Carmichael rose to a platform in Greenwood, Mississippi, and told his audience that "every courthouse in Mississippi should be burnt down tomorrow so we can get rid of the dirt." Black sheriffs, he said, should preside over black counties and black citizens should demand "Black Power."

"We want Black Power!" Carmichael shouted, and the crowd roared back, "We want Black Power! We want Black Power!"

Thus began a revolution within the civil rights revolution. The venerable slogan of "Freedom now!" was being shoved aside by the new call for "Black Power!" The rise of Black Power created excitement, fear, uncertainty, confusion. Martin Luther King's initial worry was that the movement was on the verge of abandoning the commitment to nonviolence that had been so central to its ethical and strategic vision. King also worried that black nationalism was leading, willy-nilly, to the exclusion of whites from the movement. "We must never forget that there are some white people in the United States just as determined to see us free as we are to be free ourselves," he said.

Yet King also understood the yearnings that lay beneath the Black Power slogan. "If we are to solve our problems," he said, "we've got to transform our powerlessness into positive and creative power." But he knew that he and Carmichael differed in their understanding of Black Power's meaning. King's view was that of a Christian theologian and preacher who was deeply suspicious of the very word *power*. The only proper use of power, King said, was "to bring about the political and economic change necessary to make the good life a reality." Neither political nor economic power could be viewed as ends in themselves, he said. The real goal of the movement was "a truly beloved society, the creation of the beloved community."

The rise of Black Power created a furious debate over the future of black America—and a sharp reaction within the white community. What became clear almost immediately was that Black Power could mean many different things. From one perspective, Black Power was no more threatening than Irish power or Italian power had been generations earlier. Far from being a radical break with America's past, Christopher Lasch argued, Black Power was quite consistent with the strategies of other ethnic groups in their quest for status and influence. "Black Power proposes, or seems to propose, that Negroes do for themselves what other ethnic groups, faced with somewhat similar conditions, have done—advance themselves not as individuals but as groups conscious of their own special interests and identity." Lasch contended that contrary to popular myths, ethnic groups such as the Irish did not rise "through the usual avenues of social mobility." Such groups could not have taken advantage of the opportunities available to them if they "had not already achieved a strong sense of ethnic solidarity."

Lasch also saw an invigorated black nationalism as a potential solution to the weakness of the Northern black community. "What the assimilationist argument does overlook," he wrote, "is that the civil rights movement owes its existence, in part, to the rise of a Negro subculture in the South." The absence of a comparable culture in the Northern ghettos, Lasch said, helped explain why blacks had made more progress in the South than in the North. Northern blacks, he said, badly needed their own sense of culture and community.

Yet there was a profound ambiguity about Black Power. At times it was proposed in Lasch's sense as a route for blacks to achieve full integration in American life. At other times, it rejected integration altogether. Carmichael himself was ambiguous about the meaning of his own slogan. In his book with Charles Hamilton defining Black Power, Carmichael said Black Power aimed at "full participation in the decision-making process affecting the lives of black people, and recognition of the virtues in themselves as black people." Carmichael and Hamilton endorsed "viable coalitions between blacks and whites who accept each other as co-equal partners," but said that "at this stage, given the nature of society, distinct roles must be played."

But Carmichael and Hamilton then veered away from this pluralist notion and declared that black people were really not part of the American system at all, but rather constituted a "colony" within the country. As a political matter, Carmichael and Hamilton were seeking to align the black cause in America with the anticolonial rebellions that had just swept the world. "Whether one is talking about the fantastic changes taking place in Africa, Asia or the black communities of America," they wrote, "it is necessary to realize that the current, turbulent period in history is characterized by the demands of previously oppressed people to be free of their oppression." Advocates of a "colonial" view of the black situation in America developed ingenious arguments demonstrating that Bedford-Stuyvesant and Tanzania had much in common. They contended that white society's main goal was to exploit cheap black labor and transfer whatever "surplus" they made in the black community back into the "metropolitan," i.e., white, economy. Under this theory, even economic growth in the broader society would not help the exploited ghetto. For the ghetto, like a colony, had to "import" most of its consumer goods from the outside. "Much as a colony is dependent on its 'mother country,' " wrote one advocate of colonial theory, "so too is the ghetto dependent on the larger society for most of its material needs."

Although aspects of the colonial analogy rang true to many in the ghetto, the problems with the theory were immense. For one thing, black neighborhoods tended to suffer not so much from "exploitative" investment as from a lack of investment altogether. And it was not at all clear that any plausible political strategy could follow from the colonial analogy. As Theodore Draper argued, "colonies rebel to throw out alien rulers and establish national independence and sovereignty." Draper went on: "If American blacks truly constituted a colony, Carmichael and Hamilton would no doubt have advocated the same course in the United States."

Over time, however, Carmichael followed just this logic and came to identify American blacks not with other Americans, but with the formerly colonized poor of the Third World. "The proletariat has become the Third World and the bourgeoisie has become white western society," he said in 1967. Carmichael's concept ruled out any hope of coalition politics between blacks and disadvantaged American whites, who were written out of the proletariat by definitional fiat. This analysis fit in neatly with the directions the New Left was taking. "The people, the majority of people in the affluent society, are on the side of that which is," the New Left's teacher, Herbert Marcuse, wrote in 1966, "not that which can and ought to be."

Most black Americans did not accept a view of themselves as a colony, but the separatist implications of Black Power and colonial theory had a wide influence. In a rather moderate presentation of the meaning of Black Power, Nathan Wright, Jr., a black Episcopal Church official, argued somewhat surprisingly that the goal of integration had been imposed upon the black community by *whites*. Blacks, Wright said, "should long ago have perceived that enforced 'integration' as a goal is a compromise of black Americans on its face. Negroes do not need the presence of white people either to give them worth or to learn." Wright's argument was representative of the new emphasis on "self-reliance," "self-defense" (the latter phrase made popular by the Black Panther movement), and pride.

Under other circumstances, Black Power might have been a logical strategy, a much-needed effort to build political solidarity. It was precisely such unity, after all, that allowed blacks in later years to achieve so many electoral breakthroughs. Even Black Power's critics, moreover, recognized that new departures were needed to reinvigorate the civil rights movement. Lyndon Johnson, no friend of Black Power when he was in office, understood its roots. "Black Power," he wrote in his memoirs, "had a different meaning to the black man, who until recently had to seek the white world's approval and for whom success had come largely on white people's terms." Moreover, moderate black leaders such as Bayard Rustin sensed that a transformation in the civil rights movement was taking place—and was necessary. "The civil rights movement is evolving from a protest movement into a full-fledged *social movement*," Rustin wrote in an important essay published in *Commentary* in February 1965. "It is now concerned not merely with removing the barriers to full opportunity but with achieving the fact of equality."

But as a practical matter, Black Power's impact was divisive and in many ways counterproductive. Conservatives seized on black separatism as a rationale for halting progress toward integration. If blacks did not want integration, the arguments went, why should whites "impose" it on them? If blacks wanted to have nothing to do with whites, the more extreme opponents of integration asked, why should whites feel obliged to have anything to do with them? Black separatism also led to the loss of liberal self-confidence. If the entire society was "hopelessly racist," liberals worried, what right did it have to impose its "white bourgeois values" on the ghetto? Even if certain values at work in the ghetto seemed "dysfunctional" to whites, perhaps that was just because the whites did not understand black culture. There were, to be sure, many things that whites failed to understand about the ghetto. But it was also true that many of the patterns of ghetto behavior were thoroughly harmful to the people who lived there. Separatism, perhaps inadvertently, thus encouraged the most subtle kind of racism: the refusal to admit that certain values were color-blind and worth promoting in the ghetto no less than outside. As William J. Wilson, the nation's premier student of the ghetto argued recently, the "black solidarity" movement encouraged scholars to focus only on "the positive aspects of the black experience" and "discouraged research by liberal scholars on the poor black family and the ghetto community." Promising scholarly efforts to solve real problems "were cut short by calls for 'reparations' or for 'black control of institutions serving the black community.' "

The argument over black family life moved from the academy to politics—with explosive results—when an internal Johnson administration policy paper written by Daniel Patrick Moynihan was leaked to the press in August 1965. The "Moynihan Report," as it became known, asserted that while working and middle-class blacks were progressing, a lower-class black group was falling steadily behind. In a memorable phrase that would forever be mired in controversy (and that Moynihan openly borrowed from Kenneth Clark, one of the nation's leading black sociologists), the young assistant secretary of labor asserted that "at the center of the tangle of pathology is the weakness of the Negro family." One-third of black children, Moynihan's statistics showed, lived in broken families. In Harlem, the illegitimacy rate was over 40 percent. In an assertion much challenged by historians, Moynihan suggested that the weakness of the black family had its roots in slavery. "It was by destroying the Negro family under slavery," Moynihan wrote, "that white America broke the will of the Negro people." Forcing black men into roles of public submissiveness "worked against the emergence of a strong father figure." Moynihan argued that the urgent need of the moment was for programs to strengthen the black family.

Moynihan was instantly accused of racism and of "blaming the victim." While some of Moynihan's critics did raise substantive questions about his use of evidence and his extrapolations from history, many of the vitriolic attacks on him amounted to politically inspired name-calling. To be sure, the political questions at stake were important: For Moynihan's critics, his emphasis on the black family was a way of directing attention away from white society's responsibility for the condition of the black poor and of downplaying the importance of political and economic inequalities. In truth, Moynihan, in his own provocative way, was pointing to the plight of the black family as a way of insisting that *more* needed to be done on behalf of the black poor. The polarization was a sign of things to come—a hint of the growing alienation between blacks and whites, liberals and conservatives, over issues relating to "values." The tragedy, as William J. Wilson has pointed out, is that the bitterness of the argument drove the issue of assisting the black family off the national agenda for nearly two decades. In the meantime, the problems grew much worse. When Moynihan wrote, a "staggering" 26 percent of nonwhite children were born out of wedlock; now, 61 percent are.

The battles of the late 1960s involved far more dangerous weapons than words and concepts. In the same month that the Moynihan Report became public, the Watts section of Los Angeles exploded into riot. Thirty-four people were killed, all of them black. What followed were three consecutive "long, hot summers"—more rioting amid a growing pessimism that was affecting even Dr. King, who was still trying to hold the line for nonviolence. "I feel that this summer will not only be as bad but worse than last time," Dr. King said in a sermon at Washington's National Cathedral on March 31, 1968. Four days later, Dr. King was murdered, and riots broke out in more than a hundred cities around the nation, including Washington, D.C. "By dawn on April 6," wrote Godfrey Hodgson, the British journalist and one of the best chroniclers of that period, "a pall of black smoke from those fires hung over the national monuments. The capital of the United States was under military occupation. For those who had dreamed the dreams of the New Frontier, and shared the hopes of a Great Society, this was perhaps the darkest moment of the entire decade."

Someone else who understood that liberal hopes were going up in the flames that enveloped the cities was the leading Republican candidate for president, Richard M. Nixon. A month before Dr. King's assassination, Nixon sharply criticized the report of President Johnson's National Advisory Commission on Civil Disorders, known as the Kerner Commission. The commission blamed the riots on unemployment, crime, drug addiction, and welfare dependency in the ghetto and concluded that "white racism is essentially responsible for the explosive mixture." Nixon condemned the commission, charging that it "blames everybody for the riots except the perpetrators of the riots." Nixon urged "retaliation against the perpetrators of violence" that would be "swift and sure." Nixon knew that his appeals for law and order were striking a responsive chord. "I have found great audience for this theme in all parts of the country," Nixon wrote Dwight Eisenhower, "including areas like New Hampshire, where there is no race problem and very little crime."

With resentment growing between blacks and urban whites, the Black Power theme had an additional effect. If Black Power initially seemed to be black America's strategy for imitating the successes of white ethnic groups, these same white ethnic groups began to use Black Power as a justification for their own assertion of ethnic consciousness. Michael Novak, at that point a radical Catholic intellectual, wrote an angry manifesto called *The Rise of the Unmeltable Ethnics*. The book denounced the liberal WASP Establishment for many sins, chief among them the hypocrisy that allowed it to embrace the civil rights movement, Black Power, and even the Black Panthers while scorning the interests of urban white ethnics. The Reverend Andrew M. Greeley complained that liberals who had long criticized white ethnic groups for clannishness in celebrating their ethnic ties suddenly approved of Black Power. "It is all right for the blacks and the Chicanos and the American Indians to have some sort of ethnic consciousness," he wrote, "but for other American ethnic groups, ethnic consciousness is, somehow or other, immoral." Orlando Patterson, a black sociologist who was critical of the new ethnic advocates such as Novak and Father Greeley, nonetheless understood their complaints and saw the roots of the new movement in the upsurge of black nationalism. "By continuing to insist on ethnicity as the only path to liberation," Patterson said, "blacks have relegitimized ethnicity as a principle of political action." Patterson captured the discontent of whites with near-perfect sense of pitch: Many whites, Patterson said, reasoned that "if it was good enough for the blacks, and the liberals supported it, it surely must have been good enough for the lower middle classes who felt most threatened by the emergence of black demands for greater equality."

In the midst of the controversy, words quickly lost meaning. Phrases such as "the blue collars," "the white ethnics," "the white working class," "the lower middle class," and "middle America" came to be used interchangeably. Despite the semantic confusion, the political implications were clear. Whites of modest income had once been content to think of themselves as "working people" and to seek economic relief through trade unions and the Democratic Party. But as politics came to be defined more and more by Black Power, class interests and the Democratic Party seemed less relevant while ethnicity and later, evangelical religiosity, became much more so. "Ethnicity is at least as much a tactic as a definition," wrote Irving Louis Horowitz, the sociologist. "The new ethnicity is a statement of relatively deprived sectors seeking economic relief through political appeals." Daniel Bell saw the new ethnicity "as a strategic choice by individuals who, in other circumstances, would choose other group memberships as a means of gaining some power and privilege."

Explaining the anger of the white ethnics became a major industry. Liberals who saw the white ethnics as reactionaries, "a vanguard of repression," tended to seek the salvation of their cause in a coalition of blacks, the young, and "enlightened" upper-class whites. That, essentially, was the coalition that reelected New York City's Mayor John Lindsay in 1969—but with only 42 percent of the vote in a field where conservatives divided the majority, much as Nixon and Wallace had done in 1968.

The notion that an enlightened upper class could save liberalism was one of the liberals' gravest mistakes. This view ignored the most basic electoral fact: that upper-income voters tend to vote their economic interests and that most of them, most of the time, will support *conservatives*. Liberals could simply not expect to substitute the votes of lower-income whites with the ballots of a "coalition of conscience." Human nature being what it is, such a coalition was simply not big enough. By ignoring or misunderstanding the grievances of lower-income whites, liberals opened up a political gulf that has still not been closed.

III

In defense of the liberals, it must be said that they faced almost insoluble political problems in the late 1960s and early 1970s. They were committed, and rightly, to rapid advancement for blacks. They were under increasing pressure from a justifiably militant black community. At the same time, hard-pressed whites who believed that government was engaged in a major effort to uplift blacks sensed that no comparable effort was being made on their behalf. Liberals contributed to their own problem by overselling what their programs were doing. They thus simultaneously heightened the impatience of blacks and the anxieties of whites.

Among the dilemmas faced by liberals was the practical meaning of the phrase "equality of opportunity." In light of the burdens of two centuries of slavery and a third century of discrimination, how could "fair" competition be possible? The most popular metaphor, used by Lyndon Johnson among others, was that of the shackled runner:

> Imagine a hundred-yard dash in which one of the two runners has his legs shackled together. He has progressed ten yards while the unshackled runner has gone fifty yards. At that point, the judges decide the race is unfair. How do they rectify the situation? Do they merely remove the shackles and allow the race to proceed? Then they could say that "equal opportunity" now prevailed. But one of the runners would still be forty yards ahead of the other. Would it not be the better part of justice to allow the other runner to make up the forty-yard gap; or to start the race all over again? That would be affirmative action toward equality.

The analogy was revealing not only for its aptness to the plight of blacks, but also for its imperfections. How does a society with a complex class structure start the race all over again? If the runner forty yards back is allowed to make up the difference, which seems only fair, what about runners who faced unfair but less imposing burdens and are, say, only ten or twenty yards back? Does fairness not demand that they, too, be moved up? The latter group included the sons and daughters of the white working class, the children in the community colleges and state schools who were certainly better off on the whole than blacks but lacked the advantages of the children of the wealthy and the students of the Ivy League. If society was so concerned about making the race fair, such whites asked, why was it not making life more fair for *them*, too?

Detailed studies of whites who moved right because of the race issue suggested that such questions played at least as much of a role in their political conversion as racism. In a study of white voters in Gary, Indiana, who had voted for George Wallace at twice the national rate in 1968, political sociologists Thomas F. Pettigrew and Robert T. Riley found that Wallace supporters were far more likely than Nixon or Humphrey voters to identify themselves as *working class* rather than as middle class. Those who identified themselves *strongly* with the working class were even more likely to support Wallace. In other words, the sort of class identification that had pushed voters *left* during the New Deal began pushing them *right* in the 1960s. Wallace understood this acutely, paying homage to "this average man on the street, this man in the textile mill, this man in the steel mill, this barber, this beautician, the policeman on the beat."

The Pettigrew-Riley study also found that Wallace voters were far more likely than supporters of either Nixon or Humphrey to agree with this statement: "In spite of what some people say, the lot of the average man is getting worse, not better." Among those who saw the lot of the average man worsening, roughly 40 percent backed Wallace; Wallace won less than 20 percent among those who did not take such a dire view of the average man's fate. Pettigrew noted that Wallace's supporters manifested "acute feelings of relative deprivation." They believed that "Negroes are unjustly making rapid strides forward at their expense, helped out by a too generous federal government, a government that has forgotten them." Pettigrew concluded that "the bitter irony for our nation is that the same powerful social-psychological mechanism—the sense of relative deprivation—is leading to racial strife on *both* sides of the color line." (His emphasis.)

Liberals, as the party of equality, were being asked to provide relief not only to blacks, for whom relief was long overdue, but also to a working-class white community that felt under siege. When liberals failed to deliver, blacks and whites turned to their own forms of separatism. For whites, that meant turning right and away from government, calculating that if the government would not help them improve their lot, they would at least try to protect what they had.

This sense of a need for "protection" was especially acute in the white ethnic neighborhoods of Northern cities. A large sociological literature has shown that working-class neighborhoods provided their residents not simply with places to live, but also with a thick web of personal, familial, community, and political relationships that eased the burdens of urban life. Yet liberals, as Daniel Patrick Moynihan pointed out, were mistrustful of "the primal sense of community." For them, Moynihan said, "the tribal attachments of blood and soil appear somehow unseemly and primitive."

The working-class enclaves, usually dominated by members of a single ethnic group, regarded themselves as autonomous and resisted the efforts of outsiders to interfere with their inner workings. Indeed, for many residents of these areas, their neighborhoods were the *only* areas in which they felt a real sense of control over events. The neighborhood was a haven in which their values and attitudes dominated the culture. As the 1960s proceeded, residents of such neighborhoods came to view racial integration as no less a threat to their self-sufficiency than the designs of urban planners who often tried to knock their neighborhoods down. Gerald Suttles, an urban sociologist, referred to these areas as "defended neighborhoods." He argued that the sense of autonomy that their residents felt often disguised their dependence on a wide array of outside forces—local governments, real estate interests, the banks, among others—to keep their communities from collapsing. "Without external allies, the local community and its defended boundaries are in a precarious position," Suttles wrote. In the 1960s, Suttles argued, many residents of these neighborhoods "felt themselves betrayed" by just such a "realignment" of forces: by the workings of open-housing laws and integration plans for local schools. They were also victimized by unscrupulous real estate agents who "blockbusted" neighborhoods by buying low from whites trying to escape black "encroachment" and by selling high to the blacks who themselves were searching for better housing in better neighborhoods.

The reaction of the white residents of such neighborhoods to the civil rights revolution instantly won them condemnations from liberals as "racists" and "hard hats." But the most astute analysts of white reaction in the big cities understood that the blue collars and the ethnics were not necessarily more racist than their social "betters." Members of the white working class reacted because they, unlike those above them in the class structure, were on the front lines of racial change. In a summary of urban migration patterns, Father Greeley provided statistical support for what common sense told city dwellers: that in their search for better housing, blacks tended to migrate to the neighborhoods inhabited by poorer whites. "No matter what the intentions of the individual citizen, racial shifts in the composition of neighborhoods affect lives, from the value of homes to the quality of schools to the nature of the playgroup in the street," Greeley wrote. Thus, he went on, "it is not surprising that both the displacers and those being reluctantly displaced find themselves in situations of confrontation."

The irony is that urban whites were battling to control their neighborhoods and schools at the very moment when the New Left was asserting the right of people "to control the decisions that affect their own lives." Blacks understandably saw the resistance of whites as a form of racism, and indeed it often was. White liberals were rightly sensitive to the struggles of blacks in such situations. But with some notable exceptions, such as Mario Cuomo, who mediated a housing dispute in the Forest Hills section of Queens in the early seventies, liberals showed little sympathy for the whites who viewed liberal-sponsored integration plans as decisions over which they had no influence. Blue-collar whites returned the favor. "The rich liberals, they look down on my little piece of the American dream, my little backyard with the barbecue here," a white carpenter in the Canarsie section of Brooklyn told sociologist Jonathan Rieder. "The liberals and the press look down on hard hats like me, but we've invested everything we have in this house and neighborhood." Such voters had long felt that they owed the opportunity to own a house to liberalism and the Democrats. But to safeguard their investment, they started to turn to conservatism and the Republicans, and in large numbers.

Liberalism, then, ran headlong into a conflict of interest between blacks and middle-income whites. What many liberals did not understand, or understood too late, was that many of their proposals to alleviate the burdens unfairly borne by black Americans were most threatening to the most vulnerable whites. William Connolly, a left-wing political theorist, argued in 1981 that it was no surprise that whites of modest income, once the primary supporters of the welfare state, turned against the welfare state so fiercely. They saw the welfare state as turning on them, undermining the values they espoused and denigrating their own struggles for self-reliance. Connolly offered an

inimical

arresting list of grievances. Working-class parents had once been able to influence the kind of education their children would get by moving into neighborhoods with good schools. Forced busing took that option away; now, only those who could afford to send their children to private schools would have such a choice. Welfare programs seemed to send the message that individuals were not responsible for their dependency. That, said Connolly, suggested to self-sufficient but poorly paid workers that they "could no longer take much personal credit for the independence they have achieved." If, in turn, affirmative action declared that blacks and women deserved special breaks in getting good jobs, then "white, male, lower- and middle-class workers are made to feel that they deserve to be stuck in the lowly jobs they now have." Connolly added: "Seen from the perspective of these latter constituencies, *everyone else* is treated either as meritorious or as unjustly closed out from the ranks of the meritorious."

Conservative Republicans were not being wholly disingenuous, then, when they argued that their campaigns around the racial issues were really about "values," not race. For too many whites, the politics of values and race had become almost indistinguishable. The epitaph for liberalism's failure to bridge the gap between blacks and whites was eloquently written by Jonathan Rieder, who said that for many urban whites, liberalism came to be seen "as a force inimical to the working and lower middle classes, assaulting their communities, their sense of fairness, their livelihood, their children, their physical safety, their values." For such whites, Rieder said, "liberalism meant taking the side of blacks, no matter what; dismissing middle class plaints as racism; handcuffing the police; transferring resources from a vulnerable middle class to minorities; rationalizing rioting and dependency and other moral afflictions as 'caused' by the environment or as justifiable responses to oppression."

Liberals could insist that racism lurked behind this list of white complaints, and no doubt racism was there. Liberals were also quite justified in arguing that conservatives often took advantage of white discontents in thoroughly shameful ways. But liberals themselves bore a burden for helping foster the polarization that Rieder described. The discontents of less well-off whites could simply *not* be written off as racism, pure and simple, especially since many of the angriest whites were themselves disadvantaged. The situation was far more complicated. As William Connolly put it, when liberals seemed to dismiss even the legitimate concerns of the less well-off whites, "these vulnerable constituencies did not need too much coaxing to bite the hand that had slapped them in the face."

IV

In recent years, liberals have tried to explain their political failures by arguing that they suffered only because they had done "the right thing" on civil rights. But the tactical implication of this apologia was that liberalism would revive itself only by doing *less* for blacks in the future—by running away from the very achievement of which liberals claim to be so proud.

But the liberal apologia not only exaggerates what liberals did for blacks; it would also have liberals give up at the very moment when so much needs to be done, especially on behalf of the most vulnerable people in the black community.

The apologia also blinds liberalism to its fundamental failures. The tragedy of liberalism is that it failed not for what it did on behalf of blacks but because of what it did *not* do. It failed to address that "tangle of pathology" in the black ghettos, and it failed to foster self-confidence and security among whites of modest means—the very people who, under other circumstances, might have been the natural allies of Dr. King's "beloved community."

Nowhere has a politics of false choices been more destructive than in America's discussion of race. Liberals and conservatives have each tried to avoid fundamental issues that might trouble their respective worldviews.

Conservatives, as we have seen earlier, are so convinced that government programs fail that they have often willfully overlooked the ones that actually succeeded. They tend to deny the simple truth that some problems *do* go away when money is thrown at them. The reduction in poverty among the elderly poor is a good example of where that strategy worked. Conservatives have often promoted ugly stereotypes, of which Willie Horton and "welfare queens" are the most prominent examples. Some conservative politicians have been shameless in exaggerating the role that racial "quotas" play in social policy. And conservatives have also been excessively eager to ascribe problems in the urban underclass—problems that conservatives have often been more willing to address squarely than liberals—to the failure of government programs. To pick one of the better-known examples, Charles Murray argued in his conservative best-seller *Losing Ground* that rising food stamp and AFDC payments to the poor had a disastrous impact on both family formation and work incentives among the poor. Yet as Robert Greenstein, director of the Center on Budget and Policy Priorities in Washington, argued, the real value of AFDC and food stamp payments to the poor has been *declining* since 1972. If

Murray's argument were right, the trends he rightly deplores should have reversed themselves "when the relative advantage of work over welfare increased sharply." They did not. In fact, the problems of youth unemployment and family breakdown grew worse in the 1970s and 1980s. That suggests that simply cutting welfare programs, though appealing from the point of view of conservative ideology, would do nothing to improve matters—and would very likely make things much worse.

Over time, more and more conservatives have been willing to admit at least some of these things. Indeed, conservatives have taught liberals a valuable lesson: that the government itself gets in the way of the working poor by taxing away some of their earnings. Conservatives have thus been willing to "throw money at the poor" by eliminating them from the tax rolls. Conservatives have also been among the leading supporters of the earned-income tax credit, which effectively subsidizes the wages of the working poor by having the federal government give money to, rather than take it from, poor people trying to earn their own livings. The earned-income tax credit is one of the few areas where liberals and conservatives have been willing to learn from each other and act in concert. That, at least, is promising.

But conservatives are still uneasy talking about another fundamental cause of the growing underclass, the change in the kinds of jobs the private economy is creating. In his exemplary book aimed at breaking the political and policy impasse on helping the poor, *The Truly Disadvantaged*, William J. Wilson has explained the problem with great clarity. Over the last two decades, "substantial job losses have occurred in the very industries in which urban minorities are heavily concentrated." The substantial employment gains that conservatives rightly point to as a significant achievement of recent years "have occurred in the higher-education-requisite industries that have relatively few minority workers." This mismatch, Wilson points out, has been especially severe in the Northeast and Midwest, precisely the regions "that have had the sharpest increases in black joblessness and female-headed families." Finally, Wilson notes that entry-level jobs in the service industries are opening up "almost exclusively outside the central cities where poor minorities are concentrated." Wilson's point is not that free markets always fail. It is simply that free markets alone cannot be relied upon to solve social problems. That this point needs to be argued at all suggests both how successful conservatives have been in dominating the popular discussion and how ideologically rigid that discussion has become.

But liberals allowed this to happen because of their own blind spots. As Wilson put it, "the liberal perspective on the ghetto under-class and inner city social dislocations is less persuasive and influential in public discourse today because many of those who represent the traditional liberal view on social issues have failed to address straight-forwardly the rise of social pathologies in the ghetto." Indeed, in some instances, Wilson writes, liberals have been reluctant "even to ac-knowledge the sharp increases" of such pathologies. This liberal fail-ure can, to some degree, be ascribed to good motives, notably a desire not to stigmatize those who live in ghettos. But the result, Wilson argues, was to abandon the field to conservatives on issues ranging from the female-headed family to crime, drugs, and youth unemploy-ment. With only conservatives talking about the importance of "val-ues," liberal values fell by the wayside.

Wilson also contends that very successes of the civil rights and affirmative action strategies have led liberal and black leaders to sup-port "race-specific" proposals when the neediest in the black commu-nity may be helped most by "nonracial" solutions. The earlier round of civil rights reform, which involved "removing artificial barriers to valued positions," was most helpful to relatively advantaged members of the minority community, since they were in the best position to take advantage of the new forms of equality. Policies of "preferential treatment," Wilson argues, "will further improve the opportunities of the advantaged without necessarily addressing the problems of the truly disadvantaged such as the ghetto underclass." The underclass, Wilson says, could benefit most from such nonracial solutions as "full employment, balanced economic growth and manpower training and education." Wilson points out that such programs have the additional virtue of being broadly popular, with blacks and whites alike.

Wilson points the way to a more fruitful dialogue about race, class, and inequality. Happily, his arguments are receiving a wide hearing. But the legacy of the wrong turns of the last two decades and of the turmoil of the 1960s is a heavy burden on our public life. "We made a serious mistake when the movement turned against its first principle: integration," said Rep. John Lewis of Georgia, a man who still bears the scars of his courage in the civil rights movement. "The seeds that were planted twenty years ago have borne very bitter fruit." The mistakes of the last two decades have been politically ruinous for liberals and disastrous for the nation. Where we need an honest and unifying discussion, we are getting division and recrimination. We have no better example of how *not* to talk about race than the Willie Horton "issue," the ultimate expression of a politics of false choices.

4

FAMILY POLITICS:

Feminism

and Its Enemies

O F ALL THE ACHIEVEMENTS of the 1960s counter-culture, none was so enduring as its success in transforming popular attitudes toward women's roles, sexuality, and the family. The changes are reflected every day in scores of ways: in the content of television shows, in the entry of women into virtually every field of work, in the growth of fast-food restaurants to cater to families in which both parents hold jobs outside the home, in the easy way in which people talk about all aspects of sexuality, in the very words men and women use when they talk with each other. The word *sexist* would have been incomprehensible thirty years ago. Now, everyone understands it and uses it. More significantly, most people think that "sexism" exists, and most think it's wrong.

Thus one of the many mysteries of politics in the 1980s: How could a time in which feminist and permissive values continued to have so much power be considered a "conservative era" at all?

One answer is that permissive and feminist values have actually declined. There is at least some evidence to support this view. The

1980s saw divorce rates edge down. Birth rates leveled off after steep declines and began rising. Conservatives pointed to a wave of self-criticism among feminists to demonstrate that even the founders of feminism were beginning to have second thoughts. Conservatives applauded feminist criticisms of "no fault" divorce laws, which tended to benefit divorcing husbands and left their long-suffering wives in desperate economic circumstances. The conservatives noted with approval Betty Friedan's arguments for the value of the family in *The Second Stage*, published in 1981. Friedan said the second stage acknowledged "women's own needs to give and get love and nurture." It involved "coming to new terms with the family" so that "we can live a new 'yes' to life and love and can *choose* to have children." In pursuit of a broader constituency, the feminist movement was increasingly casting its demands as part of what it called "the work and family agenda." Conservatives, who had gained so much ground by casting themselves as "profamily," complained that feminists had "stolen" their favorite words, but counted it as a victory that their foes felt a need to pick up conservative language. Conservatives took comfort in the fact that the language of politics generally was backward looking. In 1988, John Kenneth White, a political scientist, wrote a book called *The New Politics of Old Values* in which he argued that President Reagan had transformed not only American politics but also that great barometer of American culture, prime-time telelvision. "Family, work, neighborhood and authority," White declared, "are rediscovered themes in entertainment, from 'Leave It to Beaver' (which has returned for yet another run) to 'The Cosby Show.' "

Some of these changes could be attributed to the life cycle: As baby boomers got older, they had children of their own. When they had children of their own, they found sixties values less appealing. But whatever the cause, the transformation of attitudes was measurable. Allan Carlson, a conservative who wrote widely on family issues, explained the change with an aphorism: "A social conservative is a liberal with a daughter in high school."

Plainly, there was a backlash against sixties values that hurt liberals. But the backlash was neither as deep nor as widespread as conservatives thought. Polls showed repeatedly that the women's movement and the word *feminism* drew positive responses from large majorities. The Reagan administration sought to curtail affirmative action programs and opposed the Equal Rights Amendment, but it did not convince women to leave the work force or give up on equal pay or government-assisted child care. Nor, except for the fear of

AIDS, was there a notable change in the country's attitude toward sexuality. If anything, AIDS itself only increased the level of political organization in the gay community, which became politically conscious in the late 1960s and early 1970s and was a powerful force for social liberalism. So important had the gay vote become in California that Republican Pete Wilson, elected governor in 1990, did battle against antigay Republicans, whom he saw driving a relatively affluent constituency into the arms of the Democrats.

It is true that television advertising shifted some in favor of monogamous, loving couples, another indication that the baby boom was settling down. But advertisers demonstrated no new inhibitions about using sex to sell things, and anyone who thought sex was out was not watching MTV. Indeed, judging from the work of young novelists such as Bret Easton Ellis, the author of *Less Than Zero*, unconstrained sex was no less popular among young people in the 1980s than it had been in the sixties. Eighties permissiveness was different from sixties permissiveness only in that the new version was shorn from any claims —or pretentions—that it was connected to a political movement. "I'm not really out to change someone's consciousness," Ellis said, "because I think writers are primarily entertainers."

But cultural politics are complicated. Even as the country as a whole shifted in favor of more liberal standards, there were substantial pockets of resistance that became key constituencies for the conservative cause. And many Americans were ambivalent about the new society they had created. That ambivalence also worked against liberalism.

II

It is the natural lot of human beings to assume that the times in which they live are unique and unprecedented. In fact, feminist revolts and sexual revolutions are common in periods of general disruption, and they have been the rule in the United States since the American Revolution. "If particular care and attention are not paid to the ladies," wrote Abigail Adams to her husband, John, "we are determined to foment a rebellion, and will not hold ourselves bound by any laws in which we have no voice or representation."

But if feminism has a long history in the United States, the roots of the current revolt lie in the Progressive Era, which saw the rise of movements for both women's rights and sexual liberation. Christopher Lasch has argued that the rise of new attitudes toward women and the family after the turn of the century could be traced to radical changes in the nature of production as farms declined and production shifted out of the home and into factories. The new family had a paradoxical effect, since it "simultaneously degraded and exalted women." On the one hand, it deprived them "of many of their traditional employments, as the household ceased to be a center of production and devoted itself to child rearing." On the other hand, as child rearing itself came to be seen as more important, society concluded that to carry out that responsibility, women needed more education "for their domestic duties." The Progressive Era, Lasch noted, taught that women "should become useful rather than ornamental," and this created a much broader revolt as "bourgeois domesticity gave rise to its antithesis, feminism." The new domestic arrangements "gave rise to a general unrest," Lasch noted, encouraging women "to entertain aspirations that marriage and the family could not satisfy." The new attitudes toward family life led to a series of remarkable changes in the position of women in society. Female college enrollment tripled between 1890 and 1910 and doubled again in the teens. There was explosive growth in the membership in women's organizations and a sharp upturn in women's participation in the work force.

Traditionalists had increasing difficulty in holding the line against experimentation in other aspects of family life, notably sex. As the family's role in production declined, its new importance lay in providing comfort and intimacy in an increasingly competitive world. As mass production took some of the joy and individuality out of work, the family came to be seen as the primary arena in which individuality could be expressed. The sexual revolution after the turn of the century, which reached its height in the 1920s, was a natural by-product of these changes. The emancipation of women meant that their own sexual needs and desires suddenly became legitimate. The triumph of the value of "healthiness" over the demands of religion and tradition emphasized individual satisfaction over adherence to communal norms. In their excellent social history of the American family, Steven Mintz and Susan Kellogg reported that the "purity crusade" of the Victorian 1880s and 1890s against prostitution and venereal disease had the ironic effect of vastly liberalizing attitudes toward sex. The crusade "broke the veil of silence that had surrounded discussions of sexuality during the nineteenth century and inspired pioneering efforts at sex research and sex education," they wrote. "For the first time, women's sexuality was publicly acknowledged."

Thus the new morality which, as Lasch wrote, "proclaimed the joys of the body, defended divorce and birth control, raised doubts about monogamy, and condemned interference with sexual life by the state or community." A 1913 magazine cover declared that the hour had struck "sex o'clock in America." Defenders of the family came to realize that full-scale resistance to the new morality would not work. "Instead of trying to annihilate the new morality, they domesticated it," Lasch wrote, celebrating "a freer, more enlightened sexuality within marriage." The result was a new theory of family life, "the companionate family." As Mintz and Kellogg put it, the new theory held that "husbands and wives would be 'friends and lovers' and parents and children would be 'pals.' " The companionate marriage, Mintz and Kellogg noted, "placed an unprecedented emphasis on the importance of sexual gratification in marriage."

The triumph of such norms was interrupted by the Great Depression and then World War II. These were followed by the domesticity of the 1950s and early 1960s, a time when the country seemed to be stepping back from an ethic of liberation. In many respects, the 1950s *were* special, marking a sharp break with the patterns of the previous half century. Marriage rates during the 1950s reached an all-time high. By the end of the 1950s, 70 percent of all women were married by the age of twenty-four, compared with just 42 percent in 1940— and 50 percent in the 1980s. The rate of increase in divorce was lower in the 1950s than in any other decade in this century. Mintz and Kellogg argued that it made perfect sense that so many Americans turned inward in the pursuit of "a house of their own and family togetherness." After the struggles of the Depression and the sacrifices and dislocations of war, nothing seemed so logical as the quest for "security and fulfillment."

But in some of the most important respects, the 1950s were not about change at all. Rather, the decade represented continuity with the patterns that had been established between 1900 and 1930. It was in the 1950s that the "companionate family" took deep root in the country. Even before the Depression, the companionate ideal had been available only to a relatively small middle class. But in the prosperous postwar years, "the luxury of mutual pleasure and companionship could be enjoyed by millions of Americans."

One of the things we remember most about the 1950s is its rigid definitions of gender roles, with women serving as "homemakers" and mothers while men worked outside the home for bread, clothing, and the mortgage payment. Indeed, it was common then for marriage experts to reduce a woman's role to "understanding" her husband and making it easier for him to achieve *his* potential. But much was written at the time about the growing power of *women* and the decline of the male role within the household. Some family experts feared that patriarchy was being replaced by "a matriarchal society, with children who know men only as nighttime residents and weekend guests." Elaine Tyler May, a historian of the American family, noted that during the 1950s, "observers of middle class life considered homemakers to be emancipated and men to be oppressed." *Life* magazine went so far in 1956 as to label the decade so often cast as a time of quiet conformity as the "era of the feminist revolution." If in practice women were assigned inferior roles, in theory marriage was supposed to be "a fifty-fifty deal," as the singer Pat Boone put it in 1958.

The proclamation of egalitarian ideals within marriage led directly to the feminist revolt. It turned out that the theory of "companionate marriage" was riddled with contradictions. In the 1950s, these contradictions manifested themselves even in the most stable and happy of middle-class households. "On the one hand, young women received the same education as men and were encouraged to develop their skills and intellectual abilities," Mintz and Kellogg noted. "On the other, women were pressured to maintain their 'femininity' and seek fulfillment as wives and homemakers, and they were cautioned against pursuing a career." The same contradictions that haunted women after the turn of the century arose again.

Betty Friedan captured that turmoil dramatically in her 1963 classic, *The Feminine Mystique:*

> It was a strange sense of dissatisfaction, a yearning that women suffered in the middle of the twentieth century in the United States. Each suburban wife struggled with it alone. As she made the beds, shopped for groceries, matched slipcover material, ate peanut butter sandwiches with the children, chauffeured Cub Scouts and Brownies, lay beside her husband at night, she was afraid to ask even of herself the silent question—"Is this all?"

Betty Friedan had some surprising company in her concerns about women's roles. In 1955, Columbia University hosted a Conference on the Effective Use of Womanpower, which had the informal support of the Eisenhower administration. Speakers at the conference called for a new approach to women's work, including increasing women's education levels, discouraging early marriage, promoting flexible hours, and encouraging women to take scientific and technical jobs. Not just rebellious feminists but also sober Republicans of the Eisenhower stripe were prepared to do some new thinking about how women could contribute to society—and themselves.

If the movement of production outside the home changed the nature of household work, so, too, did the technological revolution in housework, everything from vacuum cleaners to electric dishwashers. By reducing the time it took to maintain a home, the new devices contributed mightily to the reassessment of women's roles that began in the 1950s.

The point is that feminism did not arise from nowhere. Nor were feminist ideas the product of some radical fringe. In ways that few realized at the time, the "domestic" 1950s prepared a new generation of women for entirely new roles. By the end of the 1950s, most Americans took the security that had eluded them during the Depression and war for granted again. They were free to return to the struggle to redefine women's roles that had begun at the turn of the century. It turned out that it was not possible for society to accord women much more formal education and then expect them to abandon the outside world for the home. Indeed, not just feminists but also businessmen and government planners were reluctant to see all that education and training "wasted" by forcing women out of the work force. In the 1950s and early 1960s, most women continued to see their most important role as involving the upbringing of children. But increasingly, it was not the only role they looked to.

It is important to understand the deep roots of the feminist revolution in order to see why feminist values became so widespread in the 1960s and 1970s. Too often in our political discussions, we treat feminism as a sudden development. Critics see feminism as a fad foisted upon women by well-educated liberal propagandists; feminism's supporters sometimes see feminism as the fruit of sudden enlightenment, the response of women whose eyes have been opened to the costs of patriarchy. It is more helpful to view feminism as part of a gradual process through which society is trying to adjust to a vast array of changes that began with the industrial revolution, including changes in the nature of production and of household work. Those changes, in turn, transformed our values about the nature of equality between men and women and about what women could and should do with their lives. The revolutions of the 1960s and 1970s can thus be seen as an attempt to bring our values and our behavior into line with each other and to think our way through the contradictory demands society has come to place on women. Understanding that the 1960s were not a onetime episode but part of a long and difficult process is one key to moving beyond a politics of false choices.

III

The way feminism was received in the United States was greatly influenced by the economic circumstances of the 1970s, the moment when feminism began to amass real political power. Feminism had the misfortune of gaining ground in the period when the American economy suffered from its most severe shocks since the Great Depression.

The coincidence of the rise of feminism and vast changes in the economy has produced a "chicken and egg" debate over what led so many American women to join the work force. Was it the power of feminist ideas? Or was it simply that middle-class families needed more than one income to make ends meet? The answer obviously involved a combination of the two. But how did the economic forces interact with the power of the feminist idea?

There is nothing new about women working outside the home—most poor women have done so since the industrial revolution drew hundreds of thousands of their number to factory work. Before the enactment of child labor laws, children also poured into the factories. The affluence of the postwar period allowed the country to change these practices on a large scale. As wages rose dramatically, the wives of even working-class men were able to stay home with their children.

In the 1970s, this became less and less easy. Real wages stopped rising in 1973, and in a display of what might be called "companionate economics," husbands and wives decided together that they could no longer maintain their standard of living on one income alone. Thus, the work force was fed by two parallel streams of women: On the one side were well-educated women who commanded relatively high salaries—even if they generally made less than men in comparable jobs. On the other side were less-educated women who took whatever jobs the economy could provide.

The return of this second group to the work force had little to do with the dreams of the women's movement for a genuinely equal society. As economist James K. Galbraith noted, "the vast bulk" of the increase in women's employment occurred in sectors of the service economy where genuinely good jobs were hard to find. "Women," he wrote, "are now accepting jobs that are, in terms of pay, prestige, potential promotion and the conditions of work itself, increasingly bad."

Conservative leaders were torn by this state of affairs. Many free-market conservatives resisted any form of state intervention in the labor market, and some insisted that the idea that there had been a decline in the average family's standard of living was a myth. But other conservatives, less wedded to free-market economics, acknowledged that the changing economic circumstances were a grave threat to the "traditional values" they held dear and urged changes in tax laws and salary structures to make it easier for mothers of modest means to escape the work force.

Conservatives and liberals alike also bemoaned changes in the tax laws that subjected a larger and larger share of family income to taxation. In 1948, the median income for a family of four was $3,468. At the time, the first $2,667 of income for such families was tax exempt —meaning that three-fourths of median family income was exempt from taxation. Over the years, inflation ate away at the value of the standard deduction and personal exemptions. The result was that average families paid more and more of their income in taxes. In 1983, the median family income for a family of four was $29,184, but only the first $8,783 of income was exempt from tax—less than one-third. "The point here is that the costs of raising a family no longer bear any relationship to the amount of income not subject to federal tax," wrote Daniel Patrick Moynihan, who cited these figures as an example of the federal government's indifference as to how its policies affected family life.

Feminism itself bore no responsibility for the new pressures on moderate-income families. Indeed, many feminists argued that working women were under pressure precisely because society put so little value on the work women did as mothers and in the home. Nonetheless, feminists found themselves answering for developments that appeared superficially to be the result of their own preachings. Feminism was victimized by a false syllogism: Feminists defended women's right to work; women from families under financial pressure were flooding into the workplace; therefore, feminism was to blame for the new pressure facing families of modest income.

The entry of women into the work force had other paradoxical effects, notably a widening of the gap between the incomes of wealthier and poorer families. As Barbara Ehrenreich among others pointed out, the tendency of professional men and professional women to marry each other increased class inequality, concentrating income in families where both professionals worked. Ehrenreich also noted that the most striking feminist successes had come in the professions. In medicine, only 9 percent of first-year students were female in 1969; in 1987, 37 percent were. The proportion of law degrees going to women rose from 8 percent in 1973 to 36 percent ten years later. In the same period, the proportion of MBAs going to women rose from 4.9 percent to 28.9 percent. "It was an achievement, however, that was sharply limited by class," Ehrenreich wrote. "The chief beneficiaries of the opening of the professions were women who already had the advantages of good schools, an encouraging home life, and the money and leisure for higher education."

The result was a class war among women. Expressing a widespread view, Betty Canellas, who founded a day-care center in Rockville, Maryland, told a reporter in 1989 that she thought the women's movement had been most helpful "to women who are vice presidents or executive secretaries, who earn more than thirty-five thousand dollars a year." Ms. Canellas said she was a strong supporter of the women's movement, but added: "I don't think they do enough for low-income women." Eleanor Smeal, the former president of the National Organization for Women, countered that women at the bottom of the economic ladder had, in fact, been more "successful" at achieving equality with men in comparable positions than had wealthier women. But this happened, she said, less because lower-income women had gained so much ground than because lower-income men had been losing so much ground. Ms. Smeal complained that the women's movement was being blamed unjustly for changes in the broader economy that had nothing whatsoever to do with feminism. Unfairly or not, feminism often did find itself shouldering blame for the gap between professional and working-class women. Conservatives successfully cast feminists as the defenders of the professionals and the scourge of "ordinary women."

The class war also raged around the abortion issue. In her exceptionally sensitive study of activists on both sides of the abortion issue, *Abortion and the Politics of Motherhood*, Kristin Luker argued that the views of prochoice and prolife activists are explained in large part by their radically different interests and life choices. "Prolife women have *always* valued family roles very highly and have arranged their lives accordingly," Luker wrote. "They did not acquire high-level educational and occupational skills, for example, because they married, and they married because their values suggested that this would be the most satisfying life open to them." By contrast, "prochoice women postponed (or avoided) marriage and family roles because they chose to acquire the skills they needed to be successful in the larger world, having concluded that the role of wife and mother was too limited for them."

Luker sees the conflict over abortion as being in part a battle between groups of women with different *resources*. "Having made a commitment to the traditional female roles of wife, mother, and homemaker, prolife women are limited in those kinds of resources— education, class status, recent occupational experiences—to compete in what has traditionally been the male sphere," Luker writes. "The average prochoice woman, in contrast, is comparatively well-endowed with exactly those resources: She is highly educated, she already has a job, and she has recent (and continuous) experience in the job market." The importance of Luker's analysis is that it allows us to see how difficult it is to disentangle values and interests. Prolife and pro-choice women had different values; they therefore made different life choices; and they thus developed different resources and different economic interests. In the abortion debate, each side defends not only a heartfelt position on a difficult moral question but also an entire way of life. Thus did a war over values become a class war. The class war was made ever more bitter by a religious war, since very religious people were much more opposed to abortion, on the whole, than others.

The political paradox in this is that feminism cost Democrats and liberals votes *even though most of the country supported feminist positions*. Polls showed that Americans overwhelmingly welcomed the expansion of women's opportunities. Typical were findings cited by Daniel Yankelovich in his book *New Rules*. Between 1970 and 1980, the proportion of Americans wanting to strengthen women's status within society rose from 42 to 64 percent. Three-fourths of Americans said that a woman who found housework unsatisfying should be able to develop her interests outside the home even if her husband wanted her to do more around the house. In 1989, a *New York Times*/CBS News poll found similarly strong support for women's rights. Two-thirds of Americans, for example, agreed that the United States "continues to need a strong women's movement to push for changes that benefit women." Seventy-two percent said that the women's movement had made relations between men and women in both romance and work "more honest and open."

Yet the workings of coalition politics produced some odd political results. Feminists had "won" many of the arguments with a majority of Americans. But many in the "feminist majority" were ambivalent about certain aspects of feminism and shared the worries if not the solutions of feminism's foes. Thus, many in this "feminist majority" did not vote *for* feminist positions, but on the basis of other issues entirely. By contrast, the minority fervently opposed to feminism was not ambivalent. It was much more willing to vote its antifeminism. The antifeminist minority thus made its votes count in a way the other side did not.

This was markedly the case in the 1980 election. Polls in 1980 showed that substantial majorities supported the Equal Rights Amendment and opposed a constitutional amendment to ban abortion. Ronald Reagan took the minority position on both issues, and only 15 percent of the electorate agreed with both his anti-ERA and antiabortion stands. Yet Reagan "won" on both issues because that small socially conservative minority voted its social convictions and gave Reagan a landslide margin. By contrast, the larger number of voters who were social moderates or liberals were much less inclined to cast ballots on the basis of the social issues alone. Thus, they gave Reagan enough votes for him to win easily in 1980 and by a landslide in 1984.

Especially harmful to liberals was where the antifeminist votes came from. Because of the class war that feminism spawned, many of the most ardent antifeminists were concentrated among lower income whites—a group that had traditionally voted for Democrats and liberals. In the late 1970s and the 1980s, Republican and conservative gains among these lower-income antifeminists more than balanced off their losses among middle-to-upper-income feminists. As we shall see in subsequent chapters, the bills are coming due for the Republicans now that well-off social liberals can no longer count on the Supreme Court to protect abortion rights and other liberal victories. But through the 1980s, the reaction of a minority against feminism and social experimentation was a powerful factor in the rise of the right.

IV

Republicans and conservatives also gained on the social issues in a more subtle way. By casting themselves as champions of "family values," men and women of the right—advocates of individualism in the economic sphere—were able to present themselves as defenders of community and to cast their liberal opponents as defenders of an "antifamily" individualism. This at least partially insulated the right from the real political dangers created by its economic doctrines.

As the 1980s drew to a close, it became an article of liberal faith that America had suffered in the Reagan years because it had become increasingly "selfish." The liberals did not make this worry up. The broader public *was* uneasy about a rise in selfishness, which is one reason why George Bush implicitly criticized the Reagan years by calling for "a kinder, gentler nation." But the public's sense of what constituted selfishness went beyond the malefactors of great wealth, the Wall Street lawyers and investment bankers of liberal demonology. That is why the language of the conservative "profamily" movement resonated with so many people, including some who disagreed with the profamily conservatives on a whole range of specific issues ranging from abortion to sex education. Despite the widespread acceptance of women's quest for equality, the public did hanker for aspects of what they perceived to be the good old days and was especially worried about how the new family arrangements affected children. Yankelovich, for example, reported that despite all the popular support for feminist positions, two-thirds of Americans said they wanted "a return to more traditional standards of family life and parental responsibility." (They could, of course, have been thinking of *male* responsibility.)

The conservatives took advantage of the public's uneasy sense that the sexual revolution, looser laws on drugs and pornography, even feminism itself, were the values of a self-centered individualism. Conservatives, who were committed to precisely such an individualism in the economic sphere, appealed to public doubts about individualism as it affected the family and child rearing. Implicit, and sometimes explicit, in the attacks of "profamily" conservatives on feminism and liberalism was the question: "And what happens to the children?" Conservatives sometimes gave this question an emotional edge by bemoaning child pornography and the content of television programs.

Many feminists were as worried as conservatives about how children were being cared for. If Americans were responding to "profamily" themes, such feminists asked, was it not in part because they sensed that marketplace values were coming to dominate in all aspects of American life, even in areas such as the family where they seemed inappropriate? Was it reasonable—or "feminist"—for women to have large incentives to take low-paid, unrewarding jobs, and no economic incentive whatever to take care of children? Thus, Alan Wolfe, a radical critic of American capitalism, argued that the quest for women's equality had combined with the workings of the economy to produce a situation that few feminists had had in mind when they embarked on their revolt. Wolfe put it succinctly: "Fathers have always spent too little time with their children. Now mothers have joined them."

Conservatives had few real answers for this problem. They were reluctant to have the state interfere with economic developments that did far more to push women out of the home than any feminist best-seller. But by linking their movement to "profamily" themes, conservatives gained ground in the short term on two fronts. They furthered their image as "populists" by identifying with "average families" against feminists who were cast as upper-class "elitists." And conservatives softened their image as advocates of rugged individualism by presenting the family as a buffer against the economy's harshness; the family was a "haven in a heartless world." Conservative thinkers such as Michael Novak, Peter Berger, and Richard John Neuhaus argued forcefully that capitalist democracy needed the "mediating structures" of family, church, neighborhood, and voluntary association to strengthen individuals in their dealings with both the state and the private economy. Such ideas had considerable merit, and they were invaluable in the battle for votes. A conservatism with a communitarian lilt was far more attractive than one that preached only the disciplines of the marketplace. It was much easier for Ronald Reagan to extoll "family, work, and neighborhood" than to defend the workings of large corporations.

Thus, conservatives escaped the contradictions of their own brand of individualism in the late seventies and eighties. Liberals did not. Liberals, the traditional advocates of community and mutuality, were left with the noble but politically difficult work of defending the individual rights of unpopular minorities. Liberals were uneasy with all the "traditional family" talk, since they saw lurking behind it a desire to push women out of the workplace, to discriminate against gays and lesbians, to censor the arts, and to enforce rigid moral standards that few Americans, in fact, lived by. Liberals also argued, plausibly, that the much-touted "traditional family" existed mainly in the popular imagination. Liberals scoffed at conservative claims that the family structure of the 1950s, which was historically unusual, represented a "traditional" norm that could be traced back to the Middle Ages or to somewhere even further back in the mists of the past.

But in their eagerness to defend minority rights and in their insistence that what the conservatives wanted could not possibly exist, liberals surrendered some of society's most evocative moral symbols—family, motherhood, selfless child-rearing—to the political right. Indeed, as Moynihan has pointed out, liberals became increasingly uncomfortable with the idea of "family," in the singular, since liberals regarded what most Americans called *"the* family" as just one among many options. Thus, the 1980 White House conference on family life was about "families," plural. "It was to be *asserted*," Moynihan wrote, "that no one set of arrangements—parents raising children—was to have social priority over alternative lifestyles, as the phrase went."

Conservatives took advantage of a tension that existed within feminism itself between individualistic and communitarian norms. In the popular mind, feminism is usually thought of as a "liberal" or "leftist" movement. That is natural, since feminists were advocates of change and most of them thought of *themselves* as liberals or leftists. Theirs was the classic appeal of a left-of-center cause: Feminism championed women as an oppressed group deserving of various forms of relief.

In the United States, we usually associate liberal and leftist politics with policies of collective provision, social solidarity, and redistribution. Liberals and leftists are usually critics of the "rugged individualism" of the marketplace. Yet the goals of the feminist movement focused necessarily on *individual emancipation*. It enlisted the solidarity of "sisterhood" in support of a highly individualistic agenda. The new women's movement demanded an end to discrimination against women where pay, benefits, or the chance of promotion were concerned. It demanded that abortion be legalized, since women had "the right to control their own bodies." Preferences in favor of marriage were to be abolished, and as the movement advanced, so were preferences in favor of heterosexuality. In a sense, feminism was a demand that the capitalist marketplace behave precisely as a capitalist marketplace—it should treat all men and women equally, as individuals. Feminists demanded that in their dealings in the labor market, women should not be encumbered by their traditional roles or traditional "protections" that the law had accorded them.

Many of the more radical and socially minded feminists were troubled by this individualistic approach. They worried that a movement that had once hoped to change the world gradually transformed itself into an effort to integrate women into the world as it was. "Surely," wrote Barbara Ehrenreich, "the aim of the struggle was not to propel a few women to the top of an unjust hierarchy, in which most women counted for cheap labor." But feminists had to take any gains they could get, since, as Ehrenreich noted, "there is no way that an economically marginalized group can be expected to 'wait for the revolution,' letting moral purity compensate for certain poverty."

The trend toward individualism was also clear in the new developments in family law. Courts showed themselves increasingly willing to intervene on behalf of children's rights against their parents, on behalf of women's rights against their husbands. To pick just one example: The growing acceptance that there is such a thing as "marital rape" represented a monumental victory for women and feminism (and decency, too). It also reflected a large extension of the government's ability to intervene within the household. Increasingly, the law treated the family less as a corporate unit than as a collection of individuals. Mintz and Kellogg grasped the trend toward individualism inherent in these decisions quite clearly. "One ironic effect of these legal decisions has been the gradual erosion of the traditional conception of the family as a legal unit," they wrote. "In the collision between two sets of conflicting values—individualism and the family—the courts have tended to stress individual rights."

The women's movement generally insisted that its animating principle was solidarity—"sisterhood"—not individualism. Insofar as feminists defended "interference" in the family, it was to stop palpable injustices, such as spousal abuse. Yet to feminism's critics, solidarity among women seemed to be at war with the solidarity within the family. Conservative critics of feminism were thus often successful in capturing the rhetorical high ground. The antifeminists cast themselves as the defenders of the warm and supportive family against those who assailed it in the name of abstract "rights."

The conservatives' success in capturing "traditional family values" also undermined what had historically been the most powerful argument that liberals and social democrats invoked in defense of the welfare state. Initially, the welfare state was seen as *a family policy*, a way of strengthening families, especially families where the breadwinning father had died. Minimum-wage laws, the WPA, collective bargaining—all were seen as vehicles for increasing the salary of the male breadwinner, to the advantage of his wife and children. Indeed, the dominant image that promoters of the welfare state sought to promote was that of the needy child. The hardest hearts softened at the specter of a child punished by the workings of a coldly efficient economic system or by the failings of his or her own parents.

But in the 1960s, the idea that the welfare state helped children and families was undermined by the rise in the number of households headed by single mothers, and particularly the increase in the number of single mothers who were on welfare. Suddenly, the welfare state became the enemy of the family, promoting dependency, illegitimacy, "permissiveness." In a typical conservative jeremiad, columnist R. Emmett Tyrrell, Jr., neatly linked a populist assault on rich liberals with an attack on welfare programs, arguing that the welfare state promoted "divorce, alcoholism, drug abuse, psychosomatic illness, neurosis, suicide, and the incidence of social problems." The result, he said with tongue planted in cheek, was to foster among the welfare poor the values of "some of the most rarified regions of the upper class," those practiced within "the Beverly Hills–Hollywood axis." A more sober statement of the same argument was offered by Charles Murray in *Losing Ground,* his statistical evisceration of welfare programs. Murray argued that welfare programs promoted such socially self-defeating behavior—especially in the area of family life—that it would be better for the poor if "the entire federal welfare and income-support structure for working-aged persons" were abolished altogether.

Liberals had ample grounds on which to defend the welfare state, and liberal scholars offered impressive statistical refutations of Murray's arguments. But committed as they were to an increasingly vague idea about what "family" was, liberals were in an ever-weaker position to respond to the conservative attack. Liberals often felt obliged to defend single motherhood on feminist grounds, and also because some of the attacks on the inner-city family smacked of racism. There was much nobility in the liberal response, but the loss of the idea of "family" to conservatives was a grievous political blow to the welfare state.

V

The battles over families and feminism—or, more precisely, a conservative parody of feminism—hurt Democrats and liberals because they put the beleaguered liberal state under pressures it could not withstand. The battle brought new issues into politics and forced the government to take a stand in favor of this or that kind of family, this or that brand of morality, this or that approach to child rearing.

The cost to Democrats and liberals was twofold. By pushing class issues to the side, the new cultural politics gave Republicans and conservatives new ways of winning votes from those with modest incomes and traditionalist values. And the new cultural politics guaranteed that a significant section of the public would be alienated from government as the state was forced to pick and choose among competing moral systems. The liberal state was well-suited to redistributing economic benefits. It was ill-suited to making fundamental moral choices for a nation that was engaged in a vigorous debate with itself over the meaning of family life and sexuality. Conservatives had no sure answers to these questions, either. But conservatives were not expected to be the guardians of the liberal state, and they were more than happy to profit from its weaknesses. They did so throughout the 1980s.

Yet if ever there were a set of issues on which Americans wanted *less* polarization and political posturing, it was surely on those involving families, children, and sexuality. Americans agreed with feminism's basic demands for equality—but worried about many of the directions that family life was taking. Americans generally welcomed less repressive sexual norms, but were concerned about the rise in teen pregnancies and uneasy that "sexual permissiveness" might be going too far. They wanted women to have more choices in the workplace, but they feared that the "new family" was increasingly less nurturing to children. Americans opposed discrimination against gays and lesbians and responded impatiently to the handful of conservative politicians who tried to use the AIDS issue to whip up antigay feeling. Yet Americans also continued to insist that there was something special about *the* family—a husband and a wife taking care of children. Americans were individualists who believed each person should be free to make his or her own choices. They were also communitarians who understood that society was more than a collection of isolated individuals. They believed in private choices, yet also saw merit to publicly proclaimed moral norms—some choices were *better*, for individuals, society, and especially dependent children, than others. Americans wanted expanded assistance for child care outside the home, yet they also believed that parents tended to do a better job of taking care of their own children than even well-qualified custodians designated by the state or by private companies.

The false choices offered by an ideologically polarized discussion made it ever harder for such nuanced views to express themselves. Liberals blamed conservatives for promoting polarization—and polarization certainly helped the conservative cause in the 1980s. Yet as the advocates of change, liberals themselves had the primary obligation to make change easier. In this, they failed. Indeed, it was not until conservatives had won two electoral landslides that liberals began to pay genuinely respectful attention to the nuances of public opinion on family life. Too often, liberals saw the world as divided between "progressives" and "reactionaries," between "the open-minded" and "the bigots." This, too, was a false choice, a form of bigotry against the conventional. It was a false choice for which liberals paid a heavy price.

5

THE LOST OPPORTUNITY:

Jimmy Carter
and the
Not-So-Vital Center

I<small>N HIS INFLUENTIAL</small> 1949 manifesto on behalf of pragmatic liberalism, *The Vital Center*, Arthur M. Schlesinger, Jr., spoke confidently of liberalism's achievements and staying power. Schlesinger had reasons for hope, writing as he did after the fifth consecutive Democratic victory in as many presidential elections. "For one's own generation, then, American liberalism has had a positive and confident ring," Schlesinger wrote. "It has stood for responsibility and for achievement, not for frustration and sentimentalism; it has been the instrument of social change, not of private neurosis." He also offered this prediction: "During most of my political consciousness this has been a New Deal country. I expect that it will continue to be a New Deal country."

The Vital Center of American liberalism, which came under such pressure in the 1960s, collapsed in the 1970s. It could not withstand the storms over the Vietnam War, race, feminism, and the counterculture. American politics has never fully recovered from the implosion of the Vital Center. The very idea that a Vital Center existed tempered American politics, and the collapse of the Vital Center and its Establishment had a high cost. If Vital Center politics could be very boring, it could also be quite peaceful. After World War II, the Vital Center came to a consensus on a globalist foreign policy that squeezed out leftists and isolationists alike. When Joseph R. McCarthy rose up against leaders of the Vital Center, he was crushed by a coalition that had the vociferous support of liberals in Americans for Democratic Action and the quiet backing of conservatives such as Dwight D. Eisenhower. Indeed, Eisenhower's role in the operation led many conservatives to doubt that he even deserved the label. On civil rights, the Vital Center responded rather slowly to the moral cries of black America, but when it did respond, it moved almost as a block. Everett McKinley Dirksen—the Senate Republican leader to whom no one would deny the conservative label—worked together with Hubert Horatio Humphrey.

The Vital Center was also rather polite. To be sure, it conducted and endured its share of negative campaigns. Franklin D. Roosevelt, who might be seen as the Vital Center's founding member, had to put up with Thomas E. Dewey's arguments that he was somehow a pawn of "communist-leaning" trade union leaders. The Vital Center's leaders were merciless when it came to opponents of anti-Nazi interventionism—the antifascist "brown scare" preceded the anticommunist "red scare," as historian Leo P. Ribuffo has pointed out. And the Vital Center, from its left to its right, dismissed opponents of Truman's anticommunist policy as neurotic apologists for Stalin. Still, the Vital Center could conduct politics within a civilized framework because from the end of World War II until the 1960s, there really was broad agreement within the country on the fundamentals: A free-market economy produced enough to underwrite a globalist foreign policy, a modest welfare state, and steadily increasing standards of living for Americans who seemed more than happy to live child-centered family lives. Few Americans questioned even a single aspect of this creed. In the 1960 presidential campaign, both John Kennedy and Richard Nixon embraced it entirely, arguing only about how to get the economy moving faster and how to fight the communists better. The differences between the two candidates were sufficiently obscure that Schlesinger himself felt moved to entitle a pamphlet in support of Kennedy: "Kennedy or Nixon: Does It Make a Difference?" The question was an adequately difficult one to engage the energies of a distinguished historian.

Yet Schlesinger's essay also revealed the problems of the Vital

Center. Seen by its critics, Vital Center politics was blandly centrist, excluding the vibrancy of both the left and right. It was a system that kept roughly the same people in power, to the dismay of both left and right. In retrospect, it is striking that the New Left and the rising right saw the enemy in almost exactly the same terms. The New Left despised "Establishment liberals." The right hated "the liberal Establishment." Yet the slight difference in labeling also revealed much—each group put the most important word first. What the New Left disliked about liberals was that they represented the *Establishment*; what the right disliked about the Establishment was that it was *liberal*.

The very existence of the Vital Center helped blind liberals to the changes they confronted in the 1960s. The Vital Center idea presumed that social class differences in the country had become increasingly less important. The American working man—the word *man* is appropriate—was regarded as affluent. The notion that he might feel severe pressures seemed absurd. This view enabled liberals to embark on a campaign in support of blacks and impoverished whites free from any thoughts that they had to do much more to appease blue-collar whites. Thus, when white workers rebelled in the late 1960s and argued that the Establishment was overlooking *their* needs, it was easy for liberals to dismiss their anxieties as irrational and racist. The Vital Center was also initially mystified by the surge of opposition to the Vietnam War. Most liberals and conservatives, after all, initially saw Vietnam as they had seen the Korean War: It was a necessary undertaking to halt communist expansion. To oppose a muscular American foreign policy was to break with everything the Vital Center had taught since at least 1940. But over time, as we have seen, a large share of the Vital Center's liberal wing abandoned the war and joined the New Left in relegitimizing political opposition to the Establishment's foreign policy. One of the first to do so was Arthur Schlesinger himself. The man who had named and baptized the Vital Center understood better than most of its members what the war was doing to destroy it.

The controversies over Vietnam and race eliminated the Vital Center as the dominant force in American politics, and we have not been the same since. The rise of the New Left and neoconservatism were the clearest signs that liberalism's Vital Center was not holding. Three men—George Wallace, George McGovern, and Jimmy Carter —owed their political careers to its collapse. Jimmy Carter's success in winning the Democratic nomination in 1976 and his subsequent failures in office both owed to the collapse of a vital liberal center.

II

It is difficult to imagine three men more different from each other than Wallace, McGovern, and Carter.

George Wallace, the former bantamweight boxer, spent virtually his entire adult life as a politician. He had run and lost for governor of Alabama as a racial liberal and pledged never again to be caught on the tolerant side of racial politics. He wasn't. He won the Alabama governorship four years later with an outspokenly racist campaign, and upon his inauguration in 1963, he pledged himself to "segregation now—segregation tomorrow—segregation forever." Wallace had no illusions about what moved electorates, and he was one of the nation's most entertaining speakers.

George McGovern, a soft-spoken preacher's son, was no less a political professional than Wallace, but his roots were in agrarian progressivism, the social Gospel, and the peace movement. Appropriately, his one federal job before going to the Senate from South Dakota was as head of the Food for Peace program during the Kennedy administration. McGovern believed in human decency and in the power of moral argument to sway voters.

Jimmy Carter, the son of a landed family, was a Naval Academy graduate, an intensely disciplined achiever, and a believer in well-organized good government. An adept political calculator, he embraced segregationist support when he needed it to win election as governor of Georgia. Upon election, he immediately reversed field, declared the days of segregation were over, hung Dr. King's portrait in the state Capitol, and sought to become a spokesman for a racially tolerant New South. Carter's view of human nature was complex. He believed that human beings *should* be moved by appeals to morality and the public interest; and it angered him that this was not the way life or politics always worked. He was exceptionally adept at getting small groups of average voters to see things his way, but he was impatient when the arguments of politicians did not turn on "the merits," as he saw them. This made him much more effective campaigning in Iowa than in negotiating with Congress.

Wallace and McGovern paved the way for Carter's triumph by destroying the Democratic Party's liberal center. Wallace struck first, running as a segregationist in the 1964 Democratic primaries against President Johnson, then as a third-party candidate in 1968, and finally returning to the Democratic Party in 1972. If Wallace represented racial reaction on the Democratic Party's right, McGovern spoke for the increasingly powerful antiwar movement on its left. McGovern, too, took on the Democratic Party establishment.

Wallace and McGovern were exceptionally important figures in our recent political history because they each gave form and leadership to forces that transformed American politics. Wallace was the bridge between the old Democratic South and the new presidentially Republican South. McGovern came to represent the middle-class reformers who began to feel their power in the Democratic Party after Adlai Stevenson's nomination in 1952. With the antiwar movement augmenting its strength, the reform faction moved from being a vigorous but isolated minority to becoming one of the dominant forces inside the Democratic Party. McGovern helped the process along with the new "participatory" delegate-selection rules he helped write for the 1972 Democratic National Convention. Although the investment bankers, lawyers, and intellectuals who governed on behalf of the Vital Center sometimes scorned the old party bosses, it turned out that the Vital Center needed the bosses far more than most of its members had known. When the reform rules took the power to select presidential candidates away from the bosses and delivered it to primary electorates, the Vital Center was squeezed out. In the charged atmosphere of 1972, the *protest* movements Wallace and McGovern represented could turn out the votes. The liberal center's favored candidates, Senators Hubert Humphrey and Edmund S. Muskie, fell by the wayside.

The liberal center's difficulties could be measured with some precision in the newspaper estimates of Democratic National Convention delegates on May 15, 1972. That was the day Wallace was shot during a Maryland campaign appearance. The estimates showed Humphrey with 305 delegates and Muskie, who had withdrawn from the race by that point, with 106. On the left, McGovern had 506 delegates. On the right, Wallace had 317. The party's left and right wings, in other words, had twice the delegate strength as the combined totals of the two members of the 1968 Democratic ticket. The center was not holding at all.

The revolt against the center led Patrick H. Caddell, George McGovern's twenty-one-year-old polltaker, to believe that alienation against the status quo was so great that only a radicalized, anti-Establishment liberalism had any hope of winning the country. In analyzing the strong anti-Establishment trend toward Wallace and McGovern in the Democratic primaries, Caddell felt that there might be a way to bring together the two streams of protest behind McGovern in an anti-Nixon coalition in the fall. As odd as Caddell's idea seems now, given the results of the 1972 election, there was some evidence to support his view.

On the day after he was shot, Wallace won sweeping victories in primaries in Michigan and Maryland, two states that have always been at the center of Democratic electoral hopes. Wallace's support in Michigan was boosted by white-voter reaction to a highly controversial school busing plan that was implemented around the time of the primary. Wallace won more than half the vote in a three-person field. But there was more to the Wallace vote than just racism. According to an exit poll of Michigan primary voters conducted for the *New York Times* and *Time* magazine, the Wallace constituency had two basic components. The poll, carried out by Daniel Yankelovich, found that Wallace won support across all classes among voters reacting against busing and other civil rights measures. And he did well among working-class voters *regardless* of their views on race. For the relatively well-off, a vote for Wallace really was a vote of white racial protest. But for blue-collar voters, Wallace represented a much broader protest against the *status quo*. The Michigan survey contained other hopeful news for McGovern: The blue-collar voters opposed to busing, the ones who were giving Wallace his landslide, preferred McGovern to Nixon by a margin of five to three. Perhaps a coalition was waiting to be born.

McGovern's hope was that he could attract alienated white voters as Robert Kennedy had done in 1968. But the differences between McGovern's appeal and Robert Kennedy's were profound. The Kennedys, after all, had disdained the Democrats' middle-class reform faction; their base had always been among blue-collar voters. McGovern's base was precisely in the professional middle class—the people who would later be dubbed "yuppies." The Kennedys' Roman Catholicism gave them a special appeal to socially conservative white ethnic voters. McGovern, on the other hand, came to represent the rebellious side in the cultural civil war. Richard Nixon's supporters captured this neatly when they declared McGovern the candidate of "acid, amnesty [for draft resisters], and abortion." Wallace supporters knew which side of those issues they were on.

Still, many of the blue-collar voters who backed Nixon were not particularly happy to do so—they *were* alienated. A Yankelovich survey for *The New York Times* and *Time* magazine in the fall found nearly half of Nixon's voters among blue-collar Southerners declaring that they would have voted for Wallace if he had been on the ballot. A third of Nixon's Northern blue-collar voters also expressed a preference for Wallace.

But Wallace was not on the ballot and most of his supporters went to Nixon. For liberals, the most disturbing trend in 1972 was the collapse of their vote among middle- and lower-income whites—the legacy of racial and cultural liberalism. As if to prove that the neoconservatives were entirely right when they said that "McGovernism" was the ideology of "the new class," the 1972 results reversed decades of voting history. McGovern was supposed to be the candidate of the young, but it turned out that he was, at best, the candidate of the college-educated young. Young people who had *not* gone to college, once a bulwark of Democratic strength, were now voting overwhelmingly Republican. More broadly, McGovern actually strengthened the Democratic vote—if only slightly—among voters of higher socioeconomic status. But he lost ground badly among voters in the middle and at the bottom of the class structure.

The McGovern inversion is revealed dramatically in Table One, based on Gallup Poll data recalculated by political scientists Everett Carll Ladd, Jr., and Charles D. Hadley. The table compares voting by socioeconomic status and educational level in the 1948 election, when Harry Truman defeated Thomas E. Dewey, with the results of 1972.

In contrast to 1948, when Harry Truman found his base among the poor and less educated, McGovern found his among the better educated. Indeed, McGovern's *worst* showing was in the socioeco-

TABLE ONE

DEMOCRATIC PERCENTAGE OF THE PRESIDENTIAL
VOTE AMONG WHITES

	1948	1972	CHANGE
ALL VOTERS			
High SES	30	32	+ 2
Middle SES	43	26	− 17
Low SES	57	32	− 25
VOTERS UNDER 30			
College educated	36	45	+ 9
Not college educated	56	30	− 26

Adapted from Transformations of the American Party System (W. W. Norton, 1975)

nomic middle. No wonder Nixon and the Republicans spoke so fondly of "middle Americans."

Nixon's fall from power in the Watergate scandal seemed to render the 1972 election results irrelevant. Democrats—and not just those of the Vital Center—certainly hoped that they could put the entire McGovern experience behind them. But in truth, the transformations that began in 1972 continued in the 1974 midterm elections, which gave the Democrats a Watergate-inspired landslide victory. When the votes were counted, the Democrats had a 291–144 majority in the House and a 61–37 majority in the Senate (with two seats held by independents). Not since the Johnson landslide in 1964 had the Democrats enjoyed such a large congressional majority.

But as William Schneider and Thomas Byrne Edsall have shown, the "class of '74" was populated by a new kind of Democrat. The new Democrats were elected disproportionately from middle-class and suburban areas. Their interests were not in the sort of New Deal economic liberalism that appealed to blacks and working-class whites alike. Rather, they shared the interest of well-educated middle-class voters in cultural liberalism and procedural reform ("good government"). One of the representative suburban reformers the Democrats elected that year was Michael S. Dukakis, the new governor of Massachusetts.

The new congressional Democrats reflected the new class bias of the Democratic coalition—or rather its lack of any bias at all toward

TABLE TWO

DEMOCRATIC PERCENTAGE OF THE CONGRESSIONAL VOTE AMONG WHITES

	1964	1974	CHANGE
ALL VOTERS			
High SES	48	57	+ 9
Middle SES	65	62	− 3
Low SES	74	67	− 7
VOTERS UNDER 30			
College educated	53	69	+ 16
Not college educated	71	69	− 2

Adapted from Transformations of the American Party System *(W. W. Norton, 1975)*

the Democrats' traditional supporters among blue-collar workers. Table Two, also drawn from Ladd and Hadley, analyzes the Democratic congressional vote by socioeconomic status and education in the two landslides of 1964 and 1974. The table shows that the Democrats actually lost ground between the two landslides among lower-status whites.

The 1974 elections, in short, did not undo the 1972 trends. A new kind of middle-class cultural liberalism was an increasingly powerful force in American politics. When, as in 1974, the middle-class liberals could forge an effective alliance with most of the working-class base of New Deal liberalism, the new liberal coalition was unbeatable. But it was not a stable coalition, and it was not to last.

III

Despite the 1972 fiasco, Caddell did not give up on his alienation thesis, and in 1976, he saw Jimmy Carter as the perfect candidate to test it. In this, Caddell was right.

Jimmy Carter's 1976 candidacy was, first, a candidacy of moral uplift. No one else has run for president offering the explicit and highly personal promise "I'll never lie to you." All presidents implicitly pledge to good government, but no one formulated it quite as Carter did, "a government as good as the American people." Carter's entire campaign was perfectly calibrated for the period immediately after Watergate, a time when Americans had lost faith not only in the government's competence, but also in its willingness to observe the elementary rules of morality. "Without the trust thing, he couldn't have made it," Caddell once said.

But Jimmy Carter needed to win the *Democratic* nomination, and many Democrats read the 1972 results as suggesting that the party's nominating process gave exceptional advantages to cultural and anti-war liberals of the McGovern stripe. Carter, however, read the 1972 results properly: that the new rules, with their emphasis on primaries and low-turnout caucuses, gave the advantage not so much to the left as to *outsiders*, so long as the outsiders understood the rules. What had been significant about 1972 was not just McGovern's victory but also Wallace's strong showing. The bias of the system was toward insurgents. Carter, who had won the Georgia governorship as an outsider, understood that his lack of national stature and Washington experience was thus an asset, not a liability. "He was an unknown quantity in Georgia and he would be an unknown quantity in the country," James Wooten wrote in his fine biography of Carter. "If

others thought running from Washington as a Senator or Representative—as someone with a record in Federal office—was an asset, he
sensed once again that it was a liability. People didn't trust people who
had had a chance to foul things up, he reasoned, and the antagonism
toward the Federal government was deep and strong."

Carter had an additional advantage in a party that had been torn
apart by liberalism's agonies: *He was not a liberal.* He could not be
tied either to the old Vital Center liberalism of Humphrey, Johnson,
or Henry Jackson, or to "McGovernism." Carter was also from the
Deep South, and that gave him credibility with constituencies that
had long since abandoned the Democratic Party in presidential elections over civil rights. This helped Carter not only with white Southerners, but also with Northern white ethnics. Carter was bitterly
attacked by blacks and liberals in the spring of 1976 for his response to
a question about the integration of ethnic neighborhoods. "I see nothing wrong with ethnic purity being maintained," he replied. "I would
not force a racial integration of a neighborhood by government action." He eventually withdrew the statement under pressure from key
black supporters such as Andrew Young. But as George Wallace might
have put it, Carter sent a message, one that many working-class whites
found reassuring.

The lay of the land in the 1976 primaries was (it is easy to see in
retrospect) perfect for Jimmy Carter. On the one hand, Carter was
the only candidate in any position to compete with Wallace in the
South. His posture as the "anti-Washington" candidate could be read
by liberals as opposition to *Nixon's* Washington. But Southerners,
seasoned in the language of states' rights, had their own understanding of what it meant to be anti-Washington. Similarly, Carter could
play Wallace in different ways for different constituencies. As the only
candidate with a reasonable chance of ridding the Democratic Party
of the Wallace specter, Carter won a certain sympathy from party
liberals—especially Southern liberals eager to bring their region into
the national mainstream. Yet to Wallace's political base, Carter could
present himself as the realistic alternative, the candidate who spoke
their language in a way Yankees would accept. He even used a variant
of Wallace's 1972 slogan, "Send them a message." Carter's riposte:
"Don't send them a message. Send them a president." Carter defeated
Wallace in the Florida and North Carolina primaries and did what
Nixon and Humphrey and McGovern and many other national leaders before him had been unable to do: He ended George Wallace's
presidential ambitions.

In the aftermath of the Vietnam War, the party's liberal wing was a shambles. The McGovern wing alone divided its loyalties among several candidates, notably Rep. Morris K. Udall of Arizona and former senator Fred Harris of Oklahoma. The right-wing liberals, soon to become widely known as neoconservatives, were represented by Scoop Jackson. Arguably in the best position was Sen. Birch Bayh of Indiana, who occupied the Humphrey-Muskie middle ground between the Jackson wing and the Udall-Harris wing. But Bayh found that that particular middle road was exactly the wrong place to stand. Support peeled off to his left and to his right—yet another sign of the Vital Center's lack of vitality.

Carter's victory was not "inevitable." He had extraordinary luck. A switch of a few thousand votes to Udall in the Michigan or Wisconsin primaries would have doomed Carter's candidacy. But if Carter's victory was not inevitable, it had a clear logic, the logic of divide and conquer. When Jackson and Wallace decided not to contest the New Hampshire primary seriously, they left Carter with the entire right wing of the Democratic spectrum. He won with 28 percent as Udall, Bayh, and Harris split the liberal vote. In the South, he was the most viable "liberal" alternative to Wallace. And liberalism's divisions helped Carter again when he won the Pennsylvania primary and eliminated Scoop Jackson. Many of the New Politics liberals vastly preferred the outsider they did not know to Jackson, the unreconstructable Cold War liberal they knew too well. Thus: In the South, Carter won all sorts of liberals who wanted to beat Wallace. In New Hampshire, Carter won the conservative blue-collar vote against a field of liberals. In Pennsylvania, he won a share of the New Politics middle class against the champion of the AFL-CIO's foreign policy and swept among rural voters who had little use for any kind of liberal.

Carter did not glide as easily to the nomination as he might have. However much liberal divisions helped him, Carter was still, liberals knew, not one of their own, and they continued to search for alternatives. Two new candidates—Gov. Jerry Brown of California and Sen. Frank Church of Idaho—entered the later primaries and handed Carter some sharp defeats. But Carter won just enough, and the day after the primaries were over, Mayor Richard J. Daley of Chicago, the man the New Politics liberals had thrown out of the 1972 convention, had the satisfaction of delivering his delegates, and effectively the nomination, to Jimmy Carter. Here again, one of the party's warring factions helped Carter by using him for its own purposes. Carter was more than happy to let different kinds of Democrats use him to settle old scores, so long as the settlements worked to his advantage.

Austin Ranney, the political scientist, was right when he said that Carter's victory "was arguably the greatest feat in the entire history of presidential nominating politics." Starting out in 1976 as the choice of just 4 percent of the Democrats in the Gallup Poll, Carter had upended some of Washington's most respected figures.

(Carter won for many reasons, but chief among them was his independence from all the party's liberal factions) Carter's triumph was a demonstration of liberalism's weaknesses. "He was clearly the most conservative of the Democratic candidates in the '76 campaign," said Stuart Eizenstat, later Carter's chief domestic-policy adviser. "He was the only one talking about balanced budgets and less bureaucracy and less red tape and themes that associate perhaps with Republicans." Erwin C. Hargrove, a political scientist and a Carter scholar, wrote that Carter "clearly believed that the central weakness of American politics and government was the dominance of special interests over social need, and though he never used the term he was an implacable foe of 'interest group liberalism.' " In this sense, Hargrove argued, Carter had much more in common with the middle-class Progressives at the turn of the century than with the New Deal liberals who were their successors.

Nonetheless, Carter also understood the "populist" issues far better than most of the middle-class liberals. In 1972, both Wallace and McGovern had gained ground by attacking the tax system as being unfair to the average taxpayer. Carter condemned the system as "a disgrace to the human race." Like many right-wing populists, Carter scored the welfare system for discouraging work and family values. But unlike the right, Carter insisted that he would make the system fair to the needy. Carter could convince blacks that he really did believe in civil rights, even though he appeased whites by opposing "forced busing." Blacks could forgive Carter a more "conservative" position on race since he was so comparatively advanced for a white Southerner. Carter's Baptist religiosity also spoke directly to the sensibilities of a large share of the black community—and to the sensibilities of socially conservative whites. Moreover conservative whites also suspected that a Southern Democrat would never be as liberal as a Northern Democrat. Carter further diffused the racial issue simply by changing the subject from race to class and by speaking out against Washington and assorted "insiders." Carter, the least "left-wing" Democratic nominee since 1924, understood the power of class resentments far better than his more liberal foes.

Jimmy Carter, the man who routed the liberals, was paradoxically liberalism's great lost opportunity. Carter was uniquely placed to solve liberalism's problems, in part because he was not readily identified as a liberal. Many voters who strayed from the liberal ranks because of cultural and racial politics sensed rightly that culturally, Carter really was quite conservative. His values were those of a traditional person who was nonetheless open to the changes wrought by the 1960s—almost exactly where the country was. He was so obviously distant from the nation's cultural elites that he could simply not be cast as a member of the "liberal establishment." Yet his views were, in the end, not far from those of that establishment.

The results of the 1976 election demonstrated both the strengths and the limits of the Carter appeal. Carter's successes showed that a version of the old liberal coalition could be put together again. His problems foreshadowed many of the difficulties he would have in governing the country.

Carter managed to achieve the dream of the old Southern populists by drawing a class line across the South. He won overwhelming majorities among blacks, and just as Caddell had dreamed, he won the blue-collar racial conservatives who had backed Wallace and Nixon. A *New York Times*/CBS News poll found Carter winning half the votes of whites who said the government had done *too much* for blacks—the sorts of racial conservatives who had been bolting the Democrats since 1948. Counties across the Deep South that had given Wallace landslide majorities in 1968 and then switched massively to Nixon in 1972 returned to the Democratic fold to back Jimmy Carter. Table Three reports the vote in eight strong Wallace counties in Alabama, Arkansas, Florida, and Mississippi. In all these counties, the 1968 Wallace vote shifted overwhelmingly to Nixon; even if one assumes that all of McGovern's gains over Humphrey came from Wallace supporters, McGovern did not get even a fifth of the Wallace vote in any of these counties.

Carter's improvements over McGovern were staggering. Half to two-thirds of Nixon's 1972 voters shifted to Carter. Carter's strength was even greater than the table displays: In all these counties, turnout increased between 1972 and 1976 as voters who decided to skip a McGovern-Nixon choice came back to the polls to back their regional favorite son.

Carter's 1976 totals suggested it was possible for a nonracist candidate to assemble a coalition of protest built on both black and lower-status white votes. But what is often ignored about Carter's triumph is that he not only won back the blue-collar vote to the Democratic

TABLE THREE

VOTE FOR PRESIDENT
IN SELECTED PRO-WALLACE COUNTIES
PERCENTAGE DEMOCRATIC
(1968 WALLACE VOTE IN PARENTHESES)

	1968 Humphrey (Wallace)	1972 McGovern	1976 Carter
Cleburne, Alabama	4 (84)	15	63
Randolph, Alabama	10 (78)	23	61
Grant, Arkansas	23 (60)	32	78
Prairie, Arkansas	25 (56)	29	78
Calhoun, Florida	13 (76)	18	68
Dixie, Florida	16 (74)	18	80
Calhoun, Mississippi	5 (88)	7	59
George, Mississippi	5 (91)	6	61

Party; he also held on to many of the party's new supporters in the middle class. In effect, Carter was the candidate of middle-class reform with a populist edge. At its core, the Carter campaign was premised on bringing "good government" to Washington much as people such as Michael Dukakis had brought good government to the states. The result is that while Carter created the traditional sort of lower-class/working-class coalition that was essential to every Democratic victory, he also did well among higher-status voters. Table Four, adapted from Everett Ladd's analysis of Gallup polls, suggests the new class alignment Carter created. It was part old, and part new.

Compared with Harry Truman, Carter did significantly better among high-status voters and among the young, well-educated voters. Reflecting the Democrats' new dependence on the middle class, Carter ran slightly behind Truman among those in the lowest socioeconomic category and among young voters who had not gone to college. But compared with McGovern, Carter was Harry Truman himself. Carter posted huge gains over McGovern in the middle and bottom socioeconomic layers and among the young who had not gone to college.

What Carter showed is that there was at least the potential to turn the Democratic Party's problems into assets. With the right mix of messages, the party could draw back lower-income voters who had strayed because of the conflicts of the sixties and bring in middle-class voters who were attracted by some of the very issues (reform, a less interventionist foreign policy, social tolerance) that had turned off traditional Democrats. It was at least possible to make liberalism's contradictions work for, rather than against, the Democratic Party—especially when the candidate trying to do so was not easily identified as a liberal.

But Carter's problems in 1976 also foreshadowed troubles later. His potential weaknesses—and those of the Democratic Party—were underlined by the fact that by election day, he lost nearly all of the 33-point lead he had enjoyed after the Democratic National Convention. After the convention, Carter led Ford in the Gallup Poll by 62 percent to 29 percent. The final results were Carter 50.1 percent, Ford 48.0 percent. It was hardly reassuring to Democrats that their margin in the first post-Watergate election was so thin. Carter also ran well behind Democratic congressional candidates, giving him little leverage in a Washington that was already suspicious of him.

It was difficult, moreover, to interpret Carter's victory as a mandate for any policies, except for a new morality in government—"a government as good as the American people." This was one of the costs of Carter's ideological suppleness. Liberals who had once

TABLE FOUR

DEMOCRATIC PERCENTAGE OF THE PRESIDENTIAL VOTE AMONG WHITES

	1948	1972	1976	CHANGE '48 to '76	CHANGE '72 to '76
ALL VOTERS					
High SES	30	32	41	+ 11	+ 9
Middle SES	43	26	49	+ 6	+ 23
Low SES	57	32	53	− 4	+ 21
VOTERS UNDER 30					
College educated	36	45	44	+ 8	− 1
Not college educated	56	30	51	− 5	+ 21

Adapted from Party Coalitions in the 1980s (*Institute for Contemporary Studies,* 1981)

thought of him as a liberal began to worry that he was a conservative; conservatives who had once seen him as one of their own began to worry that he was really a liberal.

There was also a patched-together quality to the Carter coalition, a sense that it was a gadget that could work only once before falling apart. He held on largely because of his near-sweep of the South, which was eager to end its isolation in American politics. It was not clear that anyone, even Carter himself, could repeat such a feat. Moreover, Carter lost key industrial states that are usually seen as essential to Democrats and had gone, albeit narrowly, to John F. Kennedy in 1960—Illinois, Michigan, New Jersey, and Connecticut. He carried New York and Pennsylvania, usually at the core of any Democratic electoral-college majority, by unexpectedly narrow margins. The results made clear that some of the working-class Democrats who had defected in 1972 were still not ready to come home, and that some of the middle-class liberals were so uneasy with Carter that they actually voted for Ford. In some suburban counties in New York, California, and Massachusetts, Carter actually ran *behind* McGovern.

Carter's 1976 victory, then, was a confusing portent. If his presidency had been successful, his coalition had ample room for growth and might have pointed the way to a future Democratic majority. In 1980, Carter could have held on to his unusual 1976 alliance and added to it those traditional Democrats who had been uncomfortable with his unique persona. Even in the West, which was swept by Gerald Ford, Carter lost only narrowly in California, Oregon, and New Mexico. In all these states, Carter's middle-class reformism had a strong appeal, and all could easily have switched to the Democratic column.

Instead, Carter got the worst of all worlds, and his administration became a model, as Carter scholar Leo Ribuffo put it, of "the ironies of liberalism." Carter demonstrated that the politics of middle-class reform and the politics of New Dealism could run headlong into each other. Rather than rebuild the old Democratic coalition, Carter provided a model for how to alienate all its various wings simultaneously.

IV

The broad reasons for the failure of Carter's presidency are well-known—the hostage crisis in Iran, the rise in interest rates, and the unprecedented inflation accompanied by increasing unemployment in his final year in office. Inflation, in turn, drove up the average

American's tax rate, fueling a conservative tax revolt. Carter was perceived as a failure quite simply because he failed in dealing with two of the most visible challenges before him: the hostage crisis and the economic crisis. In the end, Carter was defeated on the issue of competence, not ideology.

The Carter years were a time when, thanks largely to the oil cartel, Americans began sensing that the nation had lost control over its economic destiny. Polls showed that only about one-sixth of the voters felt better off; two-fifths felt worse off. When the abrupt actions of a group of foreign sheiks have more impact on how much gas is available at the corner station than all the programs proposed by the President, popular confidence in the government's ability to manage the economy is bound to decline.

In fact, the economic news from the Carter years was not all bad. Unemployment was kept low for most of Carter's term. The nation's foreign-trade accounts were in balance or surplus, and there was real growth in the high-profit export sectors—in capital goods, for example. Thus, Herbert Stein, the Republican economist, argued that when Ronald Reagan urged voters to ask themselves, "Are you better off now than you were four years ago," many might objectively have answered yes, since real per capita income rose between 1976 and 1980. But such raw statistics meant little with gas lines, soaring inflation, and interest rates that put home ownership out of the reach of millions.

The sense that the country had lost control over its economic destiny was reinforced by its seeming loss of influence over events abroad. If Vietnam created a popular view that the United States had become "a pitiful, helpless giant," then the taking of the hostages in Iran reinforced that feeling with a vengeance. Carter's own sharp U-turns in foreign policy did little to build confidence, either. At the beginning of his administration, in May 1977, he sounded a theme highly appealing to liberals: "Being confident of our own future, we are now free of that inordinate fear of communism which once led us to embrace any dictator who joined us in that fear." That lost him the friendship of all the Cold War liberals, the Scoop Jackson Democrats, who had expected something tougher from this moderate from Georgia. But when the Soviet Union invaded Afghanistan, Carter expressed the surprise of an innocent whose trust had been abused: "This action of the Soviets has made a more drastic change in my own opinion of what the Soviets' ultimate goals are than anything they've done in the previous time I've been in office."

On human rights, Carter's much-debated policy had many positive effects, notably in the movement across Latin America toward democracy. The problem for Carter was that the full impact of his policy was felt only after he left office. During Carter's own term, his human rights policy appeared inconsistent, almost incoherent. The historian Stephen Ambrose captured the contradictions of Carter's policy by juxtaposing two of the more memorable sentences Carter spoke. In 1977, he declared: "Human rights is the soul of our foreign policy." The same year, he said of the Shah's regime: "Iran is an island of stability in one of the more troubled areas of the world."

Carter's inconsistencies had a high cost. In the end, hard-liners mistrusted Carter for what they saw as his misplaced idealism and his willingness to let friendly dictators fall in Iran and Nicaragua. Doves opposed the arms buildup that began in the final years of his administration. The already alienated hard-liners did not return to Carter's side. Support fell away to Carter's left and right.

Carter's foreign policy difficulties can be traced in significant part to the breakdown of the consensus within the Democratic Party's liberal establishment, caused by the Vietnam War. Carter, who might under other circumstances have been a credible "Vital Center" president, had no Vital Center to rely on. Carter's contradictions were, in many ways, those of his party. James Fallows, who served for a spell as Carter's chief speechwriter, reported that the Carter inner circle believed that the two main ingredients of a successful presidency were to avoid another Watergate and to avoid another Vietnam. That made the administration deeply skeptical about using military power and about supporting unpopular dictators. Carter's Wilsonian sense of morality—or in the eyes of his critics, moralism—echoed the idealism of the McGovern wing of his party. But Carter was no McGovernite. What foreign policy background he brought with him to office came from his experience at the Trilateral Commission, surely no training ground for pacifism. Carter was enough of a "realist," for example, to accept almost immediately the Nixon-Kissinger view that the stability of the Shah's regime in Iran was central to America's interests in the Middle East. And the implications of Carter's human rights policy often led him "right" as well as "left." His calls for human rights in the Soviet Union angered Soviet leader Leonid Brezhnev and complicated arms-control negotiations.

The foreign-policy split within the Democratic establishment—and within Carter himself—was exemplified in a most public way in the battles between Cyrus Vance, Carter's secretary of state and a relative dove, and Zbigniew Brzezinski, a classic Cold War liberal. Carter's lack of any ideological definition made such skirmishing com-

mon. His administration became a battleground in which all the tendencies of the Democratic Party, and all of the wings of liberalism,
struggled for influence. Carter's appointees to regulatory commissions
tended to be younger liberals much influenced by Ralph Nader–style
public advocacy. Thus, on issues such as occupational health and
safety, the environment, and consumer protection, the Carter administration had a decidedly progressive tinge. Carter himself was not
always comfortable with this, commenting once that he was the most
conservative member of his own administration. The ambivalence of
the Carter administration about its own liberal achievements did little
to build support among liberal constituencies.

On the social issues, the contradictions were between Carter's
conservative personal behavior and his deep and genuine religious
feeling, which had made him so attractive to Southern conservatives
in his election campaign, and his relatively liberal views on issues
relating to civil rights, women's rights, and civil liberties. The classic
Carter compromise was on abortion: He favored keeping abortion
legal and opposed federal financing of abortions for poor women. In
principle, his was the popular position: Majorities opposed an outright
ban on abortion and also opposed having the federal government pay
for abortions. But the position left those who felt most strongly about
cultural issues—the very people whose votes were most influenced by
such matters—uncomfortable. Social liberals mistrusted Carter's religiosity and his "Southernness," sensing that he did not fully share
their cosmopolitan worldview. Social conservatives, in the meantime,
saw Carter as betraying them.

Carter was much criticized for having no priorities, for believing
many things but no one thing deeply, for offering a long menu of
"comprehensive" programs while giving Congress no guide to the
menu. James Fallows chronicled these failures in an influential article
titled "The Passionless Presidency." Insofar as Carter did have domestic priorities, they tended to involve what might be described as "passionless issues." The choices he made were revealing both about
himself and about the style of politics associated with the middle-class
reformers who became so powerful in the Democratic Party after the
1974 elections. His highest priority, his energy program, was a classic
technocratic program put together with little regard for constituency
interests. That came naturally to a middle-class reformer who disdained "special interest" politics and yearned for what political scientist Erwin Hargrove called a politics of "the public good." Although
complicated, the program was relatively coherent. It sought both en-

hanced conservation and enhanced domestic production. But the environmentalist constituencies that favored conservation were often at odds with the industry constituencies that favored production. Carter sought simultaneously to raise the cost of energy to consumers and maintain price controls on oil and gas. "It was too liberal for conservatives in its willingness to continue price regulation," Hargrove wrote, "and too conservative for liberals in its plan for price increases." Perhaps the most fundamental error Carter made was in his claim that the struggle for energy independence should be seen as "the moral equivalent of war." Energy independence was a laudable goal, but it was not easy for him to convince Americans that his program deserved to be seen in such bold terms. Since Carter's plan, almost by design, offered few immediate benefits to particular constituencies, he needed to rely on the public's faith in his own sense of the public good. But since his heavy emphasis on the energy issue led him to deemphasize measures that might have built him a loyal constituency, there was no basis for the popular trust Carter needed to convince the country to "go to war" on the energy issue.

Carter's handling of his potentially popular welfare-reform initiative was also revealing. It demonstrated how hard it was for Carter to balance his liberal and conservative instincts. In fairness, it also showed the difficulties any president of even modestly liberal temperament will face in overhauling the welfare system.

Carter's mandate to Joseph Califano, his secretary of health, education, and welfare, was clear: He asked him to develop "a comprehensive plan that was prowork and profamily." Rewarding work required giving additional assistance to the working poor, who in many cases were no better off—or even worse off, since they often lacked health benefits—than people on welfare. And work or job-training requirements meant creating new work and training programs. Yet Carter was committed to a plan that involved "no higher cost than the original system."

Eventually, pieces of a welfare-reform package were approved, but they did not amount to the sort of "comprehensive" reform that Carter had promised. It is easy to fault Carter for his tactics, but his difficulties went to the heart of the problems of the modern welfare state. Carter's basic problem was that prowork welfare reform is inevitably *more expensive* than the current system. Providing jobs and job training for welfare recipients and lifting the incomes of the working poor—all essential ingredients to a program that would encourage and reward work—will require new spending and shifts in the tax code that will cost the government revenue. To have a system that promotes *conservative values* would require *more liberal spending*. Carter's fiscal conservatism made him reluctant to accept this reality.

Politically, any effort to lift the standard of living of the poor will require an entirely new program that is seen as encouraging work. The word *welfare* will simply have to be buried, so demonized has it become. A 1977 *New York Times*/CBS News poll found that even among Americans who favored a guaranteed annual income for the needy, a majority expressed disapproval of "welfare programs." A majority of Americans have come to associate "welfare recipients" with values they reject, notably single motherhood and the "absent father" who refuses to take responsibility for his children. "Welfare people" are thus seen as having nothing in common with the rest of the country. One of the most revealing findings about how Americans viewed welfare emerged in the National Opinion Research Center's 1980 General Social Survey. The survey asked respondents whether they thought the government was spending too much, too little, or the right amount in eleven different program areas. The public favored current levels of spending or spending increases in nine of the eleven areas. Majorities said too much was being spent in only two areas: welfare and foreign aid. For many Americans, welfare recipients are not part of the community they regard as their own. They are viewed as the equivalent of foreigners.

Carter's anti-Washington campaign and the skepticism of his closest advisers toward Washington's traditional leaders made for difficult relations with Congress. But Carter also had the misfortune of arriving in power at a time when party solidarity both within Congress and between the Congress and the White House had already broken down badly. The breakdown of parties hurts both Republicans and Democrats. But it hurts Democrats more, since Democrats are normally elected to change things and pass programs. Doing so requires party discipline. Yet as Martin P. Wattenberg showed in his study *The Decline of American Political Parties*, party-line voting in the House of Representatives—that is, the percentage of votes in which a majority of Democrats voted in opposition to the majority of Republicans— dropped from 59.5 percent during Roosevelt's presidency to 34.5 percent in the Nixon-Ford years. It rose to only 39.7 percent in Carter's term, which is not at all impressive when one considers that Nixon and Ford governed with Congresses under the control of the opposition and Carter governed with a Congress of his own party. The proportion of party-line votes cast during the Truman, Eisenhower, Kennedy, and Johnson administrations were all higher than during the Carter years. The vacuum created by the decline in parties was filled partly by the rise of political action committees, especially those associated with corporations and trade associations. The result was to push both parties to the right. Thus, another irony of Jimmy Carter's presidency is that the very popular revulsion with partisan politics that helped him into the White House made it much harder for him to govern once he was there.

The Carter administration was certainly not without achievements. The treaties turning the Panama Canal over to Panama helped lay the groundwork for improved relations between the United States and Central America. The Camp David accords initiated the first peace agreement ever between Israel and an Arab country. Carter established full diplomatic relations with Communist China and negotiated a new strategic arms limitation treaty with the Soviet Union.

It is significant that conservatives did not reverse any of these policies. They opposed the SALT treaty, yet Ronald Reagan largely lived by its provisions. Yet as historian Leo Ribuffo has pointed out, all of these successes worked to Carter's disadvantage. Carter was embarrassed by resistance to the SALT treaty among conservatives in his own party. The Panama Canal treaties gave the emerging New Right precisely the sort of nationalistic issue it needed. And many Jewish leaders criticized Carter's "evenhanded" approach to the Middle East as far too sympathetic to the Arab countries.

In the end, Jimmy Carter frustrated liberals and conservatives alike. The transideological appeal that helped make him president also helped undo him. As the 1980 campaign approached, both sides were ready.

V

The frustration of liberals with the content of Carter's presidency and the frustration of less ideological Democrats with his performance led to Sen. Edward M. Kennedy's challenge to Carter's renomination in 1980. As in 1976, Carter and his political advisers proved exceptionally adept in organizing a nomination campaign. But once again, Carter was also helped by luck—if the taking of American hostages can be called "luck"—and by the mistakes of his opposition.

Throughout 1978 and 1979, Kennedy had enjoyed large leads over Carter among Democrats surveyed by the Gallup Poll. The November 2–5 Gallup Poll gave Kennedy 54 percent, Carter 31 percent. But on November 4, the Iranian students seized the U.S. embassy in Tehran and the hostages. Carter's approval rating soared. In a month, it moved from around 30 percent to about 60 percent. This was, in the words of Nelson W. Polsby, the political scientist, "the most dramatic rally-'round-the-flag effect ever recorded."

What was striking about voting in the Democratic primaries was how negative the voters' motivations were. A large constituency opposed Kennedy and would vote for anyone, including Carter, to beat him. A large constituency opposed President Carter and would vote for anyone, including Kennedy, to beat *him*. On balance, Democrats disliked Carter less. Carter did best in the early primaries, held when voters thought there was a chance that Kennedy could win the nomination. But once a Kennedy nomination seemed a mathematical impossibility, Kennedy started winning votes. Democrats could safely vent their spleen at Carter without any fear that they would make Kennedy the nominee. As Patrick Caddell, the President's polltaker, put it at the time: "If it's Carter versus Kennedy, we win. If it's Carter versus Carter, we lose." Outside the South, Kennedy tended to do best with blue-collar voters, who were clearly in a surly mood. In 1976, disaffected blue-collar voters had turned to Carter. They were still disaffected in 1980 and turned against him.

Blue-collar anger could not be defined (or contained) by ideology. In the primaries, Kennedy won a consistent one-third or more from Democrats who called themselves conservatives. Many of these voters later turned to Ronald Reagan, so eager were they to be rid of Jimmy Carter. In the *Times*/CBS News postelection poll, roughly one-third of all voters who said they had supported Kennedy in the primaries voted for Ronald Reagan. Among blue-collar Kennedy supporters, nearly half backed Reagan over Carter. Thus did a familiar pattern reassert itself: In 1968, frustrated blue-collar voters had been willing to turn to both Robert Kennedy and George Wallace; in 1972, to Edward Kennedy (in the public opinion polls, at least) and Wallace. It should not have been a surprise, then, that in 1980, so many of them turned to Ronald Reagan after Kennedy was defeated.

Although Ronald Reagan's base of support was among the well-to-do, his *gains* over Gerald Ford's 1976 showing came almost entirely among blue-collar voters. According to the *Times*/CBS News poll, Reagan ran one percentage point behind Gerald Ford's 1976 showing among voters in professional occupations. He ran five percentage points behind Ford among the white collars. But he ran six percentage points *ahead* of Ford among blue-collar voters. Among families in which at least one member belonged to a trade union, Reagan ran five points ahead of Ford. Reagan ran even with Ford among independents and behind Ford among Republicans. Reagan's gains over Ford came among Democrats.

If blue-collar voters were disaffected, so, too, were the middle-class progressives. Carter's moderation on cultural issues, which had allowed him to do well with cultural conservatives in 1976, had created doubts among cultural liberals. These doubts were, if anything, stronger in 1980. In the primaries, some of the cultural liberals backed Kennedy. In the fall, many in their ranks found comfort in John Anderson, a liberal Republican from Illinois who dropped out of the contest for the Republican nomination to run as an independent.

Anderson's campaign was aimed squarely at the New Politics constituency of middle-class reformers who were equally uncomfortable with New Deal trade unionists and Moral Majority preachers. In an advertisement in *The New York Times* on June 27, 1980, Anderson emphasized five issues dear to the reformers: protecting the environment, extending civil rights, passing the Equal Rights Amendment, restoring federal financing for abortions for the poor, and reducing excessive government regulation. Anderson positioned himself to Carter's left on the cultural issues and to his right on economics. The latter was much more difficult, since Carter was quite moderate on economics.

What the polls made clear is that the Anderson *constituency* was well to the left of Carter's on the social issues, notably the Equal Rights Amendment and abortion. These issues were of particular concern to upper-middle-class and well-educated voters, and in these groups, most of the voters who defected from Carter backed Anderson, not Reagan. Thus, among college graduates, *both* the Democratic and Republican shares of the vote declined between 1976 and 1980. Among college graduates, Carter lost ten percentage points from his 1976 total, according to *Times* and CBS News polls, and Reagan lost four points from Gerald Ford's totals. The exit polls showed that Carter lost considerable ground among Democrats who described themselves as liberal. In this group, Carter lost sixteen percentage points, going from 86 percent in 1976 to 70 percent in 1980, according to *Times*/CBS News polls. Anderson, who got 13 percent of the liberal Democratic vote, was the main beneficiary. A similar shift occurred among liberal independents. Yet despite Carter's sharp losses among liberal Democrats, they were still his strongest supporters. Carter's paradoxical relationship with liberalism thus continued right through the end of his term. It was a paradox of which Carter himself was well aware. In a January 1978 diary entry, Carter had written: "In many cases I feel more at home with the conservative Democrats and Republican members of Congress than I do with the others, although the others, the liberals, vote with me much more often."

If Kennedy and Anderson challenged Carter for left-of-center constituencies, Reagan challenged him for conservative constituencies, especially the evangelical Protestant voters who had been a unique source of strength for the Democrats in 1976. We will examine how conservatives prepared the ground for this Reagan triumph in subsequent chapters. But it is worth noting here that Carter's losses among liberals were matched by losses among conservatives. Thus, Carter lost considerable ground in the white South. In 1976, he had won 46 percent of the white Southern vote against Ford. He managed only 35 percent in 1980—and almost all his losses went directly to Reagan, since John Anderson got few Southerners' votes. Although the patterns were mixed, Carter suffered especially heavy losses in some of the white, rural counties that had been Wallace strongholds, another sign that the alienated voters who flocked to Carter in 1976 abandoned him four years later. Even running against a Southerner, Ronald Reagan showed that the Republicans' "Southern strategy" based on conservative ideology could be made to work. In the Old Confederacy, only Carter's native Georgia stuck with him in 1980.

VI

It continues to infuriate liberals that Jimmy Carter's defeat and Ronald Reagan's victory were interpreted as a rebellion against liberalism. How, liberals asked, could a vote against *Jimmy Carter* be interpreted as a vote against liberalism? He was, as Arthur Schlesinger, Jr., has reminded us repeatedly, the most conservative Democratic president since Grover Cleveland.

Certainly Carter and his closest allies resisted the idea that he was a liberal. Carter's supporters argued that only someone as conservative as he, and only a Southerner, could have won the 1976 election—and there is reason to believe they were right. Without the South, Carter would not have won. Thus, the most ardent Carterites have come to hate the liberals for their failure to appreciate Carter's unique contributions to the Democratic cause. The Carter loyalists felt utterly betrayed by liberals and their hatred of Ted Kennedy endures into the 1990s.

But what neither Carter nor his supporters understood was that Carter's political base was a *liberal* coalition, and that their political task was to nurture that coalition. Instead, the Carter administration blew that coalition apart.

Even the most superficial examination of the 1976 results shows that Carter was elected by a version of the classic New Deal coalition: an alliance of white working-class voters, North and South, the culturally liberal middle class, and blacks. Carter needed to keep this coalition intact, but he performed only half of the task that its preservation required.

He succeeded brilliantly in reassuring the party's culturally moderate working-class base on issues relating to "values," and he did so without moving so far to the right as to lose the party's gains in the upper middle class. Carter understood what many liberals did not: that many of the working-class voters who had drifted toward the Republicans were angry but not necessarily racist; and that they felt alienated from traditional political leaders for reasons that transcended ideology.

But the second half of Carter's task was to offer tangible benefits to this wary constituency. This is where the Carterites failed, because they misunderstood the reasons for liberalism's troubles: Carter failed to deliver on the very parts of the liberal agenda that were broadly *popular*: national health insurance, full employment, fairer taxes for the people in the middle and bottom of the income structure. Carter's support for Paul Volcker's harsh anti-inflationary program at the federal reserve was certainly brave, but it was politically disastrous. Carter fought inflation at the cost of rising unemployment suffered primarily by lower-income voters who formed his political base. This allowed Ronald Reagan to steal what had traditionally been the Democrats' best issue: full employment. Working-class voters weighed Carter's policies of retrenchment against Reagan's buoyant optimism and decided that Reagan really did sound more like Franklin Roosevelt than the Democratic nominee.

Carter forgot that when Franklin Roosevelt waged not the moral equivalent of war but the real thing, his economic policies lifted the standard of living of millions at the bottom of the class structure. World War II had required the kind of sacrifices that Carter preached so urgently. But Roosevelt had made sure that the sacrifices fell most heavily on those most able to bear them; even in a time of sacrifice, Roosevelt still delivered tangible benefits to his political base, which returned the favor with its votes.

Carter took a different course. Robert Kuttner, the liberal economic analyst, has noted that as the economic crisis deepened, Carter "took refuge in a rhetoric that disparaged both government and constituent politics." Far from battling *for* liberalism, Carter increasingly laid the groundwork for the conservative revival that took full flower in Reagan's term. Carter did not realize that his own political fortunes were closely linked with those of the liberalism he was disparaging.

In the end, it was a bad case of unrequited politics: Liberals never appreciated what Carter had done for their coalition; Carter never appreciated what the coalition had done for him.

Liberals could blame their defeats on Carter's tactical errors and personal weaknesses. But in fairness to Carter, their difficulties were more fundamental. The failure of those liberal initiatives that Carter did undertake—labor law, tax, and welfare reform—could be traced to forces that operated well beyond the confines of the White House. Liberals effectively admitted their own political weakness by relying increasingly on the courts, not the democratic process, to win many of their most important victories. Moreover, in the 1980 elections, not just Carter but some of liberalism's most able champions went down to defeat. In the Senate alone, liberals lost Church, Bayh, Culver, McGovern, Magnuson, and Nelson.

Liberals suffered in part because they were no longer perceived as speaking for the public interest, but for a series of particular interests—labor, peace activists, blacks, women, gays, teachers, cities, government employees, among others. All these groups had legitimate interests. Their concerns were certainly no less legitimate than Republican interest groups that ranged through big and small business, doctors, real estate developers, and Moral Majority preachers. But the "special interest" tag hurt liberalism far more than conservativism. Liberalism had always based its claim to power on representing the interests of the *community* as a whole against individualism. It could thus not easily survive criticisms that it had come merely to represent a series of egoistic special interests. The New Deal, of course, had also represented an amalgam of interest groups. But in part because Roosevelt faced two severe national crises, the Depression and World War II, his approach was seen as representing the *national* interest. Because the Depression created so many "needy" people, speaking for the needy could be seen as speaking for the nation. By the 1960s, the needy had become a minority—rightly labeled by Michael Harrington as "the other America." As a result, advocates of the poor were easily cast by conservatives as advocates of mere "special interests." As Arthur Schlesinger, Jr., noted, the New Deal worked because it was seen as representing a "concert of interests," not a collection of "sectarian veto groups." When liberals began to look more like the second than the first, they lost their legitimacy as advocates of the national interest. Jimmy Carter was certainly concerned about this. Yet by fleeing from even a positive concept of interest group politics, he failed to represent the most basic building blocks of his own coalition.

Carter was not alone in failing to understand the need to integrate interest-group politics into a broader national vision. The middle-class Democrats elected in the classes of 1974 and 1976 also disdained interest-group politics. They were liberals in the cultural and foreign-policy spheres, yet many in their ranks disparaged the achievements of the old economic liberalism. Like Carter, they were more interested in procedural reform than social reform. Thus, the Carter administration and the procedural reformers did succeed in some of their more ambitious "good government" programs, including changes in the campaign finance laws, a toughening of ethical standards for public officials, more open congressional rules, civil service reform, and government reorganization. Had such programs been linked to social reforms, they might have done much to strengthen liberalism's coalition of middle-class progressives, working-class whites, and blacks. But Democrats in Congress, who by the late 1970s were already becoming increasingly dependent on the campaign contributions of business interests, found it impossible to agree on even the most mildly populist social or tax measures. Prounion labor-law reform, which would have strengthened one of the most important components of the liberal coalition, failed in an overwhelmingly Democratic Congress. When the Democratic Congress got around to taxes in 1978, it cut them on the wealthy by reducing the capital gains tax. Whatever the economic merits of doing this, it was hardly the sort of working-class tax reform that Carter had promised in his campaign.

In foreign affairs, Carter did not have John F. Kennedy's luxury of dealing with an America that had reason to feel itself invincible. Vietnam had been liberalism's war, a Democratic war. Americans were decidedly unwilling to pay prices and bear burdens if the prices and the burdens meant another Vietnam. A significant chunk of the Democratic Party's base constituency had sworn off foreign intervention entirely. If Carter looked "weak" and "vacillating," that was in part because the country and the coalition he led felt uncertain and uneasy. Liberals lost what had once been one of their most powerful assets: a broad and relatively enlightened view of America's interests in the world, and the political support to put it into practice.

Thus did liberalism shatter into pieces. The victims included Jimmy Carter and the liberals who despised him. Cultural issues threatened liberalism in its traditional base among the lower-middle and working classes. Economic issues divided the party's increasingly powerful upper-middle-class component from the rest of the liberal constituency. Political action committees tied nominal liberals more closely than ever to conservative constituencies. Foreign-policy issues created yet another set of divisions.

At times, it seemed that liberals had taken the very worst lessons from the New Left and the neoconservatives and ignored the best. At the beginning of the sixties, the New Left had been right on the need to invigorate political participation, to expand democracy's writ, to give citizens in their local communities real power to affect the conditions of their families, neighborhoods, and schools. What many liberals drew from the New Left instead was its latter-day suspicion of working-class people and their values, its fundamental mistrust of the United States' role in the world, and the emphasis of many in its ranks on the relative importance of culture over economics.

The neoconservatives had been right to urge liberals to be more attentive to how government programs could promote or discourage virtue, and they had been right, too, in arguing that programs should be judged by their results and not by the motives or ideologies of their sponsors. But insofar as liberals concluded from the neoconservative critique that "big government" had failed, always and everywhere, that markets always worked better than government and that the unintended consequences of programs would always overwhelm intended ones, they backed away from the most appealing aspects of their political legacy.

In short: The New Left, which had sought to deepen democracy, increasingly taught liberals antidemocratic lessons. The neoconservatives, who had wanted a more rational approach to social policy, increasingly taught them the futility of social policy.

In the end, it was the inability of liberals to articulate a coherent sense of the national interest that was decisive in creating a politics of false choices. When the poor are seen as a "special interest" while the wealthy are not, something very peculiar has happened to the national political dialogue. When such values as family and work are perceived as the exclusive province of one party to the political debate, the other party has clearly made some fundamental blunders. When the party of racial harmony creates conditions that encourage racial divisions, something is awry in its program. When constituencies who had gotten jobs, gone to college, bought houses, started businesses, secured health care, and retired in dignity because of government decided, of a sudden, that "government was the problem"—when this happened, it was clear a political revolution was in process.

The conservatives had done so much to prepare the way for this revolution, and they were ready to lead.

PART TWO

The Conservative Impasse

6

IDEAS HAVE CONSEQUENCES:

Conservatism's Contradictory Origins

THE WORLD OF 1945 was not a happy place for American conservatives. Though virtually all conservatives shared in the general celebration over the collapse of the Nazi and Japanese empires, they watched with horror as a new Soviet empire arose from their ashes. At home, World War II had exactly the results that conservatives such as Robert A. Taft had predicted and feared: It bequeathed new power upon the state. The power was gathered willy-nilly, in accord with the needs of war, but Americans accepted the government's new role as legitimate, since the American state had been so successful at war. Gone, forever it seemed, was an older America that had disdained global garrisons and centralized power. "War is the health of the state," Randolph Bourne had written in opposition to World War I. Antistatist conservatives feared that World War II had proven Bourne right.

Conservatives complained with some justice that the war, not the New Deal, had ended the Depression. But that was precisely their problem: The war had ended the Depression as part of what the historian Geoffrey Perrett called "the closest thing to a real social revolution the United States has known in this century." While many noted the favorable impact of the war on the economy, few noticed its other consequences. In fact, Perrett argued, the war demolished "barriers to social and economic equality which had stood for decades," ending "the old pyramidal class structure" and creating a "genuine middle-class nation." The war created "enormous new groups of government beneficiaries." During the war, "access to higher education became genuinely democratic for the first time" and "the modern civil rights movement began." The "greatest gains in longevity occurred" during the war and so did "the only basic redistribution of national income in American history."

Conservatives were not necessarily against all of these developments, but they were uncomfortable with the breakdown of old hierarchies and decidedly against the newly powerful state. A young sergeant in the Army who was later to become one of the postwar era's most important conservative intellectuals was one of many who saw a globalist foreign policy as Roosevelt's way of enhancing the government's power. In letters he wrote as a member of the Army's Chemical Warfare Unit, young Russell Kirk complained about military inefficiency, government paternalism, and what he called liberal "globaloney." He especially despised military conscription and wrote an article in 1946 that asserted: "Abstract humanitarianism has come to regard servitude—so long as it be to the state—as a privilege."

The political paradox of the period was that at the very same time that the war was unleashing a social revolution, it was also, on the surface at least, heralding a political resurgence of the right. In the 1942 midterm elections, the Republicans gained 47 seats in the House, for a total of 209. It was the largest number of House seats the Republicans had won since 1930, and the Republicans would exceed that total only twice between 1944 and 1990. Some of the Republican gains could be attributed to a low turnout caused by wartime dislocations. But the New Deal was being rolled back by Roosevelt himself as "Dr. New Deal" made way for "Dr. Win-the-War." Many New Deal programs were scrapped or scaled down. Business got a much larger role in the war effort than many liberals would have liked, and the taxes to pay for the war, though progressive, fell more heavily on taxpayers of modest incomes than liberals wished. The elections of 1942 were the first sign that the new prosperity, the new disorder it induced, and America's new global role could all help revive a Republican Party that had been shattered by the Depression.

Though conservatives did not pay much attention at the time, the war had actually transformed New Dealism into something much less noxious from their point of view. As the historian Alan Brinkley has shown, the war experience led New Dealers to believe that promoting prosperity "need not involve increased state management of capitalist institutions." New Dealers who in the 1930s had questioned whether capitalism was capable of rapid growth came to see that it was, *provided* the state intervened through stimulative fiscal policies and aggressive social welfare programs to expand consumption. The Keynesian revolution thus assigned government a *central* role in keeping capitalism afloat—this is what conservatives objected to—but not an *intrusive* one.

Liberals could accept this new and more conciliatory stance toward capitalism because it still allowed them to get much of what they wanted—acceptance of the government's role in prosperity, a redistribution of income toward the poor, federal aid for education, even a (temporary) form of socialized medicine through the military's vast medical network. While many liberals were distraught at the decline of the New Deal, Stuart Chase asked: "So what?" Chase, the liberal whose book in the early 1930s may have given the New Deal its name, argued that "the facts show a better break for the common man than liberals in 1938 could have expected for a generation." Conservatives noticed this, too, and they worried. Indeed, by accepting so many of capitalism's virtues, the new liberal economics gave conservatives an ever smaller target to shoot at. It was harder and harder to argue that the New Deal liberals were preaching a form of socialism.

Nor was the news from abroad good from the point of view of the right. Not only were Soviet troops occupying large parts of Eastern Europe; not only were communists on the march in China; but even in American-occupied Western Europe, socialists and communists were showing extraordinary new strength. In Italy and France, Communist parties were gaining ground rapidly, winning acclaim for their underground war against the fascists and the Nazis. Americans were shocked by the Labor Party's landslide victory in the 1945 elections in Britain, which resulted in Winston Churchill's ouster. State power appeared triumphant. George H. Nash, the author of the definitive history of the conservative intellectual movement after the war, cites a 1945 article by the historian Mortimer Smith as thoroughly typical of conservative anxieties. "Through the cacophonous chorus of the postwar planners," Smith wrote, "runs one harmonious theme: The individual must surrender more and more of his rights to the state, which will in turn guarantee him what is euphemistically called security."

For conservatives, the academy was no less dangerous a place than the outside world. The ruling ideas within the universities, it seemed, were those of liberals and socialists. Keynesian economics thoroughly dominated free-market ideas. Conservatives quite agreed with the assertion of Arthur Schlesinger, Jr., in *The Vital Center* in 1949 that "progressives, on the whole, create our contemporary climate of opinion." Conservative preaching against statism was being done mainly by the chamber of commerce and the National Association of Manufacturers, as William F. Buckley, Jr., pointed out. These were hardly groups with broad credibility for disinterested analysis. Traditional ideas, especially those associated with religion, seemed to have no place whatsoever in the intellectual worldview. Liberals, as Lionel Trilling asserted in the fifties, did not even sense that a serious conservative intellectual opposition existed. In *The Liberal Tradition in America*, the historian Louis Hartz asserted that liberalism was the *only* real political tradition in American life. Conservatives were liberals, too—a position Robert A. Taft agreed with, since he called himself a "liberal" throughout his political life. The sort of disdainful question American conservatives faced from the academy was posed by Schlesinger: "Why has American conservatism been so rarely marked by stability or political responsibility?" His answer: "In great part because conservative politics here has been peculiarly the property of the plutocracy." In the United States, the conservatives could not even count on the aristocrats, who, since the days of the Federalists, had often "allied themselves with the left against business rule." If American conservatism did not have even the support of the good *aristocrats*, what in the world did it have?

No one was more aware of conservatism's weakness and isolation than the conservatives themselves. The defining view of American conservatism as fundamentally embattled—a view conservatives continued to hold even after they were in power in the 1980s—was Albert Jay Nock's theory of the right as a redemptive "remnant." Nock, one of William F. Buckley, Jr.'s intellectual heroes, described the remnant in 1937, the year after Roosevelt's greatest triumph at the polls, in an essay called "Isaiah's Job."

"They are obscure, unorganized, inarticulate, each rubbing along as best he can," Nock wrote. "They need to be encouraged and braced up, because when everything has gone completely to the dogs, they are the ones who will come back and build up a new society, and meanwhile your preaching will assure them and keep them hanging on." (Could Buckley have taken such words as a definition of his personal mission?) In what might be taken as a prophetic warning to liberals of the things to come, Nock declared: "You do not know and will never know who the remnant are, or where they are, or how many of them there are, or what they are doing or will do. Two things you know, and no more: first, that they exist; second, that they will find you."

Two things in particular were agonizing to the conservatives. First, they were prophets without honor in their own party. To conservatives, the history of Republican politics from 1940 on was a history of betrayal. One of the best-selling books among conservatives during the Goldwater campaign of 1964 was Phyllis Schlafly's A Choice Not an Echo, which might have been called How the Liberals Stole the Republican Party. The book, which established Schlafly as a conservative heroine long before her crusade against feminism, detailed the ways in which the Republican "Establishment," the big Eastern bankers and Wall Street lawyers, repeatedly "stole" the Republican nomination from Robert Taft and bequeathed it to Establishment choices—first Wendell Willkie, then Thomas E. Dewey, and finally, Dwight D. Eisenhower. Intellectual conservatives of the Buckleyite persuasion might disdain Mrs. Schlafly's prose style, but they fundamentally agreed with her analysis. For conservatives, America had become something akin to a one-party state in which liberals managed to so dominate the nominating process that on election day, they had nothing to fear from either party. In an odd way, the conservative view had certain Marxist overtones; conservatives quite agreed with Schlesinger that the "aristocrats" were liberals and kept the remnant out in the cold. For one wing of conservatism, which wanted to see America as an aristocratic republic, the notion of an aristocratic defection to the left was akin to treason. They were to shout "treason" at one such aristocrat, Alger Hiss.

The conservatives' other problem was more fundamental: that there was no clear body of conservative doctrine. Conservatives were, quite literally, "reactionaries." Conservatism was defined almost exclusively as a reaction against Roosevelt and the New Deal. With the exception of Senator Taft, conservative politicians in the Congress were not an intellectually gifted lot. Insofar as the intellectual leadership of the right came mainly from the business class, both its motives and its prescriptions were suspect. "History thus gives little reason to expect organized political intelligence from the dominant forces of the business community," Schlesinger wrote. ". . . Terrified of change, lacking confidence and resolution, subject to spasms of panic and hysteria, the extreme right-wing elements keep the American business community in far too irresponsible a condition to work steadily for the national interest, at home or abroad."

Nor was there any consensus among the intellectuals of the conservative remnant. Some worried that Hartz might be correct, that there was no "usable past" in America on which the right could draw, that the American tradition *was* hostile to conservatism. Such conservatives looked increasingly to Europe for models. Others, such as Richard Weaver, the author of *Ideas Have Consequences*, sought their model in the American South, the one place where there was a real tradition of aristocracy and a deep-seated opposition to liberalism. Still others found both kinds of traditionalism unappealing and embraced the liberal idea as the truest form of conservatism. It was a liberalism defined in the nineteenth-century sense, as opposition to all forms of statism and as support for free-market economics above all else. And some thought the essence of conservatism was the war against communism, a battle to which all other goals were to be subordinated.

Could any order be brought from this philosophical chaos? To many in the late 1940s, it appeared that conservatives were doomed, as Schlesinger thought they were, to crankiness, incoherence, and irrelevance. It took some remarkable philosophical footwork and brilliant intellectual entrepreneurship to reverse this trend. Much of the credit for this labor goes to two men, Frank Meyer and William F. Buckley, Jr. But along the way, many others made contributions.

II

George Nash rightly sees the publication of Friedrich A. von Hayek's *The Road to Serfdom* in 1944 as the first shot in the intellectual battle that was to turn the tide in favor of conservatism. Geoffrey Perrett saw the book as "the intellectual success story of the war." Hayek, an Austrian economist who became a British subject in 1938 and taught at the London School of Economics, argued that to understand National Socialism, one needed to accept that the Nazis did represent a brand of *socialism*. He contended that "the rise of fascism and Nazism was not a reaction against the socialist trends of the preceding period but a necessary outcome of those tendencies." For Hayek, "democratic socialism" was an impossibility, since state planning led inexorably to collectivism and dictatorship. "Economic control is not merely control of a sector of human life, which can be separated from the rest," Hayek wrote, "it is the control of the means for all our ends." When it was published in the United States in the fall of 1944, the book became an instant best-seller and one of the most debated books of the postwar era. (The business classes may not have been quite as foolish as Schlesinger thought they were: *The New Republic* charged that chambers of commerce, advertising interests, and other businesses boosted sales of the book by ordering it in bulk. Business leaders may have been as aware as Schlesinger was of their lack of, and need for, intellectual respectability.)

Hayek's book was important to the still-disorganized right because it allowed it a means of escape from charges by liberals and the left that fascism and Nazism had been "right-wing" movements that had much in common with conservatism. Much of the right had opposed American involvement in the war against Nazism, after all, and some on the left used this fact to allege conservative sympathy for Hitlerism. The fact that some on the right *had* been sympathetic to Hitler and Mussolini was used to shore up the indictment. The view that fascism and Nazism had been brought to power by a frightened business class gained wide currency, well beyond the Marxist circles in which the idea originated. What the conservatives needed, and needed quickly, was a way to disentangle themselves from such charges and to claim a strong philosophical basis for having made the war effort their fight, too. By tying together socialism, communism, and the Nazis into a neat package of "collectivists," Hayek—who had strong credentials as an early anti-Nazi—gave the conservatives a powerful political weapon. As the Cold War went on, the effort to link communism and the Nazis became an intellectual cause for liberal and democratic-socialist intellectuals, too. They prefered Hannah Arendt's formulation that communism and Nazism were forms of "totalitarianism." This cast both ideologies into the outer darkness, while placing not only democratic capitalists and traditional conservatives but also democratic socialists and liberals on the right side of history. But before Arendt there was Hayek, and for conservatives, his doctrine was far more useful.

Hayek was also a godsend for conservatives because they needed a powerful rationale for dismantling the planning structures of the war effort. In a 1956 essay, Hayek said that he believed his book made a much larger stir in the United States than in Britain because planning was still popular among American intellectuals. They still had high hopes, he said, for a "new kind of rationally constructed society."

Hayek was only the best-known academic advocate for the libertarian war on the modern state. Conservatives also gravitated to the thinking of another Austrian economist, Ludwig von Mises. (John Kenneth Galbraith, a searing critic of the Hayek-Mises school, once remaked that the revenge of the Austro-Hungarian Empire for America's intervention in World War I was the export of its free-market economists to our shores.) And battling at the margins of American intellectual life were journalists and thinkers such as Nock, whose best-known book was called *Our Enemy, the State*, Frank Chodorov, John Chamberlain, and Henry Hazlitt. In the fall of 1950, Chamberlain, Hazlitt, and Suzanne La Follette, a former associate of Nock's, founded *The Freeman*, an unabashedly free-market journal that paved the way for William F. Buckley's *National Review*.

The intellectual rebirth of free-market conservatism was no doubt made easier as the Great Depression receded into the past. Indeed, the very social revolution that occurred as a result of World War II made capitalism an increasingly appealing idea, even to liberals. The growth of the middle class, the spread of home ownership and higher education as a result of the GI Bill—these created a new and previously nonexistent constituency for free-market ideas, even if the new middle class owed much to the benevolent state. If capitalism had been made to work only because of war and large-scale government intervention, by the 1950s it really did seem to be working. Liberals lived for a long time off their economic achievements during the war; but eventually, capitalism itself began to share credit with the liberal planners and economists.

If liberals were surprised by the new vibrancy of free-market ideology, it was, at least, the enemy they knew. But the postwar period also saw the revival of an entirely different branch of conservatism. This new conservatism was genuinely conservative in a way free-market thinking was not, since it harkened back to the days before free markets. Among its champions were Richard Weaver and Russell Kirk.

Weaver was a Southern agrarian and a vigorous foe of all forms of materialism. For Weaver, modernity's problem was its abandonment of transcendent and universal values in favor of a position that denied, as Weaver put it in *Ideas Have Consequences*, that "there is a source of truth higher than, and independent of, man." Weaver, it should be noted, was the author of a definition of conservatism that Buckley regards as being "as noble and ingenious an effort as any I have ever read." Weaver declared conservatism to be "the paradigm of essences toward which the phenomenology of the world is in continuing approximation." It is not the sort of phrase that would prompt conservatives to die willingly on distant beaches for the cause, but the idea behind the phrase certainly was. Weaver's assertion was that there existed an objective truth beyond man and that there were, as Frank Meyer put it, "objective standards for human conduct and criteria for the judgement of theories and institutions." That higher truth transcended the transitory assertions of commercial and democratic societies. For many conservatives, that higher truth was to be found through Christianity and Christianity's God.

The thrust of Weaver's thinking was consciously antidemocratic. Democratic politicians, unlike the aristocratic kind, catered to the majority's cruder preferences. Though Weaver insisted on the dignity of the individual human person, which he said could only be guaranteed by a reverence for tradition, he was not an individualist in the sense that most Americans, left or right, generally understand the term. Weaver saw the corruption of modernity dating back to the Middle Ages with the rejection of transcendent values to which all were expected to give allegiance. "For four centuries, every man has not only been his own priest, but also his own professor of ethics," Weaver wrote, "and the consequence is an anarchy which threatens that minimum consensus of value necessary to the political state." Weaver hated the mass media, particularly its violation of the privacy of individuals. Weaver's war was a war for absolutes and against mass society, against egoism, against an instrumental view of life. His was, in the end, a preference for the ancient over the modern. One reviewer slammed Weaver as "a propagandist for the return of the medieval papacy."

Weaver assailed American life in a way that Hayek did not. Hayek, after all, was a rationalist. Hayek's emphasis was not on absolutist "essences," but on *freedom*. Much that Weaver attacked, including jazz, impressionist art, and industrialism itself, was the product of the same undisciplined modern individualism that produced the free-market idea. Weaver disliked commercialism and the mere satisfaction of wants. Man, Weaver said, "perfects himself by discipline, and at the heart of discipline lies self-denial." Weaver defended private property as "the last metaphysical right." But what he had in mind was *personal* property, not the sort of property dear to most practicing capitalists. "For the abstract property of stocks and bonds, the legal ownership of enterprises never seen, actually destroys the connection between man and his substance . . . ," Weaver declared. "Property in this sense becomes a fiction useful for exploitation and makes impossible the sanctification of work." Weaver was, and remains, a revered figure among conservatives. But his writing pointedly suggests the uneasiness of traditionalists with free-market doctrine.

So, too, did the work of Russell Kirk. Kirk's saga, like Hayek's, was an intellectual success story. His book *The Conservative Mind*, published in 1953, drew widely favorable reviews and much popular attention. Kirk argued, against those who saw liberalism as the only valid American tradition, that conservatism had defined the American experiment. In fact, Kirk relied heavily on the philosophy of the non-American Edmund Burke and in the process helped fuel an American Burke revival. But he also traced the conservative influence through such figures as John Randolph, John Adams, John C. Calhoun, and Henry Adams.

Kirk also laid out six "canons" of conservatism that were important signposts for the development of conservative doctrine. These included "belief in a transcendent order, or body of natural law, which rules society as well as conscience" and an "affection for the proliferating variety and mystery of human existence, as opposed to the narrowing uniformity, egalitarianism and utilitarian aims of most radical systems." Kirk vigorously defended hierarchy and the "conviction that civilized society requires orders and classes." He argued that "freedom and property are closely linked" and that "economic leveling . . . is not economic progress." He put his "faith in prescription," arguing that "custom, convention and old prescription are checks both upon man's anarchic impulse and upon the innovators' lust for power." Finally, in the most fundamental declaration of the essence of conservatism, he asserted that change and reform are not identical and that "hasty innovation may be a devouring conflagration, rather than a torch of progress."

Like Weaver, Kirk defended property but emphasized virtues decidedly different from those that the market of a consumer society rewarded. Like Weaver, Kirk openly expressed his misgivings about the market as the sole determiner of value. "Conservatism is something more than mere solicitude for tidy incomes," he wrote in 1954. In a critique of Von Mises, he argued that "once supernatural and traditional sanctions are dissolved, economic self-interest is ridiculously inadequate to hold an economic system together, and even less adequate to preserve order."

The distance of the "New Conservatism" of Kirk from the free-market variety drew the notice of liberals, among them Schlesinger.

In his 1954 work, A *Program for Conservatives*, Kirk quoted Schlesinger's praise for the New Conservatism with some pride. Schlesinger wrote that "the aim of the New Conservatives is to transform conservatism from a negative philosophy of niggling and self-seeking into an affirmative movement of healing and renewal." Schlesinger praised the New Conservatism for being "based on a living sense of human relatedness and on a dedication to public as against class interests." The New Conservatism, he said, had the admirable aim of creating "a serious and permanent philosophy of social and national responsibility."

Insofar as the New Conservatism emphasized values over profits, the community over pure individualism, self-discipline over consumerism, there was much in it that liberals could admire—and free-market conservatives fear. Indeed, one free-market conservative charged that far from being conservatism, the New Conservatism of Kirk could drift to "Fascism" or to "a mild socialism" and favored "not freedom, but an exchange of power, from the present bureaucrats to an 'aristocratic elite.' "

Postwar conservatism was thus conceived in contradiction. Virtue and freedom are not necessarily in conflict, but they are radically different starting points for political philosophy and are destined to create different creeds. Those who value aristocracy are destined to be as disappointed with the leadership thrown up by commercial elites as Schlesinger often was. And as Kirk recognized, nothing is so disruptive of "the proliferating variety and mystery of traditional life" as the dynamism of modern capitalism. The battle between "libertarians" and "traditionalists" was to rage within conservatism with greater or lesser ferocity for the next three decades.

But for all the contradictions between Hayek and Kirk, both represented the new intellectual vigor of a right finally finding its footing after the years of Roosevelt Democracy and Willkie-Dewey Republicanism. And for many conservatives, there was much common ground to be found. Kirk and Weaver could provide correctives to Hayek and Von Mises, even as the libertarians could correct the traditionalists. Among those who saw the potential for such a happy marriage were the founders of *National Review*.

III

Despite the right's intellectual advances between the war and the beginning of Eisenhower administration, the mid-1950s were hardly a promising time. "At no time did the fortunes of the American Right appear as dim as they did in 1954," wrote John B. Judis in his excellent biography of Buckley. "Taft was dead; McCarthy had been discredited; the Democrats had recaptured Congress; Eisenhower, by his hostility to McCarthy and acceptance of the New Deal, had repudiated the Republican Right." For most of the public, the most visible organizations of the right were "anti-Semitic and neo-isolationist throwbacks to the thirties and forties like Gerald L. K. Smith's Nationalist Christian Crusade and the Congress of Freedom." But a Yale graduate not yet thirty who had scandalized his alma mater with his attack on its values in a right-wing best-seller, *God and Man at Yale*, thought the time was exactly right for the foundation of a new conservative magazine.

As Judis recounts the story, William F. Buckley, Jr., had been contemplating a new magazine for some time when he was approached by Willi Schlamm, an émigré who had once belonged to the Austrian Communist Party but quit in response to Stalin. When Hitler seized power in Austria, Schlamm and the left-wing, anti-Stalinist magazine he edited moved to Prague. When Hitler seized Czechoslovakia, Schlamm moved to the United States. He joined Time, Inc. and rose quickly, becoming Henry Luce's chief foreign-policy adviser. Schlamm steadily moved right in response to Stalin, though his interests lay in anticommunism, not in conservative economic theories. Schlamm and Luce made plans for an intellectual magazine called *Measure*, but Luce's interest in the project declined during a recession. Schlamm moved to Vermont to run an inn with his wife, but he had not lost what Whittaker Chambers called "the worst case of magazinitis" he had ever encountered. Schlamm approached Buckley and found the man he was looking for—someone young, filled with a passionate intensity against communism, possessing both family money and a desire as great as Schlamm's to give America a magazine that would answer the liberalism of *The New Republic* and *The Nation*. In a significant move, Schlamm insisted that Buckley assume full ownership and control over the magazine. Schlamm wanted Buckley to own all the stock to save the magazine from the factional wars that had torn up so many other ideological publications, including *The Freeman*, which was then cracking under the pressures of conservatism's contradictions.

Buckley started with $100,000 for the magazine from his devoutly conservative father, but encountered substantial difficulty in raising the rest of the money. Judis contends that two of the main obstacles

Buckley faced were a loss of heart on the part of many conservatives, who felt the project was doomed to fail in a climate of unrelenting hostility to their cause, and the anti-Catholicism of some big conservative donors who could not abide Buckley's religious background. After considerable debate, and some difficulty in assembling a group of editors, they launched *National Review* in November 1955.

Among the noteworthy aspects of the magazine was the presence of so many ex-Communists on its masthead. Except for Frank Chodorov, the magazine excluded the old free-market isolationists. It also excluded the leaders of the anti-Semitic right while embracing leading Jewish conservative writers. This would later bring the magazine attacks from right-wing anti-Semites—which served to enhance its credibility outside extremist circles. And *National Review* welcomed contributions from the new traditionalists, including Weaver and Kirk. The intellectual coalition represented by Buckley's editors and contributors was to lay the basis for the conservative political coalition of the future.

Despite his radical differences with the left, Buckley had much in common with the young New Leftists who would arise in the early 1960s. He rebelled against the conformity of the 1950s no less than they did. "Middle-of-the-road, *qua* Middle of the Road, is politically, intellectually and morally repugnant," Buckley and Schlamm wrote in their prospectus for the magazine. Asked by Max Eastman to exercise discretion in the magazine, Buckley replied: "All I can say to satisfy you is that I want discretion in the sense that I want intelligence, and no crackpottery. But I want some positively unsettling vigor, a sense of abandon, and joy and cocksureness that may, indeed, be interpreted by some as indiscretion."

Buckley's radicalism could be seen in his feelings about Dwight D. Eisenhower. No figure seemed to annoy Buckley quite so much as Eisenhower, a sign of things to come, since moderate-to-liberal Republicans tended to trouble Buckley much more than liberal Democrats, who at least stayed in the party where they belonged. Eisenhower, Buckley wrote in *Up from Liberalism*, is the "symbol of the modulated age." Buckley went on:

> It has been the dominating ambition of Eisenhower's Modern Republicanism to govern in such a fashion as to more or less please more or less everybody. Such governments must shrink from principle: because principles have edges, principles cut; and blood is drawn, and people get hurt. And who would hurt anyone in an age of modulation?

The struggle these days, if that is the word for it, is toward blandness; toward a national euphoria. Leadership consists in giving people everything they want.

The "Eisenhower program," Buckley went on, is "an attitude, which goes by the name of a program, undirected by principle, unchained to any coherent idea as to the nature of man and society, uncommitted to any sustained estimate of the nature or potential of the enemy." *National Review* saw its task as battling against such an unprincipled pursuit of politics.

In later years, Buckley's importance to the conservative cause would be explained by his mastery of the language and of television, of the quip and the elegant put-down. But his greatest contribution may have come long before his was a household name. Buckley and his colleagues on *National Review* sought nothing less than to define a new conservatism, to give the movement an intellectual coherence it had lacked. *National Review* brought together Hayek and Kirk, Von Mises and Weaver, in an alliance sanctified by anticommunism.

The primary architect of this "fusionism," as the new doctrine came to be called, was Frank Meyer. Meyer, educated at Princeton, Oxford, and the London School of Economics, had joined the Communist Party in the 1930s, but like many ex-Communists, he drifted right in the mid-1940s. Meyer was neither a conventional intellectual nor a conventional journalist: He rarely left his home in Woodstock, New York, conducting his business on the telephone and working during the night. He took over the book section of *National Review* and wrote a column, significantly titled "Principles and Heresies." If *National Review* had a Sacred Congregation for the Doctrine of the Faith, Meyer was its prefect.

Meyer's lifework was the development of a coherent doctrine for the right that incorporated the insights of both the libertarians and the traditionalists. Meyer himself was at heart a libertarian, drawn to the right by its emphasis on freedom. One of his most important works, published in 1962, was called *In Defense of Freedom*. Many of Meyer's ideas developed in argument with Russell Kirk over the merits of classical, free-market liberalism, which Meyer endorsed. The "central and primary end of political society," Meyer insisted, was "the freedom of the person." Yet Meyer also believed that the classical liberals with whom he agreed on so much were insufficiently attentive to the importance of *virtue*, to the existence of the "organic moral order" about which Kirk and Weaver were so concerned. The free-market conservatives failed "to distinguish between the *authoritarianism* with which men and institutions suppress the freedom of men, and the *authority* of God and truth."

Meyer was thus acutely aware of the "continuing tension" within conservatism "between an emphasis on tradition and virtue, on the one hand, and an emphasis on reason and freedom, on the other." Meyer saw this not simply as conservatism's problem, but as a problem inherent in all Western culture—"a tension *within* a basic civilizational consensus." The key error of the traditionalists, Meyer believed, was their confusion of the legitimate authority of tradition with the illegitimate power of the state. Virtue is the ultimate goal, but virtue is meaningful only if individuals seek it and arrive at it *voluntarily*. When "it is a mere surface acceptance imposed by external power, it is without meaning or content," Meyer wrote. "Nineteenth century conservatism was all too willing to substitute for the authority of the good the authoritarianism of human rulers, and to support an authoritarian political and social structure." On the other hand, the mistake of the nineteenth-century liberals (i.e., free-market conservatives) was their failure to see that utilitarianism had not provided freedom with a sufficiently firm underpinning. Belief in an "objective moral order," Meyer declared, was "the only firm foundation of individual freedom." And the only legitimate goal of freedom was the pursuit of virtue.

Thus was born the "fusionist" consensus. Fusionism was appealing in large part because it rationalized what so many conservatives— notably Buckley himself—believed already. Free markets could be compatible with virtue, indeed could promote virtue, and virtue was the only proper end of freedom. Donald Devine, a conservative political scientist who served in the Reagan administration, neatly summarized that fusionism meant "utilizing libertarian means in a conservative society for traditionalist ends."

The glue that held the fusionist consensus together was anticommunism, and here was the other revolution in conservative thought that *National Review* led. From the late 1930s until the 1950s, conservatism in America had been associated with a firm and principled isolationism. Since conservatism's posture was essentially antistatist, conservatives such as Robert Taft—and for that matter, the young Russell Kirk—saw a large welfare state and the burgeoning military establishment as equally dangerous. And conservatives had quite clearly seen that nothing had done more to enhance state power than World War II. Moreover, notions such as "collective security" were anathema to those who believed in national sovereignty. Had not the

Founders warned against "entangling alliances"? The battle over isolationism divided the forces that had been so powerful in building Republicanism from 1896 on—Main Street in the Midwest, which favored isolation, and Wall Street, which favored engagement. The isolationists' sense of grievance was heightened by their accurate sense that they were battling not only the usual set of liberals, but also the most powerful economic forces in the country.

Those economic forces had been able to dominate the Republican Party's nominating process, as we have seen, from 1940 through 1952. In one presidential nominating fight after another, Taft went down to defeat. The nominating battles reflected the regional divisions in the Republican Party: Half or more of the Republican National Convention delegates won by Willkie, Dewey, and Eisenhower came from the Northeast; only a fifth to a quarter of their delegates came from the Midwest, even though Midwesterners counted for about a third of the Republican convention delegates.

The rise of a new conservatism seemed to promise hope for the beleaguered isolationist right. But Buckley and his allies ensured the defeat of isolationism. For them, the issue was not the old fight over interventionism or isolationism; it was whether or not the United States would be willing to wage war against the evils of communism. For the *National Review* conservatives, the rise of the Communist empire completely changed the nature of the debate. Some of the sources of *National Review*'s particular commitment to anticommunism were obvious. The magazine's masthead, after all, was heavily laden with members of the two groups most inclined toward ferocious anticommunism: ex-Communists and Roman Catholics, and in some cases, combinations of the two. (Frank Meyer became a Catholic at the end of his life.) Moreover, some of the *National Review* conservatives had never been isolationists at all. William A. Rusher, for example, had campaigned for Dwight Eisenhower over Taft. But *National Review* was by no means isolated on the right in its rejection of isolationism. Broader forces were at work.

Frank Meyer summarized the new conservative position on foreign policy this way:

> In their devotion to Western civilization and their unashamed and unself-conscious American patriotism, conservatives see Communism as an armed and messianic threat to the very existence of Western civilization and the United States. *They believe that our entire foreign and military policy must be based upon recognition of this reality.* As opposed to

the vague internationalism and the wishful thinking about Communist "mellowing" or the value of the United Nations that characterizes Liberal thought and action, *they see the defense of the West and the United States as the overriding imperative of public policy.* [Emphasis added.]

Meyer's statement is significant in several respects. It seems to mark the complete break between the new conservatism and the old isolationism. To declare that the nation's "entire foreign and military policy" should be based on anticommunism gave American foreign policy an ideological basis that the isolationists had always mistrusted. For the isolationists, the only justifiable ends of foreign policy were those that could be defined in terms of the national interest, conceived in the narrow, old-fashioned way. The isolationists, after all, had vigorously rejected liberal claims that the battle against Nazism had transcendent, philosophical purposes. Nor could the conservative isolationists accept "the defense of the West and the United States as the overriding imperative of public policy." For them, the overriding purpose of public policy was to contain or reduce the size of the state. Messianic globalism threatened, instead, to enhance state power.

Meyer's statement is also significant for the way in which it attempted to distinguish between the new conservative internationalism and liberal internationalism. In truth, the foundations for America's postwar anticommunist policy had been laid by *liberals*. Many conservatives opposed Truman's plans for the North Atlantic Treaty Organization and his pursuit of the Marshall Plan. Indeed, the initial reaction of Senate Republicans to North Korea's invasion of South Korea had been hostile to American intervention. Sen. H. Alexander Smith of New Jersey declared that it was "just downright idiotic" for the State Department to be upset by Korea. Taft warned that the country "shouldn't get stampeded into war." Sen. Eugene D. Millikin of Colorado said that the congressional Republicans were unanimous in believing that the invasion should not be a provocation for war.

As the historian William O'Neill reports, "barely twenty-four hours later, they were still unanimous, though in reverse, having found time to read the papers." The shift in the Republican stance on Korea no doubt owed in part to simple patriotism, the natural tendency to rally in support of the flag when the nation finds itself at war. But it was also part of a transformation that was taking place within conservatism—a transformation *National Review* reflected. In condemning "the vague internationalism and the wishful thinking" of the liberals, Meyer was making the point that there was still a distinction between conservative internationalism and the liberal kind. In a po-lemical sense, Meyer was asserting that the conservatives were simply *tougher*. In attacking the United Nations, he was also implying that conservative internationalism was really a form of *nationalism*. Con-servative anticommunists were just as mistrustful of international or-ganizations as the old isolationists had been.

But that was because many of the new anticommunist interven-tionists were really old isolationists. In this sense, *National Review* was preaching in large part to the converted. The key transitional figure was none other than Joseph R. McCarthy. As Fred Siegel, the historian, put it succinctly, "Joe McCarthy was the tribune of re-venge." In McCarthy's hands, anticommunism became a mighty weapon for the isolationists to use against their old adversaries in the liberal foreign-policy establishment—the very people who had sent American boys off to fight World War II. Among those giving Mc-Carthy support, Samuel Lubell noted, were German Americans "with a burning desire to vindicate their opposition to the last war." Lubell noted that among such Americans, "the way the peace turned out was cited as proof that 'Germany and Russia should have been allowed to fight it out among themselves.' " To be *interventionist* against the Soviet Union in the 1950s, in short, was a way of vindicating one's *isolationism* in the early 1940s. Siegel, following the analysis of Peter Viereck in the 1950s, also notes that many of the old isolationists had been part of the "Asia First" lobby, those who felt that America's interest lay in involvement with Asia, not Europe. With "the fall of China" to the Communists, this group, whom Siegel labels "Asiala-tionists," could make the leap from isolation to anticommunist inter-vention and hardly notice the change. Following Siegel's analysis, one might remark on Richard Nixon's eagerness to get America involved in Vietnam in 1954 and argue that Vietnam was not liberalism's war, after all, but *isolationism's*—or perhaps, Asialationism's—war.

National Review, then, accomplished a great deal in the first years of its existence. The simple fact that it existed and survived gave testimony to the fact that there was a newly articulate conservatism in the land. The successes of Hayek and Kirk were not mere fads, but reflected a yearning for an intellectual alternative to New Deal liber-alism. At the very moment when Lionel Trilling was declaring the absence of a serious intellectual conservatism, it was in the process of being born. Meyer and Buckley, moreover, took the competing strands of conservative thought and sought to weave them into a coherent whole. And they did not seek an artificial unity. *National*

Review became a forum in which the various wings of conservatism could acknowledge and argue out their differences. Yet the magazine also became a place where orthodoxy was tested and established. Almost immediately, *National Review* was inhospitable to isolationists who would have America shirk its role in the war against communism. The magazine also came out squarely against the anti-Semitic right, against Ayn Rand's brand of individualism (a selfish and atheistic brand, in the eyes of *National Review*) and over time, against the John Birch Society.

And when Buckley and his colleagues applied their philosophy to civil rights, the most important moral and political issue in postwar domestic life, they endorsed white resistance to racial integration. They also gave currency to James Jackson Kilpatrick's theories of "interposition," which rationalized state resistance to the Supreme Court's *Brown* decision. In *Up from Liberalism*, Buckley declared flatly that "yes, there are circumstances in which the minority can lay claim to preeminent political authority, without bringing down on its head the moral opprobrium of just men." Buckley went on:

> In the South, the white community is entitled to put forward a claim to prevail politically because, for the time being anyway, the leaders of American civilization are white —as one would certainly expect given their preternatural advantages of tradition, training and economic status. . . .
>
> A conservative feels sympathy for the Southern position which the Liberal, applying his ideological abstractions ruthlessly, cannot feel. If the majority wills what is socially atavistic, then to thwart the majority may be the indicated, though concededly undemocratic, course. It is more important for the community, wherever situated geographically, to affirm and live by civilized standards than to labor at the job of swelling the voting lists.

Buckley suggested that the South could strengthen its case if it applied "voting qualification tests impartially, to black and white." It could be accused of being undemocratic, but not racially discriminatory. And being undemocratic, in Buckley's eyes, was by no means the worst sin: "The democracy of universal suffrage is not a bad form of government; it is simply not necessarily nor inevitably a good form of government. Democracy must be justified by its works."

Buckley modified his stand over the years and became somewhat more sympathetic to the cause of civil rights. He also played down— though did not repudiate—his skepticism about democracy. But

Buckley and *National Review* anticipated by several years the Republican Party's turn to a "Southern strategy" and its effort to build a new majority with the votes of angry white Southerners.

What is significant about Buckley's reasoning (beyond his almost gleeful flouting of liberal norms) is how much it bore the imprint of the traditionalists who mistrusted both the masses and democracy and saw preserving "civilization" and its absolutes as the priority of politics. As created by Meyer in theory, fusionism seemed to lean heavily in the direction of the free-market conservatives, the classical liberals. But in practice, many who espoused the fusionist cause as their own fell back constantly on traditionalist thinking.

IV

The fusionist consensus proved durable, providing a philosophical rallying point for conservatives right through to the 1980s. But the fusionists did not convert all their foes, and the early arguments on the right against the *National Review* conservatives are significant because they pointed to problems the fusionist consensus would face later.

The libertarian remnant, led by the economist Murray Rothbard, saw the *National Review* conservatives as brigands who had hijacked the right. Typical of the libertarian attacks on Buckley and *National Review* was an essay by Ronald Hamowy, an associate editor of *New Individualist Review*, a magazine for student libertarians that Buckley himself had warmly endorsed. Hamowy's essay and Buckley's reply were published in the November 1961 issue of the *Review*, and they are worth citing for what they revealed about both the extent of Buckley's triumph and the fury this aroused among the hard-line libertarians.

"Since its inception in 1955," Hamowy wrote, "*National Review* has gradually assumed the leadership of the Right in America until today it stands practically unopposed as the intellectual spokesman of conservatism throughout the country." Buckley himself had become so identified "with everything intelligent on the Right," Hamowy said, that if Barry Goldwater could justly be portrayed as conservatism's "sword," then Buckley was "without doubt, the pen."

But *National Review* and its editors, Hamowy contended, "have succeeded in remoulding the American Right until it travesties the intent of its original founders." The magazine, he charged, "has time and again exerted its considerable intellectual influence *against* individual liberty." Hamowy's brief against the Buckley crowd was heartfelt:

Where once the Right was fervently devoted to the freedoms propounded in the Bill of Rights, it now believes that civil liberties are the work of Russian agents. Where once it stood for the strict separation of Church and State, it now speaks of the obligation of the community to preserve a Christian America through a variety of Blue Laws and other schemes for integrating government and religion. Where once the Right was, above all, dedicated to peace and opposed to foreign entanglements, it now is concerned with preparing for war and giving all-out aid to any dictator, Socialist or otherwise, who proclaims his unbending "anti-Communism."

The Buckleyites, Hamowy charged, had replaced the libertarians' faith in nonintervention with "the heroics of a barroom drunk who proudly boasts that 'he can lick anybody in the room.'" *National Review*, he wrote, had "become a leading minion of the State" and was guilty of "a devotion to imperialism and to a polite form of white supremacy." In his peroration, Hamowy said that *National Review*'s conservatism was "the conservatism of Metternich and the Tsar, of James II and Louis XVI, of the rack, the thumbscrew, the whip and the firing squad."

"Dear me," Buckley wrote in his breezy reply, "thumbscrews, whips, firing squads, war, colonialism, repression, white supremacy, fascism—what a lot of things for *National Review* to have foisted upon the Right in a mere six years!"

Buckley struck back by charging that the libertarians could pursue their goals only because of the conservatives' vigilance against the Soviet Union. "There is room in any society for those whose only concern is for tablet-keeping," Buckley wrote, "but let them realize that it is only because of the conservatives' disposition to sacrifice in order to withstand the enemy that they are able to enjoy their monasticism, and pursue their busy little seminars on whether to demunicipalize the garbage collectors." At length, Buckley declared his firm opposition to statism—"it took government to translate *Mein Kampf* into concentration camps"—while also defending his stand on colonialism. "While it is true that freedom is good," he wrote, "it is not true that freedom can be promulgated in any given country by saying, Ready, Set, Be Free." Buckley declared that "one man, one vote" was not necessarily the surest way to maximize freedom. "We cannot, merely by renouncing colonialism instantly, write a script that will bring eudaemonia to Upper Volta," he said. Buckley concluded by suggesting that there might be something defective about Hamowy's conservatism, given news that Hamowy had joined the National Committee for a Sane Nuclear Policy, an antinuclear group. "I hope he will find there is still a difference between him and the moral and intellectual emasculates among whom he mingles," Buckley said.

A slightly different line of attack on the Buckley–*National Review* right came from Peter Viereck, whose *Conservatism Revisited*, published in 1949, was heralded before Kirk's book as the real foundation of the "New Conservatism." Viereck had much in common with Kirk and Weaver, notably in his attacks on "the century of the common man." Nash credits Viereck with first popularizing the term *conservative*, and Viereck wrote in 1962 that he was attracted to conservatism precisely because of its unpopularity. At times, Viereck seemed to anticipate Frank Meyer's fusionism. "Ahead," he wrote in 1955, "lies an American synthesis of Mill with Burke, of liberal free dissent with conservative roots in historical continuity."

Yet Viereck broke fiercely with the *National Review* conservatives, and they with him. The proximate cause of the break was McCarthyism, which Viereck (along with the future neoconservatives) condemned as a form of antielitism and thus not a form of conservatism at all. Viereck called McCarthyism "the revenge of the noses that for twenty years of fancy parties were pressed against the outside windowpane." Viereck was one of the first to notice how New Deal liberalism, as the defender of the established order, had really become a form of conservatism. Here is where Viereck broke must fundamentally with the *National Review* conservatives, since he welcomed the New Deal and trade unionism as conservatizing forces. He also praised the Supreme Court for its role in "frustrating the will of the masses." The McCarthyite "pseudoconservatives" did not appreciate the Court when it protected the civil liberties of liberals and leftists, but in doing this, Viereck argued, it was performing a profoundly conservative task.

Viereck had some sympathy for Russell Kirk and the Southern agrarians. Still, he scored the agrarians, revered by Weaver, for engaging in "a synthetic substitute for roots, contrived by romantic nostalgia. They are a test-tube conservatism, a lab job of powdered Burke or cake-mix Calhoun." Viereck praised Kirk for his "sensitive, perceptive rediscovery" of a humanistic conservative tradition. But Kirk's conservatism, he said, was nonetheless guilty of being an "unhistorical appeal to history" and a "traditionless worship of tradition."

Both the libertarians and Viereck, then, saw *National Review*'s fusionist conservatism as being more an artificial compromise than a genuinely coherent philosophical system. From different points of view, both the libertarians and Viereck opposed the willingness of the Buckleyites to subordinate concern for civil liberties to the struggle against communism. Many of the libertarians were uncomfortable with *National Review*'s emphasis on tradition and its mistrust of reason. Viereck understood and sympathized with the emphasis on tradition, but saw the Buckleyites as decidedly untraditional in their mistrust of the liberal elites who, in Viereck's view, had become the "true conservatives."

But by the early sixties, Viereck's was an idiosyncratic, though brilliant, voice, and the libertarians were isolated on the right—so much so that by the mid-1960s, Rothbard had begun searching for libertarian recruits on the *left*. The organizations that were flourishing on the right were groups such as Young Americans for Freedom, founded at the Buckley family home in Sharon, Connecticut, and no less committed than Buckley to militant anticommunism. The conservative politician who had replaced Robert Taft as the conservative hero was Sen. Barry Goldwater of Arizona, a militant anticommunist—significantly from the West and not the Middle West. Goldwater's best-selling political testament, *The Conscience of a Conservative*, was ghostwritten by Buckley's brother-in-law and onetime coauthor, Brent Bozell. Buckley, with the same glee that was to animate the New Left, was busy tearing down the walls of the liberal establishment he loathed.

The contradictions of fusionism were to become a problem for the conservative cause, but much later. By the early 1960s, conservatism had a working philosophy and a growing following. Next, it needed to capture a political party.

7

MODERATION IS NO VIRTUE:

The Troubled Life
of
"Modern Republicanism"

WILLIAM F. BUCKLEY, JR., and his allies on the right had good reason for their mistrust of Dwight D. Eisenhower, for Eisenhower deeply mistrusted the Republican right. When Eisenhower looked to Congress, he often found more enemies in his own party's conservative leadership than among the Democrats. On foreign policy issues especially, Eisenhower was more comfortable with the old internationalist establishment, of which he had been a part as FDR's most important general. One of Eisenhower's personal heroes was George C. Marshall, a man the Republican right, especially Joe McCarthy, had made its enemy. Eisenhower himself detested McCarthy and after some delay, maneuvered to curb the senator's power, further enraging the right.

In private, Eisenhower would rage against conservatives. "If the right wing wants a fight, they're going to have it," an angry Eisenhower told his press secretary, James Haggerty, in 1954. " . . . before I end up, either this Republican Party will reflect progressivism, or I won't be with them anymore." If the Old Guard right tried to nominate a candidate of its own for the presidency, Eisenhower went on, "I'll go up and down this country, campaigning against them. I'll fight them right down the line." The nation needed Republicanism, Eisenhower believed, but it needed *modern* Republicanism, not the reactionary stuff that the Old Guard or the New Conservatives were selling. But what was the "Modern Republicanism" that Eisenhower repeatedly endorsed? It proved to be as difficult to define philosophically as was Eisenhower himself.

On the one hand, Eisenhower was a more conservative president than either his rhetoric or his conservative opponents suggested. Eisenhower, according to Gary W. Reichard, a student of Eisenhower's dealings with Congress, was "very conservative in fiscal affairs and devoted to the principle of local responsibility in power and resource development." Eisenhower "acquiesced in certain New Deal programs," but "remained philosophically opposed to much of the spirit of both the New and Fair Deals." Stephen E. Ambrose, Eisenhower's premier biographer, noted that Eisenhower frequently characterized himself as "liberal on human issues, conservative on economic ones." But Ambrose noted that Eisenhower's liberalism "was usually connected with national security." Eisenhower favored improved educational opportunities, for example, "not so much for their own sake as for creating the scientists and technologists who could keep America ahead in the arms race." Ambrose concluded that "when there was no direct Cold War connection on a domestic issue, his liberalism faded." Ambrose noted Eisenhower's insistence that his approach to public problems was to "apply common sense—to reach for an average solution." Ambrose added dryly: "But when basic decisions affecting the economy were involved, his average solutions usually came down on the side of business."

Moreover, for all the complaints that Republicans in Congress had about Eisenhower's program, they still supported their President. Gary Reichard's study of the 1953–54 Congress—which was the only Congress after the Great Depression to operate in a thoroughly Republican environment involving GOP control of the House, the Senate, and the White House—found that Republicans were far more consistent in their support of Eisenhower than Democrats.

Yet Reichard added a significant caveat: "Only in foreign policy (where Eisenhower was admittedly tugging Republicans in a new direction) and welfare policy (where he attempted some 'middle way' measures) did Democrats support the President nearly to the extent that Republicans did." The point, of course, is that for many Republican conservatives, those deviations were the decisive ones. The ardent anticommunists of the *National Review* school cared less about Eisenhower's fiscal caution and much more about his hostility to Senator McCarthy's crusade. Their domestic goals involved rolling back the welfare state, not accommodating it. Eisenhower, on the other hand, was quite willing to expand government in certain areas. Ambrose notes that Eisenhower told his top fiscal aide that in preparing his first budget (for submission in 1954) he wanted to appear "forward-looking and concerned for the welfare of all our people." He thus asked that room be made for slum clearing and public housing, for dams on the Western rivers, and for the extension of social security.

If Eisenhower had a driving philosophy, it was that moderate brand of conservatism best defined as prudence, which was later to become one of George Bush's favorite words. Eisenhower's prudence was precisely what Buckley saw as a "blandness" designed "to more or less please more or less everybody." (By Buckley's definition of Eisenhower's goals, Eisenhower was an immensely successful president; he *did* please almost everybody.) If one looks to Eisenhower's performance as president for an understanding of what he meant by "Modern Republicanism," it was quite consciously a centrist conservatism that sought to split differences, to find what Harold Macmillan, the British Conservative prime minister, had called "The Middle Way."

The clearest effort to lay out a philosophy of Modern Republicanism was made by Arthur Larson, a close adviser to Eisenhower. In two books, *A Republican Looks at His Party*, published in 1956, and *What We Are For*, published in 1959, Larson described a Republican philosophy that was willing to come to terms with what the New Deal had wrought, while opposing its excesses. Larson's view had a fair claim to being called conservative, since it was, precisely, a defense of the status quo. Larson wrote:

> Now we have as much government activity as is necessary, but not enough to stifle the normal motivations of private enterprise. And we have a higher degree of government concern for the needs of people than ever before in our history, while at the same time pursuing a policy of maximum restoration of responsibility to individuals and private groups. This balance, together with a gradual restoration of a better balance between federal and state governments, is allowing all these elements in society to make their maximum contribution to the common good.

Though his language was a bit strained, Larson's formula was certainly a plausible and respectable brand of conservatism. Indeed, it was precisely the sort of accommodation to postwar welfare-state realities that conservative parties in Europe were pursuing with considerable success. Thus, Peregrine Worsthorne, one of British Toryism's most loyal journalistic advocates, preached to conservatives the necessity of "staunchly" defending the welfare state. In a 1958 essay, Worsthorne argued that the welfare state, "by reducing class antagonisms, creates precisely the right climate of opinion for strengthening the middle class." Worsthorne continued: "Those conservatives who would dismantle the Welfare State overlook the fact that a secure working class, far from being a challenge to the middle class, is its indispensable condition. For only if the many are spared economic hardship can the few expect to enjoy economic and social privilege."

Ultimately, of course, even Ronald Reagan and the Republican right were to adopt a version of the Worsthorne formula in proclaiming their allegiance to a "social safety net." In that sense, the Modern Republicans were exactly right in proclaiming that their party had to accept aspects of the New Deal as irreversible. The problem was that in an American context, it was not easy to see how Modern Republicanism differed on any fundamentals with what modern Democrats were saying. As Western European socialists and social democrats moved toward the center, that became an increasing problem in Western Europe, too—which was why Daniel Bell and his allies could plausibly proclaim "the end of ideology." But in Western Europe, at least, the opposition was in theory, if not in practice, socialist, so even a moderate brand of procapitalist politics could be seen as differentiating the right from the left.

The Democrats, on the other hand, could hardly be cast as socialists, and throughout the Eisenhower period, Democrats moved ever closer to the center. To the consternation of liberals, America was entering what one of their number, Karl Meyer, aptly dubbed "the era of the smooth deal," a time when all sides fled ideological conflict. Writing in 1961, Meyer anticipated problems that would trouble American politics for many years and demonstrated that it was not only the Buckleyites who rebelled against the blandness of fifties consensus politics. Meyer praised the "Smooth Dealers" for their style, wit, and sophistication. Then he added bitingly that "the Smooth Dealer is too obsessed by the problems of his 'image' to explore the controversial issues of his time; he is too impressed by opinion polls and lacking in interior conviction; he is too prone to conceive of electoral survival as an end in itself; his nose is so implanted in the middle of the road that his eyes lose sight of the horizon." Meyer concluded unhappily that "the gain in manners among the new liberals has at times been overbalanced by a melancholy loss in gumption."

The rise of Meyer's "Smooth Deal" Democrats made Modern Republicanism an even less distinct philosophy than it might have been a decade earlier, when the Democrats were more clearly a New Deal party and were more audacious in their proposals for direct intervention in the economy. Modern Republicanism was declaring itself courageously opposed to forms of government intervention in American life *that the Democrats were not even considering!*

Indeed, Lyndon Johnson and Sam Rayburn, the Democratic congressional leaders, made heroic efforts in the 1950s to ensure that voters would see *no* real differences between themselves and Eisenhower. As David Broder recounts in his book *The Party's Over*, Eisenhower made "an uncharacteristically partisan comment" at the beginning of the 1954 midterm election campaign, warning that a Democratic victory might lead to "a cold war of partisan politics." Johnson and Rayburn, Broder notes, "deliberately turned the other cheek" and even suggested that Democrats were better friends of the Eisenhower program than Republicans. Casting themselves as wounded men, they sent Eisenhower a telegram condemning his attack as "unwarranted and unjust," since Democrats had "done so much to cooperate with your Administration and to defend your program from attacks by members and leaders of your own party." They promised that there would be "no cold war conducted against you by the Democrats when we gain control of Congress." As Broder added, "And there was not."

Such bipartisanship only fed the feeling of Buckley-style conservatives that Larson's Modern Republicanism was a way of ensuring that the right would not even be represented in national politics. Buckley devoted a portion of *Up from Liberalism* to Larson, crediting him with "verve and spirit." Unable to resist taking a poke at his least-favorite Republican, Buckley also declared that Larson's book "had the singular distinction of being read by President Eisenhower." That was all the credit he would give Larson. The fate of Modern Republicanism, Buckley said, "was to stay a radical impulse for a year or two, in exchange for a considerable erosion in the conservative position." The sin of the Modern Republicans, Buckley declared, "consists in permitting so many accretions, modifications, emendations, emasculations, and qualifications that the original thing quite recedes from view." Arguing against Worsthorne, Buckley declared that simply to prevent the welfare state's expansion, conservatives needed to express a consistent and principled opposition to the welfare state as a whole. "How oppose free false teeth (I almost said compulsory false teeth) or free psychoanalysis (compulsory?) without making a case against social security?" Buckley asked.

Eisenhower remained personally popular throughout his term, but he failed to create a political base for Modern Republicanism. Stephen Ambrose attributes this to Eisenhower's failure to groom appropriate successors and to his reluctance to start divisive fights within his own party. Richard Nixon, who ran a decidedly moderate campaign against John Kennedy in 1960, might have laid a firmer basis for Modern Republicanism had he won, and the closeness of the 1960 contest suggested that Nixon's style of moderate Republicanism had considerable electoral appeal. But Nixon lost the election in part because Modern Republicanism was not so much a philosophy as a balancing act. Nixon sought to placate both the liberal and conservative wings of his party, and the result was that neither trusted him.

Nixon's difficulties spoke to Modern Republicanism's deeper problems. Modern Republicanism, said historian David Reinhard, "was first of all a hazy concept that left Republicans and pundits alike arguing about its true meaning. Modern Republicanism amounted to little more than a *smorgasbord* of liberal and conservative feelings. It lacked a philosophical backbone." In his excellent study *The Decline and Fall of Liberal Republicans*, political scientist Nicol C. Rae argued that the successors to the Modern Republicans in the 1960s allowed the conservatives "to win the intellectual argument by default." With some notable exceptions such as the late Jacob K. Javits, Rae argued, the liberal Republicans did not even try to challenge the conservatives on first principles. Rather, they framed their appeals "in terms of personality or electability, rather than of political principle, frequently acknowledging the validity of most of the right's doctrines, while arguing that they would have to be modified to win votes for the party."

Modern Republicanism was less an idea than an instinct—Eisenhower's instinct of prudence. Prudence is a plausible, even wise approach to politics, but it is not a fighting faith. It was an especially unlikely rallying point since Democrats in the late 1950s and early 1960s were offering their own slightly more populist brand of prudence. For Eisenhower himself, it was just the right approach: Many Democrats who admired Eisenhower personally wanted to find reasons for supporting him, and the soothing noises of Modern Republicanism told them that they would pay little cost for doing so. Indeed, such voters made sure they got the government they wanted by splitting their tickets in unprecedented numbers and electing Democrats to Congress. David Broder has noted that large-scale ticket-splitting began in the 1956 election when many Democrats liked Ike but preferred voting for their own kind for Congress. Modern Republicanism thus failed to produce congressional majorities. Once Eisenhower was gone, Modern Republicanism, having accomplished its historic mission on his behalf, receded. Theodore H. White understood why Eisenhower so frustrated Republican conservatives. What triumphed with Eisenhower, White wrote, "was neither a moral purpose of Taft extraction nor the commercial pragmatism of Harding, Coolidge and Hoover." What Eisenhower provided instead, White wrote, "was an extended pragmatism of the Roosevelt-Truman descent, directed by a man who had been made great under Democratic administrations and whose thinking, with a few budgetary changes, continued their policies." No wonder, White added, that there was such a "violent, almost explosive appeal" to Barry Goldwater's slogan "A choice, not an echo."

II

The early years of the Kennedy administration were good times for conservatives, though they didn't seem so on the surface. On the one hand, the conservatives looked back to the Eisenhower era as a great lost opportunity. Eisenhower created peace and prosperity, but left no discernible conservative landmarks. Except for their negotiated withdrawal from Austria, the Communists occupied all the same places they had in 1952. Indeed, Eisenhower's foreign policy was so cautious that it was John F. Kennedy who managed to make a campaign issue out of a promise to be more aggressive against communism.

But conservatism had much to feel good about. Fusionism had largely united the conservative factions, and Nixon's defeat opened the way for a conservative challenge to take over the Republican Party. Around the country, conservative troops were sufficient to make such a challenge plausible: The "remnant" was growing and its members were finding each other. Conservatives were seen as doing especially well on the college campuses; the right-wing rebels drew notice before the New Left rebels did. As Karl Meyer noted mournfully in 1961, "a flock of little Buckleys now torment social scientists in colleges large and small. By the end of the 1950s, the 'revolt on the right' had achieved somewhat the same position in campus politics as the old leftist movement." And perhaps most important, the conservatives had Barry Goldwater, stumping the country for their creed.

Goldwater and his troops found their field marshal in F. Clifton White, a young businessman whose real love was "back room politics" —a phrase he used without prejudice. The tactical and organizational work that Cliff White did for Goldwater was, as Theodore White called it, "a masterpiece of politics." The skeleton of Cliff White's organization grew out of the National Federation of Young Republicans, in which he had been active since 1950, when he was a Dewey liberal. By the early 1960s, he had converted to conservatism and was ready to turn his skills and his machine over to Goldwater. White organized the first meeting of his cadres—twenty-two friends at the Avenue Motel in Chicago—on October 8, 1961, a full three years before the 1964 election.

Thus, eight years before the New Politics of participation allowed middle-class liberals to triumph in the Democratic Party, White and the Goldwater loyalists saw the potential of a middle-class conservative politics of participation in the Republican Party. Before the moderate and liberal Republicans realized what was happening, White and his friends seized control of Republican organizations—and thus control over the election of national-convention delegates—all over the country. The result was a new kind of activist and a new kind of convention delegate. Much of the commentary on the 1964 Goldwater convention previewed what would be said about McGovern's 1972 convention. Goldwater's delegates, wrote Robert D. Novak, were "not merely the run-of-the-mill party workers under the command and the bidding of regular party leaders. Here was a new breed of delegate, most of whom had never been to a national convention before. . . . They were going there for one purpose: to vote for Barry Goldwater. To woo them away to another candidate would be as difficult as proselytizing a religious zealot."

But if the country was basically satisfied with consensus politics, as all surface indications, including Goldwater's overwhelming defeat, suggested that it was, where did this conservative insurgency come from? In good Vital Center fashion, John F. Kennedy had declared in 1962 that the social changes that had taken place since the war meant that the United States had no further need for "the great sort of 'passionate movements' which have stirred this country so often in the past." Was Kennedy wrong?

Kennedy's approach to his own campaign in 1960 suggested that at some level, he himself did not believe that the days of "passionate movements" were over. At the heart of Kennedy's "get this country moving again" campaign was a sense that something *was* wrong in

America, but that "something" was not easy to define. John Steinbeck observed in 1960 that the country felt "a nervous restlessness, a thirst, a yearning for something unknown—perhaps morality." The social critics of the 1950s certainly sensed this void. Books such as William Whyte, Jr.'s *The Organization Man* and David Riesman's *The Lonely Crowd* scored the successful American's "inner-directedness" and conformity. And when the Soviet Union launched *Sputnik* in 1958, Americans came to feel that whatever was wrong with their nation might be having a real impact on its security. At that moment, wrote political scientist Samuel P. Huntington, "complacency began to deteriorate."

This uneasiness with the state of the nation, as we have seen, created the New Left. It also created the Goldwater right, the flip side of the coin of middle-class protest.

Ideologically, Goldwater represented the purest strains of Frank Meyer's fusionism, and many of the *National Review* intellectuals, including Russell Kirk, Brent Bozell, and Harry Jaffa, a noted historian who was a follower of Leo Strauss, worked on the campaign. Goldwater's acceptance speech, partly written by Jaffa, included a remarkably academic passage on the meaning of freedom, a series of carefully constructed paragraphs that reflected the inner balances of fusionism:

> This Party, with its every action, every word, every breath and every heartbeat, has but a single resolve and that is:
> *Freedom!*
> *Freedom*—made orderly for this nation by our Constitutional government.
> *Freedom*—under a government limited by the laws of nature and nature's God.
> *Freedom*—*balanced* so that order, lacking liberty, will not become the slavery of the prison cell; *balanced* so that liberty, lacking order, will not become the license of the mob and of the jungle.
> [Punctuation and emphasis drawn from the candidate's text, as published by Theodore H. White in *The Making of the President, 1964.*]

Unsurprisingly for a candidate who had once labeled the Eisenhower administration a "dime-store New Deal," Goldwater made absolutely no concessions to the sensibilities of the party's moderates. In one of the most memorable and politically destructive passages of any speech in American history, Goldwater declared: "I would remind you that extremism in the defense of liberty is no vice. And let me remind you that moderation in the pursuit of justice is no virtue."

But if Goldwater put heavy stress on freedom, he also emphasized the other side of fusionism's equation, *virtue*. And this was at the heart of what mass appeal Goldwater had: As Steinbeck sensed in 1960, the country's restlessness stemmed in part from its sense that modernity had undermined the nation's sense of morality. Goldwater's battle was nothing if not a moral crusade, and he made this clear over and over again during his campaign.

Thus Goldwater's acceptance speech: "Tonight, there is violence in our streets, corruption in our highest offices, aimlessness among our youth, anxiety among our elderly, and there's a virtual despair among the many who look beyond material successes toward the inner meaning of their lives." Presidential candidates usually focus precisely on "material successes." What was this talk, especially from a firm advocate of the free market, about "inner meaning"?

Or again from a Goldwater speech during the California primary: "Ask yourself before going to bed tonight: Did I live today with hate? Did I steal, cheat, hate, take shortcuts? If you answered yes, you haven't been a good American." Was this a political speech?

"I deplore those far-out partisans of principles that are trying to tear the American people apart," he went on in that California speech, "trying to tear the home apart, trying to assume that they can do such things better for your children as care for their education and health better than you can."

"There is a stir in the land," Goldwater said in his opening speech of the general election campaign. "There is a mood of uneasiness. We feel adrift in an uncharted and stormy sea. We feel we have lost our way."

"What good is prosperity if you are a slave?" he asked toward the end of the campaign. "We have had rich slaves. What good is justice if you are a slave? You can find justice in some jails."

Goldwater said he got angry "when I think of the pornographic literature that runs around this country today, when I think of some of the novels that I have read thinking that they might be good but find them nothing but the worst kind of filth."

And at the very end of the campaign, speaking in his home state of Arizona, the candidate came back again to the indestructible link between freedom and virtue: "I have been speaking about man, the whole man, about man's rights and man's freedoms. I've been speaking about man's obligations to himself and to his family, to accomplish things himself, and only take help when everything else has failed. . . . These are the things, the simple things that I have talked about, and I will continue to talk about them as long as I live regardless of what God has in mind for me to do."

Long before the presidency of Ronald Reagan—whose political career bloomed because of a television speech he made for Goldwater in the closing days of the campaign—Goldwater sensed a popular desire for recapturing lost certitudes. Long before Jerry Falwell, Goldwater felt the uneasiness of a "moral majority" that worried about pornography and government "interference" with family life. Before there was much talk about "welfare queens," Goldwater saw a nation longing to recapture a frontier sense of self-reliance.

Goldwater used the issues of law and order and morality as much as he could, but not as much or as effectively as Cliff White wanted. White believed that the Democrats had been effective in turning the 1964 campaign into a campaign about fear—fear of Goldwater's "trigger-happiness" with nuclear weapons, fear that social security would be ended, fear that Goldwater was an "extremist." As White saw it, the Republicans needed to counter fear with—fear. His analysis led him to produce a documentary called "Choice," which catered to American fears about domestic violence and change. It featured barebreasted women, reveling "beatniks," and black rioting. The film was formally sponsored by "Mothers for a Moral America," essentially a front for Cliff White. As Theodore White tells the story, Goldwater found the film so inflammatory and racist that he refused to authorize it and suppressed it completely. But the film contained the root ideas of many future Republican campaign commercials.

The episode reflected Goldwater's personal decency. Still, Goldwater's campaign appealed openly for the ballots of racists and segregationists. It was this aspect of his campaign that had lasting political consequences for the Republican Party. Here, one must understand the fundamental realignment of power within the Republican Party that took place in 1964.

Among the many things that Franklin D. Roosevelt subsidized was the creation of a new Republican political base. The mass movement of Americans to the South and the West began in World War II, following the patterns of military spending set in Washington. The defense buildup in the South sent many Northerners into the Old Confederacy and sent many rural Southerners into the region's metropolitan areas. Many of the Northern migrants were Democrats, to be sure, but they were not the die-hard sort who were still voting against Reconstruction. The Northern migrants were prepared to vote for the Republicans and so over time, were the rural Southerners, who gave up some of the old ways, including glandular loyalty to the Democrats, once they moved into cities or suburbs.

Defense money also flowed to California, creating a new kind of prosperity that continued long after the war was over. In true Keynesian fashion, it was a prosperity dependent on government. But it was the one part of government that the conservative new nationalists approved of: The money was spent in the war on communism. In California, spending on military and aerospace was concentrated in Los Angeles, San Diego, Orange, and Santa Clara counties. These counties accounted for 83 percent of the new manufacturing jobs in California from 1950 and 1962, and 62 percent of the net influx of new residents. "This military-aerospace complex dovetailed nicely with the political style of the new Republican right," wrote Michael Miles in his history of American conservatism. "Republican foreign policy was traditionally Pacific-oriented, while its strategic doctrine was slanted toward air power. The new nationalism was overriding old-guard inhibitions about military might."

In the California primary, Goldwater lost almost all the state's counties to Nelson Rockefeller and was defeated especially badly in the northern part of the state in and around San Francisco. Thus, out of 2.17 million votes cast, Goldwater defeated Rockefeller by just 68,350 votes statewide. But in two counties alone, Los Angeles and Orange counties, Goldwater's margin of 207,000 votes was more than enough to offset the results in the rest of the state.

The California primary was a parable about the transfer of power in the Republican Party from North to South, and also from East to West, from Frostbelt to Sunbelt, from older industries, Wall Street, and small-town bankers to newer industries and the newly rich car salesmen and real estate tycoons of Easy Street. These shifts were reflected not only in the California primary, but in the party as a whole, as measured by votes at the Republican National Convention. At the 1940 convention, when the Eastern establishment triumphed with Wendell Willkie, the South and the West together cast only 34.9 percent of the convention's votes; in 1964, when the establishment was upended, the two Sunbelt regions cast 43.4 percent of the votes. It was a formidable base for Goldwater.

The demographic shifts not only transformed the balance of power between regions; they also altered the balances within them, nowhere more so than in the South. Through 1952, the Southern Republican Party was basically a "post office" party—a tiny organization that existed mainly to win patronage benefits (such as postmasterships) for its members. The legitimacy of these Southern Republican parties had always been in question, and at the 1952 Republican Convention, Eisenhower successfully challenged Taft delegations from the "post office" parties of Texas, Louisiana, Florida, and Georgia. By the late 1950s, real Republican organizations were replacing the post office parties across the South. In 1956, Eisenhower carried five of the eleven states of the Old Confederacy (Texas, Louisiana, Tennessee, Florida, and Virginia). Even in states he lost, Eisenhower won an unprecedented share of the vote for the Republicans and carried metropolitan counties such as Jefferson (Birmingham) and Mobile in Alabama. In 1952, Eisenhower nearly carried South Carolina, where as recently as 1944, Roosevelt had won 88 percent of the vote. In 1956, Stevenson carried South Carolina with only a minority share; the combined vote for Eisenhower and Sen. Harry F. Byrd, the conservative Democrat from Virginia who was put on the ballot as an independent, amounted to 54 percent.

In 1960, conservatives and liberals in the Republican Party feuded over whether Nixon should put his energy into winning the big states of the North and Middle West, the liberal position, or battle instead for white Southerners, as conservatives urged. Nixon settled the issue by campaigning everywhere and endorsing civil rights, though not as boldly as the liberals wished. Nixon held Florida, Virginia, and Tennessee for the Republicans (and on an honest vote count may actually have won Texas). But the rest of the South was lost, either to Kennedy or in the case of all of Mississippi's electors and five of eleven in Alabama, to unpledged slates representing segregationist Democrats. Some of Kennedy's Southern victories, however, were extraordinarily thin, and he was no doubt hurt in the region by his Roman Catholicism. In South Carolina, Kennedy got just 51 percent; in North Carolina, just 52 percent.

For Southern Republicans, the prospect of a staunch conservative such as Goldwater at the top of the Republican ticket in 1964 offered the opportunity of a lifetime. Goldwater had always personally been against segregation and had once belonged to the Urban League. But his views on civil rights reflected his strict view of property rights. Goldwater argued that the federal government could not tell individuals whom to hire or whom they must allow into their restaurants and hotels. The issue, he said, was one for the states, which was just as the Southern segregationists wished.

The opportunity Goldwater offered Southern Republicanism was understood clearly by two young Southern Republican politicians, John Grenier of Alabama and Peter O'Donnell of Texas, who were early members of Cliff White's inner circle. They sewed up the South for Goldwater early and fully: He won a majority of the delegates in every Southern and border state.

In the election campaign, Goldwater struggled to differentiate what he saw as his principled opposition to civil rights *legislation* from racism, of which he was not personally guilty. One of Goldwater's best efforts was a speech at a fund-raising dinner in Chicago in October 1964. Although the speech did nothing to turn the tide of the campaign, it contained all the elements of future conservative and neo-conservative critiques of affirmative action and busing. It also played heavily on the "family, work, neighborhood" themes that Ronald Reagan used so effectively. Thus, although some would speak of the Reagan campaign's representing a break with certain aspects Goldwaterism, the fact remains that Goldwater, the conservative prophet, actually did say it all first. It is thus worth quoting him at some length:

> Throughout this land of ours, we find people forming churches, clubs, and neighborhoods with other families of similar beliefs, similar tastes, and similar ethnic backgrounds. No one would think of insisting that neighborhoods be "integrated" with fixed proportions of Anglo-Americans, German Americans, Swedish Americans—or of Catholics, Protestants, and Jews. . . .
>
> Our aim, as I understand it, is neither to establish a segregated society nor to establish an integrated society as such. It is to preserve a *free* society. . . . Freedom of association is a double freedom or it is nothing at all. It applied to both parties who want to associate with each other. . . . Barriers infringe the freedom of everybody in society, not just the minorities.
>
> Now the removal of such barriers enhances freedom. . . . But it is equally clear that freedom is diminished when barriers are raised against the freedom *not* to associate. We must never forget that the freedom to associate means the same thing as the freedom not to associate. It is wrong to erect barriers on either side of this freedom.
>
> *One thing that will surely poison and embitter our rela-*

tions with each other is the idea that some predetermined
bureaucratic schedule of equality—and worst of all, a sched-
ule based on the concept of race—must be imposed. . . . That
way lies destruction. [Emphasis on the last paragraph added.]

And what of the Republican moderates and liberals, the Modern
Republicans? Of all of them, the one to act with true courage was
Nelson Rockefeller, who campaigned to the end to defeat Goldwater,
long after his own chances of winning the nomination were gone. And
if there was one issue that galvanized the Moderns, it was civil rights;
their stand against Goldwater on that issue was clearly one of principle, and it gave Modern Republicanism a philosophical toehold it had
lacked before.

But the Modern Republicans did not realize until much too late
the miracles that Cliff White had worked. The Moderns did not rally
to Rockefeller in California, where a firm stand against Goldwater
might have prevented his victory and thus his nomination. Eisenhower especially was guilty of equivocation, seeming at times to
encourage the anti-Goldwater forces (and the candidacy of
Pennsylvania's moderate governor, William Scranton), and then backing away from a fight (and leaving Scranton stranded and embarrassed). Nor did the party's governors, a force for the moderation of
practicality and electability, rally effectively. In the fall campaign,
many of the Moderns withheld their support from Goldwater, which
may have hurt him but also hurt their own credibility within the party.
Conservatives, who had been loyal supporters of Modern Republican
nominees, felt betrayed. Among those who stayed loyal to Goldwater
and his party was Richard Nixon, and the conservatives would remember that, too.

Two things were notable about the results beyond Goldwater's
overwhelming loss. First were his breakthroughs in the South. Goldwater carried Alabama, Georgia, Louisiana, Mississippi, and South
Carolina. With the exception of Louisiana, none of these states had
voted Republican since Reconstruction. Alabama, which had not
elected a Republican member of the House since Reconstruction,
sent a delegation of five Republicans and only three Democrats to the
Eighty-ninth Congress.

There was, however, an unusual character to Goldwater's Southern vote. Goldwater's gains came overwhelmingly in rural, segregationist counties that had never before voted Republican. In many of
the South's metropolitan areas, as the Ripon Society, a liberal Repub-

lican group, pointed out, Goldwater actually lost ground on Eisenhower and Nixon. In Florida, for example, which Nixon carried in 1960 and Goldwater lost in 1964, the Republican vote in small, rural Calhoun County jumped from 28 percent for Nixon to 65 percent for Goldwater. But in populous Pinellas County, Nixon had won 64 percent; Goldwater got just 45 percent. In Georgia, which Nixon lost and Goldwater won, Nixon got just 30 percent in rural Sumter County (Jimmy Carter's home county); Goldwater got 69 percent. In urban Fulton County, which includes Atlanta, the Republican share dropped from 49 percent for Nixon to 44 percent for Goldwater. "The Goldwater strategy succeeded in trading off the progressive, industrialized, urban areas of the New South," the Ripon Society concluded, "for the segregationist rural regions of the Deep South." Over the longer run, however, much of the urban vote would come back to the Republicans. Goldwater's legacy was to give the Republicans a chance to win places they had always lost in the past.

In the Northeast and Middle West, some Republicans, such as Ohio's normally shrewd Governor Jim Rhodes, had thought that "white backlash" would allow Goldwater to cut into the white ethnic vote. Rhodes's argument would have its day, but not in 1964. Although Goldwater posted some gains over Nixon among white ethnics, they were scattered (and perhaps inevitable for *any* Republican who was not facing a Roman Catholic Democrat such as Kennedy).

Goldwater's landslide defeat was taken as a victory by the Modern Republicans, who saw their own approach to politics vindicated. Robert J. Donovan, the Washington bureau chief of the *Los Angeles Times* and a close student of Republican politics, reported in late 1964 that "party professionals" felt that "the right wing had its chance with its most attractive candidate and that in light of the disastrous results the party must move back to its old ground." Donovan added: "The folly of the Goldwater nomination has sunk in. Republicans must campaign as a modern party, and many of those who may not have realized this before realize it now."

Donovan's prediction proved only partly true. The real lesson of the Goldwater campaign was drawn by the historian Richard Hofstadter, who could not be accused of having any sympathy for Goldwater or his allies. "The right-wing enthusiasts were justified, I believe, in the elation they expressed, even in defeat, over the Goldwater campaign," he wrote. "They had less than nothing to show in practical results, but it is not practical results that they look for. They have demonstrated that the right wing is a formidable force in our politics and have given us reason to think that it is a permanent force."

III

The immediate aftermath of the Goldwater campaign gave the Modern Republicans some cause for hope.

In 1965, Rep. John V. Lindsay, a liberal Republican and one of Congress's staunchest defenders of civil liberties, was elected mayor of New York City. But even that campaign was not without a hopeful sign for the right: Running with wit and ardor against Lindsay's liberalism, William F. Buckley, Jr., won national attention for himself and his cause when he ran on the Conservative Party ticket and got 13 percent of the mayoral vote.

In 1966, the Republicans won sweeping victories around the nation, picking up forty-seven new House seats, three Senate seats, and eight governorships. Among the big victors on election day were Republican moderates such as Governors George Romney in Michigan, John H. Chafee in Rhode Island, Raymond P. Shafer in Pennsylvania, John A. Volpe in Massachusetts, Spiro T. Agnew, who ran as the civil-rights candidate against a Democratic segregationist in Maryland, Winthrop Rockefeller in Arkansas, and Nelson Rockefeller in New York. Among the Senate victors were Charles Percy in Illinois, Edward W. Brooke, the first black senator since Reconstruction, in Massachusetts, Clifford Case in New Jersey, and Mark O. Hatfield in Oregon. Many of these moderates, unlike their predecessors, showed a real capacity to help their fellow Republicans lower down on the ticket. In Michigan, Romney was credited with helping to sweep in five new U.S. House members. In Massachusetts, Volpe and Brooke led a Republican ticket that also elected a lieutenant governor and an attorney general—the strongest Republican showing in that Democratic state since 1954.

But for all the good news for the moderates, the 1966 sweep was more a party victory as any indication of where the Republicans were going ideologically. Even as moderates could tout their triumphs, conservatives could justifiably interpret the results as a wholesale repudiation of Johnson, his Great Society and civil rights policies as well as his Vietnam policies. And conservatives did well at the polls, too. Among the new members of the House were ardent Goldwaterites, some of whom regained seats they lost in the 1964 landslide: Donald G. Brotzman in Colorado, M. Gene Snyder in Kentucky, Donald

"Buzz" Lukens, a former president of Young Americans for Freedom, in Ohio, and George A. Goodling in Pennsylvania.

Also carried into the House by the Republican sweep was the young George Bush in Houston. And the two most important victors on election day in 1966 were Ronald Reagan, swept in as governor of California, and Richard Nixon, who revived his political career by campaigning as hard as if he himself had been on the ballot. Nixon stumped for 105 Republican candidates in 35 states.

The nonideological nature of the 1966 Republican victory was a triumph most of all for Nixon, that most nonideological of Republicans, who campaigned for every kind of Republican candidate. The 1966 results unsettled the philosophical balance inside the party without resolving it, which also served Nixon's interests. By carrying the Republican Party in 1964, the Goldwater conservatives had already frightened the moderates and liberals into a new respect for Nixon's essentially centrist posture. But by rebuilding themselves in 1966, the moderates scared the conservatives enough to make them appreciate Nixon's ability to save them from someone far more liberal than he. Nixon was to play each wing of the party with brilliance, demonstrating a skill at factional politics that only one Republican in this century has come close to matching. In 1988, George Bush, who shared Nixon's feel for the Republican Party in all its variety, also showed an exceptional ability to win support from all the party's factions.

The mid-1960s saw the last major effort by Modern Republicans to establish a respectable intellectual foundation that might serve them in their battle with the Republican right. Probably the best liberal-Republican book of the period was Jacob K. Javits's *Order of Battle: A Republican's Call to Reason.* Javits's work was an attempt to rescue an older Republican tradition of nationalism—that is, a preference for national interests over state or regional interests. In a lively historical section, Javits announced his own "choice of ancestors." They included Alexander Hamilton, the father of a strong national government and the first advocate of national economic planning; Henry Clay, the Whig supporter of "the American System," involving large-scale federal spending for dams, roads, bridges, and canals; and of course, Abraham Lincoln and Theodore Roosevelt. The thrust of Javits's claim was that the lineage of the Republican Party gave it a stronger basis for being the party of federal action than the Democrats, latecomers to that cause in the New Deal.

Javits's was a worthy effort, but it went against the trends in Republicanism going back to at least 1920. Indeed, Javits's reliance on the political traditions of the Federalists and the Whigs suggested how far he had to reach to justify his brand of Republicanism. Javits's policy prescriptions were not far from those of Arthur Larson, or from those of most Democrats. His major innovation was to call on Republicans to be proud of being "the party of business" and to advocate a "people's capitalism" to encourage profit sharing and employee stock ownership, rather advanced ideas in 1966. In the end, *Order of Battle* is best seen as Javits's eloquent explanation for why he remained in the Republican Party even though he voted with the Democrats most of the time.

More systematic efforts to justify a moderate-to-liberal course for the party came from the Ripon Society, a group of young Republican intellectuals and professionals based in Cambridge, Massachusetts. The location of Ripon's headquarters and the Harvard connections of most of its leaders were enough to make the Society suspect on the right. Founded in 1962, Ripon, named after the city in Wisconsin where the Republican Party was founded, modeled itself after the Bow Group, the organization of liberal Tories in Britain that served as a center of much creative Conservative thinking. Ripon was consciously *not* a mass organization, something the moderates badly needed at the time; it was to be a center of ideas and research.

Ripon members turned out to be an unusually creative bunch, and many of their proposals ended up being accepted not only by party liberals, but also by conservatives. They were among the first in the 1960s to make the case against the military draft (which was, of course, Robert Taft's old position) and to show how an all-volunteer army could work. They were among the earliest supporters of federal revenue sharing and sought other ways to turn the Republicans' preference for state and local government into practical programs. They endorsed the negative income tax as a better way of helping the poor than the existing welfare system. The negative income tax, which provided strong work incentives by paying not just those on welfare but also the working poor, was designed to distribute money as efficiently as the Internal Revenue Service collected it. The negative income tax was originally the work of Milton Friedman, the thoroughly conservative economist, and it lives on today in the earned-income tax credit, the most effective program assisting the working poor. On other issues, Ripon was uncompromising in its support of civil rights, proposed normalizing relations with Communist China, and opposed the Vietnam War.

Ripon was one of the first political organizations to understand the political importance of young professionals. "From the outset," Ripon said in its first public statement, "Ripon members have seen as their most important contribution to American politics a bridging of the gulf that has separated much of the GOP from the intellectual and professional community for the past fifty years." Ripon said it was aiming for support "from the new middle classes of the suburbs of the North and West—who have left the Democratic cities but have not yet found a home in the Republican Party, the young college graduates and professional men and women of our great university centers. . . . These and others like them hold the key to the future of our politics." If it chose to, Ripon could lay legitimate claim to having discovered the yuppies before anyone knew they existed.

In the narrowest of political senses, Ripon failed. Some of its heroes, notably John Lindsay and Rep. Ogden Reid, the former publisher of liberal Republicanism's most important organ, the *New York Herald Tribune*, abandoned the Republican Party to become Democrats. Ripon-style Republicanism was also badly hurt by the growing strength of the young professionals inside the Democratic Party. The "amateur Democrats" who followed Adlai Stevenson were precisely the kind of people Ripon was hoping to bring into the Republican Party. Ripon's difficulties were augmented by Eugene McCarthy's 1968 presidential campaign, which not only gave the Stevenson amateurs a new rallying point but also created a whole new generation of young-professional Democrats. McCarthy's low-key cerebral style, his opposition to a strong presidency, and his ironic approach to government had an unusual appeal to liberal Republicans. Nicol Rae reports that McCarthy won 25 percent of the vote of Republicans in the Wisconsin primary, which allowed voters in one party to vote in the other's primary. A poll in August of 1968 showed 18 percent of Republicans favoring McCarthy over Richard Nixon. Ripon might have won many young professionals to the Republican Party had a plausible antiwar candidate emerged. But George Romney's candidacy collapsed before it got going, and antiwar Republicans such as Mark Hatfield resisted pleas that they challenge Nixon. As a result, the antiwar movement, in 1968 and beyond, carried out its work almost entirely inside the confines of the Democratic Party.

Over the longer run, though, Ripon played a much more important role than a narrow electoral analysis would suggest. Richard Nixon and his successors translated many of Ripon's ideas into policies (revenue sharing, the opening to China) or used them as the basis for

serious policy proposals (Nixon's Family Assistance Plan). In seeing a
need for a Republican opening to the intellectual world, Ripon acted
as an advance guard for the neoconservatives, whose perspectives
(notably those of Daniel Patrick Moynihan) they often shared. Ripon
also contributed some important individuals to Republican politics
who later emerged, surprisingly, as leading thinkers behind the Reagan Revolution. The most notable of these was George Gilder, one of
Ripon's founders who had worked for two of the most liberal Republicans in the Senate, Javits and Charles Mathias of Maryland. Gilder's
1981 book, *Wealth and Poverty*, was a powerful manifesto for Reaganism. In his poetic, even prayerful, defense of capitalism, Gilder clearly
took seriously his old boss Jack Javits's argument that Republicans
should be proud of their role as "the party of business." Ripon's philosophy also included a heavy dose of libertarianism—reflected in its
position on the draft—and the Society served at times as a conduit for
libertarian ideas.

But these developments occurred over time. The immediate and
predominant force in the Republican Party was Nixon, who managed
to make Republican lions and lambs, Riponites and the right, lie down
together. Nixon understood where his virtues lay, and he accepted
that it was not love that motivated many who came to his side. "I can
get different factions to sit down together," he said. "I know the liberal
fringe and the conservative fringe have no use for me, but they tolerate me, where they don't tolerate others."

After 1964, Nixon understood which of these two fringes was
more influential in the Republican nominating process. His priority
was the right. Stephen Ambrose notes that in his 1966 campaign
swing, Nixon visited all eleven former Confederate states. In stumping
the South, Nixon was careful to reiterate his support for the Civil
Rights Act of 1964 and the Voting Rights Act of 1965. He said he was
"firmly opposed to any segregationist plank in a Republican platform"
and pledged to "fight" any efforts to insert such a plank in a national
party platform. The pledge was safe enough, since even the most
racially conservative Southerners did not expect either national party
to back segregation. At the same time, Nixon would reiterate his support for states' rights and declare his opposition to having Washington
"dictate" to the South.

The Southern conservatives accepted all this, Ambrose argued,
because they understood that after Goldwater's defeat, a national candidate needed to sound more moderate than Goldwater. For once,
Nixon's reputation for "trickiness" worked in his favor. Ambrose

quotes an Atlanta Republican explaining his reaction to a George Romney speech endorsing civil rights: "This fellow really means it," the Republican said, referring to Romney. "Dick Nixon comes down South and talks hard on civil rights, but you know he *has* to say what he does, for the Northern press."

Nixon's courting of the right succeeded admirably. He won an early endorsement from Goldwater and also from such leading conservatives as Sen. Strom Thurmond of South Carolina and Rep. John Ashbrook of Ohio. Especially revealing of Nixon's understanding of where power lay on the right was his active and successful courting of Buckley. It was clear to Nixon that the *National Review* conservatives were an important constituency because of their influence in testifying to someone's bona fides with the rest of the movement. *National Review* was once again in its characteristic role as the adjudicator of orthodoxy. And no one was more important in this than Buckley himself, who by the late 1960s—because of his New York City mayoral campaign, his column, and his television show—was the right's premier celebrity.

Buckley had not supported Nixon in 1960, and according to John Judis, Nixon seemed to resent this. In October 1965, while Buckley was in the midst of his mayoral campaign against John Lindsay, columnists Rowland Evans and Robert Novak asked Nixon about the John Birch Society. Nixon replied that "the Birchers could be handled but that the real menace to the Republican Party came from the Buckleyites." In December 1965, when Nixon interviewed Pat Buchanan to offer him a job as speechwriter, Nixon asked: "You're not as conservative as William F. Buckley, are you?" Buchanan may have been *more* conservative than Buckley, but he was hired anyway, partly to create an opening to the right. "Nixon realized that just as in 1960, he had to make his peace with the Rockefeller wing of the party," Buchanan recalled. "In 1968, to be nominated, he had to make his peace with the Goldwater wing of the party." One of Buchanan's early tasks was to appease Buckley for Nixon's comments to Evans and Novak. In January 1967, Nixon invited Buckley, William Rusher, and other conservatives to his home to discuss politics and world affairs. Nixon gave what Victor Lasky, the conservative columnist, called "one of the most brilliant *tour de forces* that I can recall." Although many conservatives, including Rusher, were pushing *National Review* to support Reagan, Buckley thought Reagan was unprepared for the presidency and was completely taken with Nixon. "I knew when we went down the elevator, early in the evening, that Bill Buckley was going to find some reason to support Richard Nixon," Neal Freeman, Buckley's friend and television producer, recalled. "Nixon not only courted Buckley assiduously, directly and through surrogates over a number of years, but I think Buckley held Nixon to lower standards ideologically and intellectually because Nixon had never been in Buckley's mind a member of the conservative movement." Buckley himself later explained his support for Nixon in the language of a pragmatic ideologue. "I'd be for the most right, viable candidate who could win," Buckley told the *Miami News* in 1967.

Buckley's stand infuriated Rusher, who wrote later that conservatives who backed Nixon owed history an accounting for this "uncharacteristic but unavoidable streak of opportunistic calculation." But Stephen Ambrose defends Buckley and the other pro-Nixon conservatives from charges of opportunism. According to Ambrose, conservatives "flocked to Nixon because they liked what he said on Vietnam—no compromise, war to the finish, total victory." It was a lesson about contemporary American conservatism that was to be taught again and again. In the end, many conservatives of the *National Review* stripe were willing to compromise on domestic issues— those issues that Buckley had dismissed somewhat contemptuously as involving "whether to demunicipalize the garbage collectors." But when the issue was anticommunism, there could be no compromise.

Nixon's strategy worked with precision, though it was a close thing. The moderate and liberal Republicans showed no more competence in 1968 than they had in 1964. George Romney, Nixon's strongest potential primary opponent, dropped out after he was hounded by the press for making the perfectly plausible statement that military and administration officials had "brainwashed" him when he had visited Vietnam. Once again, it was Nelson Rockefeller into the breach. But Rockefeller announced his candidacy too late to compete in the primaries, and Nixon got a virtually free ride. Rockefeller's central contention, captured in a campaign button that read "Only Rocky Can Win," broke down when some preconvention polls showed him doing no better than Nixon against the Democrats. Ronald Reagan announced his candidacy at the last minute, but Thurmond and Sen. John Tower of Texas worked hard to keep Southern conservatives in line for Nixon. In the end, Nixon's Southern strategy was the key to his nomination: Nixon won 74 percent of the Southern delegates to only 18 percent for Reagan.

The South was by far Nixon's strongest region, and he needed every one of its votes. On the first ballot Nixon won 692 votes to 277 for Rockefeller, 182 for Reagan, and 162 for various moderate favorite sons—a total anti-Nixon vote of 621. Rockefeller told Nixon after the balloting that Reagan had not kept up his end of the operation, failing to crack Nixon's strength in the South. But that meant that Nixon owed his nomination to the party's conservatives, who proved again that they were the decisive constituency in Republican nominating politics. William A. Rusher was exaggerating only a bit when he wrote later: "In effect, the 1968 Convention remained under conservative control, but the control was exercised gently." Nixon's choice of Spiro Agnew as his running mate was aimed at satisfying the South. Though elected with black support, Agnew had become increasingly conservative on the issues of race and law and order. Nixon felt he could win without the Republican liberals.

He did, barely. On the one hand, the country overwhelmingly rejected the Democrats and liberalism—Hubert Humphrey won just 42.7 percent of the vote. But Nixon split the conservative and antiadministration vote. Nixon got 43.4 percent, Wallace 13.5 percent. Nixon's pattern of support in 1968 was fairly similar to his 1960 pattern, but this time, enough of the close states fell his way. Nixon won every state he had carried against Kennedy except for Maine, which was represented on the Democratic ticket by Humphrey's running mate, Sen. Edmund S. Muskie, and Washington State. In the South, Nixon picked up North and South Carolina, again failing by the narrowest of margins in Texas. Illinois, which Republicans always suspected was stolen from Nixon in 1960 by Mayor Daley, was actually counted in the Nixon column this time. To his 1960 total, Nixon also added New Jersey, Missouri, New Mexico, and Nevada. Nixon had run another cautious campaign, balancing carefully between moderation and conservatism. With Nixon's victory, the Republicans had another chance to try to establish just what sort of party they were.

IV

All discussions of Richard Nixon are laced with words such as *paradox* and *irony*. Mostly, the words are used to refer to Nixon's complex personality. What concerns us here are the complexities of his *politics*. In recent American history, no politician was more adept at following former California governor Jerry Brown's injunction about the need to move "left and right at the same time."

In his time in office, Nixon laid down a record that might well have provided a basis for a genuinely popular brand of Modern Republicanism. Because Nixon's personal interest was almost exclusively in foreign policy, he was capable of being flexible, even creative, when it came to domestic policy. For Nixon, the primary purpose of domestic policy was its value in maintaining an electoral majority. In this sense, he was not that different from British Tories such as Worsthorne, who believed that a little bit of welfare state could go a long way toward keeping the right people in positions of authority. When Daniel Patrick Moynihan compared Nixon with Benjamin Disraeli in a 1972 profile, Moynihan seemed guilty of trying to curry favor with a man who had appointed him to high office and would do so again. But the notion of Nixon as a liberal Tory capable of creating a modern and popular conservatism was not just the product of Moynihan's ambitions.

Thus, at a 1987 conference at Hofstra University on Nixon's presidency, the generally liberal scholars present were torn in their assessments of the Nixon era. Their views depended on their area of concern. Scholars who focused exclusively on foreign policy spoke of Nixon's difficulties in Vietnam, but were forced to emphasize the achievements of détente with the Soviet Union and Nixon's opening to China. Scholars who examined domestic policy spoke of Nixon's disrespect for civil liberties and his use of the race issue to court the backlash vote, but they were forced to acknowledge such liberal achievements as the creation of the Environmental Protection Agency and the Occupational Safety and Health Administration, revenue sharing, the indexing of social security benefits—perhaps the most effective antipoverty program ever passed in Washington—and his proposed Family Assistance Plan. Those who looked at economic policy could argue the costs and benefits of Nixon's wage and price controls and his single-handed creation of a new international system of fluctuating exchange rates, but no one could deny the boldness of these moves. A thoroughly negative view of the Nixon presidency was offered only by those who concentrated almost exclusively on Watergate—though of course Watergate, for good reason, came to define the Nixon presidency.

In the end, the Nixon record, far more than the Eisenhower record, had the potential of putting substance on the bones of Modern Republicanism. Far more than Eisenhower, Nixon believed in using executive power (which, of course, proved to be his downfall when he abused it). He believed in activist government. He could be thoroughly pragmatic in assessing his program. And he was, as everyone knew, acutely *political*. Emmet John Hughes, a journalist who served as an Eisenhower speechwriter, observed in the early 1960s that Nixon was neither "a lion of Republicanism and reaction" nor "a fox of ambition and guile." Nixon, Hughes argued, was the ultimate pragmatist. "Indeed, the philosophy of any policy interested him, quite evidently, far less than its efficacy; he judged any declaration of speech not by its content but by its impact." Nixon, Hughes said, was "at his intellectual best in offering tactical counsel."

This tactical approach led Nixon first to his series of liberal domestic initiatives and then away from them. On domestic issues, many of Nixon's first-term initiatives were astoundingly liberal. At times, he supported forms of New Deal–style government intervention that many liberal Democrats had turned against. For example, Nixon backed federal subsidies for the Boeing Corporation's supersonic transport aircraft, the SST. The project was a favorite of Washington State's two old-style Democratic senators, Henry Jackson and Warren Magnuson, who were eager to help Boeing, their state's largest employer. But the project was killed because many Senate liberals raised environmental objections to the plane and were uneasy about giving a large subsidy to a large corporation. These increasingly antidefense liberals saw the SST as they saw military boondoggles. Yet the SST was precisely the sort of Keynesian project that Democrats had supported for years to keep the economy humming. A new kind of liberalism—environmentally oriented, skeptical of certain kinds of government spending—was born with the SST vote. Nixon, in the meantime, sounded like an old New Dealer, calling the Senate vote "a devastating mistake" and complaining that the project would have provided precisely the stimulus needed by the aerospace industry, which was suffering from high unemployment because of defense cutbacks. Drawing on the themes of Hamiltonian nationalism that Jacob Javits so admired, Nixon said the Senate action meant that the United States would be "relegated to second place in an area of technological capability vital to our economy and of profound importance in the future." That was exactly the sort of argument that liberal advocates of national planning—of using the government to "pick winners and losers" in industry—would be making a decade later, to the scorn of the free-market Reaganites. Yet Nixon's position was quite consistent with the interests of the constituencies that had gravitated to the right in the postwar period. As Michael Miles had noted, the aerospace industry was one of the mainstays of the economy of newly Republican regions such as California's Orange county. Nixon had supported these interests as a young southern-California congressman, and he continued to do so after he was president.

Revenue sharing was a simple proposal of some genius. On the one hand, it signaled that Republicans, like the Democrats, believed in active government. But it also demonstrated that, unlike the Democrats, Republicans believed that much of the action should be at the state and local level. Revenue sharing took a chunk of federal tax revenues and returned it to the states and cities to spend as they wished. This was a spending program with important conservative implications. It gave concrete support to the decentralist themes Republicans had been pushing for years. And it offered localities the opportunity to use the federal money not to expand programs, but to cut the property tax. This tax fell heavily on existing Republican constituencies among the well-off *and* on the lower-middle-class and working-class constituencies that Nixon was ardently wooing. Nixon himself said that revenue sharing would lead to a 30 percent cut in property taxes, which he described as the most "unfair, unpopular, and fastest rising of all taxes."

Nixon's Family Assistance Plan was his boldest initiative, an attempt to set up a national welfare system. The maximum payment under the plan was only $1,600 a year for a family of four with no income—at a time when the poverty level was $7,500. But the plan would still have raised payments to the poor in many states, notably in the South, and it would have established in law an unmistakably liberal principle: a federally guaranteed annual income. Moreover, the proposal included the work incentives contained in the Milton Friedman/Ripon Society negative income tax proposals: Some federal payments would continue to the working poor, with the federal subsidy trailing off as a family approached the poverty line. And most important from the point of view of the plan's architect, Daniel Patrick Moynihan, the proposal would help intact families and thereby discourage family dissolution.

The Family Assistance Plan passed the House, but bogged down in the Senate, where it was opposed by Southern Democrats, notably Sen. Russell Long of Louisiana, and by the most conservative Republicans, notably Sen. John Williams of Delaware. Liberals split on the plan, some supporting it as an important first step, others opposing it because it offered inadequate assistance to the poor or because it contained work requirements they regarded as too stringent. The plan eventually died, and Moynihan, in a blistering account, held an unprincipled coalition of Northern liberals and Southern reactionaries responsible for its defeat. But when the plan got into trouble, Nixon himself seemed to lack enthusiasm. Stephen Ambrose suggests that Nixon felt he had already won credit for offering a bold initiative and might suffer losses among conservatives if the plan was actually enacted into law; "after his dramatic introduction of the plan, Nixon was nearly motionless," Ambrose wrote.

On economics, Nixon was perhaps the *least* ideological president elected in this century. That is, he was willing to borrow concepts from his political enemies and use them more boldly than his enemies would ever dare. Nixon was especially sensitive to the demands of "the political business cycle," the need to get a strong economy right at the moment when it would have the maximum impact in helping the incumbent administration (in this case, his) win reelection. Nixon had rightly felt victimized in his 1960 campaign by the Eisenhower administration's cautious response to the 1958 recession. Once in office, Nixon was not about to be tagged as a Herbert Hoover Republican.

His August 1971 economic plan, crafted by his secretary of the treasury, John Connally (then still a Democrat), was astonishing in its boldness. To free-market conservatives, it was frightening. It was a mishmash of ideas that, taken together, showed just how aggressive Nixon was willing to be in his use of government. Besides the wage-price controls and the destruction of the Bretton Woods currency system that had been in effect for twenty-seven years, Connally proposed income-tax cuts, an investment tax credit, a cut in the excise tax on cars (to help Detroit), and a 10-percent tax on imports. As Michael Barone put it, "Connally's program brought more state direction to economic policy and did more to undercut the operation of free economic markets than anything done, except in war, by the Roosevelt, Truman, Eisenhower, Kennedy, or Johnson administrations." This was Modern Republicanism with a vengeance.

Abroad, Nixon's policies were no less bold. The man who had made his name on anticommunism, who was among the leading critics of the "loss of China," became the champion of an entirely new approach to world communism. So radical was his change in direction that the phrase "doing a Nixon on China" is now a standard part of the political lexicon to refer to all dramatic breaks from a politician's past positions. As Ambrose points out, Nixon laid hints during the 1968 campaign that he was preparing a new approach to the communist world and looked forward to an era of negotiation. But the nation was so obsessed with Vietnam, race, and other issues that Nixon's remarks drew little notice. Volumes have been written on the diplomacy of Richard Nixon and Secretary of State Henry A. Kissinger, clearly the most important legacy of Nixon's term of office. What concerns us here is Nixon's Modern Republican–style pragmatism.

Nixon, editorialists noted with some amazement, abandoned a set of positions that had defined his political persona for more than two decades.

But Nixon did keep faith with his promises to the Republican right on Vietnam. Here, Nixon refused to follow any policy that resembled immediate withdrawal—he refused, as he would say, to "cut and run." Hence, Nixon escalated the war with his Cambodian "incursion" in 1970 and with stepped-up bombing on North Vietnam. But he also moved, with some success, to undercut political opposition to the war by replacing the existing draft system with a lottery and by reducing draft calls through his "Vietnamization" program of gradually withdrawing American combat forces. The mix proved politically popular, yet it infuriated opponents of the war who saw no substantive change between the Nixon and Johnson policies and who wanted an immediate end to the conflict. With the war now established as "Nixon's war," many wavering Democrats in the Vital Center —Humphrey and Muskie among them—switched sides and opposed it.

Nixon's refusal to "cut and run" in Vietnam helped him politically, over the short run, in two quite different ways. By keeping the war as a central political issue, Nixon strengthened the left wing inside the Democratic Party and promoted the nomination of McGovern, whom Nixon regarded as his weakest potential opponent. (His dirty tricksters were pursuing less subtle ways of helping McGovern by undermining the candidacy of Edmund Muskie, the man Nixon saw as his strongest general-election foe.) The war, moreover, polarized American politics and cast Nixon, despite his détente policies, as the firm anticommunist who was resisting the countercultural foes of American resolve. This helped keep the increasingly rebellious right in line.

For the right had much to rebel against. Nixon's domestic initiatives were bad enough. So were his substantial cuts in military spending. But the opening to China and the détente policy toward the Soviet Union were, in their eyes, positively treasonous—to right-wing doctrine, if not to the country. It was enough to make conservatives long for the good old days of Dwight Eisenhower. At a meeting at Buckley's New York apartment, a group of conservatives, including Buckley, Rusher, and Meyer, issued a statement in which they "resolved to suspend our support of the Nixon administration."

Buckley, increasingly a "realist" when it came to electoral politics, was somewhat less eager than the others to break with Nixon. His brother James, running on the Conservative Party ticket, had been elected to the U.S. Senate in 1970 with considerable help from the Nixon administration. The administration had made clear that it preferred him to the very liberal Republican incumbent, Charles Goodell, and sent in Vice President Agnew to denounce Goodell. Nixon, in turn, was grateful that the Buckleys had helped him rid the Senate of Goodell, one of the administration's harshest critics, and sought to strengthen his relationship with Bill Buckley after the election. Buckley also remained close to the administration because of his admiration for Henry Kissinger.

Still, Buckley was sickened by much of what the administration was doing. Before leaving to cover Nixon's visit to China, Buckley taped radio commercials on behalf of Rep. John Ashbrook of Ohio, who challenged Nixon from the right in the New Hampshire primary. Ashbrook's candidacy went nowhere. He received just 9.7 percent of the New Hampshire vote to 68 percent for Nixon and about 20 percent for Rep. Paul McCloskey of California, who challenged Nixon from the left on Vietnam. That McCloskey outpolled Ashbrook seemed to prove what Buckley had feared all along, that Ashbrook's candidacy would demonstrate the weakness of the right, not its strength. Ashbrook withdrew and Buckley ultimately supported Nixon, his decision made easy since the alternative was George McGovern. (William Rusher, however, refused to support Nixon.)

Viewed from the perspective of Modern Republicanism's failures at the end of the 1950s, Nixon had accomplished something quite remarkable: On issue after issue, he had positioned the Republican Party well to the left of where anyone would have expected it to be just a few years earlier. And in doing so, he kept the Republican right in check. If anyone seemed on the verge of giving Modern Republicanism life, it was Richard M. Nixon.

Yet to say this goes against all of our common understandings of who Nixon was and what his presidency was about. For Nixon, ever shrewd when it came to counting votes, decided in the course of his first term that while some moves to the left—especially on economics —would be helpful to his reelection, the flow of events was really to the right. The contradiction is unraveled by understanding that it was only when measured by the issues of the 1950s and early 1960s that Nixon seemed so liberal. On the issues that came to define politics in the late 1960s and early 1970s—race, student disorders, the cultural issues—Nixon was thoroughly conservative.

A key event in Nixon's own understanding of his political situation was the publication of Richard Scammon and Ben Wattenberg's *The Real Majority* in 1970. They argued that to win, the Democrats needed to finesse the social issues and emphasize economics. For Scammon and Wattenberg, the key to winning American elections lay among those who were "unyoung, unpoor, and unblack." Their heroine was the forty-seven-year-old housewife from Dayton, Ohio, who, they argued, held the key to America's future in her hands. The book was intended mainly as advice to the Democrats by two analysts closely tied to the party's hawkish center—Wattenberg had been an aide to Lyndon Johnson. But no one took their book more seriously than Nixon, who was sold on its importance by Pat Buchanan. Buchanan and Nixon understood that the Republicans had as much of an interest in *emphasizing* the social issue as the Democrats had in putting it to rest. Referring to the Scammon and Wattenberg thesis in his memoirs, Nixon wrote that "if this analysis was right, and I agreed with Buchanan that it was, then the Republican counterstrategy was clear: We should preempt the social issue in order to get the Democrats on the defensive." Nixon went on: "We should aim our strategy primarily at disaffected Democrats, and blue collar workers, and at working class white ethnics. We should set out to capture the vote of the forty-seven-year-old Dayton housewife."

Nixon moved immediately to do so. Noting Wallace's successes in the 1972 Democratic primaries, Nixon went on record strongly and repeatedly as opposed to busing. He contrasted student radicals and those who burned the flag with the "silent majority" of law-abiding, tax-paying, patriotic Americans. He spoke about law and order. He emphasized traditional values and his opposition to drugs and abortion. And he condemned those who would surrender to the Communists in Vietnam.

He thus ended up giving a relatively liberal record a decidedly right-wing cast. Nixon's liberal foes, who could not help but endorse much of his foreign policy, drew comfort from the fact that at the end of it all, he still seemed to be the same old Nixon. And so they continued to wage war on him. The Ripon Society's hope that the Republican Party could be the party of the young professionals was dashed. Nixon spurned the yippies and the young professionals and embraced the forty-seven-year-old Dayton woman instead.

V

Watergate destroyed Richard Nixon. It ended what chance there was that Nixon could lay the groundwork for a reinvigorated Modern

Republicanism. But it did not destroy the Republican Party. And it did far more to help build the American right than to resuscitate liberalism or the Democratic Party.

Watergate was in no way inevitable, but it did follow logically from two aspects of Nixon's worldview. Nixon, after all, became a hero to elements of the right because of his war on Alger Hiss and other domestic opponents of an anticommunist foreign policy. At the heart of the anticommunist zeal of the postwar period was the view that domestic opponents of anticommunism could be as dangerous to American interests as the Soviets themselves.

But in the 1940s and early 1950s, most of those who opposed anti-Soviet policies were on the far left. It was politically painless to outlaw the Communist Party and to infiltrate pro-Soviet groups. Because of the Vietnam War, however, opposition to American foreign policy entered the mainstream. Now, it was not just the Communist Party, but the Democratic Party of George McGovern that was challenging the very basis of America's world strategy. In the 1950s, a "third-rate burglary" of a Communist-front headquarters would have gone unnoticed and might even have been cheered. But when such a burglary involved America's oldest political party, it was suddenly seen as a much greater threat to constitutional liberty.

Watergate thus permanently undermined the underpinnings of McCarthyism. The popular revolt against Watergate suggested that domestic dissent from the country's foreign policy was once again acceptable and that government efforts to undermine the dissenters would no longer win popular approval. It was one of the ways in which Vietnam and Watergate profoundly changed the postwar political order. Nixon himself hastened this process through his détente policy, which suggested that America's old Soviet and Chinese enemies were not quite the enemies they once were. The ratification of that change came during Ronald Reagan's administration. Partly because of his optimistic and conciliatory nature, but also because political reality had changed, Reagan resisted demonizing the enemies of his foreign policy. Reagan, even more than Nixon, believed for much of his term that the Soviet Union was an "evil empire," yet he rarely implied that those who disagreed with him were traitors or proto-communists. Although there was some government surveillance of groups opposed to Reagan's Central American policy, the mere revelation that such surveillance was taking place was enough to limit or end it entirely. Thus, one of the most profound changes of the period, ratified by the reaction to Watergate, was that American foreign policy was debatable again. Some would see this as the breakdown of the "postwar consensus" and regret the change. But the transformation also meant that the United States was rediscovering political freedoms that had been curbed during the postwar era.

Watergate also had more recent roots, in the political polarization caused by the Vietnam War, and in Nixon's embrace of polarization as the key to a new electoral majority. His administration even coined the term *positive polarization*, to refer to the beneficial political outcome that accrued when a right-wing majority was polarized against a left-wing minority. William Safire said this approach came naturally to a politician who, both politically and psychologically, was taken with the "us-against-them syndrome." Watergate was the pursuit of the Scammon-Wattenberg strategy carried to extremes.

What is so odd in retrospect is that Nixon was polarizing American politics at the very moment when he was depolarizing all the important political issues. Before Watergate brought him down, Nixon suggested that his second term would be more devoutly conservative than his first. Yet he was clearly not about to reverse his foreign policy initiatives, which did so much to reduce the distance between himself and his liberal foes. On economic policy, Nixon was still a pragmatist who might have tried to undo some of the damage the Connally policy had caused, but only because aspects of it had not worked as planned. Nixon remained deeply loyal to Connally himself and to his eclectic and highly political approach to economics. Nor despite Nixon's doubts about environmentalism, did he seem likely to abolish the EPA. As for government spending, Nixon might have tried to cut this or that liberal program, but he had already decisively shifted the government's spending priorities in a liberal direction, because of his generous approach to social security and the decline in defense spending as the costs of the Vietnam War dropped. Thus, between the 1968–69 budget, the last budget fully crafted by Johnson, and Nixon's 1971–72 budget, social security spending was up 55 percent, nondefense spending was up 44 percent—and defense spending was down by 3 percent. Ronald Reagan was to make much of the declining share of federal spending that was going to defense. That trend began under Richard Nixon, and the first steps toward reversing it were actually undertaken by Jimmy Carter.

By choosing to emphasize conservative social-issue politics over the liberal achievements of his administration, Nixon led himself to Watergate and gave up his chance to be the architect of a working Modern Republicanism. Nixon's decision was decisive for the future of American politics because it promised that politics would become polarized and that false choices around the social issues and race would become a normal part of the political process. Nixon could have changed this by ending the Vietnam War earlier or by resisting the obvious temptations laid before him by the logic of the Scammon and Wattenberg analysis. Liberals could have avoided this by pursuing a less divisive politics of their own—by not handing Nixon advantages on the issues of "patriotism" or the white-ethnic rebellion. In the event, both sides opted for polarization.

But political actors do not usually choose the circumstances in which they must make choices, and there was a logic to the choices made by both Nixon and his foes. Since the beginning of the 1960s, large parts of the nation had been yearning for what Samuel P. Huntington, the political scientist, called "a politics of creedal passion." Huntington defined "creedal passion" periods in American history as involving "intense efforts by large numbers of Americans to return to first principles." The Goldwater campaign and the New Left were just that. Both were movements of the engaged middle class and both emphasized the importance of morality in politics. Both saw the United States as lacking a clear sense of ethical direction, and both saw the battle for political power as a struggle to define the nation's moral goals. Although the pragmatist in Nixon was viscerally uncomfortable with this style of politics, he understood its increasing importance inside the Republican Party and saw the uses to which it could be put. Nixon's enemies, especially those opposed to his Vietnam policies, defined politics almost entirely in moral and cultural terms. For them, Nixon's fall in Watergate was a vindication of political morality—especially their own.

Yet surprisingly, Watergate ultimately worked in favor of the conservative right, not the left. It did this first by destroying Modern Republicanism's best chance for success, which was Richard Nixon's administration. Many on the right understood this, which is why so many conservatives had given up on Nixon long before Watergate. After the 1972 election, Buckley wrote a column that was more prophetic than he could ever have realized at the time. Buckley warned that Nixon, lacking any ideological direction, was already mistrusted not only by the liberal opposition, but also by many in his own party. "Mr. Nixon will fill the void quickly," Buckley wrote, "or he will suffer the fate of Harold Macmillan, who in 1959 won the most triumphant reelection in modern English history, and eighteen months later everything lay in ruins around him."

Conservatives, of course, had no sympathy for the "liberal

media," who were seen as destroying Nixon. Indeed, many conservatives came to see Watergate as a liberal coup d'état, seizing power away from the man on whom it had been legitimately conferred and postponing a conservative political realignment. This was a case of sharing Nixon's enemies without necessarily sharing Nixon's goals, but the conservatives' point had implications for the Democrats and the liberals. For the Democrats gained less from Watergate than did institutions outside government altogether. "The press won in Watergate," said Benjamin C. Bradlee, executive editor of *The Washington Post*, which played such a decisive role in Nixon's troubles. He was correct, and in more than just the obvious way. Insofar as credit for the workings of democracy went to the press—and also to the judiciary—it was credit that did not go to Democratic politicians. Indeed, Watergate encouraged an increasingly adversarial journalism, which helped undermine government's credibility. The criticisms were often directed against Republicans, but the net result was to hurt liberal Democrats, since they rested their claim on the idea that government was a positive good. After Watergate, few Americans believed that anymore. The one Democrat who emerged as the biggest winner from Watergate was one of the most conservative members of Congress, Sen. Sam Ervin of North Carolina, a long-standing advocate of "limited, constitutional government."

It was common after Watergate to declare that "the system had worked." But what had worked was not so much government itself, and certainly not the political process; the "victor" was a series of checks on government power. Not surprisingly, many of the Democrats swept into office in the 1974 anti-Republican landslide were the young, new-style liberals who differed most notably from their elders in their skepticism about the workings of the institutions of government.

The revulsion against Washington that Watergate unleashed thus played right back into the conservative argument. When Ronald Reagan announced his candidacy against Gerald Ford for the 1976 Republican nomination, he made opposition to Washington and all its works as much a part of his campaign as Jimmy Carter made it part of his. "Our nation's capital," Reagan declared, "has become the seat of a buddy system that functions for its own benefit—increasingly insensitive to the needs of the American worker, who supports it with his taxes. Today, it is difficult to find leaders who are independent of the forces who have brought us our problems—the Congress, the bureaucracy, the lobbyists, big business, and big labor." Reagan said not a word about Gerald Ford or his pardon of Nixon. Nor did he explicitly attack Nixon's "big government" Republicanism. He didn't have to.

Gerald Ford, with more adeptness than he is usually credited for, took on the Modern Republican mission. He angered the right by keeping Henry Kissinger on as his secretary of state and by faithfully following Nixon's détente policies. In keeping with his Midwestern Republican roots, Ford was more fiscally conservative than Nixon and used his veto against Democratic spending bills more aggressively than any postwar president. But Ford's tone was moderate, and if he tried to keep spending down, he did not try to fundamentally reshape the federal budget. Richard Reeves, the able political writer, offered a book about the new president called A Ford Not a Lincoln. He might well have called his book An Eisenhower Not a Lincoln. Ford lacked Eisenhower's stature, but he shared Eisenhower's sunny disposition, his dislike of federal spending, and his moderation in pursuit of conservative goals.

Above all, Ford utterly lacked Nixon's love for the social-issue jugular, and if Ford was uncomfortable with divisive social issues, his wife, Betty, was even more so. During an interview on CBS News' "60 Minutes," Mrs. Ford was asked what she would do if her eighteen-year-old daughter came to her and said she was having an affair. "Well, I wouldn't be surprised," Mrs. Ford replied. "I think she's a perfectly normal human being, like all young girls." For good measure, Mrs. Ford suggested that premarital sex might cut the divorce rate. She also praised the Supreme Court for legalizing abortion (which brought it "out of the backwoods and put it in the hospitals where it belongs") and said that marijuana experimentation for the young was like "your first beer or your first cigarette." With the Fords in the White House, there would be much tolerance and little in the way of "positive polarization."

It was a sign of how conservative the Republican Party had become that Ronald Reagan almost deprived Ford, the incumbent, of the Republican presidential nomination. Although Ford won some of the key early primaries, Reagan staged a comeback in North Carolina, with help from Sen. Jesse Helms, and actually pulled ahead of Ford in the delegate count in the spring, mainly on the strength of sweeping Southern-primary victories. Among Reagan's issues: his firm opposition to turning over the Panama Canal to the Panamanian government. "We built it, we paid for it, and we're going to keep it," Reagan would say. Reagan also jabbed continually at Kissinger, which greatly annoyed the secretary of state. In the course of the primaries, Kissinger had his department put out a ten-page refutation of Reagan's points, which only served to give Reagan's charges more publicity.

Ford beat Reagan at the Kansas City Convention by 1,187 to 1,070. Reagan tried a last-minute gamble by announcing that he would choose the very liberal Pennsylvania senator, Richard Schweiker, as his running mate. But the move may have turned off the handful of Southern conservatives not yet committed to Reagan. The remarkable thing is that a politician as conservative as Gerald Ford could ever be tagged as representing "liberal" Republicanism at all. That he was so labeled reflected the importance party conservatives placed on foreign policy and the new social issues, on which Ford was temperamentally moderate. As a result, Ford's 1976 victory depended on a very different nominating coalition from Richard Nixon's in 1968, as illustrated in Table Five.

Where Nixon had won 74 percent of the Southern delegates in 1968, Ford took only 27 percent in 1976. Nixon had essentially split the West with Reagan in 1968; Ford's delegates there were outnumbered four to one by Reagan's. Ford made up for these losses by depending on a near sweep of the party's old liberal region, the Northeast. These states had gone for Rockefeller and other moderates in 1968, but swung in mass to Ford. He also ran slightly better than Nixon in the Midwest, which was home to Ford himself and to the kind of Republicanism with which he was most comfortable.

Viewed in historical terms, the 1976 coalitions were entirely new. Traditionally, it had been the Northeastern Republican internationalists pitted against the Midwestern isolationists, with the two sides scrambling for support in the South and West. Now, the Republican Party was divided along a diagonal splitting the country into Sunbelt and Frostbelt.

Yet even at Kansas City, a convention in which the East and Middle West nominated their choice, the conservative South played a kingmaker's role. One of the most crucial battles—and certainly the most publicized—was for the delegation from Mississippi, historically the least Republican state in the Union. While he lost most of the South, Ford won the battle of Mississippi. The power of conservatives at the Convention was such that Ford also felt obliged to pick a running mate acceptable to the party's right wing, Sen. Bob Dole of Kansas. "Though he was the incumbent, Ford was treated almost as if he were an interloper," wrote Jules Witcover in *Marathon: The Pursuit of the Presidency 1972–1976*, his definitive account of the 1976 campaign. "The phenomenon of delegates openly threatening to with-

TABLE FIVE

REGIONAL VOTING PATTERNS AT REPUBLICAN NATIONAL CONVENTIONS 1968 AND 1976
(PERCENTAGE OF DELEGATES)

	Nixon 1968	Rockefeller and moderate favorite sons 1968	Reagan 1968	Ford 1976	Reagan 1976
South	74	8	18	27	73
West	48	12	40	18	82
Midwest	52	45	3	68	32
Northeast	32	68	*	88	12

* = less than one percent
Source: Adapted from Nicol C. Rae, The Decline and Fall of the Liberal Republicans (Oxford University Press, 1989), pp. 98, 117

hold support from him if he chose a running mate not to their liking was a telling commentary on how shaky his hold on the party was."

That Ford came so close to defeating Jimmy Carter in the fall— even though Carter reversed recent electoral history by sweeping ten of the eleven states of the Old Confederacy—was a tribute to Ford's brilliant general-election campaign and to popular doubts about Carter that grew as election day approached. But Ford's showing also suggested that a conservatized Modern Republicanism still had a chance of creating a national majority.

Even in defeat, Ford made inroads into the upper-middle-class professional areas that the Ripon Republicans had wanted to target. Ford actually ran ahead of Nixon's 1972 share in such new liberal strongholds as Marin, Yolo, and San Francisco counties in California, Pitkin and Summit counties in Colorado, Johnson County, Iowa, and Suffolk County (Boston), Massachusetts—all places where John Anderson would do well in 1980. Ford bested the *combined* 1968 Nixon and Wallace totals across much of New England and upstate New York, in Washington State, and in his home state of Michigan. In such areas, Ford's moderation on social issues (and Carter's Southernness) helped restore some of the old Eisenhower Republican vote that had been straying Democratic since 1960.

But conservatives drew a different lesson from Ford's defeat, using it to pronounce the death of Modern Republicanism. The conservatives were quick to trace Ford's defeat to his failure to win the lower-income social-issue conservatives who had gravitated to Nixon or Wallace in 1968 and to Nixon in 1972. In analyzing the vote, Kevin Phillips found that even outside the South, Ford's heaviest losses came in poor, white rural areas. Looking at Phillips's numbers, William Rusher argued that "it is simply purblind not to recognize that the Democratic Party's recapture of a substantial part of the social conservative vote was what narrowly elected Carter." The Republican future clearly lay in polarization around the conservative social issues.

Ford's defeat was Modern Republicanism's decisive setback. After 1976, all of the energy in the Republican Party would be on the right. Ronald Reagan was ready again, and the next time, he would be the favorite. And new forces at work in the country were strengthening the conservatives' hand even more.

8

HELL
HATH NO FURY:
The Religious Right
and the
New Republican Party

IN 1965, A YOUNG Baptist minister explained why he felt it inappropriate for fundamentalists such as himself to become involved in politics. "We have few ties to this earth," the minister explained. "Believing in the Bible as I do, I would find it impossible to stop preaching the pure saving Gospel of Jesus Christ and begin doing anything else, including fighting communism or participating in civil rights reforms," he said. "Preachers are not called upon to be politicians but to be soul winners. Nowhere are we commissioned to reform the externals." The minister who spoke these words was the pastor of the Thomas Road Baptist Church in Lynchburg, Virginia, the Reverend Jerry Falwell.

Falwell's statement is remarkable only in light of his subsequent history. At the time he spoke, his words were well within the fundamentalist and evangelical mainstream. Until the 1970s, a polite disrespect for politics characterized much of the fundamentalist and evangelical movement. If Christ's Kingdom was not of "this world," then His followers had no political obligations beyond a relatively narrow definition of what they should "render unto Caesar." Baptists, whether fundamentalist such as Falwell or not, had long been the most ardent advocates of separating church and state, even on the touchiest issues such as prayer in public schools and abortion. The Baptists' dissenting, popular tradition and their mistrust of state religion had deep roots. In colonial America, the Established churches had been the churches of the upper classes. Baptists, with their deep belief in individual conscience and their disdain for hierarchy, knew instinctively that if a religion was established by the state, it would not be theirs.

But there were other reasons for the fundamentalists' mistrust of politics.

Fundamentalism was plunged into crisis by its two great public crusades of the teens and twenties, the wars against evolution and alcohol. Ironically, both wars initially appeared successful. Prohibition was enacted into law, passed with the support of the culturally "advanced" as well as the culturally "backward." Much support for Prohibition came from "enlightened" liberal social reformers of the upper classes who bemoaned the damage liquor inflicted on the lower orders (and who, conveniently, were often Roman Catholics, whom both upper- and lower-class Protestants mistrusted). Prohibition, of course, proved to be a disaster and was forever after invoked by all who insisted that government efforts to regulate personal morality were doomed.

The Scopes "monkey trial" actually ended in the conviction of John T. Scopes for teaching evolution, another fundamentalist victory. But few victories better deserved to be called Pyrrhic. The fundamentalists' claims about evolution were held up for scorn throughout the nation. "Respected 'evangelicals' in the 1870s, by the 1920s they had become a laughingstock, ideological strangers in their own land," wrote George M. Marsden, a leading historian of evangelicalism. "The philosophical outlook that had graced America's finest academic institutions came to be generally regarded as merely bizarre."

And so the fundamentalists went underground, disdaining a presence in public life that had done their movement so much harm. Modernity was indeed just as inhospitable to the truths that fundamentalists proclaimed as they had feared. If the world of great universities, big cities, Hollywood filmmakers, and the acid commentary of H. L. Mencken was destined to be hostile to the cause of righteousness, then that world—"this world"—could be left to its own corruptions.

Yet in 1980, the entire nation was discussing the fundamentalists and the evangelicals—vaguely aware that the two groups overlapped but were not quite the same. A religious movement that the broader society had dismissed as hopelessly unsophisticated proved exceptionally adept at using the tools of modern politics: television, precinct organization, direct mail. The religiously hip and liberal had drawn much notice in the 1960s. But by the 1970s, the declining churches were the liberal churches, which had rejected the "fundamentals" of Christianity, as the fundamentalists saw it. The churches on the rise were the most *conservative*—those preaching the most old-fashioned Gospel, those demanding adherence to the strictest moral codes. In the mid-1960s, the provocative young theologians who proclaimed "death of God" Christianity created a clamor, their cause even making the cover of *Time* magazine. But a Protestant churchman warned that the funeral procession in the Christian churches was not for God after all. "The real candidate for interment is a lesser chap by the name of Liberal Protestantism," wrote Robert E. Fitch.

Still, the growth of conservative churches was one thing; the rise of a *politicized* Christian right was something else again. The apparent power of the Religious Right caused alarm around the nation. Books with titles such as *God's Bullies* and *Holy Terror* warned that tolerance and individual freedom were in jeopardy.

Some of the Religious Right's leaders did indeed sound alarming. "God Almighty does not hear the prayer of a Jew," said the Reverend Bailey Smith, speaking at a news briefing conducted by the right-wing Religious Roundtable. Others sounded threatening. "We have enough votes to run the country," said the Reverend Pat Robertson. "And when the people say, 'We've had enough,' we are going to take over." Fears about the Religious Right went well beyond liberalism's confines. In 1984, according to Reagan campaign aide John Buckley, the political commercial for Walter Mondale that helped the Democrat most scored Ronald Reagan for the overwhelming influence Falwell was reputed to have on his policies and his judicial appointments. Buckley said he was relieved that the Democrats made so little use of the commercial. The commercial's success was not surprising: Polls consistently showed Falwell to be one of the most unpopular public figures in America.

If Americans outside the fundamentalist and evangelical communities were worried by what was going on, they were also baffled. After all, most of what had happened in the 1960s and 1970s moved the country in a *liberal* direction. In this "greening of America," sexual attitudes were freer, drugs were more widely used, abortion was legal, women were marching toward equality. If America was indeed as dangerously secularized as the leaders of the Religious Right proclaimed, how could their movement sneak up on the country and become so powerful, so suddenly?

II

There was, of course, nothing sudden about the development of fundamentalism. Nor can fundamentalism be dismissed as the irrationalist faith of the unenlightened. The conflict around the Scopes trial obscured the rich intellectual tradition of a movement that began as a rational response by conservative Christians to the rise of modern ideas within their churches.

Fundamentalism's first intellectual home was not an obscure Bible college, but at the Princeton Theological Seminary. Fundamentalism's intellectual giant was J. Gresham Machen, a theologian who took modern theology with great seriousness and found its claims troubling. "The great redemptive religion which has always been known as Christianity," he wrote in 1923 in *Christianity and Liberalism*, "is battling against a totally diverse type of religious belief, which is only the more destructive of the Christian faith because it makes use of traditional Christian terminology." For Machen, the great battle of the twentieth century was between Christianity and modernism. Those Christians who were making their peace with modern ideas were not enriching Christianity at all, he insisted. They were going over to the other side. In the interest of intellectual honesty, Machen declared, the two strains of thought within the Christian church—liberals who proposed to accommodate modernity and conservatives who opposed accommodation—needed to divorce each other. "A separation between the two parties in the Church," he wrote, "is the crying need of the hour." Machen helped bring about the divorce. Many liberals outside the churches regarded Machen's argument as compelling. Unlike liberals within the churches, the secular liberals saw no need to rationalize Christianity along modernist lines. For secular liberal spokesmen such as Walter Lippmann, Machen's argument had the virtue of intellectual honesty. How much could Christianity accommodate modernity, liberals such as Lippmann reasoned, and still remain Christianity?

From the outset, fundamentalists had much in common with other traditionalist critics of modernity, including such postwar critics as Russell Kirk and Richard Weaver. "Fundamentalism is an offshoot of the tradition of antimodernism which has fought against the modern world since its inception," wrote Harvey Cox, a theologian whose liberalism has not prevented him from expressing respect for fundamentalism's achievement. "The focal thesis of the conservative religious critics of modern theology is that since the modern world is a spiritual disaster area, theology should never have come to terms with it in the first place. . . . Nearly all conservative critics agree that ours is a *uniquely* fallen or deranged age, that it was much easier to be religious at some other time."

Though some fundamentalists were given to conspiracy theories, fundamentalism itself was not based on paranoia. Its enemy was real: a development within Christian theology in the late nineteenth century known as the New Christianity. The New Christianity was based on the meditations of liberal church thinkers on the relationship between their faith and a world rapidly being transformed by industrialism and modernity. "When I began to apply my previous religious ideas to the conditions I found, I discovered that they didn't fit," wrote Walter Rauschenbusch, the founder of the Social Gospel movement, which emphasized the church's commitment to social reform. Advocates of the Social Gospel rejected the idea that individual conversion and repentance were adequate responses to modern injustice. Only a wholesale, collective attack on social injustice could purge the world of social sin and pave the way for the coming of God's Kingdom. Many advocates of the Social Gospel aligned themselves with the rising Socialist Party of Eugene Debs. Many more were Progressives. The founding of the Federal Council of Churches of Christ in America in 1908 at the height of the Progressive Era gave organizational form to this interchurch movement of the left. The foundation of the Federal Council, the precursor to the National Council of Churches, signaled an important change in American religious life. The crucial distinctions among Christians were no longer those among the different denominations, but *within* the denominations, which were split within themselves in their attitudes toward modernity and liberalism. The ecumenical movement declared that the old divisions should be overcome—and in the process created new ones. Significantly, as James Davison Hunter, a sociologist at the University of Virginia pointed out, the "new theology" of the New Christianity sought accommodation with science, including Darwin's theories of evolution.

The Christian traditionalists were alarmed by these developments, but not because of their political direction. Indeed, John

Dewey, who could not be accused of harboring any sympathy for fundamentalist ideas, credited fundamentalists such as William Jennings Bryan with being "the backbone of philanthropic social interest, of social reform through political action, of pacifism, of popular education." Not political but spiritual concerns animated the fundamentalist revolt against the Social Gospel. "What troubled conservatives about the Social Gospel in particular was not the new movement's endorsement of social concern, but the Social Gospel's emphasis on social concern to the seeming exclusion of the spiritual dimensions of faith," Hunter has written. Conservatives, he wrote, "feared the growing popularity of the New Christianity as a threat to the apostolic faith."

In 1910, the conservatives launched a counterattack on the religious liberals by publishing *The Fundamentals*, twelve volumes that sought to define the traditional creed and defend it from the attacks of the New Christianity. The fundamentalists' priority was defending the authority of the Bible. They did so, Hunter wrote, believing that if the founding document of the Christian faith could be seen as "the inerrant and infallible word of God, they would maintain an adequate basis for dismissing all erroneous teachings." The emphasis on biblical inerrancy, so puzzling to liberals, was at least in part a *rational* search for a form of authority strong enough to resist encroachments on traditional doctrine by liberal and modern ideas.

Thus was the groundwork laid for a conflict that would tear at Christianity into the present day. Hunter believes that the fundamentalists were already on the defensive before the 1920s dawned. The Scopes trial administered a decisive blow, holding fundamentalism up for national scorn. But Prohibition struck a blow to Protestantism as a whole, since it was the one issue on which fundamentalist and modernist Protestants agreed. For the fundamentalists, Prohibition was a way for the state to enforce high *individual* moral standards. For the modernists, it was part of a program of *social* reform, aimed at lifting the urban poor. (The unusual coalition prefigured the alliance between secular liberals and conservatives against drug abuse in the 1980s and 1990s.) With the failure of Prohibition, Protestant and rural dominance in American culture ended. Cultural power passed to a heterogeneous urban America in which Catholics, Jews, and nonbelievers played decisive roles. Although Al Smith, the champion of this new America, lost the 1928 election to Herbert Hoover, his candidacy laid the groundwork for its ultimate triumph. Smith ratified the Democratic Party's shift into the camp of modernism and pluralism. The party left behind the America of William Jennings Bryan. H. L. Mencken accurately characterized the troubles facing America's once dominant religion when he wrote in the 1920s that "Protestantism is down with a wasting disease." The 1920s were unkind to the Protestants not only in the public sphere, but in the private realm as well. The relationship of the 1920s to the Victorian age was not unlike that of the 1960s to the 1950s: In the roaring twenties, the old moral standards collapsed into an era of fun, frolic, experimentation, and (despite Prohibition) booze. What America experienced, as the conservative writer Terry Eastland has put it, was "the cultural disestablishment of the old faith."

After the 1920s, fundamentalism went underground and sought to revive itself. The Great Depression helped the fundamentalists in their task, since that catastrophe seemed to justify their pessimistic view of modern life. "The Great Depression was in their view a sign of God's vindictive punishment of an apostate America, and also a sign of Christ's imminent return," Hunter wrote. Fundamentalism provided comfort and meaning for millions whose world had collapsed. As Hunter put it, "personal salvation and the variable degrees of holiness attainable by the believer served as compensations for the privileges denied him in the social and economic sphere." The 1930s also saw the first stirrings of the "electronic church" that was to receive so much notice in the 1970s. The fundamentalists moved quickly to make radio a central part of their ministry. In May 1931, the *Sunday School Times* listed over a hundred different religious radio programs available on seventy different broadcast outlets. A poll in 1932 by the *Kansas City Star* found that the most popular local program was "The Morning Bible Hour." A program called "Miracles and Melodies," which combined preaching and music, was heard on 197 stations in 43 states in early 1942.

Although some fundamentalist Protestants veered into right-wing, anti–New Deal, and even fascist politics, the movement was characterized far more by that form of conservatism that looks down on all worldly political movements. It is true that many fundamentalists subscribed to doctrines that seemed utterly strange to those unschooled in the faith—notably the idea that God would sweep up all His followers into heaven at the moment of the "secret rapture" before Armageddon. But doctrines that seem bizarre to nonbelievers are not automatically "dangerous," either politically or socially; and many of the evangelical doctrines were no stranger than the assertions of some of the "new religions" that received favorable attention in the 1960s.

In any event, radio listeners who were searching their dials for religious instruction had an array of religious worldviews at their fingertips; some believed in the "rapture" and the imminent end of the world and some did not.

If radio helped fundamentalists renew their public presence, the movement also consolidated itself organizationally. A. James Reichley, a senior fellow at the Brookings Institution and a close student of the relationship between religion and politics in America, traced the rebirth of conservative Protestantism to the formation of the American Council of Christian Churches (ACCC) in 1941 and the National Association of Evangelicals (NAE) in 1942. Both organizations were in basic agreement doctrinally and saw themselves as conservative alternatives to the liberalism of the Federal Council of Churches. But whereas the ACCC was unrelenting in its criticism of liberal Protestantism, the NAE insisted that the rules of Christian charity ought to apply even to battles within the church. The NAE promised that it would be "no dog-in-the-manger, reactionary, negative, or destructive-type organization" and would "shun all forms of bigotry, intolerance, misrepresentation, hate, jealousy, false judgment, and hypocrisy." In effect, evangelicalism was an attempt to uphold the old doctrines, but in a way that would rid the conservative Protestant movement of the reputation fundamentalism had given it for rigidity and intolerance.

The decisive figure in the rebirth of conservative Protestantism was Billy Graham. Reichley argues that Graham's "great social achievement" was "to move most evangelicals back into the mainstream of American life." Although Graham was an ardent anticommunist and a political conservative who made no secret of his admiration for Richard Nixon, he mostly steered clear of politics. Even for the intellectuals, Graham was reassuring. "Graham was no bigot," historian William L. O'Neill wrote by way of explaining his respectability. "His call for Americans to rediscover their traditional beliefs did not stir up old hatreds. Graham asked only that the individual rediscover Christ. If that was a far cry from the Social Gospel, it was a far cry too from the chauvinism and provinciality of that old-time religion."

The 1950s saw the first stirrings of a new engagement between conservative Protestantism and politics. Carl McIntire, president of the ACCC, and Billy James Hargis of the Christian Crusade led an assault on communism that laid heavy stress on fundamentalism's liberal foes inside the churches. Anticommunism had many uses, and one of them was in the ongoing battle against modernism. Mainstream conservatives, including those who gathered around the *National Review,* welcomed these evangelical allies to the battle against communism. But fundamentalism itself had little influence on the *National Review* conservatives, a high-church crowd.

Most fundamentalists and evangelicals still remained wary of political engagement. A politicized Christianity had, after all, been the project of the Social Gospel movement. Politics remained a distraction from the church's real tasks and inevitably meant excessive entanglement with the corruptions of the modern world. In his autobiography, Jerry Falwell noted that "most of the early Southern circuit-riding preachers and tent-evangelists condemned lawyers, politicians, abolitionists and suffragettes alike." The message of such preachers, Falwell said, was that "we are here to serve Jesus" and "don't get bogged down with unbelievers and their unrighteousness." For conservatives such as Falwell, such views were only reinforced by the fact that the civil rights revolution was being led by ministers preaching the Gospel. This provided conservatives with yet more evidence that the engagement between the church and politics was an affair of the left. (Falwell's own attacks on politicized clerics were made against the civil rights leaders.)

Even if they had been inclined to political action, the churches, both mainline and fundamentalist, were too busy growing in the 1950s to become too heavily engaged. The United States, at last prosperous and at peace after the challenges of the Depression and war, experienced a religious boom during the Eisenhower era. In 1940, only 64.5 million Americans belonged to churches—50 percent of the population. By the end of the 1950s, there were 114.5 million church members, 63 percent of the population. The new religiosity affected Congress, which accorded God new forms of official recognition. It was in the 1950s that the words *under God* were inserted into the Pledge of Allegiance and that "In God We Trust" was stamped onto coins.

It was not surprising that the new religious enthusiasm manifested itself most visibly on the nation's coinage. The religion of the 1950s was very much about celebrating America's strength and prosperity. The faith of the fifties did little to challenge the country's values. In 1955, Will Herberg, a sociologist who had moved from communism to a devout Judaism, wrote his influential *Protestant-Catholic-Jew.* Herberg sought to explain the paradox that "mounting religiosity" was accompanied in the 1950s by "pervasive secularism."

The real American religion, Herberg wrote, was "the American way of life," which was represented by the inner-directed middle class. Religion for the typical American, Herberg said, "is not something that makes for humility or the uneasy conscience." Rather, he argued, "it is something that reassures him about the essential rightness of everything American, his nation, his culture and himself." Religion "validates his goals and his ideals instead of calling them into question" and "enhances his self-regard instead of challenging it." The signal expression of American religion's lack of content was President Eisenhower's famous declaration: "Our government makes no sense unless it is founded on a deeply felt religious belief—and I don't care what it is."

Yet if such a view seemed to denigrate the intellectual content of religious faith, it also promoted a greater tolerance, which served many interests. For evangelicals, it meant reentering the mainstream of American life. A country that was celebrating once again the value of religiosity appreciated the efforts of preachers such as Billy Graham. Fundamentalist and evangelical churches grew along with the other churches, blossoming not only among the rural poor, but also in the middle-class neighborhoods of the new suburbs. The new domesticity that the nation celebrated in the 1950s correlated well with a conservative Protestant morality. It is no wonder that in the turbulent 1960s, so many fundamentalists would look back to the 1950s as a time when the nation was a more godly place.

The new tolerance also spelled the end of confrontation between the Protestant majority and the Catholic and Jewish minorities. If, as Herberg asserted, the dominant commitment of all the American faiths was to the nation's way of life, then the differences between the churches could not be all that important. Eisenhower's "I don't care what it is" approach to religion helped mightily to elect John F. Kennedy in 1960. Although many fundamentalist preachers, notably Carl McIntire, preached against the election of a Roman Catholic president, the religion issue turned out to be more helpful to Kennedy than not. His losses among Protestants were more than offset by gains among Roman Catholics eager to tear down social and political barriers. Kennedy himself may have been the ideal Roman Catholic to achieve the breakthrough. As Garry Wills observed, he was "officially" Catholic and "functionally" non-Catholic. "One can find little organic intellectual connection between his faith and his politics," declared Arthur Schlesinger, Jr. Kennedy was the quintessentially Secular Man, celebrated by Harvey Cox as the embodiment of *The Secular City*, a place where religion's importance was receding.

Kennedy's breakthrough signaled the end of fundamentalist and evangelical opposition to American Catholicism. In the 1970s and 1980s, one of the most remarkable (and little noticed) facts about the Religious Right was its friendly relationship with conservative Roman Catholics. Just as the liberal-fundamentalist split at the turn of the century had rendered denominational differences within Protestantism far less important, the cultural cleavages of the 1960s would lower the barriers between Protestantism and Catholicism—and even those between Christians and Jews. Indeed, the political communion between conservative Catholics and Protestants in the 1970s was foreshadowed by the growing closeness of Protestant and Catholic liberals in the 1960s. Harvey Cox, who was surprised by the popularity of *The Secular City*, his celebration of secularization, was especially impressed with how many Roman Catholics took his book to heart. Catholics, with the Second Vatican Council, were undergoing their own Reformation, and their own version of the fundamentalist-modernist debate. Cox's bold endorsement of "the loosening of the world from religious and quasi-religious understandings of itself" thus resonated even more among Catholics, for whom the debate was something quite new, than among Protestants, who had gone through it all before.

But the 1960s did not result in more secularization, but less. Religion, far from receding to the most private corners of individual lives, reasserted its public role with a vengeance. Cox, an exceptionally honest self-critic, acknowledged that he had been at least partially in error. Yet one of Cox's assertions in *The Secular City* proved to be quite prophetic. "In secular society politics does what metaphysics once did," Cox had written. "It brings unity and meaning to human life and thought." Politics, which had been the downfall of conservative Protestantism in the 1920s, gave it new unity and meaning in the 1970s and 1980s. But the process began in the 1960s.

III

The relationship between the Religious Right and the sixties was thoroughly paradoxical. The Religious Right arose in reaction to "sixties permissiveness." Yet the rise of the Religious Right and more generally, the growth of evangelical Christianity were also very much part of the revolt during the 1960s against the status quo—in the churches no less than in the broader society.

During the 1960s, much attention was lavished on the more exotic religious or quasi-religious movements that young people imported from abroad—Zen Buddhism, transcendental meditation, Hare Krishna, the teachings of the Swami Muktananda. But many among the young did not go abroad for new religions. Rather, they turned to new forms of homegrown Christianity, which in many cases turned out to be the *old* forms, which looked new only because mainline Christianity had become so resolutely modern.

Both Peter Clecak and Harvey Cox have argued that the resurgence of the old-time religion was part of the broader revolt against modernism and scientific rationality that can be traced to the counter-cultural and New Left movements of the 1960s. As Lutheran pastor Richard John Neuhaus put it, "the counterculturalists have served the moral majoritarians by whom they feel threatened." Like the New Left, both the new religious movements and the new manifestations of old-time Christianity were skeptical of the bland pragmatism of the 1950s. Like the New Left, the new religious enthusiasts were suspicious of the ease with which the nation's moral leaders, including those in the churches, had adapted themselves to the status quo. But if many on the New Left rejected religion—or never took it seriously in the first place—many among the new religious enthusiasts sought to transform the nation's religious life, to reject "cheap grace" and turn religious faith into a challenge once again.

Even among those who turned to religion more for good vibes than for ethical guidance, there was a sense that the old modernist authorities had failed them. Leonard Sweet, an evangelical church historian, saw both the new religions and the new turn to the old ones as part of a "subjectivist search for authority" to replace forms of authority that were rejected during the 1960s. "People began to journey with anyone who promised them some new insight about the self or some escape from the burden of building a self," he wrote. Both the Jesus movement ("Jesus people") and the charismatic movement (with its emphasis on the inspirations of the Holy Spirit) were similar to new non-Christian movements of the 1960s, Sweet wrote, in that "both movements were obsessed with feeling and exhibited the strong desire to romp spiritually through new forms of consciousness and new dimensions of experience."

The rebellion against mainstream religion, like the rebellion against liberal politics, developed both left and right tendencies. Like many liberals in the political sphere, many religious liberals lost faith in the liberal religious project and in the assertions of the mainline churches. They became more radical, questioning whether the church or even God Himself, whom some pronounced "dead," had anything at all to say to modernity. If earlier mainline liberals had sought to accommodate modernity, some of their successors embraced modernity completely; whereas the church was once expected to set the standards for the culture, now the culture set the standards for the church.

In truth, what the theological radicals did in the 1960s was not all that different from what conservative conformists had done in the 1950s. The culture had set the standards for the conservative churches in the 1950s, too. In the 1960s, the radicals had the honesty to admit culture's role in shaping the content of religion and the courage to rebel against the superficiality of religion's cultural accommodations. Yet the embrace of the 1960s ethic of change was so complete that the churches were often left as empty vessels, with little to assert that was independent of the culture. "The sixties cliché that 'change is the only constant' got thrown around rather thoughtlessly," Sweet wrote. He adds that "if the cliché is true, then change itself changes, there is no stable ground anywhere, and those who seek relevance face defeat from the start."

This, of course, is what the early fundamentalist critics of Christian liberalism had predicted all along—that modernity was a virus that would, if allowed inside the Christian churches, ultimately sap them of all content. In Sweet's view, the evangelical churches became increasingly important in the 1970s and 1980s because they remained bold enough to continue asserting the basic truths of Christianity at a time when the mainline churches "often seemed more dogmatic about doubt than about faith." (Richard John Neuhaus argues that Roman Catholicism shared these advantages since it preserved itself from many of the ravages of modernity by being so late in opening itself up to the modern world.) "When many churches found the going hard, those who still saw the face of God had a tremendous appeal," Sweet wrote. The evangelicals had an advantage in a time of crisis: They could assert, as Billy Graham did, "I know where I've come from, I know why I'm here, and I know where I'm going."

The religious revival of the late 1960s and early 1970s was not solely an evangelical affair. Some who had left the strict, conservative churches in the early 1960s returned to religion by way of the liberal churches, forging personal compromises between the religiosity of their youth and the liberalism of their teens and twenties. Among Roman Catholics, church attendance had plummeted in the 1960s; the decline leveled off and attendance eventually began to creep back up in the 1970s. Some of the mainline churches also began to stem their decline, occasionally in surprising ways: In the Episcopal Church, for example, black membership grew rapidly.

Nonetheless, evangelical Protestantism was the greatest beneficiary of the religious awakening, and the evangelical style influenced the entire Christian religious spectrum. Even within the Catholic Church, a new Pentecostal movement whose approach resembled Protestant revivalism enjoyed rapid growth. Within the traditionally liberal mainline Protestant denominations, many local churches took on an evangelical coloration.

The religious revival did not automatically move in a politically conservative direction. Some Christians sought to integrate the radical lessons of the 1960s into orthodox religious faith. A thriving example of this philosophical marriage is the Sojourners Fellowship in Washington, D.C., which combines a deep evangelical Christian faith with pacifist and radical politics. The Catholic Worker movement drew thousands of new supporters by offering a similar mix of religious and political challenge.

But the rebellion against modernity and the attempt to assert religious and ethical certainty were more likely to turn right. An especially militant brand of the new evangelical politics took root in Kanawha County, West Virginia, in the mid-1970s when parents rebelled against school textbooks they saw as obscene and mocking of their values. Many liberals saw the protestors as a group of bigots demanding censorship. But supporters of the rebellion drew on language popularized by the New Left and Black Power movements. Like their leftist forerunners, the rebels of Kanawha County saw themselves battling distant and powerful interests, the educational and cultural establishments based in New York City and Washington, D.C.

"The people of Kanawha County saw the struggle as a question of community self-determination and cultural integrity," said Robert J. Hoy, a spokesman for New Right causes. Hoy said the battle involved "basic questions of power and cultural destiny." Alice Moore, the leader of the protests, used similar language. "What is at issue here, what we are fighting for," she said, "is simply who is going to have control over the schools—the parents, the taxpayers, and the people who live here, or the educational specialists, the administrators, the people from other places who have been trying to tell us what is best for our children." She added, in the sort of phrase Tom Hayden might have used in his community-organizing days, "We think we are competent to make those decisions for ourselves." It was an argument, in the New Left's famous phrase, for controlling the decisions that affect your own life. Thus did even the Religious Right learn from the 1960s; thus did the leftist and rightist rebellions against liberalism elide into each other. One left-of-center Protestant who expressed sympathy for the West Virginia protestors was Harvey Cox, who responded positively to the language of self-determination. Cox subsequently noted that just as black Americans sought recognition for their culture, so did "rednecks" begin to use that term of opprobrium as a badge of pride, a symbol of their rebellion against the learned folks in the big cities. After years of political quiescence, the fundamentalists were on the move.

But the Kanawha rebellion symbolized another kind of interaction between sixties culture and the Religious Right. The 1960s and early 1970s transformed the mass media—most importantly television —in ways that the upholders of traditional values found objectionable. In the 1950s, television adhered to a strict (and in the eyes of its critics, stultifying) moral code. Programs such as "The Adventures of Ozzie & Harriet" and "Leave It to Beaver" celebrated domesticity and 1950s "traditional values." The moral lessons of such programs were thoroughly consistent with the preachings of the conservative churches. In the 1960s, television slowly became more daring, partly in response to the tastes of the baby boom, which began to assert its influence on the culture. Those tastes increasingly ran to the countercultural. James Hitchcock, a conservative historian, captured the anger of religious conservatives in a critique of the influence of "secular humanism" on the media. "Put simply," Hitchcock wrote, "those who controlled the media realized that there was a substantial audience which had broken with traditional moral values and wanted entertainment which ventured into forbidden territory in hitherto forbidden ways." As a result, he said, "traditional moral values were ridiculed, assaulted, and ground into dust." An increasingly secular audience "wanted to experience the thrill of the forbidden" even as it "sought confirmation that its own break with the past was justified."

The rise of the televised church in the 1970s was one response to the evangelicals' sense that their values had been closed out of mainstream media in the 1960s. Like so much in contemporary conservatism, the Religious Right's attack on the media betrayed a certain nostalgia for the ordered world of the 1950s. In its search for entertainment that was morally acceptable, Pat Robertson's Christian Broadcasting Network became a showcase for the revival of television shows from the 1950s, including "Leave It to Beaver."

In light of the growth experienced by the evangelical and fundamentalist movements through the 1970s, a political reassertion by conservative Protestantism was inevitable. But the insurgency need never have been as loud, as widespread, or as right wing as it proved to be. The sparks that inflamed the Religious Right came from the judiciary —specifically, the Supreme Court's decisions on issues such as school prayer, abortion, pornography, and government aid to religious schools. *The paradox of the Religious Right is that it became an important factor in American politics primarily because of liberal victories.* "It is the great successes of secular and liberal forces, principally operating through the specific agency of the courts, that has in large measure created the issues on which the Fundamentalists have managed to achieve what influence they have," wrote the sociologist Nathan Glazer. "They may be on the offensive, but it is, if I may use the phrase, a 'defensive offensive,' meant to get us back to, at worst, the 1950s, and even that is beyond the hopes, or I would think the power, of Fundamentalist faith."

Jerry Falwell himself wrote in his autobiography that he began changing his mind about the involvement of preachers in politics on January 23, 1973, the day the Supreme Court issued the *Roe* v. *Wade* decision that struck down the nation's abortion laws. If advocates of the Social Gospel had spoken of "social sin," Falwell began to speak of "national sin." A new Prohibitionist movement was about to be born. And this time, conservative Protestant preachers and Catholic bishops would frequently find themselves on the same side. In light of fundamentalist-Catholic history, it is truly remarkable that Falwell declared that it was the willingness of the Catholic bishops to speak out, as he put it, "courageously" on abortion that inspired his decision to enter politics himself.

IV

The first evangelical breakthrough in American politics since Prohibition was not Jerry Falwell's movement, however, but Jimmy Carter's election. As we have seen, Carter won in significant part because he was able to win back Southern constituencies that had been moving Republican since the 1950s, and many of Carter's Southern votes came from his fellow Baptists and from the overlapping groups of fundamentalists and evangelicals. Carter was thus the first (and through 1988, the only) Democrat after Harry Truman to carry a clear majority among Southern Baptists. In the nation's ninety-six most heavily Baptist counties, Carter won 58 percent of the vote, more than doubling George McGovern's 1972 tally.

Carter's victory was as important to the self-esteem of evangelicals and fundamentalists as John Kennedy's victory had been for Catholics. The Carter campaign played explicitly on the evangelical quest for legitimacy. An advertisement in the evangelical magazine *Christianity Today* ran under the headline "Does a Dedicated Evangelical Belong in the White House?" For many evangelicals, the idea that one of their own had outplotted and outorganized the entire secular establishment was a source of considerable satisfaction.

Carter demonstrated the personal and intellectual self-confidence of a new generation of evangelicals. By speaking so openly about his religious beliefs, Carter made clear that his was a serious and rigorous faith, something more than the superficial religion described and condemned by Will Herberg. Though some intellectuals—notably Arthur Schlesinger, Jr., and Garry Wills—found Carter's understanding of theology shallow, his theological reading was certainly broad. He was devoted to the thinking of Reinhold Niebuhr, the liberal Protestant theologian who was a hero to many liberals, notably Schlesinger himself. Carter's strong espousal of civil rights, equal rights for women, and the separation of church and state challenged the stereotypes of "born-again" Christians that had been formed in sophisticated urban America.

Yet Carter's experience during the 1976 campaign and after also suggested that there was a cultural chasm between the evangelicals and a large part of America. It was Carter's religious experiences that contributed most to what Hamilton Jordan, his top aide, called the "weirdo factor." As Jules Witcover put it in his shrewd chronicle of the 1976 campaign: "It was not something specific, but rather a general uneasiness about this rather strange man who had strode boldly onto the political landscape, speaking unabashedly about love and compassion and being influenced in his conduct of public office by God's word and guidance." Carter's highly public religiosity was a particular source of concern for American Jews, who were understandably worried whenever public institutions and organized Christianity became too intimately involved with each other. He also made many urban Catholics uncomfortable. And many Americans of all faiths were simply not as deeply grounded in religious language as Carter was. Thus, when Carter confessed to *Playboy* magazine that "I've looked on a lot of women with lust, I've committed adultery in my heart many times," a nation guffawed. It did Carter little good that he was simply paraphrasing one of Jesus' better-known injunctions on sexuality. Carter's religiosity and his musings about lust were especially strange to the mediators of American culture. Peter Clecak noted that "critics and journalists tried to explain Jimmy Carter's born-again experience to each other as if it were as alien to American culture as a Balinese cockfight." When such cultural critics examined the Christian revival, Clecak noted, they did so with "an almost anthropological detachment."

Understanding Carter's experience is central to understanding both the extent and the limits of the evangelical revival. The United States was *not* becoming a secular nation as fast as many intellectuals had predicted--that is what the rise of the evangelicals demonstrated. But neither had the United States escaped secularization or a liberalization of its values. That is why Jimmy Carter's religiosity was viewed by so many as "weird." Yes, polls showed that the United States was an unusually religious nation. Among Western nations, only the Irish matched the Americans in the proportion of their numbers who believed in God, prayed regularly, and looked forward to life after death. Yet Americans were also uniquely uneasy with expressions of religion in the public realm. As Richard John Neuhaus observed, Americans did not want their "public square" to be naked, devoid of any spiritual meaning. But they were reluctant to see the public square dominated by religion, and they especially did not want to see it controlled by any one faith. On balance, Americans agreed with Eisenhower that their country needed to be guided by a "deeply felt religious belief." But they also agreed with Eisenhower in not wanting that "belief" to be defined in too much detail. Similarly, Americans wanted high moral values enshrined in their government. But they were not always happy to see those values enforced too stringently. There was much truth to the line in the old folk song that went, "They pray for Prohibition, but then they vote for Gin." Americans were profoundly Niebuhrian in understanding that human beings would often fall short of the high ideals they might publicly proclaim.

Carter himself probably understood this better than any recent politician. He struggled hard to show that while he was a man of deep religious conviction, he was not seeking to impose his religious views on the nation. That was the message he tried to convey, imperfectly as it turned out, in the *Playboy* interview. In the 1976 presidential campaign, Carter succeeded and gained from religiosity without losing too much. But by 1980, he was alienating voters on both sides of the religious divide. Many of his evangelical brethren, especially the most conservative among them, felt sold out by Carter. To them, as Richard Neuhaus put it, Carter "seemed pathetically eager to prove that his faith did not make him a redneck reactionary." This view is unfair to Carter, but he gave his religious opponents concrete issues to use in backing up their subjective view of him. Carter opposed a constitutional amendment to restore prayer to public schools and opposed tax credits for parochial schools. On both issues, he was simply clinging to the old Baptist belief in separatism. But the fundamentalist and evangelical right no longer shared that position.

Yet Carter also made the sophisticated and the secular, both Christian and non-Christian, uncomfortable. Early in his presidency, Carter met with leaders of the Southern Baptist Convention at the White House and urged his denomination to expand its missionary work. To Carter's critics, as historian Leo P. Ribuffo noted, the President seemed to be using the White House to support a narrow denominational cause. The protests were loud.

No issue illustrated Carter's dilemma better than abortion, as we have seen. Like the liberals, Carter believed in upholding the Supreme Court's decision legalizing abortion. But Carter himself was personally opposed to abortion and sided with the conservatives in opposing government financing of abortions for poor women. Carter's position displeased both sides.

Carter did not lose the presidency in 1980 because of religious issues. The hostages in Iran and high interest rates were much more important. But Carter was caught in a religious vise, squeezed between his evangelical coreligionists and the Catholics and Jews who were usually the most loyal supporters of his party. Carter lost substantial ground on both sides. White born-again Christians who had given Carter at least half their ballots in 1976 went nearly two to one for Ronald Reagan in 1980. In 1976, Carter had won 64 percent of the Jewish vote and 54 percent of the Catholic vote in 1976. In 1980, he got just 45 percent of the Jewish vote and 40 percent of the Catholic vote—the worst showing by a Democrat in either group since 1924.

In the end, the Religious Right might never have emerged if Jimmy Carter's success had not prepared the ground for the evangelicals' reentry into national politics. Carter's failure, in turn, allowed the Religious Right to emerge as Evangelicalism's loudest voice.

V

If Jerry Falwell began moving toward political action in 1973 because of the *Roe* decision on abortion, an influential group of conservatives were ready to encourage him. Falwell arrived on the scene at precisely the point when conservative political operatives were searching for new political constituencies and new ways to move them.

The New Right had learned this lesson well from Richard Nixon himself, who had used "social issue" politics so effectively against George McGovern. "Acid, amnesty, and abortion" became a symbolic battle cry that was, in one form or another, to dominate Republican politics for many years.

Although Nixon's collapse proved to be only a temporary setback for the conservative cause, it sent the *National Review* conservatives into crisis. Nixon's fall was especially disheartening to William F. Buckley, Jr., who had encouraged conservatives to embrace Nixon in 1968. In the *National Review* circle, the angriest man of all was William A. Rusher, the magazine's publisher, who may have been an Eisenhower Republican but had never shared Buckley's warm feelings about Nixon. In Rusher's view, Nixon finished off the Republican Party. Rusher was less worried about Watergate than about Nixon's apostasy on Soviet and Chinese policy and his liberal initiatives in domestic policy. If Watergate demonstrated Nixon's alleged character flaws for the broader public, Nixon's faithlessness to the conservative agenda was the character flaw that most bothered Rusher. In Rusher's view, conservatives needed to abandon the Republican Party and form a new party based on an alliance between well-to-do Republican conservatives and the working class, mainly Democratic, supporters of George Wallace. Buckley was as skeptical of Rusher's project as he was of Wallace and Wallace's populism. But both Buckley and Rusher agreed on the identity of the man they would like to see lead a conservative revival, either inside or outside the Republican Party. Their choice was Ronald Reagan.

But by the mid-1970s, the *National Review* circle no longer defined conservative politics to the extent that it had in the early 1960s. The dominance of the old fusionist conservatism of *National Review* was being challenged by group of activists who self-consciously proclaimed themselves a "New Right." The New Right was less solicitous of intellectuals than the *National Review* conservatives and much more taken with George Wallace–style "populism."

The relations between the New Right and the Old Right affiliated with *National Review* were complicated and often rocky. Rusher himself shared the New Right's political analysis and cooperated with elements of the Wallace campaign, to Buckley's discomfort. As for Buckley himself, some New Right leaders continued to speak of him with respect, but others, notably Kevin Phillips, spoke of him as a has-been or worse. For Phillips, Buckley was guilty of "abandoning Middle America to load up his yacht with vintage wines and sail across the Atlantic." Once an anti-Establishment backer of Joe McCarthy, Phillips said, Buckley now "primed his magazine with cast-off Hapsburg royalty, Englishmen who part their names in the middle, and others calculated to put real lace on Buckley's Celtic curtains." The *National Review* published a critique of Phillips under the headline "To the Nashville Station," drawing on Edmund Wilson's reference to Lenin and the Finland Station. The magazine accused Phillips of "country and Western Marxism," which amused Phillips, who had no qualms about his hard-edged class analysis. Buckley himself dismissed Phillips as a philistine and "an eccentric theorist writing orotund stuff."

Class resentment clearly played a key role in New Right politics and its founders. They were eager to identify with George Wallace and his followers among both the working class and the unvarnished new rich. Among the key figures was Richard Viguerie, a onetime direct-mail fund-raiser for Young Americans for Freedom who was hired by George Wallace to handle his mail solicitations. "Compared to a William Buckley or Jeffrey Hart," wrote Paul Gottfried and Thomas Fleming, two conservative historians, "Viguerie resembles a car salesman attending, uninvited, a formal dinner." Among Viguerie's direct-mail clients and allies was Paul Weyrich, a former congressional staffer who helped found two new conservative institutions in the early 1970s. The Committee for the Survival of a Free Congress was the forerunner to the dozens of conservative political action committees that would proliferate in the 1970s. The Free Congress operation was to spin off dozens of conservative committees and institutes, all headquartered in the same Capitol Hill brownstone. Weyrich's other creation was the Heritage Foundation, which he set up with Ed Feulner, another Capitol Hill veteran. Heritage was to be a militant think tank that would feed ideas directly to the conservative movement and to its allies in Congress. Weyrich and Fuelner saw their organization as an alternative to the American Enterprise Institute, a conservative research institute that was a trifle too solicitous to the views of liberals and not in the thick of the congressional and electoral trench war that Weyrich and Fuelner wanted to fight. Heritage wanted political victory *now!* Weyrich saw little point in the niceties of academic debate, since he took the warfare analogy to heart. "It may not be with bullets," he was once quoted by Viguerie as saying, "and it may not be with rockets and missiles, but it is a war nevertheless. It is a war of ideology, it's a war of ideas, and it's a war about our way of life. And it has to be fought with the same intensity, I think, and dedication as you would fight a shooting war."

Clearly, the stylistic differences between *National Review* and the

New Right were profound, and they betrayed a fundamental difference in emphasis between the two schools of conservatism. For *National Review* conservatives, the centerpiece of postwar conservatism had been anticommunism. Despite *National Review*'s traditionalism, it was still more comfortable with libertarian antigovernment themes than with the New Right's "populism." Following their hero George Wallace, the New Rightists were much more prepared than the older conservatives to use government for their own ends. Kevin Phillips noted that the New Right, while sharing with the Old Right a sympathy for a strong military and a suspicion of government, believed that the primary political questions were "domestic social issues." What he really had in mind were domestic social *resentments*. He listed these as "public anger over busing, welfare spending, environmental extremism, soft criminology, media bias and power, warped education, twisted textbooks, racial quotas, various guidelines and an ever-expanding bureaucracy." It is no accident that Phillips's list seemed to define the difference between Barry Goldwater and George Wallace.

Weyrich never disguised the fact that his attraction to Jerry Falwell was initially based on calculation and strategy. Though Weyrich himself was a devout Christian, he viewed Falwell more in Machiavellian than in Christian terms. "The New Right is looking for issues that people care about," Weyrich said. "Social issues, at least for the present, fit the bill." The Moral Majority was born out of a series of meetings among Falwell, Viguerie, Howard Phillips, another early New Right leader, and others. Falwell credits Weyrich with coming up with the name, though Howard Phillips appears to have used it first. "Jerry, there is in America a moral majority that agrees about the basic issues," Weyrich told Falwell in 1979. "But they aren't organized. They don't have a platform. The media ignore them. Somebody's got to get that moral majority together."

For the New Right, religious issues offered an opportunity to expand the movement's social-issue repertoire. Abortion had emerged first during the Nixon campaign in 1972. After the 1973 Supreme Court decision, all the pressure on the issue moved right, since the *Roe* v. *Wade* decision gave liberals what they thought was the decisive victory; now it was the conservatives who had to organize against the status quo.

The Falwell movement also allowed the New Right to speak more effectively on a host of other issues. Where George Wallace's attacks on the educational establishment could not help but smack of racism, the Religious Right's approach emphasized not race but values—the right of parents to influence the content of their children's education, the right of schoolchildren to recite prayers. The Moral Majority was also a natural complement to the antifeminist movement. Support for Phyllis Schlafly's campaign against the Equal Rights Amendment was especially strong among women with conservative religious commitments. With Schlafly concentrating her efforts in states where the ERA was up for ratification, the Moral Majority helped give her sympathizers elsewhere an alternative organizational voice.

The Moral Majority gave bite to the political approach that F. Clifton White had proposed to Barry Goldwater when he made his "Choice" documentary on declining American values. White's film spoke to a generalized unease that many Americans felt about the country's moral direction. But in 1964, those Americans were unorganized, and the evangelicals and fundamentalists had still not achieved their political breakthrough. Falwell's activities gave Weyrich and his allies a chance to turn vague discontent into a real lever of political power. And with the growth of the evangelical and fundamentalist churches, such a movement had more political potential than ever.

It is a sign of the distance between the Old and New Right that in 1980, Ronald Reagan was not the first choice of many of the conservatives who gathered around Viguerie and Weyrich. For them, Reagan was a throwback to the Goldwater campaign, a champion of the Buckleyite past rather than the populist future. The New Right's alternative candidates were Rep. Phil Crane of Illinois and former Treasury secretary John Connally. The New Right's attraction to Connally was particularly revealing in light of Connally's highly interventionist and protectionist economic policies, which were anathema to the economic conservatives. Kevin Phillips made much of this difference, noting that *nationalism* was far more important to the New Right than *laissez-faire* purity. The distinction between Buckley and the New Right also emerged in the battle over the Panama Canal treaties. The New Right opposed treaties on nationalist grounds. The Canal was *American*—end of argument. Buckley and Henry Kissinger favored the treaties, seeing the question of who controlled the Canal as being of little strategic importance. What mattered was maintaining American popularity and strength in a Latin America where the main enemy was Cuba and its Soviet sponsors. Turning the Canal over to Panama would strengthen America's image and its hand on more important issues. The New Right understood the visceral appeal of nationalism to the conservative constituency and so did Ronald Reagan, who broke with his friend Bill Buckley and opposed the treaties, to his great political benefit.

In the Republican primaries, Reagan proved to be far more in touch with the conservative base than the New Right's leaders. Not only did they overestimate the political potential of figures such as Connally and Crane; they also underestimated how much the conservative base inside the Republican Party was still defined by Goldwaterism—by the older traditions of the right. For all the talk of a new populist conservatism that would encompass working-class voters, the fact remained that most of those voters still regarded themselves as *Democrats*. They were not voting in Republican primaries. To be sure, Reagan ran extremely well in the primaries against Gerald Ford and George Bush among working-class Republicans. But Reagan could not have won with working-class Republicans alone. The base for Republican conservatism was still largely middle and upper-middle class (something George Bush would remember in 1988). Reagan's base was among the businessmen and the accountants, the car dealers and the contractors, the dentists and the physicians, who had rallied to Cliff White's Goldwater organization in 1964.

Once Reagan's nomination was assured, the New Right joined the crusade, and Jerry Falwell became their most visible spokesman. The nation was treated to a wave of news reports about the entirely "new" and alarming political phenomenon that was Moral Majoritarianism. When the exit polls showed that white born-again Christians had provided Reagan with a two-to-one margin, Falwell was credited by some with having "elected" Ronald Reagan. Such claims did not come only from the Religious Right's friends. Among those who said the Moral Majority and its supporters had elected Reagan was Louis Harris, a liberal who had been John Kennedy's polltaker.

The populism of the Religious Right made the conservatives affiliated with *National Review* uncomfortable. Russell Kirk, for one, detested the very idea of a "populist conservatism," calling populism "the ignorant democratic conservatism of the masses." But the *National Review* conservatives could put their doubts aside because they understood the political potential of the Religious Right and its electoral sympathizers. Here, at last, was the mass constituency that traditionalist conservatism had lacked. In the 1950s, traditionalism seemed to be a hopelessly antiquated creed, an antidemocratic doctrine supported by a handful of marginal conservative intellectuals. It turned out that traditionalism had a genuine base among those who looked to the Bible rather than Edmund Burke for authority.

Thus, Kirk managed to embrace those whom others labeled "conservative populists" by renaming them "popular conservatives." The first characteristic of the popular conservatives, Kirk said, was that "they take a religious view of the human condition" and "believe in a moral order of more than human contrivance." The popular conservatives, he said, "grow alarmed at increasing secularization of American society, both through the agency of the state and through commercialized sensationalism." This is a fair description of what the evangelical right believed. It was also very much what Kirk himself had proclaimed in the 1950s.

One of the most unlikely defenders of the Moral Majority was the devoutly Roman Catholic Buckley. Yet the author of *God and Man at Yale* was ready to take the side of the God-fearing, especially when the opposition to them came from his alma mater. Thus, Buckley scored Yale president A. Bartlett Giamatti, whom he admired, for an address in the early 1980s in which Giamatti warned incoming Yale freshmen of the dangers posed by the Moral Majority. "To be lectured against the perils of the Moral Majority on entering Yale," Buckley wrote, "is on the order of being lectured on the danger of bedbugs on entering a brothel."

For conservative evangelicals and fundamentalists, the elections of 1976 and 1980 created a sense of triumph. The first had allowed evangelicals to rejoin the political mainstream. The second confirmed their power. Even if much of the attention the Religious Right received in the media was negative, the important fact was that an America that had scorned and ridiculed fundamentalism since the Scopes trial once again had to take it seriously. Now, fundamentalist Protestantism would have a voice in the White House. The movement had not died with William Jennings Bryan. Ronald Reagan had picked up Bryan's mantle, while rejecting the Great Commoner's commitment to economic equality.

Yet in retrospect, it is clear that the Religious Right was never as powerful as it claimed to be, or as its liberal critics feared. "The truth is that Falwell had for months made fools of the press—it was purely and simply a case of the country boy taking the city sophisticates for a ride," wrote University of Virginia sociologist Jeffrey K. Hadden. Not all journalists fell into the trap. But many who wrote about the Religious Right, especially liberals who sounded alarms, did exaggerate its influence.

For example, the notion that the Moral Majority had "elected" Ronald Reagan is almost certainly wrong. The evidence suggests strongly that Reagan would have won with or without the Moral Majority. According to the *New York Times*/CBS News poll surveying over 12,000 voters after they had cast their ballots in 1980, "born-again white Protestants" accounted for 17 percent of the electorate. Reagan carried this group over Carter 61 percent to 34 percent. *Even if Carter had defeated Reagan by the same 61 to 34 percent among born-again white Protestants, Reagan would still have won.* And this analysis makes every effort to *exaggerate* rather than underestimate the Moral Majority's influence. For example, it assumes that *all* born-again white Protestants were influenced by the Moral Majority, which was certainly not the case, since polls showed that substantial numbers of born-again white Protestants actually disagreed with the Moral Majority on many issues.

In fact, Ronald Reagan did not do nearly as well among the evangelicals and fundamentalists in 1980 as Richard Nixon had in 1972. Although hard evidence on the evangelical vote is hard to come by before 1976, Albert J. Menendez, a careful student of religious voting, estimated that Richard Nixon defeated George McGovern among evangelicals and fundamentalists by a margin of 13 million to 3 million —a percentage for Nixon of about 80 percent. In the nation's ninety-six most heavily Baptist counties, Menendez found that Nixon won about 75 percent of the vote, compared to just under 60 percent for Reagan in 1980.

What happened in 1980, then, was not a Republican breakthrough but a ratification of earlier trends toward the Republicans that had been interrupted by Jimmy Carter in 1976. White evangelicals and fundamentalists had begun backing Republicans long before anyone outside of Lynchburg, Virginia, had heard of Jerry Falwell. These shifts did not occur because a group of preachers told their followers to abandon the party of Roosevelt. Nor did Republican politicians win the evangelical vote on the basis of conservative religious themes alone. Most of the evangelical conservatives were white Southerners *who began voting against the Democrats because of civil rights.* Many of them did so when not a campaign word was spoken about faith or morals. Even in his 1964 landslide victory, Lyndon Johnson could not manage a majority in the nation's most heavily Baptist counties. Johnson's share of the Baptist vote was 13 percentage points *lower* than his share in the nation as a whole. Barry Goldwater thus did at least as much as Jerry Falwell to promote the political conversion of evangelicals.

But if the Moral Majority's influence was exaggerated, its achievement was still important. Since Reagan was running against an evangelical Protestant who, like many evangelicals, was from the South, it was inevitable that Reagan would do less well than a Richard Nixon running against a George McGovern. In the eyes of the Religious Right's supporters (and of more critical analysts such as Lou Harris), the crucial fact about 1980 was not Reagan's overall percentage among the born-agains but the *gains* he posted in their ranks on Gerald Ford's 1976 vote. The swing away from Carter between 1976 and 1980 was, indeed, much greater among fundamentalists and evangelicals than it was in the rest of the country. Menendez estimates that in the heavily Baptist counties, Carter ran eighteen percentage points behind his 1976 showing; in the nation as a whole, Carter ran only ten behind his 1980 performance. There is also evidence that the Religious Right increased voter registration and turnout among evangelicals and fundamentalists, to Reagan's advantage.

The Moral Majority also received considerable credit for the Republicans' success in winning control of the Senate for the first time since the 1952 elections. Here is where the Religious Right could legitimately claim a major impact. Its power loomed especially large in the cases of the most unlikely Republican triumphs, notably those of Senators Don Nickles in Oklahoma and Jeremiah Denton in Alabama. Both states were heavily Baptist. Both candidates had actively courted the Religious Right. And the most remarkable fact of all, as Kevin Phillips noted, was that *both men were Roman Catholics.* Just twenty years before, it would have been inconceivable that two Catholic Republicans would be sent to the Senate from the South; all the more inconceivable that they would be sent there on an avalanche of conservative evangelical and fundamentalist ballots. Thus did the Moral Majority help the nation overcome old denominational prejudices in the interest of a new conservative politics.

Haley Barbour, a former Reagan-administration official and a Republican national committeeman from Mississippi, believes that the Religious Right's main contribution to his party was below the presidential level. Since World War II, he says, Southern evangelicals did move steadily toward the Republican Party in presidential elections, but continued to vote Democratic for lower offices. "After 1980, they not only voted for Republican presidential candidates, but *began thinking of themselves as Republicans,*" Barbour said. "Before, if they didn't know either candidate in a race, they'd vote for the Democrat. Now, if they don't know either candidate, they usually vote for the Republican."

What is important about the Religious Right, then, is not that it created new political facts, but that it reinforced trends that had begun long ago because of the reaction of conservative Southern whites to civil rights. In the process, the Religious Right transformed both the Republican Party and the conservative movement. At least as late as 1976, it was possible for a candidate with moderate—which is to say nonconservative—views on social issues to win the Republican nomination. By 1980, that had become virtually impossible. As late as 1976, conservatism was largely defined by the issues of anticommunism and limited government. By the 1980s, conservatism was defined more and more by issues such as abortion, pornography, prayer in schools, and the content of elementary-school teaching. In the past, religious conservatives were content with an Eisenhower-style piety devoid of much content. By the 1980s, arguments among Republicans had taken on a heavy theological content. Not only did George Bush consider it prudent to change his position on abortion, he also felt a need to suggest that he had gone through a profound religious experience not unlike Jimmy Carter's. In Republican politics, it was no longer "weird" to be born-again; it was almost essential.

VI

The Religious Right gained even more attention during the 1984 campaign and on election day when it seemed to deliver more to Reagan than ever. The *Times*/CBS News poll showed white fundamentalist and evangelical Christians backing Reagan 78 percent to 22 percent over Walter Mondale. Little notice was paid to the fact that this margin was not far from Reagan's 72 to 27 percent lead over Mondale among all white Protestants. Reagan's share of the evangelical vote in 1984 was no greater than Richard Nixon's had been in 1972 —the last time the Democrats had nominated a Northern liberal. Nonetheless, the highly visible leaders of the Religious Right continued to get and accept credit for transforming American politics. Getting credit is a luxury that accrues to those who find themselves on the winning side.

The Religious Right could take considerable satisfaction at the extent to which its goals and values were being taken seriously at the highest levels of government. To the guffawing of liberals, Attorney General Edwin Meese did wage war on pornography—and his Justice Department stepped up prosecutions in obscenity cases. Congress passed legislation to authorize federal spending to promote chastity as a form of birth control. The bill passed with the support of Sen. Edward M. Kennedy, who proved that his faith in government's ability to improve things extended across a broad area. Congress also enacted the "equal access" act, to allow religious clubs to meet on public-school property. Some liberals enthusiastically embraced the proposal, agreeing with Rep. Barney Frank that the bill expanded the civil liberties not just of religious students but of followers of all dissenting creeds.

At the National Endowment for the Humanities, William J. Bennett shifted monies from experimental and leftist projects toward more conventional and conservative undertakings. As secretary of education, Bennett proclaimed a "back to basics" philosophy in elementary education and a "back to the classics" philosophy in higher education. Both themes articulated well with the Religious Right's criticism of exotic influences on the nation's curricula. If a onetime teacher at Harvard could make this cause his own, then surely something was shifting in the culture. Bennett's position was representative of a powerful current that ran through the neoconservative movement. Although the neoconservatives were as culturally distant from the people in the pews of most evangelical churches as liberals were, they spoke with great sympathy for religion and for the values that religion fostered. And even if Ronald Reagan did not get abortion outlawed or prayer returned to the classroom, he spoke out repeatedly on behalf of these causes, giving them a legitimacy they had never before enjoyed.

In the two areas where liberal dominance had most aggravated the Religious Right, in the courts and in the media, the causes espoused by the Religious Right made some noticeable progress. Slowly but steadily, Ronald Reagan was carrying out a judicial revolution, transforming the majority on the Supreme Court and stocking the lower levels of the federal judiciary with conservatives. Over time, the seeds planted by Reagan would flower into court victories for the Religious Right's causes.

The media was also undergoing considerable change—even if, as we have seen, some of the changes were caused more by the aging of the baby boomers than by anything that was happening in politics. The rise of cable television brought MTV into many homes, but it also eased the way for the creation of new broadcast outlets, including those run by the Religious Right and its allies. Cable television ate away at the dominance of the three big networks and gave America's subcultures more opportunity to make their voices heard. Even network programming was changing, at least a little. If much on television remained offensive to the Religious Right, some of the most popular programs seemed to ratify conservative values. Writing about "The Cosby Show," "Family Ties," and "Cheers," conservative scholar Michael Novak noted "the remarkable treatment of classic family values." The humor on these programs, he said, "is directed against the sorts of values that were common in the 1960s and 1970s. . . . Those with traditional values could get the feeling—at least temporarily—of being in on the jokes rather than being the butt of them."

In a sense, the nation had taken some large steps back toward the 1950s. The Reagan administration was giving conservative religion a great deal of public honor—and unlike Jimmy Carter, who had to worry about the Democratic Party's liberal base, Ronald Reagan could do so without paying much political cost. Yet Reagan, like Eisenhower before him, was careful not to give offense to the irreligious. Reagan offered this brilliantly balanced sentiment to an ecumenical prayer breakfast: "Our government needs the church because those humble enough to admit they are sinners can bring to democracy the tolerance it requires in order to survive." In one sentence, Reagan placated both the Religious Right and those who feared that it would promote intolerance. For his part, Bennett proclaimed that the Founding Fathers had "envisioned a Federal government neutral between religions in particular, but sympathetic with religion in general." It was a far more eloquent formulation than Eisenhower's expression of fealty to a religion about whose content he did not care. But the sentiments expressed by Bennett and Eisenhower were actually quite similar.

For some on the Religious Right, this was not enough. Preachers such as Pat Robertson often spoke as if the liberals had continued to run the country all through the Reagan years. "The greatness of America is departing us," Robertson proclaimed. The "secular humanists" were forcing textbooks onto "impressionable young children" that "just do away with God and theism entirely." The thrust of such textbooks was "toward radical lifestyles." Children, Robertson declared, were "being subjected to psychological manipulation which moves them away from their Judeo-Christian mind-set and moves them into a humanistic mould and from the humanistic mould into the socialist worldview and ultimately into the Communist International." Where in the world had Ronald Reagan and George Bush been while all these terrible things were happening?

Robertson's views can easily be dismissed as cranky, but underlying his anxieties and those of his followers was an accurate realization that for all the much-touted strength of the Religious Right, the movement's successes during the 1980s were actually quite modest. Reagan proved himself to be very much a man of the Old Right, just as some of the New Right leaders had feared. Although Reagan could speak as movingly about traditional values as he spoke about everything else, his priorities were elsewhere: in cuts in domestic programs, in reductions in marginal tax rates, and in large increases in military spending to counter the Soviet threat. In the meantime, abortions continued, women kept flooding the workplace—and not a word of prayer was recited in the schools to petition the Almighty to turn these trends around.

Reagan himself, moreover, seemed to embody the broader society's ambivalence in the battle between modernity and traditionalism; he seemed very much the sort of person who could pray for Prohibition and vote for Gin. He was the nation's first divorced president. He rarely attended church. He had been formed by Hollywood and demonstrated enormous personal tolerance for "alternative" lifestyles. As one Republican put it, young voters who liked Reagan but were liberal on the social issues always sensed that Reagan was winking at them when he tossed a rhetorical bone to the Religious Right. How serious could a man of his experience and background really be about Jerry Falwell's agenda?

Indeed, the 1980s could hardly be seen as a time when the nation embraced the old Protestant virtues of thrift, self-denial, and self-discipline. The Republican Party abandoned dour, if "responsible," fiscal policies for deficit spending. The dominant ethos of the age seemed to be acquisitive, materialistic, self-indulgent. The clichés of the 1980s were Madonna's "Material Girl," insider trading, MTV, MBAs, BMWs, yuppies. The traditionalists who streamed to evangelical churches could no more identify with these symbols than they could with the Rolling Stones, LSD, or the yippies of the 1960s.

If the secular world was still a bastion of sin, the Religious Right faced problems in its own ranks. A series of religious broadcasters, notably Jim and Tammy Bakker, were discredited in scandals involving sex and money. For some on the Religious Right, history was repeating itself as even more farcical than ever. The fundamentalist cause had been hurt before by scandals involving promiscuous and avaricious preachers. It was not really so shocking that those who preached the most about sin were often especially familiar with it themselves. But never before had television existed first to bring the preachers' words and faces into millions of living rooms and then to spread word of their obloquy just as widely. If the Religious Right had risen to influence through the power of television, it was in danger of being consumed by that merciless medium. New television preachers arose to give comfort to a confused flock. But into the 1990s, the Religious Right was still trying to heal its wounds.

The problems faced by the Religious Right went deeper than the troubles faced by a few preachers. The religious and social conservatives had always been torn by fundamental differences between the "maximalist" demands of their core constituencies and the "minimalist" demands of their sympathizers. The Religious Right arose largely in reaction to liberal triumphs and to a sense that secular society was increasingly intolerant of those who brought their religious views to the public arena. The goal of many who sympathized with the social and religious conservatives was not to have conservative religious values dominate government policy, but simply to have religious voices accepted as part of the democratic chorus. Many religious conservatives were simply seeking the legitimacy that conservative religion had lost after the Scopes trial. The quest for such legitimacy became all the more urgent in the 1960s, when so many other voices were raised in the moral debate. In the eyes of moderate supporters of religious conservatism, traditional religious values had a right to at least as much deference as countercultural values.

"The religious person is entitled, if not to prevail, at least to be heard," wrote Terry Eastland in an essay defending Christian political activism that appeared in *Commentary*, the neoconservative journal sponsored by the American Jewish Committee. "The religious person can expect to be allowed a voice in matters of public policy," Eastland continued. "He can expect that his religion will not disqualify him from speaking on political matters, and that if he offers a religious or ethical justification for his position on a public issue, it will not *ipso facto* be considered out of the bounds of public discourse." The Religious Right was destined to become weaker as soon as these minimal demands were met, since many social conservatives—among the voters, if not among the leaders—shared Eastland's modest goals. Once the moderates of what Eastland termed "Religious America" had found their voices in the national debate, their support for conservatism would become less automatic, their need to mobilize less urgent.

On the other hand, for the more ardent religious conservatives, many of whom repaired to Pat Robertson's candidacy in 1988, the Reagan years had meant little progress at all. They were not content with Eastland's modest definition of Religious America's goals. They sought much firmer commitments from conservatives to social and religious traditionalism. To the extent that they pressed their demands too forcefully, they threatened the Republican coalition and conservatism's delicate philosophical balance. For the rise of the Religious Right had strengthened the hand of the traditionalist wing of conservatism—the wing that had always seen values as more important than markets, religious faith as more important than economic growth, tradition more important than progress. As a result, the old conservative war between traditionalists and libertarians that Frank Meyer and *National Review* conservatives had tried to settle was raging with greater ferocity than ever. For the libertarians, who profoundly disagreed with the traditionalists on many issues, had also made real gains under Reagan. Many conservatives sensed danger ahead.

But where did the new libertarian drive come from? How did the libertarians, so battered and isolated in the late 1950s, return in such strength in the 1980s?

9

THE DEMAND FOR SUPPLY SIDE:

Conservative Politics, New Deal Optimism

Good POLITICIANS rarely worry much about consistency. Effective democratic leaders frequently ignore contradictions, paper over differences, win the trust of groups who despise each other. Ronald Reagan was a genius at making a virtue of contradiction. Young investment bankers who looked kindly on cocaine and fundamentalist factory workers who saw a world full of sin and corruption could vote for Ronald Reagan with equal enthusiasm. And they did.

Reagan himself understood clearly that building a conservative majority required the votes of both factory workers and investment bankers. In this sense, he was only following the teachings of his friends at *National Review* who sought to unite the libertarians and the traditionalists, the Wallace voters and the Nixon voters. But Reagan's presidential campaigns did more than follow a formula; they actually helped create a new politics out of what had once been just a theory.

If the rise of the Religious Right gave new strength to the cause

242

of traditionalism, the rise of supply-side economics strengthened the cause of libertarianism. If the works of the Austrian free-market economists such as Hayek and Von Mises had been buried during the years of Keynesian triumph, they were unearthed in the 1970s and reread with new enthusiasm.

The new libertarianism in economics had a broader potential constituency than the new traditionalism of the conservative churches. The "moral breakdown" to which the Religious Right responded was not obvious to everyone. One person's moral breakdown was another's outbreak of freedom. But the "economic breakdown" of the 1970s was obvious to everyone. And with the possible exception of a few Marxists who looked forward to capitalism's collapse, no one liked what they saw.

Without the economic troubles of the late Carter years, Ronald Reagan's presidency would have been impossible. And without the economic troubles of the 1970s as a whole, the *ideas* that dominated the Reagan presidency would certainly never have become so powerful.

The New Deal coalition was fractured in the 1960s by the rise of racial and cultural politics. But until the late 1970s, its pieces could still be rallied by the memories of Herbert Hoover and Franklin D. Roosevelt. Even working-class Democrats who suspected liberalism's sympathy for civil rights and cultural experimentation still believed, on the whole, that Democrats brought good economic times and Republicans brought recessions. The whole premise of the influential Scammon and Wattenberg thesis was that Democrats could win if they finessed the social issue and emphasized the *economic* issue. What Scammon and Wattenberg were saying is that for many voters, casting a ballot against Herbert Hoover was still, all things considered, a good idea.

The economic chaos of the late 1970s exploded that assumption and destroyed the foundations of loyalty to liberalism and the Democratic Party. Jimmy Carter became the Herbert Hoover of the last part of the twentieth century. The Great Inflation of the 1970s destroyed the political constituency behind the New Deal idea.

II

Inflation had always been an issue in American politics, but because of the Great Depression, most Americans were instinctive Keynesians. Inflation was bad, but mass unemployment was worse.

When Republicans acted on their worries about balanced budgets and the integrity of the currency, they usually threw people out of work. Roosevelt had not cared whether the dollar was backed with gold. He had not worried about balanced budgets (in fact, he had at various points, but that was not part of the legend). And Roosevelt did not worry about inflation, since *deflation* was the problem of the 1930s. Roosevelt's policies seemed to work—even if conservatives were right to complain that the war did more to end the Depression than the New Deal. The mantra of the New Deal coalition became the word (*jobs.*)

Under Jimmy Carter, the Republicans at last had their chance because inflation at last became a mass concern. Democrats would mournfully note that inflation became a consuming worry because so many Americans had been lifted to prosperity by Keynesian economics—*by liberal, Democratic economics.* The "ordinary American" who was as likely as not to be unemployed in 1933 now had a decent job, owned a home, paid a mortgage, received social security. Such voters could now *afford* to worry about inflation.

But that version of events underestimates the alarm that rampant inflation can inspire even among voters who don't have large bank balances. Rampant inflation creates rampant anxiety. It makes the most basic forms of economic planning impossible not only for big corporations but for average citizens. And it can put the basic components of the American dream—home ownership and college education—out of the average American's reach.

During 1980, inflation reached a high point of 18 percent—up from 4.8 percent in Gerald Ford's last year in office—and it stood at 15.5 percent on election day. The prime interest rate was at 21 percent. Such numbers gave ample credibility to the Republican Platform's claim that inflation was "the greatest domestic threat facing our nation today."

But Jimmy Carter had the worst of all worlds. Voters had always expected that Democrats might produce a little more inflation than the Republicans, but would at least keep unemployment low. In 1980, the Democrats not only produced staggering amounts of inflation; they didn't even deliver jobs. On election day in 1980, 8 million Americans were out of work. The unemployment rates were the result of the harsh (and ultimately successful) anti-inflation policies pursued, with Carter's blessing, by Paul Volcker at the Federal Reserve. Ronald Reagan—and in some important ways, the economy—were to profit from Volcker's policies. But in 1980, the result was the worst of all possible worlds: high inflation *and* rising unemployment. Carter paid the price at the polls.

Carter was not alone in paying the price. New Deal liberalism paid the price, too. The 1970s taught Americans that inflation could be as fearsome as unemployment. They taught that Democrats could mismanage the economy no less than the Republicans. And Republicans succeeded in arguing that *big government* was responsible for the mess. This last lesson has become so much a part of our political folklore that it seems like common sense. But it was not intuitively obvious. The genius of conservatives lay in selling this part of their message.

For whatever else was true of Jimmy Carter, he was hardly a big-government Democrat. He had won his party's nomination as the *least liberal* alternative to George Wallace. Even Scoop Jackson, who stood to Carter's "right" on foreign policy, was an old friend of New Dealism and federal spending. In office, Carter did *not* embark on big new spending projects. Indeed, his stringent budgets enraged liberals and helped prompt Kennedy's challenge to Carter in the Democratic primaries. In his final years in office, Carter actually *reduced* spending, in real terms, from their levels in the Nixon and Ford administrations in a host of domestic areas. A partial list of areas cut back includes housing development, transportation, community and regional development, education, and family welfare.

If it was hard to paint Jimmy Carter as a big-government Democrat, it was also by no means automatic that high inflation would lead voters to oppose activist government. Voters worried about inflation can be just as inclined to look for *more* action from government, not less. When Richard Nixon slapped on wage and price controls in 1971, his decision was controversial, but many voters welcomed the relief. (He did, after all, get reelected.)

But events prepared the way for conservatives to make their anti-government case. New York City's fiscal crisis in the mid-1970s was one turning point in popular attitudes toward government. The crisis itself had complex origins, as Martin Shefter made clear in his masterful account *Political Crisis/Fiscal Crisis*. Not the least of the city's problems was the recession of 1974–75, which devastated the economies of the Northeast with a force not felt in the rest of the country. But the popular lesson taken from the fiscal crisis was that *liberalism had failed*. New York City's problems had to do, as Charles Morris put it in the title of his influential book, with *The Cost of Good Intentions*. Liberalism had become the party of undisciplined government spending on behalf of undisciplined interest groups. The result was fiscal chaos. In 1980, it was easy for conservatives to argue that New York City offered a cautionary tale for the rest of the nation. That conservatives could suggest between the lines that all this profligacy had been committed on behalf of unpopular minority groups only made their case more politically potent.

Another turning point was the tax revolt embodied in California's Proposition 13, passed in 1978. The Proposition 13 rebellion had its roots not in economic distress, but in prosperity. California's rapid growth had led to an exceptional inflation in property values. As property values went up, so did real estate taxes. Between April 1974 and April 1978, the price of an average house in Los Angeles County went from $37,800 to $83,200—an increase of 120 percent. In California as a whole, property tax assessments on single-family houses increased by 110.9 percent between 1975 and 1978. The government's tax windfall extended well beyond the property tax. Between 1973 and 1977, personal income in California increased by better than 50 percent. But personal income *taxes* increased by more than 150 percent, sales taxes by 188 percent. As Robert Kuttner argued, such figures made a tax revolt inevitable. "When inflation blended with tax schedules to push up tax rates," Kuttner wrote, "hard-pressed consumers were in no mood to tolerate rising taxes, as they might have a decade earlier when times were good." As Kuttner has made clear in his many writings, liberals inadvertently helped conservatives create an alliance of the middle class and the wealthy to cut taxes because they moved too slowly to create an alliance between the middle class and the poor to make taxes more progressive.

For middle-class voters did not suddenly turn against big government's benefits. Indeed, polls showed right through the tax revolt that voters were willing to pay higher taxes for a whole range of specific government services. But inflation raised tax rates on the middle class so high and so suddenly that its members could not believe that what they were getting out of government had any connection with what they were paying. The New Deal had taught that government was the middle class's friend. The inflation-tax surge of the 1970s taught that government was the enemy. A letter writer to the *Los Angeles Herald-Examiner* called Proposition 13 "the Watts riot of the white middle class." Like the rioters in Watts thirteen years earlier, the white middle class had reason to feel that its grievance against government was legitimate. And it was not just whites who felt this way: 42 percent of blacks voted for Proposition 13.

Thus did events from coast to coast conspire against government. When inflation crested during Jimmy Carter's final year in office, voters were ready to blame not simply his stewardship, but government itself. As Theodore H. White put it, voters, in large numbers, came to believe in a breathtakingly simple and insurrectionary proposition: "The government is cheating you." The theoreticians of supply-side economics and libertarianism agreed completely, and they had answers.

III

Critics see supply-side economics as an elaborate intellectual ploy through which old ideas that were discredited by the Great Depression got smuggled back into political circulation wearing flashy new clothes. Supporters of supply-side economics agree that many of their theories are based on old insights. Their claim is that those old insights represented a form of common sense that was lost in the false sophistication of Keynesianism and Marxism. Jude Wanniski, the leading promoter of supply-side economics, suggested that his ideas were so straightforward and so basic that they simply described *The Way the World Works*, which is what he called his supply-side manifesto. The demand for supply-side economics was created by the apparent failure of Keynesian/New Deal economics in the 1970s.

Keynesian economics declared that the Great Depression had been caused by falling *demand*. As the purchasing power of the citizenry collapsed, the economic slump built on itself. Unemployment rose, frightening investors, who saw no market for their goods. The investors stopped investing, which further increased unemployment. This vicious cycle produced mass unemployment. In Keynes's view, the key to breaking the cycle was to restore mass purchasing power. If the government put money in the hands of consumers, they would spend it, setting up a chase for new goods. Investors, their confidence restored, would start investing again in plant and equipment, slashing unemployment. Thus could government save the private economy from itself. Keynes once asserted that even if the government paid people to bury bottles of currency under huge piles of rubbish and left it to entrepreneurs to dig up the bottles, a stagnant economy could still benefit. Those burying and then unburying the bank notes could use their wages to buy goods and thus spur new production.

Keynesian economics was specifically intended to counter the views of the original "supply-sider," Jean Baptiste Say. Say's most important contribution may have been to give Adam Smith's ideas wide currency in France—and in John Kenneth Galbraith's view, to present Smith's ideas more clearly and concisely than Smith had himself. Say also celebrated, as Galbraith put it, "the distinctive, even decisive role of the entrepreneur, the man who conceives or takes charge of an enterprise, sees and exploits opportunity and is the motive force for economic change and improvement." For this reason alone, Say would win reverence from the economists who supported the Reagan Revolution. But Say was most famous for "Say's law," which is usually summarized as "supply creates its own demand." Say argued that an economic system could not "overproduce" goods, which is to say that it could not lack for purchasing power. The natural equilibrium of a free economic system was for supply and demand to match up at full employment. Keynes argued that the Great Depression had proven Say wrong—that an economic system could find "equilibrium" at far less than full employment. Keynes turned Say on his head, emphasizing the role of demand rather than supply.

Keynes's view was highly congenial to those who would redistribute income, since it held that the key to prosperity was the purchasing power of the masses. Huge sums of money concentrated in the hands of the rich did not automatically go to investment, Keynes asserted; and there was a limit to what even the most extravagant among the rich could consume, so their wealth did not necessarily stimulate demand. Keynes thus rationalized what egalitarians had always wanted to believe: that spreading money around equitably was the key to prosperity. Keynes also destroyed the view that the government should be asked to behave like a household and never run a deficit. In times of economic trouble, nothing was *better* for the common good than deficit spending. If, as Daniel Bell asserted, installment-plan buying destroyed the puritan ethic of thrift among individuals, Keynes struck a blow against puritanism as a principle of government.

But in the 1970s, the simultaneous rise of inflation and unemployment—the phenomenon became known as stagflation—left Keynesians confused and politically weak. In the past, there had always been a trade-off between unemployment and inflation. When unemployment went up, inflation went down or disappeared. Therefore, during hard times, the economy could easily absorb the modest inflation that accompanied job-producing government deficits. But when unemployment and inflation were going up at the same time, the Keynesian solution was suddenly dangerous. Pump priming of a Keynesian sort might bring unemployment down, but only at the cost of exacerbating already raging inflation.

The difficulty Keynesians experienced in solving this problem created the opening that conservative economics needed. The biggest winner among the alternative conservative theories was monetarism. Monetarists believed that the key to economic policy lay in control of the money supply. In a time of high inflation, choking off the money supply and raising interest rates would ultimately choke inflation— although it would also choke off economic growth. Monetarism effectively worked in the United States in the early 1980s—but at the cost of the highest unemployment rates since the end of World War II.

Supply-side economists offered a happier vision than monetarism. They believed in an unusual mix of policies, "tight money and fiscal ease." Choke inflation with tight money, yes, but encourage economic growth by cutting taxes. Economics did not have to produce dismal outcomes.

Supply-side economics waged full-scale war against the New Deal/Keynesian consensus. It got its name because one of its central goals was to restore the credibility of Say's law, that supply, not demand, was the predominant economic force. Supply-siders argued that the Great Depression had *not* been caused by a breakdown in demand, as the Keynesians claimed. In his book, Jude Wanniski explained it all in a simple declarative sentence: "The stock market crash of 1929 and the Great Depression ensued because of the passage of the Smoot-Hawley Tariff Act of 1930." What had caused all the problems was *government*'s getting in the way of the natural workings of markets through high tariff barriers. Government had kept Say's law from working. Not only that: Wanniski asserted that the bull market and fast growth that had come before the Depression in the 1920s had been caused by the decision of President Calvin Coolidge and Secretary of the Treasury Andrew Mellon to slash the top income tax rate to 25 percent. Ignoring the lessons of his Republican predecessor, Hoover made the Depression much worse, Wanniski argued, by raising taxes.

If the Great Depression had not been caused by slack demand and the mistakes that caused it lay with government, then a wholly different view of government policy emerged. Demand-side economics was, at its heart, egalitarian in wanting to fuel demand by spreading purchasing power around. But supply-side economics was consciously antiegalitarian. It emphasized investment and the importance of increasing the rewards accorded to capital. If the heroes of

Keynesian economics were the politicians and the planners who kept business healthy by taxing, spending, and redistributing, the supply-side heroes were the entrepreneurs who built the plants and factories that kept the people employed.

More than anyone, Wanniski created the very idea that there was a "school" that could be called "supply side." He emphasized the work of Arthur Laffer and Robert Mundell. It was Laffer who became the more famous of the two, partly because his great insight, the Laffer curve, could be drawn on any napkin. Laffer's point was that the government would receive no revenue if taxes were set at 0 percent, for the obvious reason, or at 100 percent, because a 100-percent tax rate would destroy any incentive for anyone to work in the money economy. Somewhere between those two numbers lay the optimal tax rate. Laffer's curve was less a breakthrough in economic thought than a public relations miracle. It allowed the supply-siders to dramatize their fundamental point that high tax rates discouraged individual effort and thus economic growth. In what might be seen as the ultimate lesson of the law of unintended consequences, high taxes designed to finance worthy liberal programs might *reduce* the amount of money available for such programs by discouraging the private economic effort required to produce wealth for the government to tax.

For Wanniski, his supply-side heroes helped demystify economics. Instead of concentrating on arcane talk about the money supply or government management, Wanniski wrote, "Mundell and Laffer go back to an older style of economic thought in which the incentives and motivations of the individual producer and consumer and merchant are made the keystone of economic policy." If government policy, and especially government tax policy, rewarded work, savings, and investment, then society would have more of all of them. If government taxed work, savings, and investment, society would get less of them. Supply side's supporters repeated those two sentences with the same conviction and frequency as devout believers recited the fundamentals of their church's creed.

As was true of so many conservative initiatives that were declared part of the Reagan Revolution of the 1980s, supply side's first victory was actually recorded during Jimmy Carter's administration in the 1970s. Following a brilliant lobbying and public relations campaign, complete with the careful academic studies that were to become so central to conservative political breakthroughs, Congress voted in 1978 to cut the capital gains tax. Wanniski, from his perch at the *Wall Street Journal*'s editorial page, was one of the leading publicists for the capital-formation ideology behind the cut. The theory was *not* that the rich "deserved" a break. It was that government would promote more investment by taxing it less and that everyone would benefit from a surge in productivity and employment. Advocates of Calvin Coolidge–style economics thus stole away New Dealism's most potent word, *jobs*. As a result, a tax cut that benefited the nation's wealthiest citizens became the central component of Jimmy Carter's tax reform, which had originally been intended as a "populist" bow in the direction of the average, overtaxed worker.

But winning on capital gains was not the same as gaining acceptance for supply side as a legitimate basis for economic policy. The capital-gains cut was in the interest of, and thus supported by, virtually every powerful private economic interest in the country. Investment houses and large corporations knew what the benefits of such a cut would be to them. But supply side's more audacious claims —notably that the government could *gain* revenue by *cutting* basic income-tax rates—seemed much chancier. And the supply-siders did nothing to comfort traditional Republicans by arguing that the basic inspiration for the benefits of a broad tax cut came from John F. Kennedy's tax-cut proposals in the early 1960s. The Kennedy tax cut, which was ultimately enacted under Lyndon Johnson after Kennedy's assassination, was followed by robust economic growth. The supply-siders wanted to do the same thing all over again. But most conservatives, including Barry Goldwater, had opposed the Kennedy-Johnson tax cut as fiscally irresponsible. In the late 1970s, most conservatives still saw balanced budgets as a central article of their creed, fiscal responsibility being for most conservatives no less of a "traditional value" than family or patriotism.

But the supply-siders had at least three things going for them: an important ally in Ronald Reagan's camp, Jack Kemp, who was later joined by one of the nation's most intelligent conservative politicians, David Stockman; a powerful political argument; and the logic of anti-statism, which appealed to some of Reagan's deepest convictions.

Wanniski had converted Kemp to the supply-side cause in 1976, and the Kemp-Roth tax bill, involving a 30 percent cut in income-tax rates over three years, became the centerpiece of the supply side's lobbying. The reasons for Kemp's openness to Wanniski's ideas were revealing. Kemp represented Buffalo, New York, whose economy had been devastated by the 1974–75 recession. As a practical politician, Kemp understood that to stay in office, he needed to offer voters a vision of economic recovery. He understood that his traditionally

Democratic constituents did not identify with conservative talk about the need for probity and belt-tightening. Moreover, like many relatively young politicians who came to conservatism later in life, Kemp had always admired John F. Kennedy. Supply side seemed to offer conservatives, usually looked upon as a collection of dour pessimists, a chance to look bold and optimistic, as Kennedy had.

Supply side thus offered conservatives a form of economic populism to match their social-issue populism. Since one of supply side's fundamental goals was reducing the top tax rates on the very wealthiest taxpayers, it was surely an unusual style of "populism." But in a time of economic trouble, voters are prepared to listen to almost any theory that embodies their anger, sounds radical, and promises relief. Moreover, the tax revolts of the 1970s suggested that the political assumptions of Americans had shifted radically. If in New Deal times voters looked for direct economic benefits from government, in the 1970s many wanted the tangible benefits of tax cuts. *Supply-side tax cuts gave conservative politicians a way of passing money around.* It gave them an approach to politics that had traditionally been the province of New Dealism or of even more radical politicians such as Huey Long. Voters with modest incomes were prepared to give large tax cuts to the wealthy, provided they got something to show from the tax cuts, too.

It is impossible to underestimate the sheer force of supply side's *optimism* in winning Ronald Reagan over to the cause. Campaigning against a president associated with "malaise" and "the era of limits," Reagan's whole approach was based on an insistence that such gloominess was out of place in the United States. Reagan's promise was to "make America great again." Having voted for Roosevelt four times, Reagan understood the appeal of a candidate who told Americans to put aside their fears and vote their hopes. Reagan put the optimistic political *psychology* of the New Deal to the service of a very different set of policies.

Supply-side thinking said there was nothing wrong with America that couldn't be cured by lower taxes and less regulation. The people would solve the problems themselves if the government would only get out of the way. Jimmy Carter had promised "a government as good as the people." Ronald Reagan trumped him by declaring that the people were *better* than the government and always would be.

In the marriage of supply-side economics to "traditional moral values" lay the genius of the Reagan campaign. Through issues such as abortion and school prayer, Reagan insisted that he was the candidate of old-fashioned virtue opposing the forces of modernism and permissiveness. Yet his economic program told voters that they could help the economy by agreeing to let him cut their taxes; they could help their country best by helping themselves. Reagan seemed to be linking personal virtue to fiscal permissiveness. For Reagan's liberal critics, his economics flew in the face of all his piety on traditional values. "Self-indulgence takes the place of self-denial," wrote Wilson Carey McWilliams in 1981. "After years of learning 'you don't shoot Santa Claus,' the Republicans decided to nominate him. Even if Reagan's proposals work as well as he hopes, they make a mockery of middle class virtues." Many Republicans took a similar view. When Ronald Reagan promised to cut taxes, raise military spending, and balance the budget, George Bush famously dubbed the program "voodoo economics."

The supply-siders dismissed such criticisms. They heartily agreed that their goal was to rid the Republican Party of what they contemptuously called "root canal" economics. They were fighting against the idea, so long congenial to Republican conservatism, that pain was good for you. If supply side was "feel good economics," the conservatives would make the most of it. Let Republicans such as Bush or Bob Dole or John Anderson defend "feel bad" economics.

Still, the supply-siders insisted that feel-good economics was also virtuous. Their low-tax policies, the supply-siders insisted, would promote such middle-class virtues as work, savings, and investment. George Gilder's book *Wealth and Poverty* was a bold effort to link supply-side ideas with traditional values. In a sense, Gilder tried to do for conservatism in the 1980s what Frank Meyer had sought to do in the 1950s and 1960s—bind together capitalists and traditionalists.

Some of Gilder's efforts to link supply-side thought with traditionalist goals were ingenious. Writing in 1980, Gilder argued that many of the disorders in family life had been caused by high inflation and yes, *high marginal tax rates*. By levying such high taxes on those who worked hard, Gilder asserted,

> [t]he result is to penalize the family that depends on a single earner who is fully and resourcefully devoted to his career. Two halfhearted participants in the labor force can do better than one who is competing aggressively for the relatively few jobs in the upper echelons. Exacerbating this trend has been a gross insufficiency of new capital investment of the sort that sustains high-productivity employment. Instead of buying durable equipment, companies have tended to hire low-paid workers, often seasonal or part-time.

Gilder was essentially arguing that the collapse of traditional gender roles was hurting the economy, even as the economy's decline was encouraging the collapse of traditional gender roles. And who was profiting from the flood of women into the work force? The government, of course. The "income" that a woman received for carrying out household chores—her share of her husband's outside earnings—had gone untaxed. "What has been happening is a drive, conscious or not, on the part of government, to flush the wife out of the untaxed household economy and into the arms of the IRS," Gilder wrote.

Gilder insisted that it was not capitalist freedom that encouraged a breakdown in moral values. Moral decay came from *a decline in popular belief in the capitalist idea*. Gilder wrote:

> It is the idea of economic futility—not capitalist growth—that gives license to the culture of hedonism and sensuality. In an imperfect and suffering world, the possibility of progress implies a responsibility to attempt it. Only in a world of socialistically managed "limits to growth," where human effort, enterprise and creativity can never long prevail over needless poverty and suffering, can the progressive dream of sexual liberation, leisure, redistribution and sensual pleasure lose its onus of decadence and injustice.

A devout Christian, Gilder turned popular assumptions about the roles of the capitalist and the compassionate liberal upside down. In Gilder's view, the activities of capitalists were the ultimately generous acts. "Capitalism begins with giving," he wrote. "Not from greed, avarice, or even self-love can one expect the rewards of commerce, but from a spirit closely akin to altruism, a regard for the needs of others, a benevolent, outgoing and courageous temper of mind." Gilder acknowledged that this benevolent view of capitalism was not widely shared, and he saw this as one of society's gravest problems. "One of the little-probed mysteries of social history is society's hostility to its greatest benefactors, the producers of wealth," he wrote. "How much easier it is—rather than learning the hard lessons of the world—merely to rage at the rich and even to steal from them. How much simpler than diligence and study are the formulas of expropriation!" For Gilder, "the war against the rich" was really a war against prosperity.

On the other hand, he argued that most welfare programs, far from helping the poor, actually guaranteed their enslavement. "The moral hazards of current programs are clear," he wrote. "Unemployment compensation promotes unemployment. Aid for Families with

Dependent Children (AFDC) makes more families dependent and fatherless. Disability insurance in all its current forms encourages the promotion of small ills into temporary disabilities and partial disabilities into total and permanent ones." After continuing through a lengthy list of the sins promoted by other government assistance programs, Gilder concluded: "To the degree that the moral hazards exceed the welfare effects, all these programs should be modified, usually by reducing the benefits."

Gilder's argument was in fact more complicated than a simple case against all government benefits. For example, he wrote with some sympathy about proposals to have the government reduce the incentives for going on welfare by providing benefits such as health care to people in poorly paid, low-skill jobs. Still, for liberals, the preachings of Gilder and the other supply-siders amounted to nothing more than an elaborate rationalization for what conservatives had always intended to do. In his history of economic thought, John Kenneth Galbraith confines his discussion of supply-side economics to a dismissive footnote. "What is called supply-side economics came forward in the United States specifically to license the tax reductions and welfare curtailments sought by the Reagan Administration," Galbraith wrote. Supply side, he said, had not "achieved a significant foothold in established economic instruction and thought" because it was "too obvious in its intent, an unduly unsophisticated accommodation to pecuniary interest."

Galbraith is largely right about the failure of supply-side economics to win the academic esteem that accrued to Keynesianism or monetarism. But as an effort to change the course of the nation's political debate, supply side has to be rated a success. Through most of the 1980s, capitalist entrepreneurs *were* viewed as heroes, even if the popular imagination did not endow capitalists with all the virtues Gilder ascribed to them. Government bureaucrats were viewed as government bureaucrats, not as public servants. Government's role in creating a social climate conducive to productivity was played down. The individual's role in fending for himself or herself was paramount. High marginal income-tax rates were eliminated. After the 1986 tax reform, the top rate of 28 percent was very close to Calvin Coolidge's magic number of 25 percent. Even among liberals who wanted to increase taxes on the rich in the early 1990s, the figures tossed about —33 percent or 38 percent—were far lower than the 70- to 90-percent nominal rates that had once actually been law.

The supply-siders and their allies also played an important role in a decidedly salutary development: a renewed emphasis in economics on analyzing the factors that make individuals, companies, and sectors of the economy more productive. Among economists concerned about public policy, it was a shift away from "macroeconomics," a concern with the broad economic policies pursued by government, and toward "microeconomics," an interest in how shop floors are organized, how goods are priced and marketed, how companies are managed, how investment is encouraged—and how government policies might affect all these particulars. The rebirth of microeconomics owes more to the challenge posed to American industries from abroad, especially from the Japanese, than to the work of any particular economic school. The Japanese challenge caused economists of all stripes to take a new interest in the details of why some forms of production seemed to create better goods than others. Still, Wanniski is right in giving supply-side economics some credit for the revival of interest in the "incentives and motivations" of individuals and companies. Some liberals, after all, renewed their interest in such things for the very purpose of countering the views of the supply-siders and other conservatives. Writing in *The Public Interest* in 1983, George Gilder praised the development of "a supply side microeconomics of the left," singling out the work of Robert Reich, Ira Magaziner, and Lester Thurow. Reich and his colleagues came to substantially different conclusions from the conservative supply-siders, but they were interested in many of the same questions.

But Gilder's efforts to link capitalism and traditional virtue were considerably less convincing. Gilder was certainly right in his insistence that there were virtuous capitalists and in his praise of risk-taking. But by the late 1980s, his vision of the heroic entrepreneur and gutsy small businessman began clashing with the unseemly world of insider trading and leveraged buyouts. Defenders of leveraged buyouts insisted that in the long run, they promoted efficiency. But in the short run, they usually produced large profits for a handful of financiers and layoffs for employees who had given their firms years of service—hardly the job-producing economics that figured so much in the rise of the right. Indeed, the impact of the debt that leveraged buyouts piled onto corporations was to force many companies to shut down large parts of their operations. These factory closings tore apart local communities—the very sorts of communities worshiped by traditional conservatives. They also weakened the sense of loyalty that workers felt toward their companies by suggesting that companies, which were forever in danger of being taken over by someone else, were not in a position to requite such loyalty. Nor did the "lifestyles of the rich and famous," which were celebrated on television and in countless magazine articles, seem to be rooted in anything like the traditions that Gilder held dear. The 1980s saw the rise of a form of conspicuous consumption that had little to do with thrift or deferred gratification.

The climax of this era of finance capitalism was the collapse of the Drexel Burnham Lambert Group the day before Valentine's Day in 1990. Drexel Burnham had done more than anyone to make words such as *junk bonds, leveraged buyouts, white knights,* and *greenmail* everyday terms. When Drexel went under, many of the chief executives whose companies had been targets of Drexel-backed junk-bond buyouts were gleeful, sounding less like capitalist titans than like Marxist economists. "They didn't create wealth, they just played with it," said Fred L. Hartley, who was chairman of Unocal Corp. when Drexel ally T. Boone Pickens sought to take it over. "They weren't really running a market, they were running a casino." The *Washington Post* captured the popular reaction to Drexel's collapse with the headline: "Drexel Financed—and Symbolized—Wall Street's Decade of Excess."

Years earlier, Gilder himself expressed alarm at some of these developments, agreeing with Robert Reich that much of the action in the economy was the empty work of "paper entrepreneurs." Writing in 1983, Gilder was as scornful of the paper entrepreneurs as anyone on the left. "Unable to create real assets, they shuffle paper assets in a symbolic economy of zero-sum maneuvering and legal and financial virtuosity," Gilder declared. "They shower the system with legal briefs and regulatory orders, merger and acquisition announcements (a record $82 billion went for this purpose in 1981), executive recruitment raids, and all the buyouts and leasebacks, stock and bond exchanges, 'defeasances' and accounting finagles which preoccupy many American conglomerates."

Still, whatever the contradictions between traditional values and "casino capitalism," Ronald Reagan profited by speaking fondly of both. The key to Reagan's popularity lay less in his ability to blend the two into a coherent creed, as Gilder tried heroically to do, than in his skill at using these two sets of ideas to send different messages to different constituencies. To the young and entrepreneurial, he was the champion of freedom, entrepreneurship, low taxes, optimism, and all the good things money could buy. To the older and the devout, he was the champion of the familiar verities of family, work, and neighborhood. Permissiveness and rigor coexisted in the Reagan coalition.

The potential contradictions between these two constituencies never became a political problem in the 1980s because to both groups, Reagan was the man of sunny disposition who presided amiably over a period of growth and prosperity. *Reagan had been right to be optimistic in 1980 and Jimmy Carter had been wrong to be such a pessimist.* Most voters did not care whether the relative economic success of the Reagan years was the result of supply-side theory, or simply of old-fashioned Keynesian pump priming through high deficits and military spending. The point was that for a substantial majority, America looked better off in 1988 than it had in 1980.

Supply-side economics served Ronald Reagan well at the crucial political moments. During the 1980 campaign, supply side gave him specific benefits, tax cuts, to promise the electorate and a strategy—or at least what looked like a strategy—to get the economy moving. Once Reagan was elected, supply side gave him a program on which he could immediately move. Reagan's victories in 1981 set the tone for the entire Reagan presidency. Yet Reagan's 1981 triumphs on the tax and budget bills can be seen as his *only* far-reaching legislative triumphs for eight years. After 1981, the administration moved much more cautiously. As David Stockman recounted in devastating detail in his book *The Triumph of Politics*, the administration never managed to match its tax-cutting virtuosity with comparable skill in passing expenditure cuts. And after the 1984 elections, the administration seemed to have no agenda at all.

But by providing the new president with a program on which he could move quickly, the supply-siders gave him a chance to take *action* in the midst of a crisis. Americans had always agreed instinctively with Franklin Roosevelt's declaration that the main thing in a time of crisis was to "above all, do *something.*" The supply-side economic program suggested that at least someone had a plan and the conviction to carry it out. Thus, supply side's greatest single gift to Reagan-era conservatism was to provide programmatic and ideological sustenance for the optimism that Ronald Reagan exuded so naturally and, it seems, so sincerely.

From the point of view of their policies, Jimmy Carter had not been Herbert Hoover and Ronald Reagan had not been Franklin Roosevelt. But the joint impact of Carter and Reagan on the national psychology was very much akin to that of Hoover and Roosevelt. Carter came to be associated with "malaise," Reagan with "morning in America." Because the psychological effects of the two administrations were so powerful, their political effects would inevitably be powerful, too.

10

POLITICS WITHOUT GOVERNMENT:

The Rebirth
of Libertarianism

FRANKLIN ROOSEVELT'S impact on the nation in the 1930s extended well beyond the specific effects of New Deal programs. Roosevelt was also the prime architect of the political culture of his era, transforming American attitudes toward the possibilities of government, the virtues of collective endeavor, and the rights of those he called "the forgotten Americans." When Roosevelt spoke of "one-third of a nation, ill-housed, ill-fed, ill-clothed," he instantly legitimized their cause. When he endorsed industrial unions, labor organizers around the nation told workers, "The President wants you to join," and by the millions, they did. American socialists often complained that Roosevelt had destroyed the possibilities of socialism in America by coopting many of socialism's most popular programs and by converting socialism's potential constituency, the industrial workers, into Democrats. But Roosevelt's relationship with the American left was symbiotic. If Roosevelt harnessed leftist currents unleashed by capitalism's collapse for his own purposes, then he also gave the cause of the left a respectability it would not otherwise have enjoyed. It is hardly accidental that the New Deal–era coincided with the only period in American history in which the Communist Party enjoyed substantial influence, growing membership, and a thriving institutional life.

Ronald Reagan's relationship with the antistatist libertarians was very much akin to Roosevelt's relationship with the American left. The libertarians knew that Ronald Reagan was not a faithful follower of their creed, much as socialists knew that Roosevelt could be an ally but never a comrade. Like Roosevelt, Reagan was not a systematic thinker. Like Roosevelt, Reagan saw no need to make all parts of his philosophy or his program consistent. Both men were skilled politicians who preferred to bend with hostile winds rather than be broken by them. Ronald Reagan was thus quite prepared to change his position on social security and endorse America's largest single welfare-state program if that was what it took to win.

For the libertarians, the Reagan record thus constituted a betrayal of the principles of limited government that Reagan claimed to espouse. Edward H. Crane, the president of the libertarian Cato Institute and the campaign manager for Ed Clark's Libertarian Party presidential candidacy in 1980, complained toward the end of Reagan's term that "the Reagan administration has failed, both in terms of its stated objectives in 1980 and in terms of the more ambitious goals my classical liberal or libertarian principles call for." Under Reagan, Crane declared, government was consuming a *larger* share of GNP than it had at the end of the Carter years, and the civilian federal work force had grown by "some 159,000 bureaucrats." One can debate the precise numbers, but it was clear that Ronald Reagan did not make much of a dent in the size of government; he had arrested its growth, but only on the domestic side of the ledger. Crane's point still stood: If the New Deal had not created the socialist paradise, then neither did the Reagan years create the libertarian utopia.

Yet as we have seen, the Reagan administration was a product of broad changes in popular attitudes toward government, and he in turn did much to promote those changes. Many of the forces that created Reaganism also helped the libertarian movement to be reborn. Reagan, by preaching against government, created fertile ground for the libertarians. And the growth of libertarianism was also aided, as we saw in Chapter Two, by the rise of the New Left and its attack on liberal government in the 1960s. By the end of the 1980s, libertarian attitudes enjoyed a prominence in the American political discussion they had not had since at least the 1940s.

What made libertarianism important was not a political party—the Libertarian Party was small, and it declined after the 1980 election, suffering in much the same way as socialists and communists suffered during the New Deal. Nor did voters themselves identify easily with the libertarian label, as they once had with the labels "liberal" and "conservative." Rather, libertarianism was important as the *latent and unconscious* ideology of millions of new voters who entered the electorate in the 1970s and 1980s. These voters shared the old conservative's skepticism of government intervention in the marketplace and the 1960s social liberal's opposition to government interference in the private lives of individuals. Such voters were, as Republican polltaker Robert Teeter put it, "prochoice on everything." They felt that *all* acts among consenting adults—whether in the marketplace or in the bedroom—should be legal, unless they demonstrably harmed others. Many of these younger voters also shared the skepticism of the 1960s New Left toward an interventionist American foreign policy. They were no more sympathetic to the American government's interference in the affairs of foreign nations than they were to its involvement in their own lives.

It would be mistaken to view the entire postwar "baby boom" as libertarian. In their pioneering study of the rise of libertarianism in the electorate, William S. Maddox and Stuart A. Lilie found that only about a fifth of voters who came to political maturity in the 1960s and 1970s could be classified as consistent libertarians. The well-off and well-educated were much more likely to be consistent libertarians than people of lower socioeconomic status. Moreover, many young voters who showed libertarian inclinations still welcomed government intervention in important areas of life, notably environmental regulation, civil rights, and equal rights for women.

Still, libertarianism was unquestionably on the rise among the young through the 1980s. In their study of public-opinion data in 1980, Maddox and Lilie found that 55 percent of consistent libertarians were under the age of forty-one. On the other hand, those they classified as "conservatives," i.e., people who opposed state intervention in economic life but favored state regulation of personal behavior to make it conform to traditional norms, were much more likely to be over forty.

The rise of libertarianism posed a direct threat to the conservative consensus that Frank Meyer, William F. Buckley, Jr., and others in the *National Review* circle had done so much to develop. The new libertarianism of the 1970s was especially troublesome to the *National*

Review conservatives because the libertarians broke decisively with a central article of the "fusionist" faith, the need for a highly interventionist American foreign policy based on anticommunism. The *National Review* conservatives had buried Robert Taft–style isolationism. The libertarians brought isolationism back to life. And the new libertarians of the 1970s and 1980s had little patience with fusionism's fondness for traditional values. Liberals and socialists— and some conservatives—frequently argued that capitalism's dynamism more often than not worked against traditional values. Capitalism often ripped apart old communities. It promoted a high level of geographical mobility, thus creating a footloose society that lacked reverence for the ties of locality, region, and even family. Libertarians did not shrink from this aspect of capitalism; they often reveled in it. Libertarians took the view of Samuel Brittan, who wrote in *Capitalism and the Permissive Society* that "to the extent that it prevails, competitive capitalism is the biggest single force acting on the side of what is fashionable to call 'permissiveness,' but what was once known as personal liberty." Jeff Riggenbach boldly entitled a 1979 article for *Libertarian Review* "In Praise of Decadence." Unlike the moral conservatives, Riggenbach hailed "decadence" as a creative force, for what was decaying most of all was *authority*, and this Riggenbach welcomed. In words that would win him star billing in a *National Review* assault on libertarianism, Riggenbach declared that "the authority of previous generations was a sorry spectacle indeed." He went on: "God was a fiction; his representatives on earth, the bishops and famous preachers, were con men who enriched themselves and their churches at the expense of their mostly poverty-stricken 'flocks'; our public men and generals had lied us into imperialism and mass murder around the globe, the Vietnam War being only the grossest of many examples."

Unlike conservatives, Riggenbach declared the 1960s an immensely positive and creative period, precisely because they were a time when decadent individualism flourished. "Like every decadent period before it, it is a period of innovation and high craftsmanship in the arts, and of passionate commitment to ideas in all the intellectual spheres," Riggenbach said. "When an individual chooses his ideas for himself, judges them for himself, and does with them what he wishes to do with them, he is much more likely to devote himself to ideas with enthusiasm and dedication than when he is forced to rely on an authority to decide for him what is worth studying and what use is made of it."

If Riggenbach sounded like one of the cultural revolutionaries of the 1960s, that is exactly how he saw himself. "All this decadent behavior is by no means a repudiation of the political ideals of the '60s," Riggenbach wrote. "The politics of the '60s were always individualistic at root, and not at all opposed in spirit to the ethos of the 'Me Decade.'"

For traditionalists such as Russell Kirk, libertarians such as Riggenbach had learned exactly the "wrong" lessons—the sort of lessons that capitalism, when uninformed by transcendent values, could teach. "The ruinous failing of ideologues who call themselves libertarians," Kirk declared, "is their fanatic attachment to a simple solitary principle—that is, to the notion of personal freedom as the whole end of the civil order, and indeed of human existence." The libertarians accepted "no transcendent sanctions for conduct," said Kirk, and thus bought into their own version of Marx's "dialectical materialism." The libertarian novelist and theorist Ayn Rand, who did so much to create the new generation of libertarians and who scorned the religiosity of Kirk and his allies, nonetheless looked with equal horror at so many who claimed to follow her teachings. She denounced them as "capitalist hippies," which is exactly what Riggenbach celebrated the new libertarians for being.

Clearly, libertarians were destined to clash fiercely with the old *National Review* conservatives, and even more with the Moral Majoritarians. Yet the libertarians, no less than the followers of Jerry Falwell, were both the creators and the products of Ronald Reagan's America.

II

Although libertarians ultimately attacked *National Review* conservatives for hijacking the right away from its old principles of anti-statism and isolationism, the new conservatism that Buckley and his allies championed in the late 1950s and early 1960s was initially helpful to libertarianism in many ways. The libertarians profited along with the rest of the right from the energetic organizing that the new conservatism and the Goldwater movement encouraged. The growth of a broad-based conservative movement inevitably exposed thousands to the libertarian "classics," notably the work of Hayek and Von Mises. Even among conservatives who loosely allied themselves with Frank Meyer's "fusionism," there were many who placed far more emphasis on liberty than on virtue or tradition. Meyer himself seemed at times to lean this way, which won him criticism from Russell Kirk and praise from some of the younger libertarians. Organizations for the young that had the blessing of the *National Review* conservatives, such as the Intercollegiate Society of Individualists (ISI), founded in 1953, and Young Americans for Freedom, founded at the Buckley family home in 1959, provided an important forum for libertarians.

Despite their differences on foreign policy, traditionalists and libertarians found it relatively easy to be fellow travelers in the 1950s and 1960s because the right as a whole felt itself isolated and embattled. Whatever their disagreements, traditionalists and libertarians knew that they shared a sympathy for market economics and an opposition to the welfare state that made them allies against conventional liberalism.

But the cracks in conservatism that were later to become chasms were already obvious at the very moment of *National Review*'s triumph. One of the most significant recruiters to the libertarian cause was Ayn Rand, whose book *Atlas Shrugged* was published in 1957 and helped create a cult around Rand and her ideas. Rand celebrated what she called "the virtue of selfishness"—a view that won her denunciations from the religiously oriented conservatives at *National Review*. Her heroes were superior individuals locked in a war against mediocrity, altruism, and the collectivist state. As one critic put it, "the Randian hero is really Nietzsche's superman in the guise of capitalist entrepreneur. He is the creator of all value, the source of all wealth, the instrument of human progress." Not surprisingly, this heroic (and cartoonlike) figure proved especially attractive to the young, and Rand's following was especially large on college campuses.

The campuses were alive with conservative action of all sorts in the early 1960s, and many of the campus conservatives were attracted to conservatism's libertarian wing. The creation of the *New Individualist Review* by the University of Chicago chapter of the ISI in 1961 was a sign of libertarian conservatism's intellectual vitality. The magazine's board of advisers boasted three of the most important conservative thinkers in the country, Milton Friedman, Hayek, and Richard Weaver, all of whom were on the Chicago faculty. The first article in the first issue was called "Capitalism and Freedom." Written by Friedman, it was a preview of his influential book, which would be published under that name in 1962.

The history of ideological movements can often be traced by the history of their magazines, and the story of *New Individualist Review* is a tale of how libertarianism gradually broke away from the broader conservative movement. The magazine's early issues showed its openness to all strains of conservative thought and suggested that its libertarianism was very much in the conservative mainstream. The magazine published articles by Russell Kirk and Hayek, as well as sympathetic reviews of books by Frank Meyer. *New Individualist Review* even criticized Ayn Rand early on, and in terms that would make most *National Review* readers cheer. "The ludicrously mistitled *'philosophy'* of Ayn Rand is a sham," a writer declared in the November 1961 issue. "To those who are traveling her road, I can only suggest its abandonment—for that way madness lies." The magazine was sympathetic to the Goldwater campaign in 1964, and many of its articles were devoted to discussions of free-market economics that conventional conservatives could only find highly congenial.

Yet from the beginning, *New Individualist Review* struck notes of libertarian skepticism about *National Review*'s foreign policy and about traditionalist conservatism's view that (Christian) religious belief provided the conservative creed with its underpinnings. Ronald Hamowy's angry attack on William F. Buckley, Jr., cited in Chapter Six, had already appeared by the third issue, in November 1961. The magazine's review of Frank Meyer's *In Defense of Freedom*, published in the autumn of 1962, was friendly, but it questioned whether the central role Meyer accorded the church was compatible with freedom of religion. In the summer of 1962, the magazine published an impassioned plea from former congressman Howard Buffett, Robert Taft's campaign manager in 1952, for the abolition of the draft. Buffett's language, astounding for a conservative at the time, explains why he later become a hero to some of the New Left. "When the American government conscripts a boy to go 10,000 miles to the jungles of Asia without a declaration of war by Congress (as required by the Constitution) what freedom is safe at home?" Buffett asked. "Surely, profits of U.S. Steel or your private property are not more sacred than a young man's right to life."

By the mid-1960s, the conflicts between the libertarians and the conservatives became sharper. One revealing sign of estrangement was an attack by Murray Rothbard, a prominent libertarian economist, on Herbert Hoover, published in the winter of 1966. Hoover, as the man who had been upended by Franklin Roosevelt and who had remained a resolute foe of New Dealism all his life, was a hero to most conservatives. But Rothbard insisted that this reverence for Hoover was misplaced. Hoover had, in fact, embarked on elaborate forms of government intrusion in the economy long before Roosevelt became an important figure on the national scene, Rothbard argued. Hoover had also supported, with enthusiasm, one of the most egregious forms of government interference with the private preferences of individuals, Prohibition. "Far from being a libertarian, Hoover was a statist par excellence, in economics and in morals," Rothbard wrote. ". . . FDR only built upon the foundations laid by Hoover." The essay was a harbinger of a role that Rothbard would play with increasing frequency: He was to be libertarianism's leading smasher of conservative icons. But Rothbard's emphasis not only on economics but also on *morals* was a sign of the growing antipathy of libertarians to conservatism's support for the regulation of personal norms and behavior. Published at the moment when the counterculture was getting off the ground, Rothbard's comment on Hoover suggested the growing common ground between the libertarian right and the New Left.

The issue of religion and morality was joined in the same issue of *New Individualist Review* in a fierce exchange between Ralph Raico, the magazine's editor in chief, and M. Stanton Evans, a leading conservative editor, over the relationship between religious faith and free-market ideas. Evans wrote in defense of an assertion basic to *National Review* conservatism, that "a regime of political freedom cannot long exist without the underpinning of religious and moral sentiment derived from Judeo-Christian revelation." With tongue in cheek, Raico replied that "if Evans could demonstrate that Christian doctrine calls for capitalism, it would represent a real landmark in the history of thought." On the contrary, Raico argued, "most of the Christians who have lived, and most Christians today, would disagree with this interpretation." All things considered, Christianity had done far more to oppose than to support capitalism. In a peroration that neatly summarized the philosophical roots of the growing impatience of the libertarians for the traditionalists, Raico declared: "I for one am finally getting bored with the sophomoric misuse of technical, philosophical terms; with sketchy outlines of the 'course' of modern history; with constant attacks on the French Enlightenment, on human reason and on the *hubris* of modern man; and with worldly-wise references to Original Sin and the absurdity of progress." Raico's argument was that libertarians were not conservative at all, but *classical liberals* who identified with the Enlightenment, with progress, and with an optimistic view of human possibilities. In all these commitments, the libertarians shared much in common with the "modernists," whom so many conservatives, especially the religious among them, loathed.

As the sixties wore on, the young libertarians at *New Individualist*

Review showed ever greater openness to the young rebels of the New Left. In the spring of 1967, the magazine devoted itself to a symposium against the draft and included an essay by SDS leader Richard Flacks. The Winter 1968 issue included a brief unsigned review of John Kenneth Galbraith's essay *How to Get Out of Vietnam* that was revealingly sympathetic. Galbraith, the magazine noted, "rather carefully demolishes" what it called "the usual anti-Communist approach to foreign involvement." The magazine spoke understandingly of "those who fear the less than pleasant prospect of a global American Empire policing the free world at enormous cost in lives, cost and domestic liberty."

Yet the note on Galbraith's book concluded with a frank statement of discord among the editors on the Vietnam issue:

> The editors of *New Individualist Review* have been divided for some time as to what editorial position to adopt on this question, and have sidestepped the issue in favor of omitting articles devoted to foreign policy. In the future, we would like to consider for publication well-written and thoroughly documented articles on these general questions. We invite our readers to assist us in this endeavor.

That endeavor never got off the ground because the Winter 1968 issue was *New Individualist Review*'s last. The Vietnam War, which did so much to divide liberalism, also led to a sharp break between a large segment of libertarianism and the conservative "mainstream" represented by Buckley and *National Review*. If the libertarians were uncomfortable with *National Review*'s anticommunist foreign policy in theory, they could not abide it when the theory was put into practice in Southeast Asia.

One of the best-publicized journeys from conservatism to libertarianism was that of Karl Hess, who had served Barry Goldwater as a speechwriter. Hess pronounced himself "a left-wing anarchist" and said his crucial break with the conservative mainstream became possible when he changed his views on foreign policy. "As soon as I educated myself to the fact that Communism wasn't just plain Stalinism, which I was hung up on," he said, "the rest was easy." Hess argued that he was doing nothing but rejoining the old Taft antigovernment tradition within conservatism. "Vietnam should remind conservatives that whenever you put your faith in big government for *any* reason, sooner or later you wind up an apologist for mass murder," he declared.

The fervor of sixties politics was felt in a most unlikely place: the 1969 convention of Young Americans for Freedom, a raucous affair at which the organization's libertarian wing broke away to form a new organization called the Society for Individual Liberty. The key issues at stake were the draft and the war.

The leading agitator, propagandist, and theorist of the libertarian breakaway was Murray Rothbard. Rothbard had begun to stray from the conservative mainstream before the Vietnam War. Indeed, he insisted that he had not moved at all; it was the right that had been hijacked, by Buckley and his friends. For Rothbard, the libertarians' best hope for winning new supporters lay not on the right, but on *the left*, since by the late 1960s, the crucial divide in American politics was over "American imperialism," and here, New Left and Old Right agreed in their opposition to anticommunist globalism.

Rothbard thus became a familiar, if somewhat odd, figure in New Left circles. He made his case to the left wherever he could, most notably in an essay in *Ramparts*, the sprightly magazine of the New Left. His essay, published in June 1968, was titled "Confessions of a Right-Wing Liberal" and began this way:

> Twenty years ago I was an extreme right-wing Republican, a young and lone "Neanderthal" (as the liberals used to call us) who believed, as one friend pungently put it, that "Senator Taft had sold out to the socialists." Today, I am most likely to be called an extreme leftist, since I favor immediate withdrawal from Vietnam, denounce U.S. imperialism, advocate Black Power and have joined the new Peace and Freedom Party. And yet my basic political beliefs have not changed a single iota in these two decades!

In what was now an increasingly familiar refrain, Rothbard blamed Buckley and his crowd for the decay of the true right-wing creed. "In the early days, young Bill Buckley often liked to refer to himself as an 'individualist,' sometimes even as an anarchist," Rothbard wrote. "But all these libertarian ideals, he maintained, had to remain in total abeyance, fit only for parlor discussion, until the great crusade against the 'international communist conspiracy' had been driven to a successful conclusion." In language strikingly similar to that used by his friend and ally Ronald Hamowy seven years earlier, Rothbard complained that "the right wing has been captured and transformed by elitists and devotees of the European conservative ideals of order and militarism, by witch-hunters and global crusaders, by statists who wish to coerce 'morality' and suppress 'sedition.' " Rothbard urged partisans of the old isolationist right to "wake up and rise up to restore our heritage." Toward this end—and explicitly choosing a name that might appeal to the left—Rothbard formed the Radical Libertarian Alliance in 1969. The organization came to little, and one sympathizer described its membership as "a multifaceted assortment worthy of inclusion in anybody's gallery of American oddities."

It was not Vietnam but the hallowed free-market idea that led to the creation of a libertarian political party. The moving force behind the Libertarian Party was a group of Young Republican renegades protesting against Nixon's imposition of wage and price controls in 1971. The Libertarian Party held its first convention in 1972 and nominated John Hospers, the chairman of the philosophy department at the University of Southern California, for president. The poorly organized party got on the ballot in only two states, and Hospers recorded but 5,000 votes, as against 76 million for the two "statist" candidates, Nixon and McGovern. But one Republican elector from Virginia, Roger MacBride, broke with his party and cast an electoral vote for Hospers. (MacBride also voted for the Libertarian Party's vice-presidential candidate, thus making Tonie Nathan, not Geraldine Ferraro, the first woman in American history to receive an electoral-college vote.) As the Libertarian Party candidate in 1976, MacBride did better than Hospers, winning about 175,000 votes. But no elector was willing to do MacBride the favor he had done Hospers.

In one sense, the history of the libertarian breakaway from conservatism through 1976 was a history of failure. *National Review* held the line for both traditionalism and anticommunism. Frank Meyer, who had always been sensitive to the dangers to freedom embodied in Russell Kirk's form of traditionalism, saw the new libertarianism as a danger to civilization itself. He attacked "the libertine impulse that masquerades as libertarianism" and scored the libertarians for disregarding "all moral responsibility" and "the minimal needs of social order." The conservative movement, even when it was most fed up with Nixon's policies on the economy and détente, remained the most faithful source of support for the Vietnam War. As George Nash argued in his history of conservatism, "for all the sound and fury and discussion of a 'burgeoning split,' one durable fact stood out: the conservative center was not disintegrating in practical terms."

But the very durability of the conservative movement suggested that for all its failures, Rothbard's strategy of appealing beyond the confines of traditional conservatism was a sensible course for libertarianism. In truth, libertarian ideas—or at least libertarian impulses—penetrated sectors of society that had little allegiance either to *National Review*-style conservatism or to New Deal liberalism. Many of the young who had protested the draft and the Vietnam War never joined the New Left. As Riggenbach insisted, they were not really "left" in any modestly rigorous definition of the term. Few of them identified with the term "libertarian," either. But their skepticism about government—born in the Vietnam era, nourished by Watergate, and confirmed by the failures of the Carter administration—was precisely the attitude that libertarianism had been trying to promote for so long. As a formal movement, Libertarianism would make only limited progress. As an attitude, libertarianism, without the capital letter, would grow much more.

III

During the 1970s, in fact, the first glimmers of a new libertarian politics inside the two major parties occurred within the Democratic Party. The antiwar protests invigorated the Democrats in middle-class suburban and university areas and created a new breed of Democratic candidate. They ran, and won, in mass in the 1974 elections. They ran and won not only against Richard Nixon and Watergate but also against the New Deal. When Gary Hart pronounced his breed of Democrat as something other than "a bunch of little Hubert Humphreys," he was declaring that Democrats of his stripe had grown mistrustful of big government, at home and abroad. As we have seen, the new Democratic breed was defined most clearly by those aspects of government that its members opposed: Watergate's violation of civil liberties, Vietnam-style intervention abroad, the use of government on behalf of "special interests," and abuses of the political process generally. Members of the New Breed, most notably Jerry Brown, who was elected governor of California in 1974, lectured voters on the need to ask and expect *less* of government. We were living, in Brown's oft-repeated phrase, in an "era of limits." It was a striking indication of New Dealism's weaknesses that so many *Democrats* were challenging two of the greatest achievements of Roosevelt liberalism: a strong welfare state at home and a military establishment with the power to intervene around the globe.

None of these New Democrats was a consistent libertarian. Indeed, though many of them spoke of the limits of government, they actually voted for a great many spending programs. But their approach to politics suggested that libertarian ideas and impulses were making themselves felt in the most unlikely places. Many of these Democrats had principled objections to the old liberalism, but one of their motivations in running away from the New Deal was the belief they shared with the libertarians that the votes were to be had elsewhere.

Libertarianism was winning new respectability in another unlikely place, the realm of academic philosophy. With the publication of Robert Nozick's *Anarchy, the State and Utopia* in 1974, advocates of the minimal state found an intellectual champion whom even their staunchest foes had to take seriously. Nozick's book could not have been better timed. In political terms, it appeared just as the war against the state was gathering steam. (What better year for an antistatist book than the year of Nixon's resignation?)

In academic terms, Nozick's work provided a riposte to another book that was widely regarded as the most important work of political philosophy in the postwar period. *Anarchy, the State and Utopia* appeared just three years after the publication of John Rawls's *A Theory of Justice*, a magisterial defense of the philosophy of the liberal welfare state. Rawls had argued that all economic arrangements had to be judged by their impact on the poorest in society. He postulated that if everyone in society sat down together before they knew what their natural endowments would be or how well-off they would be, they would want to establish a society that would ensure that their basic liberties and well-being would be protected, regardless of how "successful" or "unsuccessful" they were in amassing wealth and power. Thus, they would permit *only those inequalities that actually improved the lot of "the least advantaged members of society."* Rawls's argument was consistent with a market economy, but only one with a large welfare state. If market outcomes produced such wealth that they enhanced the well-being of the poor, they were acceptable. Wherever market outcomes produced another result, they were to be altered.

The rigor with which Rawls made his case won him something more important than praise: Whether they agreed with Rawls or not, political philosophers knew that they had to come to terms with his work. In the English-speaking world and ultimately beyond it, political philosophers were forced to take a stand on Rawls. And Rawls came along at a point when advocates of the welfare state realized that their political position was weakening and that they very much needed the bold defense of their project that Rawls had provided.

Nozick came along to refute Rawls and *Anarchy, the State and*

Utopia was hailed as no less a breakthrough for libertarianism than Rawls's book was for welfare liberalism. As Jude Wanniski put it, Rawls and Nozick became the "yin and yang" of political philosophy. Welfare staters and libertarians each had their own Harvard philosopher. If Rawls's argument was based on what kind of society individuals would create *before* they knew what the outcomes of life's race would be, Nozick declared that outcomes were not the issue. Nozick's starting point was that individuals "may not be sacrificed or used for the achieving of other ends without their consent. Individuals are inviolable." Nozick offered a compact summary of his philosophy:

> Our main conclusions about the state are that a minimal state, limited to the narrow functions of protection against force, theft, fraud, enforcement of contracts and so on, is justified; that any more extensive state will violate persons' rights not to be forced to do certain things and is unjustified; and that the minimal state is inspiring as well as right. Two noteworthy applications are that the state may not use its coercive apparatus for the purpose of getting some citizens to aid others, or in order to prohibit activities to people for their own good or protection.

Within the world of philosophy, Nozick was to be taken with the same seriousness as Rawls. Within the world of politics, libertarians could rest secure that their own genius had thought matters through to first principles and had come out just where they were. Supporters of the minimal state, so easily dismissed in the 1940s as mere apologists for the economic interests of the rich, now had a philosopher making a *moral* case for libertarianism that their foes could not ignore. The libertarians set to work to turn this intellectual conquest into political victory.

IV

Libertarians believe in the importance of individuals, and one of the most important events in the recent history of libertarianism was the conversion of one man to their cause. The man was Charles Koch, and his importance lay in his personal wealth and his willingness to use it on behalf of libertarian ventures. Koch was the head of one of the largest family-owned businesses in the nation, Koch Industries, a conglomerate based in oil, chemicals, and real estate. His personal wealth is estimated upward from $500 million. A former member of the John Birch Society, Koch had been converted to the libertarian cause by the writings of Von Mises. Guided by Ed Crane, a former financial manager who abandoned his business career for the peculiar task of putting a bit of order into libertarian politics, Koch helped to establish a string of libertarian institutions after the 1976 campaign.

Among the Koch-Crane ventures in the late 1970s were two think tanks, the Cato Institute, which became the Washington base of their libertarian empire, and the Institute for Humane Studies in Menlo Park, California; two magazines, *Inquiry* and *Libertarian Review*; the Council for a Competitive Economy, a business group pledged to opposing all forms of government interference in the economy, even those that were "good" for business; and Students for a Libertarian Society, a youth group.

Although Rothbard, ever the individualist, suspected Koch and Crane of dangerous tendencies toward "pragmatism," the Koch-Crane strategy reflected Rothbard's central political insight: that libertarianism's political base was to be found outside the realm of the conservative movement. The Koch-Crane approach was embodied most notably in *Inquiry* magazine, which counted editors of the *New Individualist Review* among its contributors, but could not have been more different from the *Review* in both style and content. *Inquiry* was breezy and irreverent, where *New Individualist Review* had been highly academic. Where the balance of *Review* articles had been about free-market economics, *Inquiry* seemed more interested in social issues and foreign affairs—the issues on which libertarians were on "the left" of the conventional political spectrum. *Inquiry* articles critical of interventionism in foreign policy were often written by people identified with the left. *Inquiry* also wrote critically about the Religious Right and included among its regular contributors such noted civil libertarians as Nat Hentoff. When *Inquiry* attacked "big government," it tended to do so in the popular forms, through investigative journalism or hip derision. The magazine sought to stay true to the libertarian faith on all issues, but in a way that made it a kindred spirit to the adversary culture of the left.

No one noticed libertarianism's "left-wing" deviationism more than the old conservatives at *National Review*, and they took the movement seriously. In exercising its traditional role as the guardian of conservative orthodoxy, the magazine published a lengthy cover story in June of 1979 attacking the libertarian heresy, especially its Koch-Crane version. For this purpose, *National Review* rolled out one of conservatism's more formidable intellectual guns, Ernest van den

Haag, a distinguished sociologist whose specialties included debating against civil libertarians on behalf of tough penalties for crime. Such a conservative could not be expected to have much sympathy for "capitalist hippies." Not suprisingly, Van den Haag turned early on to the issue of crime: "Conservatives believe in limited government. But in some respects, state power might be extended. Most conservatives would strengthen the ability of government to apprehend and punish criminals, to impose the death penalty, and to control pornography."

But Van den Haag's attack went beyond specific "issues." His essay was a full-dress discussion of the fundamental differences between conservatism and libertarianism. He neatly summarized all of the traditionalist objections to the libertarians:

> Libertarianism is opposed to all conservative traditions, to tradition itself. It is inconsistent with the conservative anti-utopian view of life and society. . . . They oppose all government, and they repudiate the need for the social cultivation of the social bond, for public authority, and for legally enforced rules. . . . Indeed, libertarians repudiate essential elements of civilization as it has historically developed everywhere. . . . They are a belated offspring of the Eighteenth Century enlightenment, of rationalism in its most virulent form. They believe that we can do away with the perennial tension between the individual and the group by denying the legitimacy of any social authority.

And when Van den Haag turned to foreign policy, he vented the rage of anticommunist conservatives at the willingess of the libertarians to make common cause with the left. Most of three full pages of the article was taken up with quotations from libertarian writers who opposed an assertive American foreign policy. On defense and foreign-policy issues, Van den Haag declared, the libertarian movement had "consistently taken extreme leftist positions." He added: "Even on issues such as the history of the cold war, or the spying of Alger Hiss, the libertarian position is indistinguishable from the Communist position." To link any movement to communism was the ultimate *National Review* anathema. Nothing else needed to be said.

The *National Review* article helped set off other polemics against libertarians from conservatives. In October 1979, *Human Events*, another bellwether of conservative-movement thinking, published an article by Joseph L. Gentili, a former Libertarian Party member who spoke of a takeover of the organization by its "left wing." Gentili was referring in part to the party's decision at its 1979 convention to nominate Ed Clark, a corporate lawyer with ARCO, as its 1980 presidential candidate on a ticket with Charles Koch's brother, David. Clark's triumph was a victory for the Koch-Crane organization (derided by its foes as the "Crane machine" and "the Koch-topus"). David Koch's presence on the ticket as the vice-presidential candidate guaranteed that Koch money would play an important role in the campaign. Under the Supreme Court's ruling on campaign contributions, there are no restrictions on what a person can contribute to his own campaign. David, and through him the Koch family, could thus contribute unlimited sums to the Clark campaign.

Clark's was a slick and skillfully run campaign, and he began with high but reasonable hopes for a breakthrough. In the 1978 midterm elections, held in the midst of the antitax boom, Libertarian Party candidates had polled an estimated 1 million votes around the country. Many of those had been cast for Clark himself. Running for governor of California on the Libertarian ticket against incumbent Jerry Brown and Evelle Younger, a competent but colorless Republican, Clark polled an astounding 377,000 votes, 5 percent of the total.

When asked to explain his political philosophy during the 1980 campaign, Clark would refer to himself as "a low-tax liberal." The phrase was a pithy summary of the Libertarians' overall strategy. On the one hand, the party sought, no less than Ronald Reagan, to capitalize on the growing tax revolt. But Clark realized that many of his potential constituents thought of themselves as liberals on issues such as feminism, gay rights, and foreign policy. The Libertarian strategy ultimately amounted to assembling a coalition of the sort of disaffected white middle-class voters who disliked New Dealism but sometimes found the younger antigovernment, antiwar Democrats appealing.

Measured by its own hopes, the Clark campaign proved a failure. True, Clark received nearly 1 million votes nationwide, an exceptional showing for a third-party candidate. In Alaska, the home for the most rugged of the rugged individualists, Clark received nearly 12 percent of the total. In the lower forty-eight, Clark's best showings came in two types of states that reflected the two sides of libertarianism. On the one side were states where middle-class liberal or reform candidacies have often been popular—Oregon, Colorado, and Washington. On the other side were states where the right-wing individualism of the "sagebrush rebellion" had a strong hold—Wyoming, Idaho, Arizona, and Nevada. Clark also did well in California, which includes places that reflect each of these two traditions: Orange County, representing conservative individualism, and Marin County, representing liberal reform.

But the libertarians had hoped for much more, given public dissatisfaction with both Ronald Reagan and Jimmy Carter. What held the Clark vote down was John Anderson's third-party candidacy. Anderson's support came from precisely the voters that the Libertarians had hoped to make their own: whites in the well-educated middle class. Though Anderson could not be described as a libertarian—he wanted higher energy taxes to discourage consumption, hardly an antigovernment idea—his campaign emphasized many themes congenial to libertarian-inclined voters, notably social tolerance, nuclear disarmament, and skepticism about government economic regulation. Anderson, not Clark, thus became the candidate of middle-class protest against the "old politics" of conventional liberalism and conservatism. Still, Anderson's strength helped prove the libertarians' point: that there was, indeed, a large potential constituency opposed to the old politics. At the height of his campaign, Anderson drew 20 percent in some national polls, suggesting that the 7 percent Anderson drew on election day understated the appeal of middle-class protest.

The Libertarian Party won much less national attention after 1980, and Crane and Koch withdrew their support in 1984 after the party spurned their chosen candidate. That was part of a broader shift in the Koch-Crane strategy. First, they folded *Libertarian Review* into *Inquiry*. Then, in 1984, they stopped publishing *Inquiry* altogether. Crane cited financial reasons for the move, but closing down *Inquiry* also had the effect of depriving "left-wing" libertarianism of a highly public voice, one that had so irritated conservatives. (Interestingly, *Reason* mazagine, a libertarian journal historically less hostile to conservatives, survived into the 1990s.) Much of the Kochs' libertarian philanthropy and Crane's energy went into the Cato Institute, which sought friendlier relations with more conventionally conservative Washington think tanks. Cato continued to take stands that unsettled the conventional right—against NATO, for the legalization of drugs. But many of its better-publicized studies concentrated on the failures of regulation and dismantling the welfare state.

The new strategy sought to strengthen libertarian tendencies inside the Republican Party, and to a lesser degree, among Democrats. Among Cato's most influential ventures was the Maddox and Lilie study of the electorate, *Beyond Liberal and Conservative: Reassessing the Political Spectrum*, which stressed the growth of a distinct libertarian constituency in the country. The study was important because it successfully demonstrated with survey data what the Libertarians had been unable to show at the polls in 1980: that they represented a large and growing segment of the electorate.

The Maddox-Lilie model divided the electorate into four groups. "Liberals" were those who supported state intervention in the economy but opposed its intervention on moral issues. "Conservatives" were the mirror image of liberals, opposing state economic intervention but supporting intervention on moral issues. "Populists" consistently supported state intervention—on economics and morals. "Libertarians" consistently opposed state intervention. The Maddox-Lilie analysis represented not so much a new idea as an intelligent way to organize the old distinction between "social issues" and "economic issues."

Their model suggested strongly that both parties were most clearly defined by their positions on *economic* issues. Two-thirds of the Democrats were *liberals* (who constituted 30 percent of Democrats) or *populists* (37 percent)—the two groups that favored state economic intervention. As for the rest, 11 percent of Democrats were conservative and 7 percent were libertarians. (Roughly 15 percent of the Democrats—and of whole sample—were impossible to categorize in any of the four ideological groups.)

A substantial majority of Republicans, on the other hand, were clearly identified with the two groups opposed to government intervention in the economy—27 percent of Republicans were *conservatives* and 29 percent were *libertarians*. Among the Republicans, only 13 percent were liberal and 18 percent were populist. Independents divided roughly evenly—25 percent liberal, 23 percent libertarian, 20 percent populist, and 17 percent conservative.

The presidential voting patterns of the ideological groups were revealing. Whereas Gerald Ford performed about as well among libertarians and conservatives—winning about two-thirds of each group—Ronald Reagan was significantly stronger among conservatives (he got 78 percent of their votes) than libertarians (66 percent for Reagan). John Anderson's coalition was, as the libertarians suspected, essentially an alliance between liberals and libertarians. Anderson got 17 percent of the libertarian vote and 15 percent of the liberal vote. On the other hand, Anderson was weak among populists (5 percent for Anderson) and conservatives (3 percent). In effect Anderson deprived Reagan of a significant share of the libertarian vote—the role Libertarians had hoped Clark would play—and took a substantial share of the liberal vote away from Carter.

The differences that Maddox and Lilie uncovered between George McGovern's 1972 vote and Carter's vote in 1976 were also instructive. Among libertarians, Carter ran only six points ahead of McGovern and among liberals only eight points better than Mc-Govern. But Carter ran eighteen points ahead of McGovern among conservatives and nineteen points better among populists. The key to Carter's election had thus been his gains among the older and the traditional, who gravitated to populism and conservatism, not among the young and the hip, who tended to be liberal or libertarian. Neither McGovern nor Carter did well among the libertarians, but Mc-Govern's *relative* strength among libertarians suggested that at least some libertarian voters cast ballots on the basis of social issues or the Vietnam War rather than economics, a sign that Rothbard's idea of seeking support on the left had at least some potential.

The Maddox-Lilie analysis demonstrated what libertarians knew all along: that while liberals felt relatively comfortable in the Democratic Party and conservatives comfortable in the Republican Party, libertarians and populists did not fit neatly into either. "For libertarians and populists, the choices offered by a two-party, two-ideology political system are problems rather than solutions to their need to express their political views," they wrote.

Their study also suggested that the political center was neither as easy to define nor as large as conventional analysts suggested. Many voters who were poised between liberalism and conservatism and called themselves "moderates" were not moderate at all in their views. Rather, many of them were either libertarians or populists whose views toward government were consistent and strongly held. They could not identify with the conventional "liberal" and "conservative" labels because they were not represented by them and often chose the "moderate" label by default. "The American public is not middle of the road," Maddox and Lilie concluded. "It is spread out all over the road, a fractionalized public facing a political system that does not translate popular opinion into public discussion very well." This view was well-received by libertarians, who were anything but centrists. It also helped explain how Ronald Reagan could defeat two men far closer to the center than he, John Anderson and Jimmy Carter. Cleaving to the center is often, but not always, good politics.

The Maddox-Lilie analysis supported the Koch-Crane strategy for libertarians in some respects, but not in others. On the one hand, their study showed clearly that a sizable libertarian constituency existed and that it was biggest in the group that represented the political future: the young. The natural foes of libertarianism, the populists, were older and declining in number.

But their analysis also showed that Republicans were already largely getting the libertarian vote and that the key to their success or failure in elections lay in winning the Democratic-oriented populists, who disagreed with the libertarians on almost everything. In House elections, the populists consistently gave Democrats over 70 percent of their ballots and thus victory. But in presidential elections, the populists gave a sizable share of their vote to Republicans (57 percent for Nixon, 39 percent for Ford, 41 percent for Reagan), producing either Republican victories or in Ford's case, near-victory. Since about a quarter of Maddox and Lilie's populists were black and reliably Democratic, their figures underestimated the volatility of the populist vote. For example, Carter's gains over McGovern among *white* populists were even greater than his gains in the group as a whole, since blacks voted for the Democrats in both elections.

Since populists were more likely to swing between the two parties, they were a more obvious group for the Republicans to woo than the libertarians. The message, uncongenial to libertarians, was that concessions to the "populists," the Wallace and Moral Majority constituencies, might pay higher electoral dividends than concessions to libertarians.

And despite the willingness of a minority of libertarians to vote Democratic, the study showed there were severe limits to the Rothbard-Koch-Crane strategy of an "opening to the left." The Maddox-Lilie findings showed clearly that the largest potential constituency for libertarianism lay inside the Republican Party, where conservatives and libertarians were almost evenly matched. Among Democrats, on the other hand, libertarians were but a tiny minority.

Still, for the libertarians to have clout in Republican circles, they needed to demonstrate that a large share of the libertarian constituency might be prepared to vote Democratic, given the right candidate. Here, Gary Hart's showing in the 1984 Democratic primaries proved exceptionally useful. Although libertarians were critical of Hart in some respects, they were quick to interpret his surprising strength against Walter Mondale, the quintessential New Dealer, as a sign that "their" constituency was making its influence felt in both parties. The libertarians argued that the young professionals who gathered to Hart's campaign in support of "new ideas" against "old arrangements" were protesting New Dealism at home and interventionism abroad. After all, Hart had been to Walter Mondale's "left" on foreign policy issues and vaguely to his "right" on economics—a positioning the libertarians found congenial, even if Hart was still too close to Mondale for their taste. In the meantime, Ronald Reagan had won reelection with strong support from young voters who liked his free-market economics far more than they liked his ties to Jerry Falwell. Was this not a signal to the Republicans that they might strengthen their majority by moving in a libertarian direction and win the lasting loyalty of the baby boomers who had found both Hart and Reagan attractive? David Boaz, vice president of the Cato Institute, summarized the libertarians' advice to the two parties at a 1985 conference organized around the Maddox-Lilie book. "The future of American politics," Boaz said, "may be determined by whether the Democrats can liberate themselves from the grip of the AFL-CIO before the Republicans break free from the Moral Majority."

The libertarians were pursuing what might be seen as the classic "second stage" approach of third-party movements. Having made their point as a third party without scoring a major electoral breakthrough, they were now seeking to move both of the major parties in their direction. In the process, they sought to reestablish ties to the Republican Party and the right—sensing perhaps, as the Maddox and Lilie analysis suggested, that their potential there was greater.

The libertarians knew that the Reagan presidency was bound to fall short of their hopes. His was not a libertarian administration but a coalition among traditionalists, libertarians, and Republican Party "pragmatists." This last group, which had once been the base for Modern Republicanism, had moved right to accommodate the new and more conservative balance of power inside the Republican Party. But the pragmatists were as aware as anyone that the libertarians were right in asserting that a constituency existed for their ideas; and on some issues, especially the social issues such as abortion, the pragmatists often found themselves arguing the libertarian case. Others inside the Reagan administration actually made the libertarian case on principle. But they didn't always win, as David Stockman learned to his dismay.

V

The resurgence of libertarianism was one of the less noted but most remarkable developments of recent years. During the 1970s and 1980s, antiwar, antiauthoritarian, antigovernment, and antitax feelings came together to revive a long-stagnant political tendency. This had an impact on many levels.

Libertarian economics—notably the work of Hayek and Von Mises—became respectable after years of derision at the hands of Keynesians. Libertarian economists even started winning Nobel Prizes, with Hayek getting his in 1974. Nozick's work conferred new respect on libertarianism within philosophy. The "law and economics" school gave libertarianism a foothold in legal scholarship, and libertarians invaded the realm of research on government administration —surely the camp of the enemy—with the rise of "public choice" theory.

The very word *libertarian*, which had largely passed out of use except when joined to the word *civil*, became part of the common political discourse again. When Lee Atwater, the ultimate political pragmatist, spoke of libertarians forming a "larger and larger" share of the electorate, it was a certainty that libertarians were no longer a fringe group.

The rebirth of libertarianism has had many salutary effects on our politics. In particular, the libertarians are especially gifted at calling the bluffs of contemporary liberalism and conservatism. Libertarians have been among the most consistent critics of business organizations that preached free enterprise loudly and then quietly accepted the benefits of government subsidies or regulatory actions that hurt their competition. They have forced conservatives to think through their commitments to a large military and to the inevitable distortions that high military spending creates in a market economy. Similarly, they have forced liberals to rethink their grounds for supporting individual liberty strongly in many areas, but not where economic regulation is involved. "Free markets" often do not automatically create "free people," but utterly unfree markets certainly do destroy human liberty, as the peoples of Eastern Europe have been telling the world.

But the rise of libertarianism was also a sign of a deep sickness in the democratic system. "If you wish to know how libertarians regard the State and any of its acts," declared Murray Rothbard, "simply think of the state as a criminal band, and all of the libertarian attitudes will logically fall into place." Libertarianism became popular because in the wake of Vietnam, Watergate, and the failures of the Carter years, the view that the leaders of America's democratic republic constituted "a criminal band" became ever more widely accepted. The resulting losses have been immense. The flight from public life over the last two decades led to a meaner, narrower kind of politics. Those who believe in democratic republics insist that the political process, the process of citizens arguing and reasoning together, is a positive good. They argue that individuals are more than just an egoistic collection of "preferences" and that our common life together can produce social goods that none of us can produce on our own. They insist that liberty is a value, but so, too, is solidarity. The growing popularity of the libertarian cause suggested that many Americans had given up on even the possibility of "a common good." They thus became more inclined to seek protections from government intrusion and less eager to become partners in the democratic enterprise. Given the failures of democratic government, that seemed a perfectly sensible choice.

The revival of libertarianism, coming at almost precisely the moment when the Religious Right came to the fore, was making the conservative movement increasingly unstable. The *National Review* "fusionist" synthesis had largely buried the differences within the right because fusionism was the ideology of the only conservative mass movement that existed. Traditionalism and libertarianism were, at best, fringes of this broad movement. In the 1970s and 1980s, the Religious Right turned traditionalism into a mass movement, and libertarianism, if not quite a mass movement, had certainly become what political scientists call "a mass belief system." As each wing of the right became more powerful, it eyed the other with increasing suspicion. Their mutual suspicions were well-founded, since the roots of the two worldviews were entirely at odds. The libertarians were Enlightenment rationalists fully prepared to overthrow tradition—and religion—in the name of individual freedom. The traditionalists, and the Religious Right, saw the Enlightenment as a wrong turn and saw the destruction of tradition as a grave danger. This was not a narrow difference over an issue or two; it was fundamental. It had a large impact on conservative politics.

11

BALANCING ACTS:

Reagan, Bush,

and the

Conservative Impasse

Since the late 1980s, American politics has been held hostage to conservatism's impasse and liberalism's past failures. The result has been immobility in government, an increasing harshness in politics, and a lack of substance in electoral campaigns.

By the mid-1980s, the conservative revolution had run its course. Conservatism completed what turned out to be its main and most popular projects by 1983: ending rampant inflation, cutting taxes, and raising military spending. As Reagan's second term showed, conservatives were hard-pressed to come up with new proposals. Even conservatism's greatest policy successes seemed to breed conservatism's political decline. Once the Reagan administration "solved" the tax and defense issues, popular support for conservative positions on these issues dropped. The Reagan income-tax cuts helped curb the tax revolt. High levels of defense spending quelled fears that America was militarily weak and thus reduced support for big defense budgets. Support for military spending had begun to drop long before the revolution in Eastern Europe made deep cuts in defense more popular than ever.

Conservatism was increasingly torn by the demands of its various wings and by its contradictory commitments. "Today, the common ground between libertarians and traditionalists is eroding," warned Donald Devine, the conservative political consultant. "Suspicion runs deep." It was clear, said Devine, "that the conservative movement will not long survive as a simple coalition."

The lack of action in Ronald Reagan's final years in office, the emptiness of George Bush's 1988 campaign and his reactive approach to domestic issues—all were rooted in conservatism's growing difficulties in organizing and disciplining its factions. While conservatism's factions might still form majorities at election time, they were finding it increasingly difficult to come together behind policies. The danger to the right was identical to that faced by New Deal liberalism in the 1960s: as its electoral coalition became increasingly incoherent, so, too, did its philosophy of government. On issue after issue, the contradictions within the conservative electoral alliance made it increasingly difficult for conservative government to act boldly—and in some cases, to act at all.

II

The troubles conservatism faced in the late 1980s were clear in the most important areas of policy: the budget, foreign affairs, and the social issues.

One can debate when the high point of the Reagan presidency and its conservative revolution was reached, but a plausible date is July 1981, when Congress passed the massive Reagan tax cut. The administration was never again to enjoy a victory quite as complete or as far-reaching.

The Reagan tax cut brought together in one place many strands of conservative strategy and philosophy. The tax cut represented, or seemed to represent, an economic strategy, which is what the country most wanted at a time of economic crisis. It satisfied the yearnings of tax rebels for deep, permanent tax cuts. It was a step libertarians welcomed, since it markedly reduced the state's income and thus its capacity to grow and meddle. Social conservatives liked the tax cuts for a similar reason—the lack of revenue made it easier to "defund" liberal social experiments. Business lobbyists, who managed to attach all manner of special-interest tax breaks to the Reagan bill, got almost everything they had been seeking for decades. Combined with the 1986 tax reform, which lowered the top tax rate to 28 percent, the

Reagan cuts revolutionized the way the federal government financed itself. The revolution (or counterrevolution) was made all the more extraordinary by the 1983 increases in social security taxes, which hit low- and middle-income taxpayers far harder than the wealthy. The supply-siders' dream had been to create a tax system that was kinder to those whose investment and risk-taking they saw as crucial to the nation's economic success—the wealthy. The Reagan years gave the tax code a mighty tilt in that direction.

Yet the revolution was over almost as soon as it started because, as David Stockman made clear in such devastating detail, the administration never managed to match the tax cuts with comparable reductions in spending. Stockman, who by nature was a believer in large doctrines, had hoped for more. At one time a young leftist, he was pushed by the supply-siders down the path that Murray Rothbard had blazed. "My soft-core Marxism had annealed into libertarianism," Stockman said. "I didn't believe in economic regulation, and I didn't believe in moral regulation." His vision, Stockman said, was of "minimalist government—a spare and stingy creature which offered even-handed public justice but no more."

The problem for Stockman was that his vision lacked the support of a political majority. Stockman's libertarian view represented the thinking not of the Reagan coalition as a whole, but of just one of its wings. What is striking about Stockman's account of the 1981 budget battles is that even the administration's greatest congressional victories had a patched-together quality; there was never wholehearted support for the entire program. It was hardly surprising that liberals opposed Stockman's vision. But as Stockman showed, deeper spending cuts became impossible because they were also strenuously opposed by Republicans and conservative Democrats. Thus, it was *conservatives* who preserved huge categories of federal spending—notably farm subsidies and veterans' benefits—from Stockman's cutting knife.

The most glaring sign of the conservative revolution's limits was the inability of conservative Republicans to agree to even modest cuts in the most important achievement of the New Deal, social security. For true fiscal conservatives and libertarians of the Stockman faith, social security was offensive because it was far more than a "safety-net" program for the poor. It was a comprehensive entitlement for which almost every American was eligible. This was big government with a vengeance. And it was the very comprehensiveness of social security that made it so politically popular. Narrowly targeted programs had narrow constituencies. Programs narrowly targeted to the

poor had narrow and relatively powerless constituencies. But social
security was supported by nearly everyone. It was the welfare state's
trump card, and Democrats used it over and over to great effect. No
one recognized that more than the leader of the conservative revolution. When Senate Republicans showed that they were prepared to
prune social security, they were stopped in their tracks by none other
than Ronald Reagan himself.

Ronald Reagan and his political managers knew a large fact that
Stockman tried to ignore: The conservatives could not afford to offend
supporters of social security and other broadly based benefit programs
because the conservative constituency included so many of them. The
genius of the fusionist-Reagan coalition was that it figured out a way
to bring together people with vastly different economic interests by
appealing to them with different sets of issues. That was also its limitation. By acting boldly on either the libertarian or the traditionalist
side of their agenda, the conservatives threatened to throw overboard
huge pieces of their coalition. On the spending issues, too many of
the "populist" traditionalists liked the New Deal just fine. They had
voted for Ronald Reagan to restore the nation's values, not to dismantle what Roosevelt had built. They kept voting the Democrats into
control of the House of Representatives to preserve those aspects of
government they supported.

The conservatives might have succeeded if Ronald Reagan had
reduced his commitment to the military buildup. Dwight D. Eisenhower, despite his moderate reputation, proved to be the most fiscally
conservative president since Calvin Coolidge because he insisted on
keeping a lid on military spending, no less than on domestic spending.
True to his libertarian inclinations, Stockman eventually turned to
the military budget in search of cutbacks. But on military cuts, as on
social security cuts, he was stopped dead by Ronald Reagan.

The result of the conservative impasse was the gigantic budget
deficit. The deficit was not the product of some technical failure in
the governmental process. *Its causes were entirely political.* Only a
high deficit could keep the conservative coalition together, since conservatives could not raise taxes on one part of their constituency and
could not cut programs that benefited another part of their constituency. In effect, conservatives turned to Japanese and German financiers to support a government that they refused to finance by taxing
Americans. That such a course transferred substantial political power
to the foreigners who bought government bonds went largely unde-
bated for a long time. If the Democrats could trump the Republicans

with social security, Republicans could still trump the Democrats with the tax issue, as Walter Mondale learned from sad experience in 1984. And so the budget debate continued at a stalemate throughout the Reagan term and into the Bush years. Each side preferred to play defense because the risks of going on the offense were so high.

On foreign policy, Ronald Reagan seemed eager to go on the offensive. His military buildup was the most notable expression of a new American assertiveness, but so, too, were the intervention in Grenada and the bombing of Libya. Reagan succeeded in convincing Western European nations to station American short-range missiles on their territory, a major political victory over the Soviet Union that set the stage for the transformations in Eastern Europe that followed. The America that had looked powerless when its hostages were held in Iran was gone. "America's back, standing tall," the President's commercials declared in 1984. Americans agreed and voted accordingly.

All this is true, but it misses the other striking aspect of the Reagan foreign policy: that the administration was deeply constrained by the past—and especially by the cultural civil war over Vietnam. Ronald Reagan did not triumph over the "Vietnam syndrome." He accommodated to it.

Nowhere was this more obvious than in the administration's approach to Central America. Direct American intervention against the Sandinista government was simply out of the question. Instead, the United States would use the contras—or as conservatives preferred, the "freedom fighters"—to do its fighting for it. But so deep was popular skepticism of American intervention abroad that even the indirect device of backing the contras proved highly unpopular. Polls consistently showed strong majorities against contra aid. That is why Congress felt free to tie the administration's hands with its frequent votes to end military aid to the rebels. It was those restrictions that set the Reagan administration up for its greatest fiasco, the Iran-contra scandal.

In the public mind, the single most unpopular aspect of the scandal was the President's apparent willingness to trade arms to Iran to secure the release of the hostages being held in Lebanon. Iran was still the enemy Americans despised most. It was galling to see Ronald Reagan, who had been propelled to power by his predecessor's failures in dealing with Iran on one set of hostages, caught giving armaments to Iran to win freedom for another set.

But if its negotiations with Iran created the administration's most serious political problems, its legal tangle was caused by the siphoning of proceeds from the arms sales to the contras. The remarkable fact was that an administration supposedly elected to pursue a more aggressive foreign policy had to use absurdly complicated forms of indirection to do what neither Congress nor public opinion would allow it to do. The Iran-contra scandal was simply a highly visible symbol of the limits of the conservative revolution. The scandal was also a sign of how the conservative political impasse was hurting American democracy. The Iran-contra scandal was, quite simply, an effort to "privatize" foreign policy. Since it could not rally Congress or the American people behind its policy, the administration had to turn to foreign governments and to a "parallel government" that was unconstrained by democratic disciplines to achieve what it wanted.

Even the invasion of Grenada, an undeniably successful if relatively minor use of American military power, was marred by the event that came just before it: the slaughter of 240 Marines in Lebanon by a suicide bomber. The Marines' experience was symptomatic of the tragic contradictions in America's view of its world role. The Marines were in Lebanon as a sign of America's power, a symbol of its commitment to the Lebanese government. Yet the Marines could not use their power at all. They complained loudly and justly about the fact that they could not respond adequately to unfriendly fire. "At least in Vietnam, you could shoot back," muttered one Marine sergeant. The administration wanted American troops in Lebanon as a "presence," but did not want to use them against any one of a number of enemies. When the administration called in fire from American ships offshore to support Lebanese government troops, it was effectively turning the Marines into allies of the beleaguered Lebanese government. But still they could not fight back. The administration was committed—sort of.

The Marines became a substitute for the administration's lack of a policy—and paid dearly. Reagan ultimately conceded the illogic of the situation by abruptly pulling the Marines out, too late to save 240 in their ranks and only after he had gone on record as insisting that Lebanon was "vitally important" to American security. For Lebanese Christians, who had counted on U.S. backing and believed Reagan meant what he said, it was no less a "sellout" than America's abandonment of Vietnam. Yet the administration could not possibly have kept its commitment to a Lebanese government with an ever-narrowing base of support unless it was willing to enmesh itself in the quagmire of Lebanese politics and risk war with Syria. President Reagan was prudent to avoid this trap, but in doing so, he sent the message that America was only partly "back." America wanted to use her power, but only if the price was low. George Bush was later to be far bolder.

What is revealing is that President Reagan paid no domestic political cost for his failed Lebanon policy. The cause of Lebanon's Christians was never popular in the United States, and Reagan, as he usually did, read public opinion correctly. As William Schneider, the political analyst, observed, polls during Vietnam had shown that Americans wanted to win or get out. Reagan followed their logic. "In Grenada, he won," Schneider quipped, "in Lebanon, he got out." The lesson was just that: Americans would support short and successful wars, but no other kind. They would arm America to the hilt as long as American troops were kept out of trouble. The long-term effect of Vietnam on American public opinion was a victory for neither the "hawks" nor the "doves." It was stalemate. Reagan pushed American opinion as far as he could, but he accepted limits that his conservative followers would have found damnable just a decade before.

If conservatives came to accept the constraints under which Reagan had to work, they could not accept his early embrace of Mikhail S. Gorbachev or his apparent rush to get an arms control treaty. Reagan saw the Soviet leader as a genuine reformer at a moment when most conservatives still viewed glasnost as a trick. The attacks on Reagan from some of his most fervent supporters were even more fierce than the assaults conservatives had directed against Richard Nixon's détente policies: It was harder to forgive Reagan, who, unlike Nixon, really had been one of their own. Reagan's conversion to détente produced some thoroughly strange political alliances. In late December 1987, the nation watched a joint debate of Democratic and Republican presidential candidates in which the Democrats praised a conservative Republican president's foreign policy, while all the Republicans but George Bush criticized their own leader. That espisode was only a preview of the thorough restructuring of the American foreign policy debate that Gorbachev would bring about as his actions became even bolder. It was also a further indication of how fragile conservative unity could be.

On the social issues, conservatives were constrained both by the divisions in their own ranks and by a shift in the popular mood that began after the 1984 elections. The Republican coalition was so badly split on the issues of interest to the Religious Right that bold moves were impossible. Ronald Reagan kept up their spirits with moving speeches on their issues—and in his eloquent pleas against abortion,

Reagan did seem thoroughly sincere. The biggest victories won by the social conservatives, as we have seen, were quiet and indirect. Within the federal bureaucracy, they got money shifted away from their foes (such as Planned Parenthood) and toward some of their favorite causes, and won victories on regulatory issues that can be important but are rarely public.

But the social conservatives got nowhere on their big-ticket items, such as constitutional amendments banning abortion or restoring prayer to the public schools. To the social conservatives' dismay, the influential "pragmatists" of the Bush administration, notably James A. Baker 3d, struggled to keep the President free from too close a connection with the Religious Right. Prayer breakfasts and the embrace of evangelical ministers were acceptable; this struck most voters as no more troublesome than Eisenhower's endorsement of religion-in-general. But the President would do nothing to offend the free-thinking conservatives among the young and well educated. The key word for the administration was not *tradition* but *tolerance*.

The uneasiness of some of the President's "pragmatic" political advisers with the demands of the Moral Majority came through loud and clear on many occasions. At a conference after the 1984 election, Lee Atwater, who served as Reagan's deputy campaign director, seemed positively apologetic about the influence of the socially conservative "populists."

"If you're a Republican strategist, your job is not to try to reeducate populists on what they should believe about social issues, but rather to concentrate on the notion of tolerance," Atwater said, suggesting, perhaps inadvertently, that the socially conservative populists were so wrong that they needed "reeducation." Atwater continued gamely: "One of the things Reagan did so well was that he often took very conservative positions on social issues, but at the same time he was able to establish the fact that he was a tolerant man. That's basically the approach you have to take on social issues." Linking conservative stands on social issues with "tolerance" was like squaring a circle. The whole point of the social conservatives' message was that liberals had been *too tolerant* of "alternative" lifestyles and value systems. Still, the formula of mixing moral absolutes and tolerance worked marvelously for Ronald Reagan on the campaign trail: On both sides of the moral debate, people trusted him. The social conservatives were at least glad to have someone in power who spoke their language; the social liberals were glad that Reagan did not seem to do much to back up his words. That, of course, was the point: Maintaining the trust on both sides meant doing little to offend either side—which meant doing little at all.

The social conservatives did win decisively in one important arena, the matter of court appointments. Liberals insisted that nothing was more ironic than the conservative quest for judicial dominance, since conservatives had spent a good twenty years accusing liberals of doing end runs around public opinion by winning so many of their major triumphs in court. Conservatives could argue that they were simply seeking to restore sovereignty to elected officials by putting an end to "judicial activism." But it was clear that the Reagan administration realized that the social conservatives' agenda was unpopular with a significant share of its own electorate, especially among the libertarian-inclined young and the well educated. Rather than fight directly for unpopular causes, the administration shrewdly chose to reshape the judiciary in a way that would give the social conservatives their victories over time, in some cases long after Ronald Reagan had left office. The immediate costs to the Reagan electoral coalition would be minimal, and the key decisions would be made at some remove—by judges rather than conservative politicians. The conservatives were copying the liberals' judicial strategy.

The conservatives thus set a series of judicial time bombs, and they began exploding soon after Reagan left office. Among the most notable was the *Webster* decision expanding the rights of states to regulate abortion. The *Webster* decision was privately mourned by scores of Republican pragmatists who realized immediately that it would unsettle the delicate balance between the libertarians and the moral traditionalists that was so vital to conservative victories. As long as abortion rights were protected by the Supreme Court, supporters of legal abortion who also wanted tax cuts and less government could safely vote for conservative candidates, even those such as Reagan who were publicly opposed to abortion. Such voters believed that the courts would protect them from any changes in the abortion law. And in the case of Ronald Reagan, they were never convinced that his heart was really in the antiabortion cause, since he conveyed, as Lee Atwater asserted, such a "tolerant" image. But as the conservative judiciary began working its will, there could be no more winking. Conservatives, finally, had to confront the deep chasm within their coalition.

The first political results of the *Webster* decision were alarming for the right. In both New Jersey and Virginia in 1989, Republicans lost contests for governor that they had reasonable hopes of winning.

In both races, abortion played an important role. In New Jersey, Republican representative Jim Courter infuriated the right-to-life movement by softening his opposition to abortion. He ended up losing ground on all sides. Foes of abortion who once viewed Courter as an ally abandoned his campaign in disgust. But Courter gained little ground among abortion-rights supporters, who voted for the clearly prochoice Democrat, Rep. James Florio. Florio won in a landslide.

In Virginia, L. Douglas Wilder became the nation's first elected black governor by making abortion rights a central issue in his campaign. Wilder dominated the dialogue on abortion by casting the issue in libertarian terms. One of Wilder's television spots on abortion featured a statue of Thomas Jefferson, the compleat Virginian, and Wilder's attacks on politicians who meddled with the private lives of individuals resonated with the antigovernment rhetoric that chamber of commerce leaders use when they discuss the minimum wage. Wilder's Republican opponent, Marshall Coleman, opposed abortion in almost all cases and was thrown off-stride, taking weeks to respond to the attacks. Unlike Courter, Coleman stuck to his antiabortion position. While noting that he had always favored abortion in extreme cases, such as those involving danger to a woman's life, he suggested that his opponent's stance was so liberal that it amounted to endorsing the use of abortion as "birth control." Coleman's response was more effective than Courter's and he lost only narrowly. But the abortion issue clearly hurt him, partly because it took him so long to respond. Coleman was beaten decisively in the Washington suburbs where affluent voters who like conservatives when it comes to taxes reject the conservatives' social agenda. Those libertarian-leaning voters were the key to his defeat.

III

But conservative problems on the social issues began before the *Webster* decision, and abortion was just one of a number of social issues that had once worked for the right and now threatened to work against it. The conservatives also began to have unexpected problems around the constellation of women's-rights issues that included day care, parental leave, equal pay, and fair access to promotions. As we saw in Chapter Three, conservatives gained ground among socially conservative constituencies in the late 1970s and early 1980s by attacking feminism. The conservatives took advantage of widespread uneasiness about the seeming suddenness of the social changes that engulfed the country and the gap between the values of professional women and those of working-class women.

But by the late 1980s, it was clear even to the most traditional that women were unlikely to disappear from the work force. Many women worked out of economic necessity, and even the most optimistic economists did not expect the wages of male breadwinners to rise quickly enough to allow women in middle-income families to return home at will. Just as important, millions of women, especially those of baby-boom age or younger, had no desire to abandon the workplace to men. For all the frustrations involved in balancing careers and families, most professional women—including many who claimed to oppose feminism—now saw their careers as being integral to their lives.

Seen from a long-term perspective, this was a huge victory for feminism. Discrimination against women was still a fact of life. Liberal political candidates supported by feminists lost many of the elections held over the last twenty years. But basic feminist values were now part of almost every American's idea of what was "right" and "normal." If discrimination against women was still practiced, it was now almost universally condemned. Even Jerry Falwell declared himself in favor of "equal pay for equal work." Working women who felt uneasy about whether they were spending enough time with their children were no longer condemned as "selfish"—except by conservative Democrat John Silber, who lost the Massachusetts gubernatorial election in 1990 in part because of his sharp tongue. Many women were working, after all, to make sure their children were adequately provided for. The problems such women faced were seen as legitimate *social* problems that needed solution.

This shift struck a fundamental blow to conservative traditionalism and created new tensions between traditionalist conservatives and those whose main interest was in the free market. Pushing women back into the home—or even just creating conditions that would allow them to go back—demanded vast changes in the workings of the marketplace. Conservatives such as Allan Carlson called for restoring a "family wage" that would allow fathers to earn enough so that mothers could devote themselves to caring for children. But this amounted to a conservative restatement of a demand in the oldest traditions of the left: asking employers to raise pay. In fact, private employers had come to depend on working women, especially on those who worked part-time and received low wages and few benefits. Chamber of commerce conservatives could hardly be expected to sympathize with the "family wage." Carlson believed he could achieve his ends in the good conservative way, through the tax system. But he was unrelenting in his criticism of what he called "an ostrichlike form of libertarianism" and charged that conservatives were "unwilling to face the enormity of recent change."

Liberals and feminists, in the meantime, took advantage of the new public sympathy for working women and the difficulties conservatives faced in confronting the problem. Happily borrowing conservative slogans, feminists and liberals recast their demands in the name of a "family agenda." The new demands were intended to call the conservatives' bluff. If conservatives cared so much about having mothers stay with their children, why were they unwilling to require employers to give leave to the parents of newborns? In opposing parental leave, were not the conservatives admitting that they gave the market priority over children?

For liberals, the new focus on the needs of children was a godsend. The reaction against the welfare state had never been a reaction against helping the disadvantaged, which was why the Reagan administration insisted it was assisting the "truly needy." But the public did react against a system that they saw as encouraging idleness over work, crime over obedience to law, self-indulgence over self-discipline. As long as conservatives kept the debate focused on the ways in which the welfare state seemed to foster antisocial *values*, their cause had a sympathetic audience.

But by the late 1980s, liberals began to gain ground by shifting the debate to the most "deserving" poor of all, needy children. Children did not ask to come into the world and could not be held accountable for the real or imagined sins of their parents. Children in ghettos did not ask to go to poor schools, nor did they create a marketplace in which a drug dealer could earn fifty times the salary of someone in a McDonald's. Children did not create the speculation in real estate in big cities that seemed to reduce the availability of affordable housing. And teenagers looking for work had no responsibility for the vast international economic changes that had reduced the availability of well-paying entry-level jobs for the unskilled.

The rise of children's issues was part of a broad but subtle shift in popular attitudes toward government and social programs. The caution of the 1980s was not transformed into an outburst of social activism, as had happened between the 1950s and the 1960s. Rather, there had been support for certain forms of government action *throughout* the 1980s, notably for education, the environment, medical insurance, programs for the elderly, public works, and day care. This underlying support for government was what made David Stockman's bold experiment in budget cutting impossible. By the late 1980s, Ronald Reagan's very successes—in steadying the economy, in shifting money to defense, and in creating the impression that government had shrunk—created a climate in which these pent-up demands for government had increasing legitimacy. This climate set the terms of the 1986 midterm elections.

IV

The 1986 midterm elections restored the Democrats to control of the Senate and provided the first concrete evidence of the decay within the conservative coalition. The Democrats scored some of their most striking victories in what had seemed to be the new Republican heartland, the South. In Florida, Alabama, Georgia, and North Carolina, Republican seats fell to the Democrats. In Louisiana, where Republicans had expected victory, the Democrats won going away. Democratic Senate candidates also won in North and South Dakota and Colorado—all states that Democratic presidential candidates lost in every election after 1964.

Election results, like the Scriptures, can be interpreted in many ways and for many different purposes. But the 1986 elections were important in shaping the strategies of 1988—and as the losers in 1986, the Republicans learned their lessons better than the Democrats. The Republicans saw clearly that the 1986 elections were bad news for conservatives in at least three important respects.

The first lesson was that conservative "social issue" politics was not a Republican elixir that would work in every election. The 1986 elections showed that the Democrats still had the ability to draw support from moderate- to low-income whites whose views on the social issues tended to be conservative. Democrats won their Southern victories by reassembling the very same coalition of blacks and moderate-income whites that had allowed Jimmy Carter his near-sweep of the South in 1976. They did so by winning back many of the evangelical and fundamentalist voters who had been straying from their ranks for so long. The Democratic Leadership Council, a moderate-to-conservative group, commissioned a study of Southern "swing voters" who had supported Ronald Reagan in at least one of his two elections but voted for Democratic Senate candidates in 1986. Among the study's significant findings: 56 percent of the "swing voters" described themselves as either fundamentalist or evangelical.

The Republicans, aware of the combustibility of their coalition, were uncertain where to turn next. The Democrats, in the meantime, had become much more adept at turning back conservative attacks on the "values" issues. One of Georgia Senator Wyche Fowler's television commercials portrayed a teacher trying to instruct a group of school-children on how to pronounce the Democratic candidate's first name. She noted that his name was "Wyche: c-h, as in church." How could somebody with *church* in his name be anything but thoroughly tradi-tional in his values? The point of the commercial seemed trivial, but it was not. Fowler's advertisement was an implicit bow in the direction of the traditionalists. It was a way of depolarizing the "values" issues. Since what many traditionalists had been seeking was simple recogni-tion of the legitimacy of their worldview, it was enough.

For the Republican right, especially the traditionalists close to the Moral Majority, the moral of the elections was that the Republicans had failed because they had not drawn the lines sharply enough. They had allowed the campaign, in the phrase widely used at the time, to be "issueless." Conservative strategists argued that only by running sharp, issue-oriented campaigns could Republicans fight the vestigial but still real attraction that many lower-income voters felt toward the Democrats. "If voters see a race as a nice-guy Republican against a nice-guy Democrat, we lose," said Rep. Newt Gingrich, the Georgia Republican. Once again, Republicans saw a need to return to Nixon's politics of "positive polarization." The struggle for the post-Reagan Republican Party began in 1986.

But the social issues were less effective in 1986 for another reason, and that was the second lesson of the elections: The Democrats were still capable, under the right circumstances, of using economic dis-tress to their advantage. The old Scammon and Wattenberg lesson, that the economic issue could beat the social issue, was still sometimes valid. Economics worked well for the Democrats in some parts of the country because of the uneven nature of the Reagan economic recov-ery. While some regions were doing exceptionally well, others were doing quite badly. Especially hard hit were the farm, oil, timber, and mining economies.

The Democrats, in a rare moment of brilliance, coined two phrases that served them well. They spoke of the Reagan economy as the "Swiss-cheese economy." It was an economy that was full of holes. They also spoke of the "bicoastal economy," arguing that while the two coasts were doing well, the nation's "heartland" was suffering. The bicoastal description was not entirely accurate—not all places on the coasts were doing well and not all places in the heartland were doing badly. But the slogan neatly tagged the Republicans as the "elit-ists" who were happy to help California and Wall Street while they ignored Main Street. Since Democrats had suffered for years as the party of the Beverly Hills and Manhattan sophisticates, the embrace of Main Street was inspired. Democratic campaigns throughout the country made effective use of "us versus them" economic populism. If it truly was "morning in America," as Reagan claimed, Democrats would keep losing. But if morning had come only to Beverly Hills and Wall Street, the rest of the nation might start thinking twice about Republican prosperity.

The third lesson of 1986 lay in the rise of new political issues to replace the old Republican standbys of tax cuts and defense buildups. Precisely because the country faced no obvious single problem, what the polltakers call the nation's "issue agenda" became highly diffuse. No single issue dominated the mind of America. Drugs rose and fell and rose again as an important concern. So did the environment, education, and child care. Taken as a package, these concerns sug-gested that voters were now more worried about domestic problems than about foreign policy or economics. And on these issues, Demo-crats had a potential advantage, since all seemed to call for *govern-ment* action. In the case of the environment, it was axiomatic that "big government" Democrats could be counted on to favor more rig-orous regulation than the Republicans. Education and child care could easily be turned into the sorts of spending issues with which Democrats were so comfortable. Most revealing was the battle over drugs. Here, it seemed, was a *social issue* tailor-made for the Repub-licans. To oppose drug use was to oppose permissiveness and crime. Drugs allowed the conservatives to offer an entirely different expla-nation for what ailed the ghetto than what liberals had offered. If the real problem in the ghetto was crime and drugs, the answer lay in law enforcement, not social programs.

But in 1986, at least, the Democrats maneuvered cleverly to make the drug issue a *spending issue.* On the criminal justice side, the Democrats came very close to matching the Republicans penalty for penalty. But the Democrats were always willing to outbid the Repub-licans in spending for police and prosecutors, for drug treatment and education. The Democrats effectively trumped the Republicans on drugs by doing what they have always done best, promising to spend more money.

Nothing better symbolized the emptiness of the conservatives' cupboards than Ronald Reagan's 1986 campaign on behalf of Republican Senate candidates. Although the President had just won an important victory on tax reform, Americans were wary of the new system and skeptical about whether it would help them very much. Even Ronald Reagan had not fully cured Americans of the mistrust of government, or the tax system, especially since the benefits to the middle class from the 1980s tax changes had been modest. As for the future, the President promised—more of the same. There was nothing left to the conservative program. So Reagan talked about drugs, and the past. He attacked "big spending, high taxes, and runaway inflation" and "policies that gave us a weak and vacillating America." He promised an America that was "strong and proud and free." And his party lost the Senate.

V

American politics had thus come full circle. By the late 1960s, it was clear that the liberal experiment was in deep trouble and that its constituency was collapsing. As the 1988 election approached, the conservative experiment was exhausted and the conservative coalition increasingly unstable. These twin failures left American politics in a sorry state.

Liberals had set the conservatives up for success. They had acted with some boldness on civil rights, but had failed to attend to the needs of their white working-class supporters and thus set in motion the destruction of the only viable coalition available to them. Ever sensitive to the need for change, many liberals were insensitive to the power of tradition and the value of local community. Liberals had lost the tax issue by failing to enact progressive tax reform on behalf of their own constituents. They had lost the jobs issue by their own economic failures and by their unwillingness to join the issues of work and welfare. This discredited the welfare state itself, by severing the link between social programs and the country's most deeply held values. Many liberals even lost faith in their own political base, the broad middle classes whom Democrats once proudly referred to as "the working people." They came to believe that "populism" was only something that hucksters such as George Wallace engaged in. The slogan "trust the people," once a liberal sentiment, fell to George Wallace and the right by default.

Now, it was the conservatives' turn to run out of ideas and to face insurrection within their coalition. They were facing liberals who, it appeared, had learned at least some lessons from their defeats. Approaching 1988, the conservatives faced a series of bad choices. They could try to respond to the public's search for a new round of government activism. But in light of the deficit, they could do this only at the risk of abandoning the tax-cut issue. They could try to heat up the social issues. But if done badly, this approach could lose the conservatives large chunks of their libertarian wing. They could argue that their stewardship of foreign affairs had been largely successful. But part of that success owed to Reagan's decision to warm relations with the Soviet Union, which drew nothing but scorn from the conservative movement.

But conservatives did have two powerful assets: a country that was at peace and on the whole, prosperous, and the liberal past. If conservatives could not offer much for the future, they could at least point to the present and run against the past. Ronald Reagan had tried this in the 1986 campaign, but in an unsystematic and scattershot way. The Republicans needed to be much more precise about exactly what liberal past they were running against. Jimmy Carter was still available as a target, but he was not enough. To win, the Republicans needed to recreate the divisions that had brought liberalism low in the first place. They also needed a Democratic candidate who would allow that to happen.

As if miraculously, all this came to pass. The result was a campaign that was, at once, one of the most brilliant and miserable in American history. The campaign gave George Bush the White House, but left American politics at a dead end.

12

ONE NATION, DIVISIBLE:

The 1988 Campaign and the Logic of False Choices

FOR THOSE WHO SAW George Bush as either a "wimp" or a "moderate," the scene was utterly incongruous.

It was a brilliantly sunny day in late August of 1988, a couple of weeks after the Republican National Convention. Bush was visiting North Carolina, the home of Jesse Helms, perhaps the most right-wing member of the United States Senate and certainly the senator who most got under liberals' skins. About two thousand people had gathered in a park on a small college campus in Rocky Mount, North Carolina to watch Helms embrace a candidate whom he had once regarded as dangerously soft on his issues, and to hear from the candidate himself.

The remarkable thing about that day was that when the time came for speeches, it was Jesse Helms who sounded like the moderate. George Bush hammered away at Michael Dukakis on one social issue after another, declaring that there was "a wide chasm" on "the question of values between me and the liberal governor whom I'm running against." The Vice President of the United States assailed Dukakis for

300

opposing prayer in public schools, for vetoing a bill that would have required children in Massachusetts' public schools to recite the Pledge of Allegiance, for supporting gun control, and for sponsoring the Massachusetts prison-furlough program that had let Willie Horton out of jail.

Indeed, Bush sought to wrap the issues together in one tidy formulation. "I don't understand the type of thinking that lets first-degree murderers who haven't even served enough time to be eligible for parole out on parole so they can rape and plunder again, and then isn't willing to let the teachers lead the kids in the Pledge of Allegiance," Bush declared. In that one sentence lay the key to Bush's campaign strategy.

Charles Black, a Bush adviser and longtime strategist for the right, watched all this with some amazement and asked the obvious question as he wandered back to the press buses. Would one have imagined even a year earlier that if Helms and Bush had found themselves speaking back-to-back, Helms would emerge as "the *second* most incendiary guy on the podium?"

George Bush's 1988 victory is one of the great comeback stories in American politics. In early 1988, after his third-place finish in the Iowa caucuses, many who watch American politics wrote George Bush off. He really *was* a wimp, they argued. He was hopelessly unacceptable to the Republican right. He seemed too much like his father, the former Connecticut senator who was a good Modern Republican in the Eisenhower mold. Bush was being cut up by Pat Robertson, the former minister who stood as the champion of the Religious Right. He was assailed by former Delaware governor Pete du Pont, who spoke the language of the libertarian right on many issues. He was attacked by Rep. Jack Kemp, who was trying to keep the lamp of *National Review*'s fusionism alight even though Robertson and Du Pont were tearing away pieces of its coalition. The beneficiary of all this, it appeared, would be Sen. Bob Dole of Kansas, a Midwestern Republican who still preached the gospel of fiscal probity and had never been much taken by the miracles of supply-side economics.

Even after Bush finally upended all those foes by winning the New Hampshire primary and swamping everyone in the South, he fell behind in the public opinion polls. The country was ready for change. The Democrats, witness their 1986 showing, were finally speaking a language the country could understand. The old Reagan constituency was hopelessly split.

Bush won the fall election going away. His victory demonstrated his acute understanding of Republican Party politics and the ease with which the old liberalism could be brought back to life as an electoral scarecrow.

II

Bush and his advisers understood a few simple things, and a number of more complicated things, about Republican politics.

The simple things had to do with the Republican Party's tendency to return loyalty to those who give it, and its fealty toward established leadership. Like Richard Nixon before him, George Bush was both the established candidate and a faithful servant of Republican interests.

He remained unswervingly loyal to Ronald Reagan. When most conservatives were assailing Reagan's embrace of Mikhail Gorbachev, Bush endorsed his President. He vigorously defended Reagan during the Iran-contra scandal. In the face of much criticism from political consultants and commentators, he resolutely pushed aside reporters' questions aimed at discovering matters on which he and the President had disagreed. Bush's loyalty to Reagan reflected his own nature, but also his understanding of conservative Republican politics. Whatever doubts conservative leaders might have had about Reagan's foreign policy, the conservative masses still revered their President. Just as Reagan had remembered that the old Goldwater right was the most important Republican constituency in 1980, so Bush understood that the Reagan right was the most important Republican constituency in 1988.

The Bush team also understood the dynamics of the party's nominating politics and the issues that mattered most to conservatives.

Lee Atwater, Bush's campaign manager, had a guiding theory: The *conservative* wing of the Republican Party had become its *nominating* wing. Outside this church, there could be no salvation. With the death of Modern Republicanism, conservatism became the Republican mainstream. But the conservatives, Atwater believed, had been transformed by their own experience of power. Because they were now in control of the party, conservatives were now much more likely to think pragmatically—they were now the party regulars. They thus wanted a leader who could unify the party and help elect its other candidates.

Bush emphasized two set issues in his quest for conservative legitimacy. In both cases, he changed his positions rather substantially to win conservative approval.

Early on, he realized the growing importance of the Religious Right to the conservative coalition. Bush embraced the Religious Right's cause as his own. He spoke at the Religious Right's meetings and paid homage to its issues, notably opposition to abortion and support of school prayer. Bush, who had once favored legal abortion, now spoke as a devout opponent. He also began talking openly about his own religious convictions and experiences, something he had not done before. Bush's efforts bore fruit, and he won an early endorsement from the Reverend Jerry Falwell.

Bush, who had once called supply-side economics "voodoo economics," also became an apostle of the supply-side creed. Taxes, in fact, were the one substantive issue on which there was a clear difference between Bush and Bob Dole. Dole was far more orthodox in his economics and suggested, without saying so directly, that he would be willing to raise taxes to close the deficit. Bush pledged himself to "no new taxes" and thereby showed he understood the importance of supply-side politics to the conservative presidential majority.

Bush was also careful in how he chose the areas where he distanced himself from the President. The care was necessary because Bush could not do anything that might suggest disloyalty; he had to keep his differences to the necessary minimum.

In two areas, the environment and education, Bush chose to paint himself as being somewhere to the President's left. Reagan's environmental policies had been broadly unpopular, and they were especially controversial within the upper middle class. This group has always been crucial to Republican victories and is often susceptible to appeals from post–New Deal reformers such as Gary Hart (who, until his troubles in May of 1987, was the Democratic front-runner). So Bush promised to be "the environmental president." Bush also promised to be "the education president." His use of the education issue demonstrated his awareness that Americans were increasingly concerned with social problems and were more favorably disposed to government programs. But Bush prevented the conservatives from thinking of him as too liberal by emphasizing a "back to basics" approach to education and by avoiding commitments to large new spending programs.

Bush's trickiest problem of all was on foreign policy, where he needed to appear slightly to Reagan's *right*. Without in any way opposing the President's Soviet initiatives, Bush wanted to make clear to conservatives that he was more skeptical of the Soviets than Reagan. Reagan gushed whenever he spoke about Mikhail Gorbachev, a man whose fights against hard-liners in the Politburo Reagan equated with his own battles with Democrats in Congress. Bush could not afford to do this, since nothing is more dangerous in conservative circles than appearing insufficiently anticommunist. Bush also needed to preserve his credentials as a hard-liner to use the issue of foreign policy "toughness" against the Democrats in the fall. If Bush had agreed that Gorbachev was all Reagan said he was, such toughness would be irrelevant.

The bloodiest and most complicated fight of 1988 took place in Michigan, which Bush aide Rich Bond dubbed "the Beirut of American politics." Michigan set up a highly complicated caucus process where the first skirmish actually took place in a Republican primary in 1986. The well-tuned Bush operation received a shock when they were outorganized by the enthusiasts for Pat Robertson's presidential candidacy. Most Republicans, including most conservatives, had regarded Robertson's candidacy as something of a joke. How could someone rise from being a television preacher (or as Robertson preferred it, "the founder of a television network") to become a serious candidate for the presidency? Robertson's success owed much to the ungainly nature of the Michigan system, which put a premium on a high degree of commitment to one's cause. What was striking about the battle between the regular Republicans associated with Bush and the outsiders associated with Robertson was the extent to which it was characterized by the harsh tones of class warfare. John Buckley, Kemp's campaign press secretary, captured the spirit of the battle in offering an explanation for why the (mainly upper middle class) Bushites so disliked Robertson's supporters. "They don't want these muddy feet on the freshly cut greens of the Republican country club," Buckley explained.

Bush finally upended Robertson in Michigan, but the acrimony suggested that there were limits to the conservative balancing act. Ronald Reagan had publicly done little for the Religious Right, but they didn't blame him. Through Robertson, they took their frustrations out on Bush. The Bush-Robertson battle revealed the fragility of the conservative coalition at the beginning of 1988.

Iowa was Bush's Dunkirk: He was routed, but he managed to escape. Bush ran third in Iowa, behind Dole (which was not surprising) and Robertson (which was a shock). Robertson's showing demonstrated that something indeed was afoot on the Republican right. Michigan had not been a fluke. Many conservatives *were* just as worried about the nation's moral state in 1988 as they had been in 1980, when they elected Ronald Reagan.

Dole looked forward to finishing off Bush in New Hampshire. Bush campaigned furiously, literally begging the people of New Hampshire to save his political career. He weighed whether to wage a negative campaign against Dole, first deciding against and at the last minute, deciding in favor. His one negative advertisement attacked Dole for straddling on the issues—on defense, on an oil import fee, and most importantly, *on tax increases*. If ever there was a state where the tax issue mattered, it was New Hampshire, which proudly had neither an income tax nor a sales tax. For good measure, on the Monday before the primary, Barry Goldwater himself flew into the state to tape an endorsement for Bush. Goldwater was not Ronald Reagan, but he was good enough. And Dole compounded his problem at a debate on the Sunday before the primary when Pete du Pont invited him to sign the "no tax" pledge that was de rigueur in New Hampshire politics. When du Pont handed him the piece of paper to sign, Dole dismissed him. "Give it to George," Dole said. "I have to read it first." In New Hampshire, a candidate *never* makes light of the tax issue.

With all this going for him, and Gov. John Sununu's organization hard at work in the neighborhoods and small towns, Bush won easily. In a five-person field, he got 38 percent of the vote, 10 points ahead of Dole. Kemp, Du Pont, and Robertson each got about 10 percent. Combined, it was a formidable showing for the right wing; but for each of the right's standard-bearers, it was a disaster.

Bush finished Dole off in the Southern primaries of "Super Tuesday." Bush won a sixteen-state sweep and picked up 577 delegates. Robertson managed a victory only in the caucuses in Washington State, and Dole won nothing. Bush's nomination was secure. He had thoroughly understood the state of American conservatism and the dynamics of the Republican Party. If conservatism wasn't in a triumphalistic mood, as it had been in Reagan's time, that was just as well for Bush, whose more plodding and methodical approach articulated well with conservatism's quiet mood.

But the conservative mood did not bode well for the general election. Something was awry on the right. The Democrats sensed it. And for the first half of 1988, they took advantage of it.

III

The 1988 presidential campaign was not a moving experience, unless one counts being moved to anger, impatience, or disgust. But one moment in the campaign was genuinely moving. It was the one time when those following the bizarre and often contrived events that constitute a modern political campaign could sense that they were part of a small bit of history. The Reverend Jesse Jackson's triumphant tour through Wisconsin the week before the state's Democratic primary was, in many ways, the campaign's high point.

What was remarkable about that moment in the Jackson campaign was not that he was headed for victory; in fact, the result in Wisconsin, a landslide for Michael Dukakis, effectively ended what chances Jackson had to win the Democratic presidential nomination. There was, moreover, some evidence that Dukakis built his lead with the support of voters who cast ballots for him simply to make sure that Jackson was kept out of the White House. But the embrace that Jackson won from almost exclusively white crowds all over the state conveyed the sense of a nation trying to heal its own racial wounds.

Typical was a scene in La Crosse, Wisconsin, a small city in the midst of farm country in the southwestern part of the state. Jackson landed at the local airport sometime after ten in the evening, and about four hundred people had jammed an airport hangar. Virtually all of them were white. Many had voted for Ronald Reagan in 1984. Yet they cheered Jackson's defense of the common people, his proclamations that what unified blacks and average whites was far more important than what divided them, his calls for a coalition of "working people" against the "merger maniacs" at the investment banking houses. In Jackson's formulation, whites of modest means were no less the victims of racism than blacks. Racism, Jackson argued, was not a sin of the white masses, but a technique used by white elites to divide the natural coalition of the downtrodden. In effect, Jackson was separating himself from white liberals who looked down upon average whites. The white liberals might blame white working people for racism, but Jackson knew that its real cause lay elsewhere. The Jackson campaign in Wisconsin was simultaneously a political drive aimed at creating a coalition of protest on the left and a quasi-religious revival in which black and whites were seeking to absolve and be absolved of past social sins.

The response to Jackson in La Crosse, no less than in other parts of the state, was thunderous. Dozens handed up their children to offer Jackson a kiss. Every hand rose to touch him. For at least one moment, in one state, white Americans took the possibility of a black man's becoming the president of the United States with the utmost seriousness.

Jesse Jackson embodies, within himself, all of the contradictions of American racial politics over the last quarter century. He has his feet planted firmly in *both* traditions of the black movement of the 1960s—the integrationist wing that sought coalitions (or in Jackson's parlance, "common ground") across racial lines, and the separatist wing that saw black solidarity and confrontation with whites as the only avenue to black advancement. At times, Jackson's central message to blacks is self-reliance: their need to advance themselves as individuals through education, self-discipline, and achievement. At other times, his rhetoric stresses the role of blacks as the primary victims in American life and suggests that only the equivalent of white "reparations" to the black community will suffice to cure the results of past injustice. Often Jackson successfully mixes the two messages —which are not, logically, mutually exclusive. But keeping the two in balance is no easier for him than it has been for other black leaders.

The rise and fall of Jackson's popularity within the white community is almost directly related to which side of his message he is emphasizing at a particular time. Jackson the integrationist who preaches self-reliance is immensely popular among whites. Jackson the separatist who preaches anger is immensely unpopular among whites. The Jackson who is seen embracing Martin Luther King's legacy is admired; the Jackson who is seen as allied with Louis Farrakhan is loathed and feared. Jackson's power as a national figure owes a great deal to this ambiguity. Within the black community, this ambiguity allows Jackson to win support across virtually every divide. His supporters range from the moderate, older supporters of Dr. King's conciliatory approach to the angry young militants who share Farrakhan's seething mistrust of white society. But Jackson's ambiguity greatly limits his appeal to whites; they want the unifying Jackson, but are never sure at any given time that that is the Jackson they will get.

Most of the time during the 1988 primaries, it was the conciliatory Jackson who was on display and his unifying message dominated the Democratic primaries. Indeed, to a considerable degree, the message the Democratic Party was sending to the nation during the primaries was more Jackson's than Dukakis's. For among the other Democratic contenders for president, both Rep. Richard Gephardt and to a lesser degree, Sen. Al Gore, were also trying to unite the party through class appeals aimed at "working people" and "average middle-class families."

Gephardt in particular tried to cast his campaign as a crusade on behalf of the standard of living of the average American. Gephardt sought to recapture patriotism as a Democratic theme by recasting patriotism as an economic issue. He would challenge the Republicans to be as "tough" in their negotiations with Japan as they were in their negotiations with the Soviet Union. Gephardt's campaign slogan was that of a crusader: "It's your fight, too."

At the early stages of his campaign, Gore explicitly tried to distance himself from liberalism's past sins by arguing that among the Democrats, only he was willing to support a tough foreign policy. He signaled this by touting his backing for the bombing of Libya and the invasion of Grenada, which the other Democratic candidates were not very enthusiastic about. The move got Gore some press attention and may have helped him with conservative Democrats. But foreign-policy issues were not moving the voters in the Democratic primaries, so Gore donned a check shirt, borrowed heavily from the populist scripts being used by Jackson and Gephardt, and began to speak out on behalf of "working men and women."

In the early going, some of the Democratic candidates, notably Gephardt and Joe Biden, also fastened on a theme that was beginning to bubble up in the country in 1986: that the United States had become too selfish in the Reagan years, that it was time for Americans to ask what they could do for their country, and each other. Sen. Paul Simon, running as the one old-fashioned Democrat in the race, tried a variation on this theme with the slogan "Isn't it time to believe again?" The echoes of John F. Kennedy were entirely intentional. Many Democrats reasoned that 1988 was just like 1960. The country was being led by a popular Republican president whose administration was running out of steam. His far less popular vice president was trying to succeed him. The country was at peace and relatively prosperous but uneasy about the future. In this view, the answer for the Democrats, in 1988 as in 1960, was not so much to run against the past as to supersede it. The Republicans were tired, the Democrats were fresh; the Republicans were the past, the Democrats were the future; the Republicans were about the old selfishness, the Democrats promised an exciting new period of public engagement.

Foreign-policy issues, as Gore found out, were not the Democrats' strong suit. Indeed, the genius of Gephardt's campaign was his effort to turn foreign policy into a domestic economic issue. It is, however, worth noting that of all the candidates in either party, only two spoke about the coming end of the Cold War in a way that looked prophetic when the events in Eastern Europe in the fall of 1989 would turn everyone's foreign policy upside down.

One of them was Gary Hart, the only candidate in either party to offer a fully thought-through alternative foreign policy. Hart, who was much taken by Gorbachev during a visit to the Soviet Union, called his plan Enlightened Engagement and suggested that in the next period, the United States and the Soviet Union might find that they had many interests in common. The real problem the U.S. faced, he said, was the proliferation of conflict in the Third World. In light of the subsequent developments, notably those in the Persian Gulf, Hart's grand vision was prophetic. But it never got much of a hearing, since his candidacy collapsed in the far from grand controversy over his personal life.

The other candidate who spoke forthrightly about the end of the Cold War was former governor Bruce Babbitt of Arizona. Babbitt's standard speech captured the euphoria of the fall of 1989 a couple of years early. "The Cold War is over," he would say. "*We've won!*" Democracy, Babbitt would argue, was "on the march" around the world and so were free-market ideas.

There was one candidate whose campaign paid little attention to bold new ideas or broad themes. His approach was to emphasize the basic workings of government and how it could be used more effectively to create a climate for "good jobs at good wages." Michael Dukakis believed in public life the way conservatives believed in free markets. He used the words *public service* without embarrassment or affectation. He believed that well-organized, practical, honest government made things better for people. There was nothing radical about Dukakis. He thought free enterprise was just fine, but that it sometimes needed nudging and regulating. He also thought that government could encourage private interests to pursue the public good. He preached "partnerships" among labor, business, and government. Dukakis believed in Reason with the faith of the eighteenth-century Enlightenment.

Michael Dukakis's political strength—and the reason he won the Democratic nomination in 1988—was that he combined within himself several different traditions of liberalism. At heart, he was an old Adlai Stevenson–style "reform Democrat." His entire career in Massachusetts politics was built on battles with the old ethnic pols, the spokesmen for Hibernian and Italian Democracy, people whom Dukakis loathed. In his style, Dukakis was much closer to the old Yankee liberal Republicans who believed in active government carried out in an honest and gentlemanly fashion. Dukakis's style was that of the upper-middle-class reformers who were now so important to the Democratic nominating process.

Yet Dukakis was also a Greek American, the "son of immigrants," as he would say over and over. His bloodlines linked him to the very sort of Democrat (outside Massachusetts) who loathed the Stevenson–

style reformers. Dukakis was an ethnic Gary Hart. Dukakis's Democratic enemies among the old Massachusetts pols would watch in amazement as a man who (so they claimed) "didn't have an ethnic bone in his body" would make connections with the Democrats' huddled masses. Dukakis's ethnic background also served a highly practical purpose: Greek Americans, one of the nation's most entrepreneurial communities, funneled millions into Dukakis's campaign coffers. The Greek connection and Massachusetts business interests gave Dukakis a far stronger financial base than any other Democratic candidate.

In many ways, Dukakis resembled Jimmy Carter—and as we have seen, this did not have to be a political liability. Dukakis's approach to government, like Carter's, was intensely serious and mistrustful of politics-as-usual. It was, finally, anti-ideological. Dukakis liked concrete talk about *this* welfare plan, *that* job training program.

It could be said of Dukakis, as it was said of Carter, that he became a kind of Rorschach test, a figure onto whom very different kinds of Democrats and liberals could project their hopes and desires.

By the late spring, Dukakis had become the dominant political figure in the country. Although George Bush and his advisers had been quite brilliant in solving his problems with party conservatives, they had not done nearly enough to improve his image with the country as a whole. Peace and prosperity, it seemed, were not enough. Reagan's own personal popularity had tumbled because of the Iran-contra mess, and this had hurt Bush. And *collectively*, the Democratic candidates had assembled a rather appealing message: that theirs was the populist party, the party of economic nationalism, the party of the future, the party that would roll back selfishness and inaugurate a new period of public engagement, the party of the family *and* day care. It was also the party that seemed, at long last, to be producing an amicable settlement between the races. For although a minority of white Democrats disliked Jesse Jackson, his popularity grew during the campaign as he spoke out for racial harmony and biracial coalition politics. Bush fell steadily behind Dukakis in the polls—first ten points behind and eventually seventeen points back. The old conservative magic wasn't working anymore. Something needed to be done.

IV

Lee Atwater, Bush's wily campaign manager, became aware as soon as Bush had clinched the Republican nomination in the spring of 1988 that something needed to be done to tear Michael Dukakis down to the level of the average Northern liberal. He thus commissioned his director of research, the towering and brilliant Jim Pinkerton, to come up with the information that would destroy Dukakis. He asked Pinkerton to make sure it all fit on one three-by-five card. Atwater generously allowed Pinkerton to use *both* sides of the card. Pinkerton and his staff of "thirty-five excellent nerds," as Atwater called them, came up with the killer issues. Dukakis, Pinkerton reported, was a "high-tax, high-spending" governor. He opposed virtually every defense program. He was skeptical of the Monroe Doctrine. There was the prison furlough program and Willie Horton's crimes. He was a "card-carrying member of the ACLU" who opposed the death penalty. He was pro–gun control and proabortion. He had, as the shorthand of the Bush campaign put it, "vetoed the Pledge of Allegiance." Dukakis, in short, was a classic, unrepentant "sixties liberal."

Like most stories in modern American politics, this one moves immediately to a "focus group," those representative citizens gathered together by polltakers to test reactions to the "themes" and "issues" thought up by the campaign professionals. The focus group may be the perfect symbol of what has happened to democracy in America. Insofar as "the people" are consulted by political leaders these days, their reactions are of interest not as a guide to policy but simply as a way of exploring the electorate's gut feelings, to see which kind of (usually divisive) message might move them most. The approach to politics is not even Machiavellian; it is Pavlovian. The focus group organized to test Pinkerton's findings gathered in Paramus, New Jersey, and was made up of conservative Democrats who had voted for Ronald Reagan but who, at the time, were supporting Michael Dukakis. While the voters talked, most of the high command of the Bush campaign listened, out of view. The results of the focus group were beyond the most optimistic imaginings of the Bush planners. About half of the group turned sharply and angrily against Dukakis when they learned about aspects of his record that they had known nothing about, such as the Willie Horton episode. The Bush planners realized immediately that they had found the silver bullets.

The truth was, Atwater said later, that most Democrats who had strayed to Reagan in 1980 and 1984 wanted to go home to the Democratic Party. They sensed that the Republicans had been in power long enough and that it was time for a change. The swing vote in the key states, Atwater said, was "conservative populist," and if such voters didn't see any real differences between the candidates, Atwater said, "guess what? They would have gone back and been Democrats again. They're always looking for excuses to be, because they are Democrats. So if we were to allow the Dukakis campaign strategy to unfold and not get on these issues, they would have prevailed."

It was a remarkable acknowledgment. After all the talk of a conservative, Republican realignment, Republicans were forced to admit that Democrats really wanted to go back home. The earthquake in American politics had not been an earthquake after all.

Bush was widely criticized, especially by Democrats and the press, for the kind of campaign he ran. The question that goes unanswered in the criticism is: What other kind of campaign could he have run and still emerged victorious? The answer is that Atwater was right in understanding that almost any other kind of campaign would have failed. Bush's own image problems were deep enough, but his standing also reflected the weakness of conservatism in 1988. Conservatism's message was neither coherent nor appealing. Indeed, no single wing of conservatism was strong enough to dictate a strategy, and no single conservative tendency was popular enough to assemble anything close to a majority.

Bush could not run a purely libertarian, antigovernment campaign because by the late 1980s, Americans perceived a need for *more* government. Bush accommodated this with his talk about the environment, education, and day care, and by promising to create, in the famous phrase, a "kinder, gentler nation." Yet Bush was unable to propose any real departures in these areas that might cost money, because he couldn't say he would raise taxes. The low-tax policies of supply-side economics were central to holding his coalition together, and his "no new taxes" pledge had been crucial to his victory over Bob Dole. Thus Bush, by temperament a Modern Republican who believed in government, was closed off from what might otherwise have been a natural strategy.

The social conservatives were certainly an important piece of the conservative coalition, as Pat Robertson had shown even in defeat. In 1988, the Republicans could not allow social conservatives to move Democratic, as they had done in so many places in 1986. Thus Bush's stand against abortion and for school prayer and "traditional values." But the social conservatives assuredly did *not* constitute anything close to a majority, either.

The issues of patriotism and military strength were promising, but support for military spending was down. And with economic nationalism, the Democrats had shown that the current national bogeyman might be not the Soviet Union but Japan. The "protectionism" that Ronald Reagan so easily attacked Walter Mondale for in 1984 suddenly seemed patriotic in 1988, given the nation's large trade deficit.

Finally, there was Dukakis himself, who seemed so adept at avoiding the traps into which so many other Democrats had fallen. He had perfectly amiable relations with all the key Democratic interest groups, but seemed beholden to none of them. Dukakis's protean persona—an *ethnic* upper-middle-class reformer, a liberal Northeastern governor who talked a lot about *efficiency* and *practicality*—made him a difficult target.

The Bush campaign thus remade Dukakis as the liberal who represented all that had made conservatism look very good to a great many people.

Dukakis helped. For one thing, he was exceptionally uncomfortable with economic nationalism, which might have shifted the ground of the foreign-policy debate. ("You can't even get him to say the *word* Japan," a frustrated adviser blurted out one day.) Dukakis genuinely was an old internationalist in the Stevenson mold, and the Republicans understood that. His *formal* foreign policy papers were realistic and a fair rendition of the post-Vietnam consensus among liberals. Late in the campaign, he did manage to turn economic nationalism to his advantage. But Dukakis's *instincts* were those of a man who never stopped believing the 1950s proclamation that the United Nations represented "the last, best hope for peace"—a theme, ironically, that Bush later made his own in the struggle with Saddam.

Dukakis also allowed the tax and deficit issues to dominate all others. Dukakis offered some creative proposals to finance the college educations of both needy and middle-class students and to expand home ownership. But both programs were less attractive and less ambitious than they might have been because Dukakis accepted the fiscal arithmetic the Republicans handed him. Dukakis was unwilling to break the impasse by talking about a more progressive tax system—or by going ahead with bold proposals that might have changed the subject from a narrowly fiscal argument to a broader debate over national goals.

The issues of crime, race, patriotism, and "values" went to the heart of liberal weakness. The remarkable fact, as Paul Taylor of *The Washington Post* pointed out in 1990, was that a man as straitlaced and family-oriented as Dukakis could be tarred with accusations of representing liberal, permissive values. It was easier to imagine Abbie

Hoffman as a Marine than Michael Dukakis as a hippy. It was impossible to find a candidate with a more profound respect for "the rule of law" than Michael Dukakis. Yet the 1960s "values issues" had cut so deeply that George Bush could speak in North Carolina with a straight face about that "wide chasm" on "the question of values" and have voters believe him.

The problem was not that Dukakis (or for that matter, George McGovern) held *personal* values that were outside the mainstream; they did not. Rather, liberals were seen as unwilling to uphold a set of *public values*; they were plainly uneasy about using government to promote, encourage, and—where violent crime was at stake—enforce the community's shared moral commitments. When Bush attacked Dukakis as "a card-carrying member of the ACLU," he was attacking a certain brand of individualism that was seen as always preferring the rights of an accused individual over the claims of the community. New Deal liberalism, which was based on the principle of social solidarity, was replaced with a new kind of liberalism based on the weaker claims of altruism. Robert Reich, the economist who made this point, argued that in Roosevelt's time the country had been bound together by the shared experiences of the Depression and war. As a result, he wrote, "society was not seen as composed of *us* and *them*; it was the realm of *we*." The new liberalism, Reich argued, lacked a strong sense of "we" and thus "lacked any definition of the public good apart from the sum of individual claims." It also "lacked a system of principles for screening and balancing such claims." In the Bush formulation, belonging to the ACLU meant never balancing an individual claim against a social claim. Fred Siegel, the historian, made a similar point when he argued that the welfare state lived on, but "without a strong ethical core." Liberals were vulnerable on the "values" issues precisely because it was no longer clear what they were asking individuals to do for their country, for their community, or even for themselves—except to pay taxes. All this worked against Dukakis.

Though the Pledge of Allegiance issue seemed trivial when balanced against such matters as the trade deficit or Soviet policy, it in fact spoke directly to the nation's split personality, which by turns emphasizes individual liberty and the importance of community. Dukakis was certainly right on the issue in one sense: Punishing the children of Jehovah's Witnesses for not reciting the Pledge is repugnant to most Americans. That, in effect, is what the original Supreme Court case on the Pledge was about. Yet Dukakis never made this point clearly. He understood the words, but not the music, of the issue. The Pledge issue spoke to Americans' sense that children above all others must be taught values in the schools. Eloquent testimony to the power of the Pledge issue was offered by Joseph Stinson, a young man who lived in a blue-collar subdivision outside St. Louis. "Little kids in school have to be taught things," Stinson told a reporter. "One of them is that there are a lot of good people who died for this country. You've got to remember your past, or you're not going to have your country anymore." Edmund Burke could not have said it better. Dukakis's failure on the Pledge issue was his inability to convince voters like Stinson that even though he had vetoed the Pledge bill, he shared their reverence for tradition and memory.

Dukakis, finally, was upended by the race issue, embodied in the Willie Horton commercials, and he chose never to confront the issue, either by attacking the Republicans' use of race head on or by trying to reassure restive working-class whites that he shared their values.

Dukakis fell behind so quickly and was beaten so decisively that many came to accept that as a liberal, Northeastern governor, he simply could not have won at all. But it seems quite clear that Lee Atwater's worries in the spring had been, in fact, well-placed, that the conservative coalition had run out of steam in 1988 and was in trouble.

For one thing, the Democrats' strength in the Senate and House elections in 1988 suggested that no large forces were at work, as they had been in 1980, on behalf of Republicanism or conservatism. In the Senate races, the sort of ardent liberals who were thrown out of office in 1980 were largely triumphant. Indeed, one of the most liberal politicians in the entire nation, Sen. Howard Metzenbaum of Ohio, breezed to victory against what was supposed to have been a formidable Republican challenge. Metzenbaum used the same economic populism that seemed to work so well for the Democrats in the spring. "Metzenbaum cast himself as the man protecting the small guy, protecting you against the big guy," said an admiring Robert Hughes, the leader of the Cleveland Republican organization. "He made himself into Horatio at the Bridge." Dukakis, belatedly, sought to run the same kind of campaign ("He's on your side"), but it was too late.

Moreover, the 1988 election returns pointed to real decay in the conservative coalition.

On the one hand, the South held for Bush, who kept the Republican vote close to 1984 levels. But outside the South, the Republican losses were large. Dukakis carried about five hundred counties that Walter Mondale had lost. Bush's losses were especially severe in areas dominated by industries that did not do well in the Reagan years—

farming, oil, natural gas, timber, and mining. The "bicoastal econ-omy" theme from 1986 still had resonance. Iowa went Democratic for only the second time since 1952. Downstate Illinois swung Demo-cratic, as did much of rural Missouri. In Oklahoma, Dukakis cut the Republicans' victory margin from 476,000 votes in 1984 to 195,000 in 1988. In Kansas, Ronald Reagan won by two to one, George Bush by just five to four. In South Dakota, Reagan had won 63 percent, Bush just 53 percent. Even in Idaho, one of the most Republican states in the union, the Democratic share of the vote climbed by 7 percentage points. Social liberalism also helped the Democrats, even though the Dukakis campaign made almost no effort to take advantage of the splits within the conservative coalition on the social issues, notably abortion. Dukakis, who was paying a heavy price for his social liber-alism on the crime issue, did little to reap the benefits of his social liberalism among younger voters. The Bush campaign was clearly petrified of the potential of the abortion issue for the Democrats. When Bush gave an equivocal answer during a debate on whether he would punish women who had abortions, his campaign chairman, James A. Baker 3d, rushed out to reporters the next morning to offer assurances that Bush's opposition to abortion did not extend to impos-ing penalties on women who had them.

The election returns suggested that the "traditionalist but toler-ant" message that Reagan had perfected worked much less well for Bush and that social liberalism had a large potential for the Dukakis campaign. Bush lost substantial ground on the 1984 vote in middle-class, socially liberal areas across the country, notably in California, Colorado, New York, Washington, and Oregon. In California, where the local Dukakis campaign ran some radio ads attacking Bush's stand on the abortion issue, the Republican losses were enormous. Reagan had carried the state by 1.49 million votes; Bush carried it by just 352,000. Reagan carried, but Bush lost, such predominantly middle-class counties as Santa Clara, Contra Costa, and Sonoma. California, the nation's trendsetter, demonstrated that in 1988, the trend was decidedly *not* in a conservative direction. Bush hung on not because of the trends, but despite them.

V

The 1988 campaign left Americans with ashes in their mouths over the state of their political process. It had been a brutish, back-ward-looking, divisive campaign. Most of the issues Americans really

cared about had gone largely undiscussed. The future had gone un-
debated. Our politics was still trapped in the past, and the voters hated
what they saw.

In 1988, half of the voters stayed away from the polls, producing
the lowest turnout since 1924. In the course of the campaign, two-
thirds of the voters, according to a *New York Times*/CBS News poll,
wanted choices other than Dukakis and Bush. It was the highest level
of dissatisfaction with the available choices ever recorded in the polls.
Half thought the 1988 campaign had been more negative than past
campaigns; only a tenth thought it had been less negative. Half said
that *both* candidates had leveled unfair charges against each other; an
additional one-quarter said that the candidate they opposed had leveled unfair charges against the candidate they supported. A majority
rated the campaign as "dull." Even in 1984, when Reagan's reelection
had been a foregone conclusion, most voters had rated that campaign
as "interesting."

In his first eighteen months in office, Bush seemed to be in a
strong position to put all this behind him. He tried to act as if the man
who had just waged a bitter campaign had no relationship with the
man who took over the White House. Indeed, he dismissed what
happened in 1988 with one of his favorite phrases, "That's history."

And at first it seemed to be just that. He negotiated with Congress
over child care and a clean air bill. He got his way on a limited increase
in the minimum wage. Prosperity largely held up during 1989. And at
the end of the year, there was the collapse of communism. This was
history's gift to Bush, though even his most severe critics conceded
that he handled the events with considerable skill.

All this did wonders for Bush's poll numbers, which appeared to
be the currency that his administration took most seriously. Boosted
by Democrats and blacks who were simply relieved to have Ronald
Reagan out of the White House, Bush's approval ratings soared. In
his first year and a half in office, Bush seemed poised to preside over
a new Era of Good Feeling.

His ratings were only strengthened in August 1990, when he committed troops to Saudi Arabia to battle Saddam Hussein. Here was an
enemy so brutal and unsympathetic that it was as if Bush's political
managers had formed another focus group to put together the precise
profile of a foreign leader who would inspire Americans to rally behind
their president.

But the conservative coalition contained some irrepressible conflicts, and these eventually caught up with George Bush.

The most striking development was the rebirth of right-wing anti-interventionism—or, as its critics preferred to call it, isolationism. The first rumblings of dissent against Bush's intervention in the Middle East came not from the left but from the right, notably from Patrick Buchanan, the former Nixon and Reagan administration official who built himself a mighty pulpit through his television shows and syndicated column. Buchanan, long a critic of Israel, was bitterly attacked, notably by *New York Times* columnist A. M. Rosenthal for his charge that the administration's anti-Saddam policy had been promoted by Israel's "amen corner" in the United States. The skirmish was only a highly publicized case of a battle between neoconservatives and traditionalists (or, as they called themselves, "paleoconservatives") that had been going on for some time.

Russell Kirk had already caused a storm with one line in a lecture he gave on neoconservatism at the Heritage Foundation in October 1988. "And not seldom," Kirk had said, "it has seemed as if some eminent neoconservatives mistook Tel Aviv for the capital of the United States—a position they will have difficulty maintaining, as matters drift in the Levant." The comment brought denunciations of Kirk from many neoconservatives, notably Norman Podhoretz. In the meantime, the Rockford Institute, a promising effort to bring together paleoconservatives with neoconservatives, was riven by an argument over nativist sentiments expressed in one of its magazines. Richard John Neuhaus, the Lutheran minister turned Roman Catholic, who combined a liberal temperament, neoconservative politics, and a strong sympathy for religious traditionalists, condemned the magazine —and was locked out of the New York office of one of Rockford's most productive ventures, the Center on Religion and Society. Neuhaus's stand was warmly endorsed by the neoconservatives and also by *National Review*, even as conservatism's leading organ continued to publish many articles by the paleocons and tried to keep lines of conservative communication open. None of this, of course, suggested that the mainstream right was about to be engulfed by anti-Semitism. Still, it was a depressing series of events for conservatives like William F. Buckley, Jr., who had worked so hard to purge anti-Semites from the mainstream right.

But the sources of dissent on the right from Bush's Iraq policy went deeper than anti-Israel or pro-Arab feeling. In the polemics that followed the collapse of the Berlin Wall, it became clear that the old conservative divisions on foreign policy were reasserting themselves.

Many conservatives who embraced anticommunism in foreign affairs had never been converted to internationalism. Once the Evil

Empire had been routed, these conservatives were perfectly prepared to follow George McGovern in inviting America to "come home." Buchanan led the way, expressing great skepticism about neoconservative proposals for a United States-sponsored movement on behalf of democracy around the world. Buchanan made his case in a provocatively entitled article in *The National Interest* magazine: "America First—And Second and Third." The ironies of the new foreign policy alignment were not lost on Vice President Dan Quayle, who spoke to *Washington Post* reporter David Broder about "the McGovern–Buchanan axis." Eventually, Buchanan decided to take his case to the voters, and although unsuccessful, his challenge to Bush for the 1992 Republican presidential nomination underscored the many fissures among conservatives.

The disputes on post-Cold War foreign policy juggled alliances all across the right. Libertarians, who had never joined the anticommunist crusade, found that they had at least as much in common on foreign policy issues with the paleoconservative right as with what was left of the left. Thus, Murray Rothbard, who had once preached an alliance with the New Left, opened a dialogue with the Old Right figures at the Rockford Institute. They shared a common enemy in the interventionist neoconservatives. The paleoconservatives accused the neoconservatives of being little more than welfare-state liberals who had joined the conservative movement to oppose the New Left and to push for an anticommunist foreign policy. Seen in one light, this "charge" amounted to nothing more than an accurate recitation of history that the neoconservatives themselves would not dispute. Still, the old Reagan coalition was fraying badly.

The disputes on foreign policy will take years to play out, especially since the isolationists are still a minority. But the political impact of conservative divisions on domestic policy were felt immediately and dramatically in the summer and fall of 1990, when Bush abandoned his "no new taxes" pledge.

For the Republicans and conservatives, the supply-side antitax message had been a political boon, whatever its problems as economic theory and policy. As middle-class voters came to expect less and less of government—and, indeed, saw government as primarily helping the poor—the one benefit they sought was the containment or curtailment of taxes. Moreover, they could accept tax cuts for the rich so long as they got their share, too.

But by the early 1990s, it became clear that the benefits voters in the economic middle got out of income-tax cuts were more than offset by sharp increases in the regressive social security payroll tax and by hikes in state and local taxes. One result of Reagan's "new federalism" was to push more responsibility down to local government—which meant more responsibility for raising taxes.

For the Republican right, the way out of the federal budget mess was clear: further cuts in domestic spending. Some on the right, such as House Whip Newt Gingrich, even called for *more* tax cuts. For Bush, however, this strategy raised a host of problems. As a political matter, large segments of government spending never stopped being popular—notably social security and Medicare. Squeezing these programs carried a very high electoral cost. And with Bush attempting a modest leftward correction in the Republicans' posture—mixing a bit of Modern Republicanism in with Reagan Republicanism—he was ill-placed to slash federal outlays. That was not the route to a "kinder, gentler" nation. On the campaign trail, Bush could mix messages freely. But when it came to making budgets, mixed messages added up to disarray.

From a political standpoint, conservatism's contradictions and the way Bush handled them left the president and his party with the worst of all possible worlds. Ever sensitive to the Republicans' business constituency, Bush continued to push for a cut in the capital gains tax. At the same time, Bush backed a slew of regressive consumption taxes—on beer, cigarettes, and gasoline. These fell precisely on the lower-middle-class constituencies that had been so crucial to Republican presidential victories. Among the cuts Bush favored was a two-week delay in paying unemployment compensation. He thus backed cuts in the welfare program that did the most for non-elderly Americans who lived by middle-class rules.

The Democrats could not have asked for a bigger opening. Simultaneously, Bush threw away the Republicans' advantage on the tax issue and painted his party as the friend of the rich. Yet it is a sign of liberal and Democratic incoherence that the Democratic congressional leadership initially bought into this regressive package. It seemed that the Democrats were bent on proving that the conservatives had been right all along: The Democratic Party seemed so interested in raising taxes that it did not care whose taxes it raised.

The Democrats were saved by the Republican right, led by Gingrich, and their own left. Together, left and right rejected the initial budget deal and opened the way for the Democrats' assault on the Republicans as the party of the rich. After a decade, the Democrats finally understood that if they had a single mission in American politics, it was to deliver something, at least, to the broad American middle. They redrafted the package to hike taxes on the wealthy—taking back about half the cuts that the rich had won in the Reagan years—and shaved the consumption taxes and cuts in Medicare. For a while, Bush continued to play the Democrats' game, holding out against one of the most popular tax measures ever devised, a levy against millionaires, a group that does not bulk large in anyone's electoral calculations. In the end, Bush largely capitulated. Having done so, he then effectively pledged himself to "no new new taxes."

Conservatives, who understood how crucial the tax issue had been to their coalition, talked of mutiny. There was certainly a point to their anger. Exit polls suggested that insofar as the budget deal hurt anyone politically in the 1990 midterm elections, it hurt Republicans. Opposition to taxes, moreover, played a role in tossing three governors from office. Fury in New Jersey at Democratic Governor Jim Florio's tax plan held down Senator Bill Bradley's victory margin to a shockingly close two percentage points. Why, conservatives asked, should they abandon the tax issue at a point when it held so much promise?

For Democrats, the news was highly positive on the surface, but less bracing in fact. At the least, the party had finally found its middle-class voice again and finally seemed willing to challenge the conservative assumption that tax cuts for the wealthy were good for everyone. After a year of evading Senator Daniel P. Moynihan's compelling argument that the social security payroll tax was the most regressive levy ever devised in Washington, the Democratic leadership began looking at ways to relieve the tax burdens on the middle class.

But as Democratic political consultant Mandy Grunwald argued after the 1990 election, the tax issue is only half of a populist program. The Democrats' real problem remained what it had been throughout the 1980s: the electorate's mistrust of government and its loss of faith in the idea that government could be the servant not just of the poor or the rich, but of the great middle, too. The voter tax revolts in 1990 were uneven. Massachusetts, for example, voted down an antitax referendum while electing an antitax Republican governor, largely because he seemed more *liberal* than his conservative Democratic foe, Boston University President John Silber. Still, voter impatience with taxes was palpable, as the conservatives contended.

At the heart of the mistrust of government and the anger at the political process was the fear that the economy was flying out of control and that those who would suffer most were the members of the great middle class. On election day 1990, roughly three-quarters of the electorate rated the economy negatively, and unhappiness extended even to states that were doing relatively well, such as California. Representative Robert Torricelli, a New Jersey Democrat who saw Bill Bradley's troubles up close, argued that while the tax revolt was real, it was only a piece of this broader anxiety over whether the middle class could maintain its standard of living in strained times. If Americans had come to hate politics, it was because politics no longer seemed to offer them a way out of this trap. Neither conservatives, who spoke the same old language about tax cuts, nor liberals with their new tax-the-rich battle cry, offered much more than slogans.

In partisan terms, the 1990 elections were largely a wash. Democrats could boast about capturing statehouses in the Republican base, notably in Florida and Texas. Republicans seized statehouses in the battleground midwestern states of Ohio and Michigan, and held on in California and Illinois. The Congress became marginally more Democratic, which was a serious defeat for the Republicans. Republicans won about as many House seats in 1990 as they had in the disastrous recession election in 1982. The much discussed anti-incumbent surge did not materialize in big turnovers in Congress. For the most part, the voters "threw the bums back in." But they did slash the victory margins of many incumbents. In 1988, only fifty House victors had majorities of less than 60 percent. In 1990, the ranks of the vulnerable more than doubled.

More striking than the actual results of the 1990 elections was the mood of the country in which they took place. The electorate was surly and anxious. Turnout levels were low. Insofar as they went to the polls, voters took out their anger at the local and state level, shifting roughly 40 percent of the governorships at stake from one party to the other. In California and Colorado, voters backed term limitations for legislators, and polls showed overwhelming support for term limits in the rest of the country.

Most alarming of all was the reappearance of increasingly nasty racial politics. In Louisiana, David Duke, the former Ku Klux Klan leader, won about 60 percent of the white vote in a contest for the United States Senate. In North Carolina, Sen. Jesse Helms closed his campaign against Harvey Gantt, a politically liberal but temperamentally moderate black Democrat, with a television advertisement that harshly attacked racial quotas. Gantt's advisers said the ad helped reelect Helms by boosting turnout among whites of modest incomes who just a week earlier had seemed inclined to stay away from the polls. In Alabama, Republican Gov. Guy Hunt held off a strong challenge from Democrat Paul Hubbert by running advertisements linking

Hubbert to black leaders. In California, Republican Pete Wilson successfully used the quotas issue against Democrat Dianne Feinstein.

Black voters were restive, too. In both Illinois and Michigan, dismal black voter turnouts doomed the gubernatorial candidacies of Democrats Neil Hartigan and incumbent Jim Blanchard. Taken together, the backlash of whites and the unhappiness of blacks present the Democrats with a troubling problem: Any direct efforts aimed at appeasing white racial fears can easily heighten the alienation of blacks, and losing the black vote is something the Democrats cannot afford.

For the nation, the problem was even graver. The elections raised the prospect that one of the most dismal traditions of American political life might soon be revived: that of scapegoating racial minorities in times of trouble. A sullen, pessimistic country is unlikely to find racial peace.

VI

This, then, is the legacy of the last thirty years: a polarized politics that highlights symbolic issues, short-circuits genuine political debate, gives discontent few real outlets, allows money a paramount role in the electoral process, and leaves the country alarmed over whether it can maintain its standard of living. Is it any wonder that Americans have come to hate politics?

Tom Mann, a political scientist at the Brookings Institution, argues that the root causes of our political discontent transcend politics. From World War II until the 1970s, he argues, Americans became accustomed to a politics of growth, which made everything easy. With economic growth, politicians could cut taxes and spend more—and still come close to balancing their budgets. When growth slowed in the 1970s, he said, the choices became harder. Ronald Reagan tried to transcend the dilemma by giving the country what it still wanted, which was more tax cuts and more government spending. But while the economy did grow in the 1980s, Reagan's hopes that he could restore the growth rates of the 1960s proved misplaced. The result is that the choices in the 1990s will become even harder.

But polarized politics will make those choices more difficult still. Representative Torricelli of New Jersey argues that political debate has become increasingly unsatisfactory because neither liberals nor conservatives have found a way to come off their old positions. Conservatives, he says, argue that everything wrong with the country can be traced to the permissive sixties and seventies. Liberals, in turn, say that all our troubles can be traced to the selfish eighties. Nobody is talking seriously about the nineties.

If conservatives and liberals have trouble facing the future, it is because doing so will require both to face up to flaws in their world-views.

The last decade has shown that conservatives are simply incapable of cutting government down to the size that would accommodate what they would like the tax rates to be. Conservatives cannot simply blame this on George Bush's lack of effort. Ronald Reagan could not do it, either—even in his very first year, when he was exceptionally popular. Nor can they simply blame it on the Democrats in Congress; voters have continued to elect those Democrats to Congress for the very purpose of protecting parts of government from conservative cutting knives. According to the polls, even among voters who disapproved of the way Congress was doing its job, roughly 60 percent of the voters who had the choice opted for their Democratic incumbent in 1990. And throughout the 1980s, when congressional seats fell open —robbing the Democrats of their incumbency advantage—the voters still picked more Democrats than Republicans.

But liberals also face a problem: Their assault on the Reagan era is not so much an attack on its practical failures as it is a rejection of its moral values. At its heart, modern American liberalism is a moral system which insists that the government has an obligation to offset the inequalities created by the market system and to force individuals to act compassionately toward each other—even when they would prefer not to. Yet liberals often become uneasy when the talk turns to the reciprocal obligations of those who receive government help. And they become uneasier still when they are asked what kinds of individual behavior the compassionate state is trying to promote. Creating the compassionate state is an inherently moral act, but liberals' uneasiness with the relationship between government intervention and moral values casts them as advocates of what might be called "value-free big government." The result, as the historian Fred Siegel has put it, is "a government whose jurisdictional reach has been dramatically extended, but whose moral grasp recedes before the privatization of life."

Put simply, conservatives highlight the government's role in promoting individual virtue but downplay the government's responsibility to create a society in which virtue can flourish. Liberals are wary of regulating personal behavior, but would give government a powerful say over the shape of social and economic life. In essence, liberals and conservatives disagree over what are the most important sins. For conservatives, the sins that matter are personal irresponsibility, the flight from family life, sexual permissiveness, the failure of individuals to work hard. For liberals, the gravest sins are intolerance, a lack of generosity toward the needy, narrow-mindedness toward social and racial minorities.

Since the 1960s, American politics has been a war over which set of sins should preoccupy government. Conservatives preached that the good society would be created if individuals could be made virtuous. Liberals preached that the good society would create virtuous individuals. Thus, conservatives sought to ban abortion, while liberals banned racial discrimination. Conservatives preached the re-creation of the "traditional family" while liberals argued that families would be improved if working mothers were given more support and more options. Conservatives said crime bred poverty in decaying inner-city neighborhoods. Liberals said poverty in decaying inner-city neighborhoods bred crime.

As abstract propositions, these are all interesting arguments. The problem for our politics is that Americans reject the false polarization implied by all of them. Americans as a whole like neither "permissiveness" nor "selfishness." But neither do they like excessive government intrusion in personal decisions nor confiscatory taxation. Americans like the idea of the "traditional family" in the abstract and worry about what new family arrangements are doing to children. But they also like the new freedom women have won and do not imagine that it is either possible or desirable to return to some idealized version of the 1950s.

Few recent studies of public opinion have better captured popular impatience with polarized politics than a 1987 poll of more than four thousand Americans conducted by the Gallup Organization for the Times Mirror Company. The poll found that 66 percent of Americans *rejected* the idea that "women should return to their traditional role in society." Yet 68 percent said that "too many children are being raised in day-care centers today," and 87 percent said they had "old-fashioned values about family and marriage." Americans are feminists *and* traditionalists. Yet the political system does not make it easy for them to express this dual view.

The survey found that 71 percent said that the "government should take care of people who can't take care of themselves" and 62 percent said that "government should guarantee every citizen enough to eat and a place to sleep." Yet only 29 percent agreed with the statement that "hard work offers little chance of success," and only 38 percent agreed that "success in life is pretty much determined by forces outside our control." Americans believe in both a compassionate state *and* self-reliance.

The poll found that 77 percent agreed with the statements that "it's really true that the rich get richer and the poor get poorer" and that "too much power is concentrated in the hands of big business companies." In addition, 65 percent agreed that "business corporations make too much profit." Yet 76 percent of those polled said that "the strength of this country today is mostly based on the success of American business" and 63 percent agreed that "when something is run by the government, it is usually inefficient and wasteful." Americans are simultaneously skeptical of business and skeptical of government; they worry about the power of corporations, and also worry about what would happen if they failed.

The trouble with American politics lies in its failure to allow these complicated feelings to express themselves. As a result, substantial numbers of Americans see the political conversation as too polarized, too remote from their concerns, too caught up in the false "consistencies" that are seen only by the political, cultural, and economic elites. As Charles Paul Freund wrote a few years ago in *The New Republic*: " 'Nothing in moderation' has been our unofficial motto for a long time, with libertine and puritan subcultures leapfrogging each other to set the tone for an unstable mainstream." The current revolt against American politics is the mainstream's rebellion against this false polarization.

For three decades, the United States has gone through a harsh but necessary debate over first principles. In their different ways, the New Left, the neoconservatives, the Buckley right, and the libertarians all understood that old Vital Center of the 1950s needed to be shaken up. The feminist and black movements saw that the political center needed to be less confining, less exclusive.

But the time has come for a settlement. Ending popular hatred of politics demands a new politics of the middle class, an approach that represents the ideals and interests of the great mass of Americans in the political and economic center. It is the politics of the restive majority.

PART THREE

Curing
the Mischiefs
of Ideology

13

THE POLITICS
OF THE
RESTIVE MAJORITY:
Healing Public Life
in the Nineties

Is IT POSSIBLE for a nation to learn from thirty years of political debate? Can partisans in the debate accept that wisdom is not the exclusive province of one side of the barricades?

The Sixties Left and the Eighties Right had far more in common than either realized. If they shared a virtue, it was their mutual, if differently expressed, hope that politics could find ways of liberating the potential of individuals and fostering benevolent communities. If they shared a flaw, it was expecting far too much of politics. For both the Sixties Left and the Eighties Right, politics became the arena in which moral and ethical questions could be settled once and for all. Partisans of the Sixties Left could not understand how anyone could reject their insistence on tolerance and compassion. Partisans of the Eighties Right could not understand how anyone could reject their insistence on hard work and personal responsibility.

In both their virtues and their flaws, the Sixties Left and the Eighties Right were caught up in the tensions and ironies that have characterized politics throughout American history. As James A. Morone argued in his brilliant book *The Democratic Wish*, American politics is characterized by both "a dread and a yearning." The dread is a "fear of public power as a threat to liberty." The yearning, said Morone, a Brown University political scientist, is "an alternative faith in direct, communal democracy," the idea that Americans could "put aside their government and rule themselves directly." Put another way, Americans yearn simultaneously for untrammeled personal liberty and a strong sense of community that allows burdens and benefits to be shared fairly and willingly, apportioned through democratic decisions.

In their very different ways, the Sixties Left and the Eighties Right reflected both of these honorable impulses—and all of their contradictions. The "if-it-feels-good-do-it" left rejected the imposition of conventional moral norms through force of law. The entrepreneurial right rejected the imposition of compassion through taxation and regulation. The New Left and the more conventional liberals who ran the Great Society believed that the federal government could strengthen and "empower" local communities to organize themselves and act on their own behalf, sometimes by fighting City Hall and the federal government itself on the streets and in the courts. The Eighties Right also took "empowerment" seriously and sought to give individuals and local communities more say, at the expense of the federal government and bureaucrats of all kinds.

In their respective attempts to break with the drabness of bureaucratic and conventional politics, the Sixties Left and the Eighties Right aspired to a higher vision of public life. The paradox of the last thirty years is that their elevated aspirations drove both left and right further and further away from the practical concerns of the broad electorate and blinded both to the challenges facing the United States at the end of the century.

The moralism of the left blinded it to the legitimate sources of middle-class anger. The revolt of the middle class against a growing tax burden was not an expression of selfishness but a reaction to the difficulties of maintaining a middle-class standard of living. Anger at rising crime rates was not a covert form of racism but an expression of genuine fear that society seemed to be veering out of control. Impatience with welfare programs was sometimes the result of racial prejudice, but it was just as often a demand that certain basic rules about the value of work be made to apply to all. Those who spoke of "traditional family values" were not necessarily bigots opposed to "alternative lifestyles." As often as not, they were parents worried about how new family arrangements and shifting moral standards would affect their children. And those who complained about the inefficiency of government programs were not always antigovernment reactionaries; in many cases, the programs really did stop working and the bureaucracies really were unresponsive.

The right was guilty of its own misguided moralism. Feminists demanding equality for women were not selfish souls who put the children second; they were rational human beings responding to a world that had been vastly transformed, and to which they wished to make their own contribution. Gays demanding tolerance were not looking to insult the heterosexual world; they were simply asking that they not be picked on, ridiculed, and discriminated against. The right's worst blind spot was its indifference to economic inequality, an indifference that the politics of the supply side disguised brilliantly. At the heart of the supply-side vision, after all, was a view grounded in common sense: That we get less of what we tax. Supply-siders proposed cutting taxes on work, savings, and investment. But the net result of the Reagan tax program was to *increase* taxes on the work done by the vast majority in the middle; supply-side tax cuts disproportionately favored the savings and investments of the better-off. Social security payroll taxes, along with state and local taxes, kept going up. When the eighties were over, the middle class felt cheated. It had voted for tax relief, but got little of it for itself. The demand for "tax fairness" was thus not class envy or watered-down Marxism; it was simply what the middle class thought it would get when it elected Ronald Reagan.

Because of the particular myopias of left and right, American politics came to be mired in a series of narrow ideological battles at a time when much larger issues were at stake. While Americans battled over the Religious Right, Japanese and German industrialists won ever larger shares of the American market. While left and right argued about racial quotas, the average take-home pay of *all* Americans stagnated. While Michael Dukakis and George Bush discussed Willie Horton and the Pledge of Allegiance, the savings and loan industry moved inexorably toward collapse. While politicians screamed at each other about the death penalty, more and more children were being born into an urban underclass whose life chances were dismal and whose members were more likely to be both the victims and perpetrators of crime. While conservatives and liberals bickered over whether the government or private enterprise was the fountainhead of efficiency, America's health system—a mishmash of public and private spending —consumed an ever larger share of the Gross National Product.

While veterans of the sixties continued to debate the meaning of the Vietnam War, communism collapsed and a new world—probably *more* dangerous and certainly less predictable than the old—was born.

Thus, when Americans say that politics has nothing to do with what really matters, they are largely right.

The Sixties Left and the Eighties Right conspired in another way to wage war against public life. Both profoundly mistrusted the decisions that a democratic electorate might arrive at. The left increasingly stopped trying to make its case to the voters and instead relied on the courts to win benefits for needy and outcast groups. The right waged wholesale war on the state and argued that government was *always* the problem and *never* the solution—except when it came to the military buildup. Over time, as Martin Shefter and Benjamin Ginsberg argued, fewer and fewer questions got settled through the electoral process. Instead, political battles were fought out through court decisions, Congressional investigations, and revelations in the media. The result has been a less democratic politics in which voters feel increasingly powerless.

In the meantime, the sheer volume of money that flooded through the electoral process made it an increasingly technocratic pursuit. Democratic politics is supposed to be about making public arguments and persuading fellow citizens. Instead, it has become an elaborate insider industry in which those skilled at fund-raising, polling, media relations, and advertising have the upper hand.

II

In the face of all this, Americans continued to hold with our republican forebears that there was such a thing as "the public good." Americans hate politics as it is now practiced because we have lost all sense of the public good. Over the last thirty years of political polarization, politics has stopped being a deliberative process through which people resolved disputes, found remedies and moved forward. When Americans watch politics now, in thirty-second snatches or even in more satisfactory formats like "Nightline" or "The MacNeil/Lehrer News Hour," they understand instinctively that politics these days is not about finding solutions. It is about discovering postures that offer short-term political benefits. We give the game away when we talk about "issues," not "problems." Problems are solved; issues are merely what politicians use to divide the citizenry and advance themselves.

Conservatives and liberals are suspicious of an ethic of "the public good" for very different reasons. Conservatives who dislike government see the revival of a civic politics as a way of invoking old language to justify modern big government. Liberals, fearful of too much talk about virtue and community, fear that civic talk will mean the creation of a homogeneous community. When liberals hear talk about "the common good," they often think of Jerry Falwell.

The lack of a coherent notion of the common good has been especially harmful to American liberalism. To rationalize its program, as Robert Reich has argued, liberalism has had to fall back on *altruism* and *conciliation* as its central goals. Reich notes that while these are perfectly worthy objectives, they are unsatisfactory as justifications for government action in an increasingly competitive world. The goal of conciliation has collapsed into "an overwhelming preference for smoothing over rather than settling conflict," Reich argues. This, he says, "contributed to an environment in which unaccountability flourished, both at home and abroad."

In Reich's view, the New Deal stood on a much stronger foundation. Roosevelt's claim was that individuals had a powerful stake in the public interest. The citizenry was motivated not by altruism, but by enlightened self-interest. Roosevelt was aided mightily in this endeavor, as Reich points out, by the nation's shared experience of the Depression and World War II. "The goals of reviving the economy and winning the war, and the sacrifices implied in achieving them, were well understood and widely endorsed," Reich wrote. "The public was motivated less by altruism than by its direct and palpable stake in the outcome of what were ineluctably *social* endeavors."

Mark Lilla, the thoughtful neoconservative writer, also saw civic life as central to the New Deal's popularity. The New Deal won acceptance "in no small part because Franklin Delano Roosevelt spoke *to* citizens, *about* citizens." The New Deal, he went on, "succeeded in capturing the American imagination because it promised to be a great act of civic inclusion."

Reich and Lilla accurately capture the primary causes of our political discontent. Lost in a narrow ideological and technocratic politics, left and right alike have abandoned their obligation to speak for what Lilla calls "the civic interest."

Talk of citizenship and civic virtue sounds utopian. In fact, it is the essence of practical politics. Only by restoring our sense of common citizenship can we hope to deal with the most profound—and practical—issues before us: How to balance rights and responsibilities; how to create a welfare state that is both compassionate and conducive to the deeply held American values of self-reliance and personal accountability; how to pay for the size of government we want; how to restore dialogue and friendship among the races; how to promote strong families while respecting the rights of those who live outside traditional family structures; how to use government—notably the educational system and the state's proven capacity to promote research and development—to restore America's economic competitiveness.

Solving all these problems requires acceptance of the notions that individualism must be tempered by civic obligation and that the preservation of personal liberty is an ineluctably cooperative enterprise. These ideas lie at the heart of the popular revolt against both the Sixties Left and the Eighties Right. If there is an uneasiness about both the counterculture and the money culture, it is that both shunned the obligations of individuals toward the broader community. "Inability to commit oneself to or believe in anything that transcends one's private interests," wrote the philosopher William M. Sullivan, "leads to a weakening of commitment in family and community and to the self-absorption that is sometimes called narcissism." The alternative, says Sullivan, is a return to "the ideals of loyalty and service based on personal trust and commitment." Americans hate politics because that trust and commitment have eroded, and with them the ideals of democratic citizenship.

In the 1990s, Americans are seeking a politics that restores a sense of public enterprise and mutual obligation—knowing that without these things, the gains in individual liberty that the last three decades produced will be imperiled. In effect, Americans are seeking a balance between sixties politics and eighties politics. With conservatives, Americans accept the idea captured in an aphorism coined by James Q. Wilson. "In the long run," Wilson declares, "the public interest depends on private virtue." Liberals are often right in seeing "structural problems," such as the changing labor market, as primary causes of social decay. But designers of social programs need to be clear about what values—and "virtues"—they are seeking to promote. Value-free social policy is a contradiction in terms.

But with the Sixties Left, Americans also accept that public problems will be solved only through public—which includes government —action. The revolt against government during the 1980s was less an ideological rebellion against all government activity than an impatience with a government that did not seem to work and that had stopped delivering tangible benefits to the broad middle class. Voter impatience with George Bush's presidency grew in the second part of his term because the president displayed manifest indifference to domestic policy. For all the antigovernment talk of the 1980s, voters expect the government to "do something," especially in times of economic stress.

In the midst of the anger about politics that characterized the beginning of the 1990s, there were signs of hope, indications that both left and right were seeking ways out of ideological gridlock. Drawing on the core ideas of both the Sixties Left and the Eighties Right, policy analysts were turning toward programs designed to "empower" individuals. That meant schemes resembling the GI Bill which sought to extend home ownership and college opportunities within the broad middle class, and experiments with vouchers and community control of schools and public housing which sought to expand the power of the poor. The virtue of the "new paradigm" of empowerment and decentralization that has captured the imagination of some young conservatives is that it takes seriously government's role in extending opportunities—even if some of the conservatives simply want to use these ideas to dismantle bureaucracies. Instead of rejecting these ideas out of hand, liberals should encourage conservatives down the path of public engagement.

Liberals, in the meantime, were rediscovering the virtues of "virtue." In an important study of welfare mothers published in the liberal magazine *The American Prospect*, Christopher Jencks and Katheryn Edin discovered that many on public assistance were "breaking the rules" by working for extra income. The study suggested that far from being "punitive," programs that sought to lift the incomes of the poor by linking work and welfare were actually what the poor themselves were seeking. Similarly, liberals were also rediscovering the virtues of the intact, mother-and-father-and-kids family. Suddenly the boldest "new ideas" in social policy involved figuring out ways of strengthening that oldest of institutions. In the early 1990s, Daniel Patrick Moynihan's hope of creating a "new political center" on behalf of social policy that is at once generous and sensible no longer seems farfetched.

III

Nowhere is the quest for a new political center and a revived sense of common citizenship more vital than in easing America's racial tensions. In the absence of new thinking, Willie Horton and David

Duke threaten to become the symbols of the state of race relations in the United States.

During the 1980s, the chasm between black and white America grew wider. When white Americans, especially those at the bottom of the class structure, stopped believing that liberal efforts to achieve social justice had anything to offer them, many in their ranks turned right.

Conservatives, often shamelessly, took advantage of this white alienation from liberalism, the welfare state, and black America. As a result, black America saw the Reagan Era as a time of growing white hostility. It is impossible to go into any black community, whether middle class or poor, and not hear talk that "Ronald Reagan gave whites license to be racist again." While there is no evidence that Reagan himself was racist, the administration's relentless war against affirmative action, seen from the perspective of black America, was animated not by a principled opposition to "quotas" but by a desire to roll back twenty years of black progress.

There is no easy escape from this growing polarization. But such hope as there is may lie in a new agenda, suggested by William J. Wilson and Theda Skocpol, that emphasizes nonracial approaches to the problems of the poor. Wilson has closely studied the politics of the 1960s and drawn out what is one of the most obvious lessons: that programs emphasizing work—full employment, education, and expanded job training—speak to the values of both blacks and whites and offer the most promise to the very sectors of the black community that have been left behind. Affirmative action, in Wilson's view, may be desirable, but the one thing it will *not* do is lift up the black poor. Skocpol makes a similar point about the need to address the concerns of the middle class and the poor simultaneously. "Past experience teaches us that targeting the poor alone fails," she argues. "Targeting within universal programs, however, can be both effective and politically sustainable." An emphasis on such practical measures has an additional virtue: It will move our politics away from the moralistic concerns of the upper middle class, whether "Goldwaterite" or "McGovernite," and toward the practical concerns of those who most need government help.

But the time is short. Black America is being engulfed by a wave of pessimism, and historically such pessimism has been accompanied by a rise in black nationalist feeling. The new nationalism is in part an assertion of black pride. But it also takes the virulent form of Louis Farrakhan's antiwhite and anti-Semitic diatribes. The source of Farrakhan's popularity is a loss of faith within the black community in white society.

No one better understood the dangers we face today than Martin Luther King, Jr. In *Why We Can't Wait*, published in 1963, King spoke of himself as standing "in the middle of two opposing forces in the Negro community." On the one side, he said, was "a force of complacency," represented by blacks who had lost their sense of "somebodiness" under the lash of oppression, or who were so economically secure that they had "become insensitive to the problems of the masses." King went on:

> The other force is one of bitterness and hatred, and it comes perilously close to advocating violence. It is expressed in various black nationalist groups that are springing up across the nation. . . . Nourished by the Negro's frustration over the continued existence of racial discrimination, this movement is made up of people who have lost faith in America, who have absolutely repudiated Christianity, and who have concluded that the white man is an incorrigible "devil."

King warned whites that "if they refuse to support our nonviolent efforts, millions of Negroes will, out of frustration and despair, seek solace and security in black-nationalist ideologies—a development that would inevitably lead to a frightening racial nightmare."

White Americans need to listen to Dr. King's warnings now at least as much as they needed to listen to them a quarter-century ago. But there is also a parallel lesson for black America. The genius of the civil rights movement as conceived by King was that it was primarily a moral undertaking. The paradox of the movement was that it realized that the most pragmatic course was the moral course. The movement saw blacks and whites as having parallel moral obligations—to each other and to themselves. Blacks had the obligation to seek and obtain freedom; individual dignity demanded that human beings be free. Whites had the obligation to join with blacks in the struggle for freedom not merely out of altruism, but also because to be an oppressor was as much of an offense to human dignity as to be oppressed.

At the heart of the civil rights cause was an old-fashioned sense of common civic endeavor. "We can easily forget or underestimate the significance of the moral persuasiveness of the normative vision generated within the movement," wrote Jerry G. Watts. "Whites were led to believe that they should act in behalf of black civil rights and blacks were led to believe that there were sufficient numbers of white

Americans of good will who wanted to see the racial reality altered. . . . And because the movement was situated in a Christian moral discourse, the movement rhetorically reinforced the possibility of the moral/political conversion of its adversaries."

This moral sense is lacking in American public life today. Americans—black or white—who have little faith in the possibilities of common endeavor will be especially skeptical of finding common ground across racial divides. Politics in many urban areas has been reduced to a crude battle for resources between blacks and whites. Worse, blacks and whites perceive little common moral ground between their communities. Large numbers of blacks, including the economically successful, see whites as hopelessly racist. Conspiracy theories suggesting that the drug plague is a plot by whites to commit genocide against blacks receive wide attention in the black media. Large numbers of whites, in the meantime, are giving a hearing to racists who condemn the black community as little more than a collection of pathologies—drug addiction, illegitimacy, and crime.

Once again, practicality and morality are on the same side. What is needed, and desperately, is a resurgence of the language of common citizenship that animated the early civil rights movement. Such a language will necessarily involve conservative values such as self-help and hard work, and the liberal values of generosity and tolerance. Only a combination of these values will lay the basis for a new social contract between black and white Americans.

IV

The creation of a new political center is also vital to resolving the conflicts surrounding family life and feminism. And that center now exists, if politicians would but find it.

In three decades of argument, we have learned two very significant things: first, that most of the time the best way to bring up children is in what we sometimes (and very misleadingly) call "the traditional family," meaning mothers and fathers who live under the same roof with their children. To want to support that kind of family is *not* to discriminate in favor of one "lifestyle" over others. It is to lend a hand to the *only* institution in society whose main purpose for existing is the full-time nurturing of children. To make this assertion is not to discriminate against other "lifestyle choices." It is simply accepting that it is in society's interest to have our children well cared for and that children are usually better off when they live with a mother and a father who have made more than a passing commitment to each other.

Following from that, liberals should see that many of the proposals conservatives make in defense of the family are, in fact, quite consistent with the liberal agenda. Conservatives who argue that the tax system should be more generous to parents with children are, in effect, arguing for a more progressive tax system that is fairer to the families that most need relief.

But conservatives need to make a comparable concession, and this is the second thing we have learned over the last thirty years: that talk about reestablishing the 1950s-style family in which women would stay home all or most of the time is just that—talk. It is ludicrous to base public policies on the hope that women will give up their social gains. It is foolish to pretend that the economy will grow so quickly that a majority of women will be able to rush back home. Today, roughly 50 percent of families would fall below the poverty line but for the wages earned by women.

As we have seen, feminism did not arise by accident. Nor did it arise suddenly. When the economy changed radically at the turn of the century, so did family life *and* our attitudes toward family life. Work left the household and so did the people who lived there—first men, later women. Over time, society made a series of new commitments to women, including a commitment to providing women with educational opportunities equal to those of men. This transformed many things, most notably women's aspirations. It took until the 1960s for these transformations to have an explosive effect, but those changes had been coming for a long time. It is simply silly to think that a society that puts so much emphasis on work and its creative possibilities will convince half of its members to stay home, just because they happen to be women.

As a society, we are not entirely at ease with all these changes, and for good reason: In our mad rush into the workplace, we have left the children behind. New words and phrases describe our discontent, phrases like "latch-key children" who come home to an empty house because both parents are out earning a living.

These problems will not be resolved easily. But almost none of the answers will come from conservatives if they insist on holding out the 1950s ideal as the solution. The 1950s ideal is, at best, an option for those who can afford to live on one income. Conservatives also render the pro-family rhetoric highly suspect when they oppose requiring businesses to give leave time to the parents of newborns. This suggests that conservative solicitude for their business allies is greater than their concern for what happens to children. Conservatives talk of making it easier for parents to live on one income by changing the tax laws to help middle-income families raising children. But when President Bush offered his major tax-cut proposal, it was not to help these families; it was to cut the capital-gains tax, which would mainly benefit the wealthy. Once again, a conservative administration betrayed where its real bias lay.

What is needed is an approach that is both pro-family and pro-feminist. Such an approach accepts two widely held values in the society: that the family is good, that men and women are equal. For both liberals and conservatives, this approach will mean overcoming a deep mistrust that twenty years of false choices have encouraged. Many traditionalist conservatives really do believe that feminism is "anti-family." Many feminists really do believe that the traditionalists are "anti-woman." Many traditionalists see feminists as having little respect for "homemakers." Many feminists see traditionalists as having little respect for professional or single women.

The truth is that activists on both sides of the traditionalist–feminist debate have far more room for agreement than they realize. In 1989, Susan Moller Okin, a feminist scholar, published a book called *Justice, Gender and the Family*. On its face, the book was radical in its feminism. Okin argued that until the division of labor between men and women within the household was made equal, feminism would be a distant dream. To achieve real equality, she called for an end to all distinctions between men and women in the workplace. Employers, she said, should not assume that the primary responsibility for the care of small children will fall inevitably to women. It was thus vital, she argued, that all leave programs designed to allow parents to spend more time for their children be applied equally to men and women.

Such a proposal would find little support from backers of the Moral Majority. But what is striking is how many of Okin's other ideas would win a hearing from Jerry Falwell's followers. For example, she argues that in divorce cases, the parent without physical custody of the child—usually the father—should be required to contribute to the child's support *"to the point where the standards of living of the two households are the same."* (Her italics.) To do anything else, she contended, was unfair both to the children and to the (usually) female parent who bore responsibility for their care. Thus, in the name of feminist equality, Okin proposed an approach that traditionalists have long sought: an end to "no fault" divorce settlements that left women impoverished. By placing such a heavy burden on the divorcing father, Okin would create a powerful economic incentive for him to consider trying to keep a marriage together.

Okin also offered the intriguing suggestion that employers issue two paychecks "equally divided between the earner and the partner who provides all or most of his or her unpaid domestic services." This idea is surely controversial, but it provides an interesting point of contact between feminists and traditionalists, *both* of whom argue that women's work as mothers and "primary caretakers" is vastly undervalued by the society.

In short, we have reached a point where not all feminist ideas necessarily work against the values of traditionalists, and not all traditionalist ideas work against feminism. Most important, both feminists and traditionalists find common ground in seeing the care of children as taking priority over the narrowest marketplace values. It is around this proposition that a new center could form.

But if any one issue is obstructing the formation of such a center, it is abortion. On its face, abortion is as uncompromisable an issue as the American political system has ever confronted. For advocates of choice, abortion is a fundamental right. For the prolife movement, abortion is murder. Between those two positions there is little room for agreement—and, in fact, the dialogue between the prochoice and prolife movements is almost nonexistent.

Yet the mass electorate sees the issue quite differently from the partisans on either side. There is no single majority on abortion in the country; there are two overlapping majorities. On the one hand, Americans are deeply uneasy with government interference in intimate decisions. Thus, when pollsters pose the abortion issue as a question of whether the choices of individual women or government policy will be binding, the results are a clear prochoice majority. Yet when pollsters put the question differently, they get another majority: Most of the country thinks too many abortions are performed, rejects most of the reasons women give for having abortions, and favors certain restrictions on abortion—such as requiring teenagers to get parental permission. Some polls have produced the rather staggering finding that a majority can support legal abortion, even as a majority *of the same group* considers abortion to be the equivalent of murder.

This mass ambivalence makes itself felt at the polls in a peculiar way. Many voters simply refuse to base their vote on the abortion issue at all. Thus in Iowa, in 1990, Sen. Tom Harkin, running on a prochoice platform was reelected, and so was Gov. Terry Branstad, an ardent right-to-lifer. In 1990, voters handed prochoice candidates the governorships of Florida and Texas—and prolife candidates the governorships of Michigan and Ohio. The 1990 elections, which were once touted as the nation's abortion referendum, turned out to be something far less. An ambivalent country cast an ambivalent vote.

If ever there were an issue on which ambivalence is understandable, it is abortion. The challenge to our politics is to find ways of promoting public policy that speaks to that ambivalence. The problem for the right-to-life movement is that the country as a whole does not accept its absolutist opposition to abortion and is wary of too much government meddling. The problem for the prochoice movement is that the country shares the right-to-lifers' moral uneasiness with abortion and would like to encourage a moral standard that would reduce the number of abortions.

For the rather long short run, the right-to-life movement needs to accept that its primary task is not political but moral: It needs to convince the country that its view of abortion is morally compelling. Even if the right-to-lifers succeeded in their goal of banning all abortions, large numbers of women would continue to seek and get them illegally. Indeed, the polls suggest that younger women are far more prochoice than the rest of the female population, suggesting that the moral trends may be moving away from the right-to-life movement.

Accepting that abortion will remain largely legal indefinitely is not a happy prospect for the right-to-life movement. But the prochoice movement could ease the way toward compromise by accepting that "choice" is not the end of the story, but only the beginning. As Daniel Callahan, a philosopher who supports abortion rights has argued, "the prochoice movement has tried to make do with a thin, near-to-vanishing idea of personal morality." This, he argues, "serves neither its own long-term interests nor those of the pluralistic proposition."

Thus, on a broad range of issues, from promoting adoption to making it easier for women who want to give birth to do so, there is a broad arena for compromise and cooperation. Also helpful, as Callahan argues, would be "a significant improvement in maternal and child benefits, improved counseling and more effective family planning and contraceptive education and services." Further, accepting restrictions on late abortions except where a mother's life is endangered—there are, in any event, few of these—would speak powerfully to the country's uneasiness with abortion. So, too, would parental notification laws with real escape clauses for teenage girls who have reason to fear the reactions of their parents.

The truth, as Callahan argues, is that abortion is about more than choice. It is, he says, "also about the welfare of families and children, about the obligation of males toward women and toward the children they procreate, and about the family and the place of childbearing within it." Americans are ambivalent about abortion because they take exactly this sort of complex view.

What I am suggesting here will surely not satisfy the right-to-life movement, since my approach assumes that abortion will remain largely legal. It is understandable that from the right-to-lifers' ethical point of view, tolerating abortion for a fixed period is like tolerating slavery for a few more years. And many pro-choice advocates will resist even the suggestion that abortion should be restricted or discouraged. They see this as a threat to a right they cherish.

But the abortion issue could provide us with a powerful example of how to deal politically with a complex moral question. The debate the country most needs on abortion is not political but ethical. The question is as unsettled as it is unsettling, and the political system is never likely to settle the matter entirely.

For three decades we have loaded up the political system with moral debates and cast political foes as moral lepers. The result, judging from the popular revulsion with politics, has not been satisfactory. A genuinely moral politics cannot be narrow and moralistic. The mass of voters understand quite well that complex moral questions do not get settled easily. They accept that both the right-to-life and pro-choice movements are animated by people of good will. Many individuals agree with arguments made by *both* sides.

The lesson here goes beyond the abortion issue: If we are to end the cultural civil war that has so distorted our politics, we need to begin to practice a certain charity and understanding. We need politics to deal with the things it is good at dealing with—the practical matters like schools and roads, education and jobs. *Paradoxically, by expecting politics to settle too many issues, we have diminished the possibilities of politics.* After years of battling about culture and morality through the political system, voters are looking for a settlement that combines tolerance with a basic commitment to the values of family and work, compassion and the rule of law. Americans welcomed many of the liberating aspects of the sixties. They also welcomed the rediscovery during the eighties that certain "traditional" rules and values were socially useful and even necessary. In the 1990s, we have a choice: We can join the old battles all over again and set the sixties against the eighties. Or we can try to move on.

If there is a positive sign in the early 1990s, it is that even ideologues are growing impatient with ideological conflict. The death of communism and the end of the Reagan and Thatcher eras all signal a new turn in world politics. And intellectuals on the left and right finally take each other's ideas seriously. There is no more talk of liberalism as America's only serious ideology and much less casual dismissal of the arguments of political opponents. After a decade in power, conservatives are coming to accept that many problems were not created by liberals, and that many of them are hard to solve.

Thus, it was a breath of fresh air when *National Review*, the creator of the ideology of the postwar right, offered a lavishly favorable review of *The American Prospect*, a liberal magazine founded in 1990 that has proven itself refreshingly unorthodox.

Writing in one of the most ideological magazines in America, Richard Vigilante of the libertarian-leaning Manhattan Institute praised *The American Prospect* as "another sign of the welcomed waning of ideology in American politics and the return to a healthier American tradition." Vigilante declared flatly that "the old ideological bundles are breaking up, in part because some of the old issues are passing away, in part because in other areas of dispute experience is overtaking theory and producing consensus, and in part because people got tired of screaming." One can only hope that Vigilante has it right.

V

America has traveled a long way from the days of the late 1940s when Arthur Schlesinger, Jr., proclaimed his *Vital Center* and from the 1950s, when Daniel Bell declared *The End of Ideology*. The old Vital Center was destroyed, partly by events—notably the Vietnam War—and partly because of its arrogant dismissal of challenges from both the left and the right. *The End of Ideology* was proclaimed a bit too early. America, it turned out, had a lot of fighting to do over the fundamentals, from war and peace to race and feminism.

But America's restive middle class is weary of a politics of confrontation that seems to have so little to do with the challenges the nation faces to its standard of living and with its uncertainty about the role it will play in a world without communism. Given the choices on offer for the last two decades, the American electorate has uneasily split the difference, looking to Republicans to set broad policy in the

White House and to Democrats in Congress for protection against Republican excess. It is an ungainly sort of compromise, and voters have come to dislike the results, even as they see few alternatives. Thus do voters increasingly look for ways to protest the *status quo* without risking too much change. Thus the success in 1990 of measures to limit legislative terms, of two Independents seeking governorships, of an independent socialist in Vermont and of a poorly financed but appealingly eccentric left-wing professor in Minnesota. Thus the rout of incumbent governors of both parties in state after state.

What all this represents is an inchoate demand for a new center that will draw on the lessons and achievements of the last thirty years by way of moving the country forward—and ending, as Vigilante would have it, the "screaming." It is a demand for an end to ideological confrontations that are largely irrelevant to the 1990s. It is a demand for steadiness, for social peace, for broad tolerance, for more egalitarian economic policies, for economic growth. It is the politics of the restive majority, the great American middle.

This great American middle felt cheated by our politics for most of the last thirty years. In liberalism it saw a creed that demeaned its values; in conservatism it saw a doctrine that shortchanged its interests. To reengage members of this broad middle, liberals must show more respect for their values, and conservatives must pay more heed to their interests.

For liberals, the preeminent tasks are to achieve greater equity in American economic life and to preserve the social and racial tolerance that is one of the greatest legacies of the 1960s. The liberal project went off track in part because so many voters in the middle stopped believing that government programs were operating in their interests. Indeed, they stopped believing that government could work at all. And when it did act, government, to those in the middle, seemed to work against values like self-reliance, responsibility, family stability and hard work.

Conservatives have long paid homage to these values. But by allowing the standard of living of so many Americans in the middle to deteriorate, partly through regressive tax policies, the Reagan and Bush administrations and the culture they promoted have sent exactly the opposite message. For the last decade we have given honor of place not to those who labored daily for wages and salaries or who built businesses through long-term, painstaking effort, but to those who reached instant wealth, instant fame, and instant luxury. If the hardworking middle felt that its devotion to the work ethic went unappreciated in the years of liberal dominance, it felt insufficiently rewarded in the years of conservative triumph.

And while all this was going on, politics focused on abstract ideological questions to the exclusion of the basics. When government was seen to fail on the basics—educating children, delivering health care, building roads and mass transit, fighting crime—the broad American middle gave up on government. This message was misread by conservatives as a demand for less government when, in fact, it was a demand for better government.

The basic flaw in the Reagan supply-side vision was that it saw the "supply side" as only the private sector; the government could only be a drain on the society, not an asset. This led the supply-siders to a disastrous fiscal assumption: it would be easy to cut taxes because it would be easy to cut government spending. Of course it was not easy, because while the government *as an institution* has become unpopular, many government functions remain broadly popular and extremely hard to cut. One result was our foolish and entirely unnecessary budget disaster. Another result is drastic underinvestment in those aspects of government that *promote* growth: Education, research and development, job training, roads and bridges, and mass transit. The country is prepared to pay for those aspects of government it believes are necessary—provided it also believes that the government actually has a chance of accomplishing what it sets out to do.

For the moment, this faith is frayed. Thus, another aspect of a politics of a new center must be experimentation. If the American people are tired of an ideological approach to divisive social issues, so also are they unhappy with placing ideological straitjackets on programs. To restore popular faith in the possibilities of government, government must be shown to work. And it must also be shown that government intervention need not be either intrusive or excessively bureaucratic.

In fact, many good policy ideas defy ideological classification. Vouchers are thought of as a conservative idea, but one of the most successful voucher programs—food stamps—was a creation of Lyndon Johnson's Great Society. The earned-income tax credit, which essentially subsidizes the wages of poor people who work, is popular among liberals, who like it because it redistributes income, and among conservatives because it is efficient and promotes work. And some policy ideas can actually be quite simple. The country would go a long way toward solving its problems with day care for children over the age of five simply by keeping the public schools open until 6 PM.

Much of the pressure for experimentation in social programming is now coming from the right, which wants to dismantle government bureaucracies. But liberals should welcome the reengagement of conservatives with social policy and simply insist that if conservatives are serious about alternative ways of helping the middle class and the poor, they will have to find money to finance their social experiments.

The restive majority is also seeking a more stable economy in which a new balance is found among the competing values of opportunity, security, and responsibility. The emphasis during the 1980s on entrepreneurship, though in many ways healthy, also distorted our view of how wealth is created. If Marx's labor theory of value oversimplified the economic process, so, too, does what might be called the "capital theory of value" espoused by many on the right. Economics in the 1980s so romanticized the brave, risk-taking souls who provide investment capital that it overlooked the much larger group that ultimately makes a company successful: the people who work for it. In our economic life, no less than in our political life, we have forgotten the old values of loyalty, hard work, and craftsmanship. If any one aspect of the economic changes of the 1980s threatened the social fabric, it was the growing loss of faith on the part of long-time employees in the companies they thought they had served faithfully. The 1980s pattern of corporate restructurings sent the message that the interests of investors nearly always took precedence over the interests of employees. At a time when Americans were wondering why Japanese workers seemed to work harder or more loyally for their companies than Americans, here was part of the answer. The United States does not need to copy Japanese management styles to become competitive. The idea of shared responsibility is surely as American as it is Japanese.

Thus, a central theme of a politics that will restore popular confidence must be: Reward the work performed by the vast American middle. There is a widening consensus over some of the steps required to do this.

First, the tax system must be made less onerous to the middle class and the poor, and the burdens must be reduced especially for parents, both single and married. Any future tax changes must be aimed at making the tax system more progressive, starting with cuts in the payroll tax and increases in the exemptions accorded to parents with young children. Money for this purpose could be freed up by levying social secuity taxes on a higher proportion of the income of the wealthy, and by limiting government benefits—including tax breaks—that flow to the well-to-do.

The first step to welfare reform must be to increase the benefits that go to the working poor. They live by all the rules society claims to believe in, but reap few rewards. A good first step was taken in 1990 when the earned-income tax credit was expanded. It should be expanded further, and all who work should be guaranteed medical insurance. At the same time, the children of the very poor must be allowed to enter the working mainstream. That means expanding health, nutrition, and education programs for preschool children, especially those who live in impoverished and broken families. Such programs have a proven record; the money that flows to them can genuinely be seen as a prudent investment. And everyone should be encouraged to invest in himself or herself. This means expanding access to college, to midcareer education and retraining programs, and to apprenticeship programs that prepare young people for the work force.

Finally, the bonds among our citizens would be strengthened if young people were encouraged to pay back student loans and other government benefits not with *money* but with *time*—a few years devoted to teaching or police work, to the military, or to providing health care for the needy. Such programs could also strengthen the morale of government agencies by providing them with a regular transfusion of young talent and idealism. And some among the young might thereby be encouraged to devote their lives to public service, surely a good thing in a society that provides few incentives for such dedication.

This short list is meant only to be illustrative. It represents back-to-basics priorities, a kind of GI Bill for the 1990s. It emphasizes the things we know that government knows how to do. It is built around the idea that when budgets are strained, new spending should be aimed at helping individuals prosper in a world economy that puts an ever higher premium on education and creativity. The broader point is that the key to successful government in the 1990s will be to find ways of combining compassion and self-reliance, rights and obligations, equity and achievement—in short, to find ways of making peace between the values of the sixties and the values of the eighties. Liberal talk about social justice need not contradict conservative talk about "choice" and "empowerment." Indeed, if conservatives are serious about empowerment, they are talking about social justice.

But voters will not look to government for such initiatives until they are convinced that the government can behave responsibly. The savings-and-loan crisis is a good example of why Americans have come

to hate politics so. If there is one area in which antigovernment libertarians have made a powerful contribution, it is in pointing out that
government subsidies and regulations are often established in ways
that enrich private interests without benefiting the public interest.
This, of course, is an old story—remember the railroad subsidies of
the 1870s? But it becomes an especially important story in an era when
economic regulation is so complex and widespread.

The dangers of an incoherent approach to regulation became
manifest in the savings-and-loan scandal. The deregulation of the
savings and loans combined with an increase in the amount of savings
covered by deposit insurance created the monstrosity of capitalism
without risk. The profits were private, the risks were socialized, members of Congress and presidential candidates received substantial campaign contributions—and the taxpayers were left with a very large bill.
The politics of a new center will thus be centrally concerned with
reconnecting government subsidies and regulations with public purposes. Cleaning up the way we finance campaigns would make it
much easier for Congress to take steps toward doing this.

Underlying the majority's restiveness is worry over what the coming decades will mean for American power in the world and for the
American standard of living at home. Before the collapse of communism, Paul Kennedy and other scholars began promoting the idea that
America faced a period of economic decline fostered by a kind of
"imperial overreach" and too much emphasis on military spending.
Ultimately, this economic decline would foster political decline as
well, no matter how many weapons America had in its arsenals.

The collapse of communism, which followed almost immediately
after the wave of "declinist" talk, was by any measure a victory for
forty years of American foreign policy. Foes of declinism noted with
some glee that with the Soviet Union's collapse, the United States was
the only nation in the world that could claim to be simultaneously
militarily powerful and economically robust—in short, the only real
superpower. The war in the Gulf, fought under American leadership
and with all the sophisticated weaponry in the great arsenal built in
the Reagan years, underscored the continuing importance of American power. Germany and Japan, it was said, could produce marvelous
consumer goods, but they still lacked America's arsenal, its influence,
and its will.

Yet the death of communism and the Persian Gulf War also
raised many questions about the future of American power and world
stability. If there was one great advantage to the United States in the

old bipolar world, it was that it gave the U.S. and the U.S.S.R. enormous influence over events around the globe. To the extent that the world was organized around East-West competition, the two superpowers could shape the behavior of scores of nations.

Iraq's invasion of Kuwait and the war that followed proved that the post-Communist world could be far more disorderly than the old. To be sure, Bush's bold moves and the strength of American arms suggested to many on the right that the United States had, at last, transcended the Vietnam syndrome. It would, once again, be possible to use American power. At the very least, conservatives and interventionist liberals could argue that the antiwar left had manifestly lost many of its most compelling arguments. It could simply not be argued that Saddam Hussein was "on the right side of history."

Still, in the wake of war, Americans had to face the fact that a decade of fiscal irresponsibility had left the United States in a position of nearly begging for foreign contributions to the war effort. And the war also showed how costly maintaining a "new world order" could be. How often will Americans be willing to mount such a vast and all-consuming operation? The Persian Gulf War may mark the end of the post-Vietnam Era, but that only means the beginning of a new, and, one hopes, more promising argument about the proper use of American power. Military tactics, even when dazzling, do not make a foreign policy. They did not even get rid of Saddam.

The most valuable lessons of the war are almost certainly those that relate to our domestic, civic life. As a nation, our political discontent grows from a nagging worry that we have lost our sense of common citizenship. Divided by bitter debates over values, torn by growing inequalities among classes and races, Americans have become increasingly skeptical about whether public engagement could ever produce much of value. A nation whose people perform brilliantly as individuals, we questioned whether we could also respond to crises collectively.

War, as libertarians remind us, may be the ultimate expression of what is wrong with collective action. Yet one could not help but be struck by the fact that after a decade widely derided as self-indulgent, there were still hundreds of thousands of Americans willing to sacrifice their lives in the service of their country. Were there not also peaceful ways of tapping this civic potential? After a period in which all government was derided as ineffectual, the combination of government money and private endeavor had produced truly ingenious weapons of mass destruction. The United States, after all, did know how to produce things. Did America's genius have to be confined to weapons of war? Did the government's ability to finance research and development have to be limited to the military sphere?

Yet the country also faced the disturbing fact that the sacrifices of war had been born in a wildly inequitable way. Many commented on the disproportionate number of black Americans who served in the Gulf. But there were other inequities as well, notably the fact that tens of thousands of reservists had their lives and careers abruptly interrupted while Americans exactly like them went on as if nothing had happened. Polls suggest that the United States is not ready to restore the draft. But the country must rethink its approach to civic duty and shared sacrifice. This is a debate that must be nurtured both by conservative ideas about service and obligation, and liberal ideas about fairness.

The aftermath of war and the end of the Soviet Union have quickened the debate over the meaning of President Bush's "new world order." What has been missing so far is much talk about that order's political content and economic implications. As both a moral and practical matter, promoting democracy around the world is in the long-term interest of the United States, if only because democracies tend to be less threatening than dictatorships and less prone to war. Yet if the United States is serious about promoting democracy, the success of that endeavor will depend in large part on whether the United States and the other wealthy democracies pursue economic policies that will allow new democracies in Eastern Europe and the Third World enough prosperity to maintain that democratic faith. Already, there are signs in the former Communist states of disaffection with democracy as economies continue to stagnate. Economic catastrophe is now threatening to strangle democracy in the former Soviet Union before it is even fully realized. It would be a profound tragedy if the Revolution of 1991 yielded not new democracies but a series of sullen, authoritarian states.

Promoting economic growth in the Third World and Eastern Europe is by no means a purely altruistic act. It is an economic imperative for the United States itself. The United States could make some economic progress in the medium term by striking better trade bargains with its wealthiest competitors, Japan and the European community. But in the long run, real economic growth at home will depend on a far more buoyant world economy. Americans will be able to maintain their high standard of living only by helping to lift the standard of living in the rest of the world. This is a complicated task.

But it is essential, and requires a seriousness of national purpose that our recent approaches to politics seems unlikely to produce.

VI

The 1990s are daunting, but they also offer an opportunity for creative political thinking not seen since the industrial revolution ushered in new intellectual systems that we now call Marxism and capitalism.

The end of Soviet-style socialism creates an enormous opening for American social and political thought since Americans were never much taken with the capitalist-socialist debate. The relative efficiency of markets over bureaucracies was never really questioned here. When Americans made the case for social reform, they did so using a presocialist language of democracy, community, and republicanism. That is precisely the language that is most relevant in the postcommunist world. It also offers an approach that could rescue American politics from its current impasse.

Taken together, the collapse of communism and the affluence of Western market societies would seem to prove conclusively that the choice between rigid state economic control and largely unregulated economic activity is, in truth, no choice at all. When it is market against bureaucracy, market wins.

This comes as a surprise to almost no one—and certainly not to most American liberals or European social democrats, who have always accepted the efficiency of markets. But the argument that the Eastern European experience proves that all bureaucracies and all governments are doomed to the same kinds of inefficiencies is simply wrong. This view, now popular on the right, assumes that all governments and all bureaucracies are more or less the same, and that public endeavor is always inferior to private endeavor.

There is a dangerous moral equivalence at work here that misses the primary difference between the Western societies and communist regimes: Western governments were *democratic.* Our bureaucracies, though at times inefficient and unresponsive, were the creations and creatures of the popular will. Communism's biggest crime was not economic failure or inefficiency but tyranny. Communism was both inefficient *and* repressive.

As Vaclav Havel has reminded us so eloquently, political repression robbed Eastern European nations of a healthy civic life and decent public institutions. Eastern Europe is in trouble today not simply because of a shortage of private investment, but because all the *public* structures, ranging from phones and roads to schools and, yes, the bureaucracy itself, are in such a state of disrepair.

The antisocial nature of the sort of socialism created in the East is most glaring in the way communist regimes treated the environment. Their environmental crimes are almost as outrageous as their crimes against human rights. It is true that the environment is cleaner in the West in part because the West had the money available to clean things up. But the *primary* cause of the West's environmental consciousness is democracy, not the market. A cleaner environment is the product of *public life*. The bureaucrats who ran industry in Eastern Europe had no fear of popular democratic pressure; the capitalists and managers who ran the economies of the West did. If you want to know the difference between communist dictatorship and democracy, it is this: In the East, government officials, *free from public pressure*, nearly destroyed the environment; in the West, government officials, *responding to public pressure*, cleaned up the environment. In the East, bureaucrats were the polluters. In the West, bureaucrats—the people at the environmental protection agencies—were the foes of pollution.

The point here is that government and public life are not abstractions; they are what we make them. The lesson from Eastern Europe is not that we must fear government and public engagement, but that we need a *democratic* public life built on enthusiastic public engagement. The communists were thoroughly wrong in seeing capitalist democracies as doomed to collapsing into dictatorships of the rich. But they were wrong not only because they underestimated capitalism's productive capacities but also because they underestimated democracy's gift for self-correction. It was democracy that fostered the growth of social movements that called attention to those aspects of capitalism that didn't work. Such movements—New Dealism in the United States, democratic socialism and social democracy in Western Europe—insisted on a broad definition of democratic citizenship. In T. H. Marshall's famous formulation, citizenship in a free society consisted not only in civil and legal rights, not only in political rights, but also in social rights. Marshall's insight was that citizens could not fully exercise their basic civil rights and civil liberties without a degree of economic security. The struggle for Marshall's social rights produced the West's social insurance systems, which preserve tens of millions from lives of desperation.

It would be tragic indeed if the welcomed collapse of communist dictatorships were to teach us that the struggle for such "social rights" has become unnecessary. The democratic idea for which the United States and the other Western nations waged a cold war for forty years includes a recognition of both political *and* social rights. The truth is that the progress of the West has depended on the friendly rivalry between the capitalist's insistence on individual initiative and the communitarian's insistence on the broadest possible definition of citizenship and the most inclusive view of the national community. The capitalist and the democratic communitarian needed each other before communism collapsed, and they need each other now.

What is required to end America's hatred of politics is an organizing idea that simultaneously accepts the efficiencies of markets and the importance of a vigorous public life. The American political tradition contains such an idea, an idea that reaches back to the noblest traditions of Western culture. The idea is what the Founding Fathers called republicanism, before there was a political party bearing that name. At the heart of republicanism is the belief that self-government is not a drab necessity but a joy to be treasured. It is the view that politics is not simply a grubby confrontation of competing interests but an arena in which citizens can learn from each other and discover an "enlightened self-interest" in common. Republicanism is based on the realistic hope that, as the political philosopher Michael Sandel has put it, "when politics goes well, we can know a good in common that we cannot know alone."

Republicanism can sound foolishly utopian. When unchecked by the libertarian impulse, republicanism can be oppressive. Rousseau's declaration that "the better the constitution of a state is, the more do public affairs encroach on private in the minds of the citizens" sends a chill up our spines at the thought of republican mind-control.

But we are a very long way from such dangers and face instead the dangers of too little faith in the possibilities of politics. Citizens in a free, democratic republic need to accept that there will always be a healthy tension among liberty, virtue, equality, and community. It is an ancient but still valid idea that liberty without virtue will collapse, and that virtue without liberty will become despotic. And without a sense of community and equity, free citizens will be unwilling to come to the aid and defense of each other's liberty. These notions are broadly accepted by Americans. Our current political dialogue fails us and leads us to hate politics because it insists on stifling yes/no, either/or approaches that ignore the elements that must come together to create a successful and democratic civic culture. Democracy is built on constant struggle among competing goods, not on an absolute certainty about which goods are paramount.

In our efforts to find our way toward a new world role, we would do well to revive what made us a special nation long before we became the world's leading military and economic power—our republican tradition that nurtured free citizens who eagerly embraced the responsibilities and pleasures of self-government. With democracy on the march outside our borders, our first responsibility is to ensure that the United States again becomes a model for what self-government should be and not an example of what happens to free nations when they lose interest in public life. A nation that hates politics will not long thrive as a democracy.

AFTERWORD TO THE TOUCHSTONE EDITION

Beyond False Choices:

The Revolt of the Voters

Two weeks after John F. Kennedy took office, the late I. F. Stone, the gifted radical journalist and relentless critic of the political establishment, published an essay that he knew would shock the regular readers of his newsletter. "At the risk of alarming steady customers, inured to a weekly diet of apocalyptic pessimism," he wrote, "I must confess I am becoming optimistic." He went on: "I feel a little embarrassed, like the prophet Jeremiah caught giving three lusty cheers."

On the face of it, little has happened since this book was first published to inspire a sudden shift in the nation's political mood. If anything, popular hatred of politics has deepened. The confrontation before the Senate Judiciary Committee between Justice Clarence Thomas and Prof. Anita Hill in the fall of 1991 showed that the cultural civil war is alive and well. Former Ku Klux Klan leader David Duke lost his campaign for governor of Louisiana shortly thereafter; but in the process, he showed the political power of blatant appeals to racial animosity. In the meantime, the recession of 1991 sent President Bush's popularity tumbling and revived worries about the government's lack of skill at economic management. Congress got into further trouble with its check-bouncing scandal, and its ratings dropped to record lows. Voters kept telling reporters and polltakers that their fundamental concerns—about economic growth and job security, health care and their children's education—were not being addressed by politicians.

All these things are true. But both despite and because of them, there are grounds for hope for the future of American politics. Popular anger at politics is, in fact, a thoroughly *healthy* sign, an indication that our democracy is going through one of its periodic phases of self-correction. If there has been a recurring theme in these pages, it is that a politics dominated by false choices and phony issues is something very much worth being angry about. That anger is beginning to have an impact.

Anger, of course, is not always a productive emotion, and voter disaffection has had some negative effects. The country could well do without David Duke's demagoguery, which struck a responsive chord partly because so many voters were so alienated from mainstream politicians. Blind attacks on democracy's political institutions can turn into attacks on the democratic process itself. Assaults on incumbents can strike the good and the bad alike.

But it's worth remembering that in the end, David Duke lost. Despite their anger at politics, Americans still show a healthy appreciation for democratic institutions; they are angry precisely because they see our politics as insufficiently democratic and responsive. As for incumbents, the good as well as the bad still seem quite skilled at protecting themselves. And all incumbents need to be reminded now and again of exactly who elected them to office.

The positive effects of the voters' revolt have been more dramatic. They can be seen most importantly in a slow but steady transformation of the political agenda: Politics is beginning to focus on real problems again. Slowly, the political debate is getting back to basics.

The 1991 upset victory of Democratic senator Harris Wofford abruptly put health care on every politician's list of central concerns, which is where it should have been in the first place. By winning the election in Pennsylvania (and overcoming a forty-point deficit in the polls), Wofford effectively used the health care issue as a way of addressing the electorate's broader economic anxieties. It turned out that even people who had jobs and health insurance were worried about losing one or the other or both. In the wake of the Wofford campaign, conservatives and liberals moved from dodging a vexing question to arguing about the cheapest, fairest, and most efficient ways of providing adequate health care to everyone. It will be a difficult debate, but at least the debate has begun.

Moreover, Wofford, a lifelong liberal, showed how a politician could overcome political stereotypes and break through the ideological fog. "If criminals have the right to a lawyer," Wofford said in one of his most celebrated campaign lines, "I think working Americans should have the right to a doctor." Wofford thus simultaneously expressed a "conservative" sentiment (that he felt little sympathy for lawbreakers) and a "liberal" sentiment (that the government should do more to guarantee health care). And liberals could be comforted by the fact that nowhere did Wofford actually *deny* that criminals had a right to a lawyer. Pennsylvania voters, naturally, were unconcerned about how Wofford's sentences parsed ideologically. They did understand Wofford's implicit argument: that too little was being done to help average Americans who play by the rules. And so they elected Wofford.

The stubborn recession, which made the electorate especially responsive to Wofford's arguments, caused much pain and hardship. The discussion the recession engendered was, in some ways, merely a replay of the old ideological songs. Some supply-side conservatives still kept pushing for more tax cuts. Some liberals spoke of old-style public works projects as a way of getting Americans back to work.

But across the political spectrum, the recession also served as a wake-up call, a harsh but necessary reminder that America's economic position in the world has changed. This was something that a large share of the electorate already understood. For years, middle-income Americans had sensed that their standard of living was stagnating or falling. Parents grew increasingly anxious as they had to choose between spending more time with their children or working an extra job to defend their family's standard of living. Massive, long-term layoffs at General Motors served as a stark reminder that losing "competitive advantage" was not an abstract proposition, but a process with large costs to real human beings.

Cyclical downturns come and go. But because the recession of the early 1990s coincided with a broader sense of public unease, it had the potential of opening up new perspectives on the economy. After years of talking about competitive challenges from Western Europe and Japan, the nation's political leaders were being forced to take those challenges seriously. As a result, the questions that became increasingly important in the political debate were thoroughly relevant to voters: How can the educational system prepare a new generation for well-paid, high-skill jobs in the new economy? How can job training ease the transition of workers from dying to thriving industries? What kinds of public investments actually produce more wealth? Can tax incentives be targeted carefully to produce more real, long-term investment and less asset-shuffling? America, belatedly but at long last, was actually grappling with the central problems it will face in the 1990s and beyond—the very sorts of questions that voters had been trying to get on the national agenda for a decade or more.

Debate over the tax issue was transformed in more fundamental ways. By breaking his "no new taxes" pledge, President Bush gave up a powerful political weapon and infuriated the Republican right. But in doing so, he woke up Democrats to the fact that their middle-income constituents felt overtaxed, and for good reasons. At last, Democrats stopped arguing that the tax issue was somehow an artificial creation of Ronald Reagan's supposedly hypnotic powers over the electorate. The tax debate thus broadened to include not only the matter of how high taxes should be, but also the crucial question of who should shoulder the heaviest burdens.

The nation's discussion of family issues was also moving along more productive paths. The economic pressures on two-earner families received ever wider attention, and across the political spectrum, politicians were seeking ways of targeting tax cuts to families with children. "Responsibility-ism" gained ground and politicians—notably Democratic presidential candidate Bill Clinton—became increasingly outspoken about the need to find ways of encouraging citizens to take their responsibilities as seriously as they insist upon their rights. This cause was also championed by a group of activist academics, led by Amitai Etzioni and Mary Ann Glendon, who issued a "Communitarian Platform," which sought to transform the political discussion by drawing on lessons from both the left and right. The new communitarian movement argued that maintaining a free society and a sound economy required strengthening the institutions of "civil society," especially the family but also the local schools, neighborhood groups, churches, and other voluntary associations. Such institutions, they argued, transmit the moral values on which both liberty and prosperity depend, and do so far more effectively than the agencies of either the government or the marketplace.

II

Perhaps the most remarkable and heartening news of all was the dissolution of the Soviet Union, the death of communism, and the definitive end to the Cold War. For the second time in the twentieth century, democracy defeated totalitarianism. Suddenly, all the old foreign policy arguments were obsolete. Defense expenditures could be reduced sharply without fear that such cuts would amount to appeasement of a dangerous enemy. A new debate on America's world role and its priorities could begin. Long-standing advocates of globalism began to argue that getting America's economic house in order had to become the nation's first priority—even if the nation could not, willy-nilly, abandon its world commitments.

The end of the Cold War was also hastening ideological disintegration and intellectual renewal on both the left and the right.

On the democratic left, virtually no one mourned the collapse of a repressive dictatorship whose very existence had done so much to discredit the progressive cause. But liberals, social democrats, and socialists were all forced to look at market economics with new respect and at command economies with renewed skepticism. The collapse of the Soviet experiment utterly discredited utopian dreams that a powerful state could repeal human nature and create a perfect society— dreams that distorted the thinking of even progressives who knew better.

The moderate left continued to assert that government still had a large role to play in easing economic inequalities, in protecting the environment, in investing in the basic underpinnings of society, and in pushing the economy along more productive paths. The moderate left also held its ground in arguing that large concentrations of economic power needed to be checked by the assertion of democratic political power. Yet the Eastern European experience reminded the left that democratic movements have their greatest impact not through the raw exercise of centralized state control but through efforts by central governments and citizen groups to strengthen popular institutions ranging from trade unions to local governments. Some on the liberal-left also used the Eastern European experience as a spur for launching a new critique of bureaucracies. As we have seen, bureaucracies in democratic countries are qualitatively different from the bureaucracies set up by dictatorships. But even democratic bureaucracies can become arrogant and narrow-minded, inefficient and unresponsive. Even democratic bureaucracies need periodic doses of glasnost and perestroika.

For conservatives, the death of the Soviet Union was a mighty victory, but also a disorienting experience—especially in the United States. Anticommunism had largely buried the anti-interventionist impulse on the right. It was a cause to which many different kinds of conservatives could repair. When it came to beating the Soviets, almost all conservatives were globalists.

Yet when Patrick J. Buchanan, the conservative commentator, declared his Republican primary challenge to President Bush in December of 1991, he used his announcement speech to call for a new kind of conservatism—or perhaps more accurately, for a return to the right-wing doctrines of the pre–World War II period: "America first!" was Buchanan's battle cry now that the Evil Empire was gone. Just as the New Left often echoed the pre–World War II right, so now did Buchanan sometimes sound like a New Leftist with his calls to dismantle "the Cold War state." And at times, he sounded like an AFL-CIO Democrat with his attacks on Japanese economic practices and his call for a much tougher American bargaining stance on trade issues.

Most Republicans and conservatives are likely to remain free traders and globalists for some time. But Buchanan's challenge to Bush was only one particularly stark example of the divisions and debates that the end of the Cold War will create among conservatives. As long as the United States was the overwhelmingly dominant economic power in the world, as it was for a quarter century after World War II, the right's nationalism could easily coexist with a commitment to free trade; free trade was manifestly in America's national interest. Buchanan was not alone on the right—or in the country—in arguing that the national interest and pure free trade might now be at odds. Among pro-Republican business groups, there were deep conflicts of interest that led to divisions over policy. Even within the Bush administration, trade "hawks," especially in the Commerce Department, did battle with free traders. And President Bush, a lifelong free trader, tried hard to sound tough on Japan as the 1992 election year opened with polls showing him in some political jeopardy. "It's your fight, too!" Rep. Richard Gephardt had declared in 1988 of his battle for fairer foreign trading practices. Bush seemed torn between joining Gephardt's crusade and continuing to insist that free trade ultimately produced more wealth.

If trade policy was symptomatic of one set of divisions among conservative constituencies, more traditional foreign policy questions also divided the right. Many conservatives criticized Bush for being slow to recognize the inevitable triumph of Boris Yeltsin over Mikhail

Gorbachev; for moving too cautiously in recognizing the new relationships between Russia and the former Soviet republics; and for failing
to stand up more firmly for Croatia in its war with the Serbian-
dominated federal army in Yugoslavia.

But all these were, in some sense, leftover issues from the Cold
War. What conservatives of every stripe recognized was how difficult
it would become in the 1990s even to sort out the lines of argument,
let alone to find new and compelling rationales for American engagement around the globe. Norman Podhoretz, as firm a supporter of
America's role in the Cold War as could be found, said long before
the Soviet Union's collapse that it would be hard to mobilize American
opinion around globalism, since "now there's no Hitler, and there's
no, as it were, Stalin." Doubting that defenders of a large American
role in the world would fare very well in the near future, Podhoretz
said flatly: "I find it difficult to imagine the speeches that will be made
on the floor of Congress to support the appropriations that Congress
would have to make. I find it difficult to imagine the editorials that
will be written to convince large sectors of American opinion."

Conservatives, and perhaps also policymakers of other persua-
sions, will now be missing what former defense secretary James Schlesinger called "the stark simplicity" and "remarkable clarity" of the
Cold War. But if this posed problems for conservative cohesion, it also
had the virtue of forcing conservatives to rethink a slew of assumptions about how large the defense budget should be, how many troops
America really needed overseas, and how to assess the trade-off between military power abroad and economic strength at home. Conservatives, in short, were free to join Dwight Eisenhower in challenging
the role of "the military-industrial complex."

On domestic policy, the conservative impasse was, if anything,
deeper. It was already clear even before the end of Bush's first term
that the right lacked both the power and the political will to make
serious cuts in the domestic budget. In its editorial pages, *The Wall
Street Journal* repeatedly chastised the Bush administration for letting
domestic spending get out of hand. There were some innovative conservative ideas around—notably in housing and education. But some
of these, especially Jack Kemp's useful housing initiatives for the poor,
required either substantial new spending or large shifts of funds that
the administration seemed unwilling to fight for. In the meantime,
basic social disorders that conservatives had bemoaned and promised
to heal—crime, family breakdown, falling test scores, welfare dependency—actually seemed to worsen. And conservatives, including

Bush himself, implicitly acknowledged that their tax programs had been tilted toward the wealthy by joining the Democrats' calls for middle-class tax relief.

For the most devout conservatives, Bush's failures amounted to betrayal. But the truth was that after more than a decade in office, conservatives, like liberals before them, had run up against the limits of ideology. With a philosophical distance not common among those who shared his strong belief in conservatism, Donald Devine, a former Reagan administration official, argued that all ideological movements eventually spent themselves after a period in power and needed a spell to regroup and rethink. American conservatism had clearly reached that point in the early 1990s.

III

Thus have both liberals and conservatives at least begun the process of rethinking that is vital to ending popular hatred of politics. Under the pressure of new circumstances—and in more than a few cases, out of genuine courage and conviction—politicians in both parties are acknowledging the overwhelming dominance of symbols over substance and the importance of seeking to substitute problem-solving for mere posturing.

But the habits of three decades are hard to break, and not all recent developments point in a promising direction.

The shame that fell on Washington after the battle over Clarence Thomas's nomination to the Supreme Court had little to do with the explicit phrases recited in a pristine Senate hearing room. What the nation reacted against was what it recognized as a display of hypocrisy and cynicism on an exceptional scale. The visible drama was the televised conflict between Thomas and Anita Hill. But the real struggle involved the nation's extended moral civil war over its cultural soul and over issues involving race and feminism. It was a fight in which the various sides were so utterly convinced of their moral righteousness that they were willing to flout all the rules in order to win. When winning is the only thing, the rights of individuals don't matter, words and what they mean don't matter.

One result was that politicians turned the tactics of highly personalized negative campaigning, which they used so often against each other, against private citizens who dared poke their heads into a congressional hearing.

Given the stakes, both sides asked: Who cares? If you're a conservative who thinks that a radical-feminist/civil-rights complex (a.k.a. the liberal special-interest groups) has been out to destroy the traditional family, unborn children, and the cultural values of the West, then isn't any tactic justified to foil such evil designs? If you're a liberal who sees a threat to a woman's right to choose abortion, a Senate indifferent to the sexual harassment of women, and a right wing intent on rolling back affirmative action and thirty years of workplace gains by minorities and women, shouldn't you fight back with everything in your arsenal?

Such strong feelings were, on one level, perfectly understandable. Yet each side painted the other in such dark shades that civility —never mind accommodation—became impossible. When it's a fight over uncompromisable moral principles, how can you compromise?

What was maddening is that each side had complaints that were perfectly understandable and were, in fact, well understood by many Americans less committed to confrontation.

Conservatives asked: Why did sexual harassment charges against Thomas that were a decade old emerge publicly only at the last minute and only after it seemed clear that the Senate was about to approve his nomination? Why were liberals, usually so solicitous of the rights of the accused and of privacy, so eager to toss charges around so freely?

Liberals asked: Why didn't the Judiciary Committee take the sexual harassment charges against Thomas seriously in the first place? Why did Senate Democrats sit by while Republicans ripped into Anita Hill's character and repeatedly charged, without any evidence to back their statements, that she was "fantasizing" her story? Why didn't the Democrats press Thomas harder?

And at the end of the whole miserable process, neither the Senate nor the country really found out all that much about what really happened between Clarence Thomas and Anita Hill. Had the Senate been truly serious about the issues at stake, it could have postponed matters for a few weeks and allowed Judiciary Committee investigators to conduct a real investigation, including background interviews with Thomas's and Hill's former associates. As it was, the Senate instead produced a television spectacle at the end of which it was possible to conclude either that Thomas had been terribly wronged or that he had committed perjury—or for all we knew, both.

Some liberals drew some comfort from the hearings, arguing that at least the country had been forced to grapple with the real problems women face as a result of sexual harassment. Some foreign journalists

I know argued that the hearings showed what a special and wonderful country America was: How many other countries, they asked, take feminism and gender issues seriously enough to go through the sort of full-scale national debate on sexual harassment that we did? And some conservatives took solace in Thomas's victory and in his bold use of national television to defend not only himself but also his conservative convictions—and by extension, the dissent of all conservative African Americans.

There is merit to each of these contentions. But if the polls are to be believed, few Americans seemed satisfied with the process, and for good reason. At its bottom, the Thomas fight was simply the latest episode in the long-running political battle for control of the Supreme Court. Republican presidents have insisted repeatedly on stoutly conservative nominees—and as a result, have tilted the Court well to the right. Liberal Democrats in the Senate want a far less conservative Court. The problem is that while Democrats control the Senate, liberals do not. Therefore, liberals seeking swing votes to defeat a conservative nominee must win support from moderate-to-conservative Democrats and moderate-to-liberal Republicans. To do this, liberals have either had to paint conservative judicial choices as dangerous extremists or had to find reasons other than philosophy—*personal* reasons—to rule a nominee beyond the pale. In other words, for liberals to have a chance of winning, the fights have to get pretty nasty.

Many of these problems would disappear, of course, if the presidency and the Senate were under the control of the same party. Until that happens again, the president would do well to take the Senate's "advise and consent" role seriously and consult actively with leading senators *before* making a nomination.

This would inevitably result in more moderate nominations, and the truth is that on the major issues at stake before the Court, including abortion, the country is neither "right-wing" nor "left-wing" but rather moderate. A real process of consultation would produce nominees who roughly reflect the consensus in the country, end the unseemly gridlock between the president and the Senate, and restore a diversity of viewpoint to the Court. The Supreme Court, after all, is supposed to be a deliberative body in which thoughtful people with different views seek something more stable than shifting 5-to-4 majorities and something more satisfying than the rejection of one precedent after another on ideological grounds. As it is, one can hardly find a clearer example of the costs of bitterly polarized politics than in the breakdown of the process through which we choose people for what we like to think of, with some justice, as the most distinguished judicial body in the world.

IV

David Duke's campaigns in Louisiana raised other questions. It was not that Duke, ex-Nazi and ex-Klansman, was himself likely to become an important national figure. In fact, he is destined to fade from the scene, as his anemic showings in the 1992 presidential primaries showed. President Bush called Duke "an insincere charlatan." It was a peculiar formulation, but over the long run, it seemed likely to stick.

But Duke's limited success showed how an economically battered country could be tempted by appeals to race hatred and division. The search for a usable "them" is common enough in politics. American history has seen many a campaign based on racism, religious intolerance, and hostility to recent immigrants.

The most recent round of race-based politics is disturbing on several counts.

First, it follows the civil rights period, a singularly exhilarating moment in American history. While it is common enough for periods of reform to be followed by eras of consolidation or even reaction, few Americans, black or white, want to roll back the progress made in the civil rights era. In its own eyes, and in the eyes of the rest of the world, the United States is a vastly better country because of those struggles.

Second, racial politics is a diversion from the much larger tasks that confront the country. Arguments about race do little to solve the economic and social problems that genuinely trouble Americans, black and white. If the economy does not grow, then the scramble for the limited number of good jobs will be bitter and easily set off racial conflict. If only a few can go to college, then the battles for the available places will be fierce. If crime remains an overwhelming problem, then everyone, black and white, will feel insecure—and more inclined than ever to search for a "them" to hold responsible for the violence. Greater peace on the streets will create greater social peace.

The third problem raised by the rise of David Duke–style politics may be the most pernicious. The decline of ideological conflict in the 1990s opens the way for a more productive national conversation over what values social policy should promote. As I have argued, voters are fully justified to look to government to promote the value of work and to do what is possible through social policy to encourage family stability and parental responsibility. Virtually all Americans—and *especially* the poor, most of whom work despite scant rewards—believe in the dignity of work. To argue that the current welfare system has failed is not to attack the poor, but to speak a truth that the poor know better than anyone else. Progressives who believe in work *and* in lifting up the poor cannot be sidetracked in their search for a better system simply because a demagogue has decided to turn *welfare* into a code word. At the same time, conservatives cannot claim they are "solving" the welfare problem simply by imposing welfare cuts and letting the poor fend for themselves. Real welfare reform means emphasizing work, but it also means providing jobs that offer decent incomes and such basic benefits as health insurance. It means guaranteeing that the majority of the poor who already work get lifted out of poverty. Liberals especially should realize that if they do not make the cause of welfare reform their own, it will be abused by those who have no concern for the poor, for social justice, or for racial equality.

Similarly, the goal of family stability should not be abandoned simply because Duke and those like him have used that issue for racist purposes. Family breakdown is a social problem that is, if anything, even more devilishly complicated than welfare reform. The forces that lead to family breakup are society-wide, cultural at their root, and do not respond easily or directly to government intervention. It is certainly possible to do much more to safeguard the health of pregnant women and of newborn children, regardless of their family circumstances. It is also possible to reduce the financial pressures on families by altering the tax code. It may be possible to require absent parents to contribute to the support of their children and to have stricter enforcement of divorce settlements. But love and responsibility cannot be decreed by the state, nor can they be conjured up easily even by the most compassionate minister, priest, social worker, or friend.

In short, family breakup and its costs to children are not problems that will ever be solved entirely, and even improving matters will be difficult. That is precisely why the country needs a responsible discussion about what *can* be done—by government, by neighborhood support groups, and by the churches, among others—to help strengthen families and thus help children enjoy the love and stability that will give them a chance to thrive later in life. What we can be sure of is that such a discussion will *not* take place if the "family issue" is left only to those whose real goals are to punish the poor, to aggravate social conflict, or to use the word *family* as an empty electoral symbol.

V

But it is a mistake, I think, to dwell on David Duke or on the nativist aspects of Patrick J. Buchanan's message. For what is clear about the American mood in the 1990s is that voters—citizens—are demanding a new seriousness from politicians. During the 1992 New Hampshire primary, one of the most popular jokes told by journalists and politicians alike was of the presidential candidate who spent twenty minutes detailing his twelve-point economic program and was immediately asked by a voter why he had not offered a thirteenth, fourteenth or fifteenth point.

Gov. Bill Clinton survived early media revelations about his draft record and his personal life precisely because he offered specificity while also expressing an intense desire to move the debate beyond the divisive politics of the 1960s and 1980s and heal the nation's racial wounds. Despite the failure of his campaign, former Massachusetts Sen. Paul Tsongas emerged from obscurity in the New Hampshire Democratic primary not only because he was a New England favorite but also because his eighty-six page pamphlet, *A Call to Economic Arms*, conveyed precisely the seriousness that many voters were looking for. Former California Gov. Jerry Brown got a hearing because his attacks on the corrupting influence of money on American politics resonated with so many Americans. But Brown's appeal was limited in part because many democrats doubted that he had detailed answers for social and economic problems, forcing him to become more specific as the campaign went on. The fact that the three Democrats to survive the early primaries were all, in their different ways, challengers of political orthodoxy underscored the depth of the country's thirst for change in the 1990s.

The developments of the spring of 1992 offered a lesson for the longer-term. Despite a profusion of personal attacks, the primaries showed that Democrats were at least wrestling with their party's central problem: how to transcend the old fights and ideological rigidities in order to offer a progressive vision that makes sense in the 1990s. It was very much a struggle to define the new political center spoken of in these pages, which is essentially an effort to create a majority coalition for a new era of reform. The 1990s offer us the real promise of doing that because there now exists an unusual opportunity to solve problems by accepting the insights that both the left and the right have offered over the last three decades. To reiterate a theme that runs through the book: We can preserve the gains of the 1960s while recognizing the mistakes of that era.

It is clear that both the feminist and black liberation movements made huge contributions to American life. We do not need to reargue the value of equality between the genders or among races—nor, in my view, should we want to. The urgent task of a new center is to consolidate advances we've made as a society while also recognizing that we have undervalued institutions and values that are too often seen as "old-fashioned." We are in desperate need of what Jim Fallows has called, after the great film maker who gave us such movies as *It's a Wonderful Life*, "Frank Capra values": loyalty, responsibility, a willingness to contain private appetites and private interests in the name of the community, a desire to do right by others simply because that's the right thing to do. Such values are often called conservative but in fact transcend ideology. Values such as taking responsibility for one's family, struggling to be self-reliant, remembering that the communities of which we are a part have a right to expect something of us are neither left nor right. They are essential.

There is also an opportunity for liberals to pick up on policy ideas that conservative intellectuals have pioneered but that conservative politicians have been reluctant to finance such as school vouchers for the poor or programs to give parents more choices within the public school system, tenant management or ownership of public housing projects, and welfare systems that put more emphasis on work. While these ideas have been developed by conservatives eager to tear down public bureaucracies they can, in fact, be seen as thoroughly consistent with the goal of sixties liberals and New Leftists to expand the power of the poor. But liberals need to remind conservatives associated with what has been called "the new paradigm" in social policy that none of these programs will come cheap. As many a social scientist has noted, part of the problem faced by poor people is that they simply don't have enough resources or money even when they work full time. Those interested in helping to lift up the poor have to face this most basic fact.

Similarly, while some of the attacks by conservatives on the workings of bureaucracies have merit, the foes of bureaucracies overstate the wonders that might be worked by overturning them. Bureaucratic approaches clearly are not the preferred way to solve social problems, and many government bureaucracies are thoroughly out of date. As David Osborne, the coauthor of *Reinventing Government* has argued, we seem to be asking 1930s bureaucracies to deal with the problems of a 1990s society. Still, in a large and complicated society, substantial bureaucracies are inevitable, and, though it's not fashionable to say so, there are a lot of people we call bureaucrats who really are hardworking and committed public servants. So by all means, let's shake up inefficient bureaucracies. Let's decentralize and give those who use government services more choices. Let's use the technologies that have expanded consumer options in the marketplace to ease the relationship between the citizen and the government. But let's not pretend that an antibureacratic utopia is just around the corner.

With the collapse of Eastern European Communism, conservatives have won important intellectual and political ground on another front. At no time since the industrial revolution began have market economics enjoyed such widespread support. Even on the left, skepticism about the workings of state-run enterprises is enormous. The idea that markets breed indispensable efficiencies is hardly under debate anymore.

But here again, there is a danger that an insight will harden into a doctrine. Lost in the current enthusiasm for markets is any sense of the role government plays in promoting economic progress. Economies atrophy not only because of a lack of private investment but also because of a shortage of public investment in transportation, education, vocational training, and environmental protection. Social breakdown, in the form of crime and neighborhood decay, can threaten prosperity as much as inefficiency. Following John Kenneth Galbraith's famous formulation, "public squalor," can lead to a decline in private prosperity.

The one-sided emphasis on the importance of capital has also bred an indifference to the role that workers play in creating wealth. Because of the challenges from Japan and Western Europe, there has been much talk about improving the performance of American workers. But to craft the social bargains needed to make the economy more competitive, we will need a strong and democratic trade union movement to help us through. The coming decades will see large changes in the American economy. There will necessarily be a lot of give-and-take between companies and the people who work for them. If the workforce is overwhelmingly unorganized, then most of the "take" will come out of employees' standard of living.

We've forgotten that the purpose of unions is to enhance the democratic rights of average people, something we were reminded of by the courage of the anti-Communist unions of Eastern Europe. As David Kusnet noted in his recent book on the problems with the Democratic Party's rhetoric, *Speaking American*, we have lost track of the simple but fundamental things that unions are supposed to be about: "to provide representation (as in 'no taxation without representation'), to protect individual workers, and to give the entire work force a voice in determining wages, hours and working conditions." What could be more democratic than that?

Yes, there are problems with organized labor. The members of public employee unions sometimes forget that they work not simply for "bosses" but for the citizenry, which has a right to exercise democratic control over what the public sector does. In the private sector, some unions continue to insist on rigid, out-dated work rules that do little to enhance an employee's work life and get in the way of productivity growth. And it will always be true that some unions are less democratic and less honest than others.

But most of the major manufacturing unions have, in fact, been more than willing to cooperate with management to save their industries. By making deals with management to transform work rules, reorganize shop floors, and give workers more responsibility, many of the leading industrial unions have actually helped increase productivity. The unions have also raised a legitimate—and thoroughly capitalist—question in asking why there is no link between the huge compensation packages enjoyed by executives and the actual performances of the companies they run. The example set by the best of the union leaders demonstrates how democracy and enhanced participation can help us solve problems not only in our politics but also in our economy.

The most important point about the new, post-Communist era was made by Vaclav Havel, the president of Czechoslovakia, who argued that the end of communism also marked the end of "an era of ideologies, doctrines, interpretations of reality." It was, he said, the collapse of "an era in which the goal was to find a universal theory of the world, and thus a universal key to unlock its prosperity." The decline of arrogant, absolutist doctrines, he argued, opened the way for a clearer understanding of how the world actually works and should work.

The collapse of the age of ideology, however, does not mean giving up on the aspirations that lay behind those ideologies. The conservatives' emphasis on the importance of individual responsibility and initiative has been vindicated, but so, too, has the left's insistence on greater social justice. The liberal's quest for limits on the government's power to impose its will on individuals proved a thoroughly worthy enterprise, but so did the democrat's goal of finding ways for the community's interest to express itself through government.

The decline of ideology, in short, does not mean the end of history. It means the beginning of democratic politics—the triumph of the idea that the deliberations of citizens matter more than the doctrines imposed from above.

VI

When President Bush returned from his visit to Japan in January 1992, his political opponents roundly and universally denounced his quest for trade concessions as amounting to little more than "begging." Naturally enough, the president saw these charges as unfair, and he had a point in insisting that many areas of the economy were, indeed, quite healthy. But the underlying assumptions of Bush's foes had wide resonance with the public—*not* because Americans disagreed with the idea that Japan needed to open its markets more, but because most saw something unseemly about an America cast in the role of supplicant. The questions Americans asked themselves less than a month after the final end of the Soviet Union were not the questions of winners but the questions of a country worried about what the outcome of the next round would be. Why in the world wasn't American industry better organized, more productive, and more innovative? Why were so many goods and products that had been *invented* in America *produced* abroad? Why were so many American consumers abandoning their own country's products for things made elsewhere? Why was it that while the United States defeated communism, Honda defeated Buick?

This last question will almost certainly invite protest from those who rightly see communism's defeat as far more important, in the grand scheme of things, than Buick's difficulties. But it is the virtue of democracies that they tend to punish smugness in their leaders. "What have you done for me lately?" is actually not a bad question for voters to pose to those they elect. Almost immediately, the triumph over communism has become *yesterday*'s victory. The economic competition with Japan and the rest of the industrialized world is today's problem, and tomorrow's.

There is no reason to believe that Americans are incapable of meeting that challenge—especially since many parts of the economy have already begun doing so. But there is every reason to fear failure in the long run if our approach to politics, which is essentially our approach to organizing ourselves as a country, does not get very serious, very quickly. Americans are crying out for exactly that kind of seriousness. Americans are furious at all politicians who would manipulate their worries without solving the problems that cause them.

Americans want to spend more time with their kids and not just hear another lecture about "family values." They want a chance to work hard and not just have to listen to one more oration about the moral value of hard work. They want the crime rate to go down and not just get politicians' promises of ever more exotic applications of the death penalty. They want their kids to go to college and get decent jobs; they are not looking for yet another misleading debate about the difference between "affirmative action" and "quotas." Americans want government to be effective again; they don't just want to look on as career politicians run against the very government they're supposed to have led. They want their roads in good shape, their teachers well trained, their doctors there when they need them, their police around when crime happens; they're tired of hearing that government is always "the problem" and never part of the solution. They'd like lower taxes, but they also want more fairness in the tax code and a sense that government is delivering a return on their tax dollars. They want to be challenged to take more responsibility for their country's future, and not just be told that society has no right to expect anything from anyone.

Americans want a politics they don't have to hate. And therein lies our hope: Democracies are uniquely open to change, and if citizens want politicians to move beyond false choices, it is in their power to demand it.

NOTES

CHAPTER ONE: FREEDOM NOW

32

The sense of the New Left as Whitmanesque and Emersonian is conveyed brilliantly in Todd Gitlin, *The Sixties: Years of Hope, Days of Rage* (New York: Bantam, 1987). See especially pp. 66–77 and pp. 200–203. My view of the New Left has been greatly influenced by Gitlin, both through his writings and in some very helpful conversations. Carl Oglesby was one of the first to declare SDS "very Emersonian." See Jack Newfield, *A Prophetic Minority* (New York: The New American Library, 1966), p. 123.

32

The basic text of conservative attacks on the New Left is Peter Collier and David Horowitz, *Destructive Generation* (New York: Summit Books, 1990).

33

Maurice Isserman, *If I Had a Hammer: The Death of the Old Left and the Birth of the New Left* (New York: Basic Books, 1987) is a very good look at how much the 1960s left owed to the intellectual ferment within the 1950s left.

33
Oglesby quote from Gitlin, p. 77.

34
"SDSers believe the savage struggles . . ." Newfield, pp. 128–29. On anticommunism as "one way of affirming one's positive belief in democracy," see Newfield, p. 198.

35
"The Port Huron Statement" is reprinted in the appendix to James Miller, *Democracy Is in the Streets* (New York: Simon and Schuster, 1987), pp. 329–374. Miller's book is the best discussion, anywhere, of the meaning of Port Huron and the ideology of the New Left.

36
Walter Berns quoted in George H. Nash, *The Conservative Intellectual Movement in America* (New York: Basic Books, 1979), p. 222.

36
Quotes from Robert A. Nisbet, *The Quest for Community* (New York: Oxford University Press, 1971 reprint), pp. xvi–xvii.

36
"The real threat to the Left . . ." Flacks quoted in James Miller, p. 172–73.

37
Buffett quoted by Carl Oglesby in Carl Oglesby and Richard Shaull, *Containment and Change* (New York: The Macmillan Company, 1967), p. 166.

38
Hayden on *Pacem in Terris* in Tom Hayden, *Reunion: A Memoir* (New York: Random House, 1988), pp. 95–96.

38
On rock and Elvis Presley, see Gitlin, p. 42. Another fine treatment of the influence of rock can be found in Charles Kaiser, *1968 in America* (New York: Weidenfeld and Nicolson, 1988), pp. 190–214.

38–39
A wonderful sourcebook on Kerouac and the Beat Generation is the Viking Critical Library edition of *On the Road*, edited by Scott Donaldson (New York: Penguin Books, 1979). The volume includes the text of *On the Road*, and a number of excellent essays. Podhoretz's essay is reprinted as "The Know-Nothing Bohemians," pp. 342–56. See especially pp. 354–56. A particularly useful book on Kerouac is Dennis McNally, *Desolate Angel: Jack Kerouac, the Beat Generation and America* (New York: Random House, 1979).

39
On distrust of language, see Gitlin, p. 41.

40
On Dylan's "Mr. Tambourine Man," see Gitlin, p. 200–201. Harry C. Boyte

also analyzes the importance of this song in *Commonwealth: A Return to Citizen Politics* (New York: The Free Press, 1989), pp. 72–73.

41

On "the democratization of personhood," see Peter Clecak, *America's Quest for the Ideal Self: Dissent and Fulfillment in the 60s and 70s* (New York: Oxford University Press, 1983). The quotation in the text comes from page 13; Clecak explains his ideas in detail on pp. 179–226.

41

Many good books have been published on the Catholic left. Two evocative and sympathetic accounts are Francine du Plessix Gray, *Divine Disobedience: Profiles in Catholic Radicalism* (New York: Vintage Books, 1971) and Robert Coles, *Dorothy Day: A Radical Devotion* (Reading, Mass: Addison-Wesley, 1989).

41

On the meaning of "Do it!": Walzer's essay is reprinted in Michael Walzer, *Radical Principles: Reflections of an Unreconstructed Democrat* (New York: Basic Books, 1980). The reference is on page 151.

42

Paul Kirk is quoted in David Burner, *John F. Kennedy and a New Generation* (Boston: Little, Brown, 1988), p. 169.

42

A good, compact discussion of Kennedy's foreign policy can be found in Stephen E. Ambrose, *Rise to Globalism: American Foreign Policy Since 1938*, fourth revised edition (New York: Penguin, 1985), pp. 180–200.

43

On Kennedy and Vietnam, the fairest statement is probably that of Herbert S. Parmet: "What JFK would have done about American involvement in South Vietnam can never be known. It is probable that not even he was sure." Herbert S. Parmet, *JFK: The Presidency of John F. Kennedy* (New York: Penguin, 1984), p. 336. Nonetheless, Kennedy was worried about the power of the anticommunist issue and fearful of "losing Vietnam" as Truman had "lost China." Thus Burner, a sympathetic biographer, concludes: "Almost certainly he would have escalated the war; it is likely that other scenarios are wishful thinking on the part of his admirers." Burner, p. 112. Ambrose discusses the American University speech on pp. 198–200. On Kennedy's serving coffee to the demonstrators, see Gitlin, p. 94.

43

On "war as fulfillment," see James Weinstein, *The Corporate Ideal in the Liberal State, 1900–1918* (Boston: Beacon Press, 1968), pp. 214–53.

43

"Free World empire," which became a common phrase on the New Left, is the title of a chapter in Oglesby's essay in Oglesby and Shaull, p. 72.

44

William Schneider told me the story of his interview in Somerville.

44

For Gitlin on the media and the New Left, see Todd Gitlin, *The Whole World Is Watching: Mass Media in the Making and Unmaking of the New Left* (Berkeley: University of California Press, 1980).

45

The definitive book on the Democratic reformers is James Q. Wilson, *The Amateur Democrat* (Chicago: University of Chicago Press, 1966). On Stevenson and the reformers, see pp. 52–58. A delightful discussion of these issues, from a point of view rather sympathetic to the regulars, is Daniel P. Moynihan, " 'Bosses' and 'Reformers,' " *Commentary* (May 1961). The essay is reprinted in Moynihan's book *Coping* (New York: Random House, 1973).

46

Charles Kaiser does an excellent job discussing the Kennedy and McCarthy campaigns. See also Arthur Herzog, *McCarthy for President* (New York: Viking, 1969).

46

On Hayden and Kaufman, see James Miller, pp. 44, 94–95, 111, 119, 142, 146. The Kaufman quotations are from Arnold S. Kaufman, *The Radical Liberal* (New York: Simon and Schuster, 1970), pp. xii–xiii.

48

On the Democratic rules changes, see Nelson W. Polsby, *Consequences of Party Reform* (New York: Oxford University Press, 1983) and Byron E. Shafer, *Quiet Revolution: The Struggle for the Democratic Party and the Shaping of Post-Reform Politics* (New York: Russell Sage Foundation, 1983).

49

The Edsall quote is from Thomas Byrne Edsall, "The Changing Shape of Power: A Realignment in Public Policy," in Steve Fraser and Gary Gerstle, eds., *The Rise and Fall of the New Deal Order: 1930–1980* (Princeton, N.J.: Princeton University Press, 1989), p. 278.

49

"We are a minority . . ." in Miller, p. 330.

52

"protest politics flourishes . . ." From William E. Connolly, "The Politics of Reindustrialization," *democracy* (July 1981), p. 17.

53

Jeff Riggenbach, "In Praise of Decadence," *The Libertarian Review* (February 1979), pp. 22–30.

CHAPTER TWO: THE VIRTUES OF VIRTUE

55

Harrington and his fellow democratic socialist intellectual Irving Howe were among the first to understand that a new philosophy was being born in neo-conservatism. See Lewis A. Coser and Irving Howe, eds., *The New Conservatives: A Critique from the Left* (New York: Quadrangle, 1974), and especially Harrington's essay, "The Welfare State and Its Neoconservative Critics," pp. 29–63.

56
Irving Kristol, *Reflections of a Neoconservative* (New York: Basic Books, 1983), pp. 74, ix.

56
Trilling on liberalism's dominance: Lionel Trilling, *The Liberal Imagination* (Garden City, N.Y.: Doubleday Anchor Books, 1954), pp. 5–6.

57–58
For Steinfels's analysis of key concepts, see Peter Steinfels, *The Neoconservatives* (New York: Simon and Schuster, 1979), pp. 32–41.

58
On ideology's end, see Daniel Bell, *The End of Ideology* (New York: The Free Press, 1965), p. 402.

58
On the role of the Congress for Cultural Freedom in sponsoring the end-of-ideology idea, see Peter Coleman, *The Liberal Conspiracy* (New York: The Free Press, 1989), pp. 108–13.

58
On "the young intellectual," see Bell, p. 404.

58–59
For Lipset on the end of ideology, see Seymour Martin Lipset, *Political Man* (Garden City, N.Y.: Doubleday Anchor Books, 1963), pp. 442–44. See also Lipset's later essay "A Concept and Its History: The End of Ideology," in Seymour Martin Lipset, *Consensus and Conflict: Essays in Political Sociology* (New Brunswick, N.J.: Transaction Books, 1985), pp. 81–109.

59
Nathan Glazer, "The Universalization of Ethnicity," *Encounter* (February 1975), pp. 8–17.

60
"a prior commitment to ideology" and "For it is the nature of ideology . . ." Daniel Bell and Irving Kristol, "What Is the Public Interest?" *The Public Interest* 1:1 (Fall 1965), pp. 3–5.

60
On "the professionalization of reform," Daniel P. Moynihan, "The Professionalization of Reform," *The Public Interest* 1:1 (Fall 1965), pp. 6–16.

60
Nathan Glazer, *The Limits of Social Policy* (Cambridge: Harvard University Press, 1988), pp. 1–17. Glazer's original article bearing that title appeared in *Commentary* in September 1971.

61

Jay W. Forrester's "law," see George H. Nash, *The Conservative Intellectual Movement in America* (New York: Basic Books, 1979), p. 325.

61

"we do not fully understand," quoted in Nash, p. 325.

61

"A program was launched . . . ," Daniel Patrick Moynihan, *Maximum Feasible Misunderstanding* (New York: The Free Press, 1970), pp. xiii–xiv, 170.

62

"a new, more aggressive . . ." Mark Lilla, "What Is the Civic Interest?" *The Public Interest* 81 (Fall 1985), p. 71.

62

On "traditional restraints," Glazer, "The Limits of Social Policy," p. 8.

62

On "a 'liberation' of personal and collective selves," Irving Kristol, *On the Democratic Idea in America* (New York: Harper Torchbooks, 1973) pp. vii–viii.

63

On the crisis of authority, see Steinfels, pp. 55–69. See also Michel Crozier, Samuel P. Huntington, and Joji Watanuki, *The Crisis of Democracy: A Report on the Governability of Democracies to the Trilateral Commission* (New York: New York University Press, 1975).

63

Novak, "hundreds of thousands of jobs . . ." Novak wrote critically about the new class before he became a conservative. See Novak, *Choosing Our King* (New York: Macmillan, 1974), especially pp. 63–92.

63

"The simple truth is that the professional . . ." Irving Kristol, "About Equality," reprinted from *Commentary* (November 1972) in Irving Kristol, *Two Cheers for Capitalism* (New York: Basic Books, 1978), p. 177.

64

Buckley on "university crowd," see Nash, p. 119; Hart on "the habitually antagonistic" intellectuals, see Nash, p. 299.

64

Walzer was a sympathetic yet extremely tough critic of the New Left. See his essays on the New Left in Walzer, *Radical Principles: Reflections of an Unreconstructed Democrat* (New York: Basic Books, 1980), pp. 109–85.

65

"It is the self-imposed assignment . . ." Kristol, *Reflections of a Neoconservative*, pp. xiv–xv.

65–66

Wilson on race prejudice, see James Q. Wilson, "The Urban Unease," *The Public Interest* 12 (Summer 1968), pp. 25–39.

66

Nixon speech. Nixon's best statement of "the forgotten American" theme was his acceptance speech. See *Nixon Speaks Out: Major Speeches and Statements by Richard M. Nixon in the Presidential Campaign* (Nixon–Agnew Campaign, 1968), pp. 277–91.

66

On neoconservatives for Humphrey: One of the best arguments made for Humphrey all year was by Kristol. Irving Kristol, "Why I Am for Humphrey," *The New Republic* (June 8, 1968).

67–68

Daniel Bell, ed., *The Radical Right* (Garden City: Doubleday Anchor Books, 1964). "The psychological stock-in-trade . . ." Bell, p. 8. Nash's comment on "abnormal psychology" appears in Nash, p. 138.

68

On "the venerable tradition," Richard Hofstadter, *The Paranoid Style in American Politics* (New York: Vintage, 1967), p. 121.

68

On "rollback," see Nash, pp. 322–23.

68

"His posture was forward-looking . . ." Kristol, *Reflections of a Neoconservative*, p. 112.

69

"Liberals must divest themselves . . ." Daniel P. Moynihan, "The Politics of Stability," *New Leader* 50 (October 9, 1967), pp. 6–10.

69

Daniel P. Moynihan, "Where Liberals Went Wrong," in Melvin Laird, ed., *Republican Papers* (New York: Doubleday Anchor Books, 1968), p. 138.

69

The phrase "the equality revolution" is used by Herbert Gans throughout *More Equality* (New York: Vintage, 1974). See especially pages 7–35. "Once this process gets legitimated . . ." Daniel P. Moynihan, "The New Racialism," in *Coping: On the Practice of Government* (New York: Vintage Books, 1975), p. 204.

69

For useful discussions of the import of LBJ's Howard speech, see Richard N. Goodwin, *Remembering America: A Voice from the Sixties* (Boston: Little, Brown, 1988), pp. 342–48, and Daniel P. Moynihan, *Family and Nation* (New York: Harcourt Brace Jovanovich, 1986), pp. 30–34. Goodwin and Moynihan were the speech's main architects.

70

"The attitude of neoconservatives to bourgeois . . ." Kristol, *Reflections of a Neoconservative*, p. 76.

70

On "cultural contradictions," Daniel Bell, *The Cultural Contradictions of Capitalism* (New York: Basic Books, 1978), paperback ed.

71

Jeane Kirkpatrick, "Welfare State Conservatism," *Policy Review* 44 (Spring 1988), pp. 2–6. Quotation appears on page 5.

71

"the overwhelming majority . . ." Irving Kristol, "Rationalism in Economics," *The Public Interest* (special issue 1980), p. 218.

72

Kristol on Carter "double standard." See Kristol, *Reflections of a Neoconservative*, p. 269. See also Jeane J. Kirkpatrick, *Dictatorships and Double Standards* (New York: American Enterprise Institute/Simon and Schuster, 1982), pp. 23–52.

73

For a critical and detailed view of the creation of the conservatives' sprawling intellectual empire, see Sidney Blumenthal, *The Rise of the Counter-Establishment: From Conservative Ideology to Political Power* (New York: Perennial Library, 1988), especially pp. 147–60.

74

"The abolition of politics . . ." Stephen L. Newman, *Liberalism at Wits' End: The Libertarian Revolt Against the Modern State* (Ithaca: Cornell University Press, 1984), p. 42.

74

Moynihan on OEO: Daniel P. Moynihan, *Family and Nation*, p. 133.

75

"There have been more successes . . ." Moynihan, *Family and Nation*, p. 87.

CHAPTER THREE: NOT BLACK AND WHITE

77

Estrich quote from David Runkle, ed., *Campaign for President: The Managers Look at '88* (Dover, Mass.: Auburn House Publishing Company, 1989), pp. 113–14. I am grateful to Harvard's Institute of Politics for giving me the chance to participate in the roundtables published in this book.

77

"It defied common sense. . . ." Runkle, p. 115. Atwater, who fell very ill after the 1988 campaign and died in 1991, later apologized to Dukakis for using the Willie Horton "issue" and came close to confirming Estrich's view of events.

78

On low-income whites bearing the brunt of racial change, see Andrew M. Greeley, *Ethnicity: A Preliminary Reconnaissance* (New York: John Wiley, 1974), pp. 201–202. For a broad discussion of these issues from a point of view that is simultaneously sympathetic to blacks and poor whites, see also Andrew M. Greeley, *Why Can't They Be Like Us?* (New York: Dutton, 1971). For a critique of the "new ethnicity" movement that Greeley helped lead—a critique that nonetheless takes seriously the complaints of the new ethnic leaders —see Orlando Patterson, *Ethnic Chauvinism: The Reactionary Impulse* (New York: Stein and Day, 1977). See also Stephen Steinberg, *The Ethnic Myth: Race, Ethnicity and Class in America* (New York: Atheneum, 1981).

79

"The struggle over patriotism . . ." Jonathan Rieder, "The Rise of the Silent Majority," in Steve Fraser and Gary Gerstle, eds., *The Rise and Fall of the New Deal Order: 1930–1980* (Princeton, N.J.: Princeton University Press, 1989), p. 251.

79

The most chilling statistic of the 1988 election . . . William Galston and Elaine Kamarck, "The Politics of Evasion," paper issued by the Progressive Policy Institute in Washington, D.C. (1989).

80

"For a decade now . . ." Joseph Duffey quoted in Michael Novak, *Choosing Our King* (New York: Macmillan, 1974), p. 219.

80

Eisenhower quote from William L. O'Neill, *American High: The Years of Confidence, 1945–1960* (New York: The Free Press, 1986), p. 253.

81

"I think we just delivered the South . . ." Michael Oreskes, "Civil Rights Act Leaves Deep Mark on American Political Landscape," *New York Times* (July 2, 1989), p. A16.

81

For superb accounts of the civil rights movement, see John Hope Franklin, *From Slavery to Freedom* (New York: Knopf, 1979); Taylor Branch, *Parting the Waters: America in the King Years, 1954–63* (New York: Simon and Schuster, 1988); and David J. Garrow, *Bearing the Cross: Martin Luther King, Jr., and the Southern Christian Leadership Conference* (New York: William Morrow, 1986).

82

"confidently felt to be historic . . ." King quotes from Martin Luther King, Jr., *Where Do We Go from Here? Chaos or Community* (New York: Harper and Row, 1967), pp. 1–2.

82

"What entitled the sharecroppers . . ." Todd Gitlin, *The Sixties: Years of Hope, Days of Rage* (New York: Bantam, 1987), p. 159.

82

"This proves that the liberal Democrats . . ." Gitlin, p. 159.

83

"every courthouse in Mississippi . . ." Carmichael quoted in Garrow, *Bearing the Cross*, p. 481.

83

"We must never forget . . ." through to ". . . the creation of the beloved community." King quoted in Garrow, p. 488.

83

"Black Power proposes, or seems to propose . . ." Christopher Lasch, *The Agony of the American Left* (New York: Knopf, 1968), p. 134. "What the assimilationist argument does overlook . . ." Lasch, p. 127. Lasch's essay on Black Power, "Black Power: Cultural Nationalism as Politics," appears on pp. 117–68.

84

"full participation in the decision-making process . . ." Stokely Carmichael and Charles V. Hamilton, *Black Power* (New York: Random House, 1967), pp. 44–47.

84

"Whether one is talking about . . ." Carmichael and Hamilton, p. 167.

85

"Much as a colony is dependent . . ." Wilfred David quoted in Michael B. Katz, *The Undeserving Poor: From the War on Poverty to the War on Welfare* (New York: Pantheon Books, 1989), p. 58. While I find the "colonial" analogy flawed, I have found few better and more persuasive summaries of the idea than that in Katz's book. See pages 52–65.

85

"colonies rebel . . ." Theodore Draper, *The Rediscovery of Black Nationalism* (London: Secker and Warburg, 1971), pp. 121–22.

85

"The proletariat has become the Third World . . ." Carmichael quoted in Draper, p. 123.

85

"The people, the majority of people . . ." Marcuse, *Eros and Civilization*, quoted in Godfrey Hodgson, *America in Our Time* (Garden City: Doubleday, 1976), p. 365.

85

Wright's view of integration: Nathan Wright, Jr., *Black Power and Urban Unrest* (New York: Hawthorn Books, 1967), pp. 131–32.

86

"Black Power had a different meaning to the black man . . ." Lyndon Johnson quoted in Hodgson, p. 266.

86

"The civil rights movement is evolving . . ." Bayard Rustin, "From Protest to

Politics: The Future of the Civil Rights Movement," *Commentary* 39 (February 1965), pp. 25–31.

86

On the impact of the "black solidarity" movement on scholarship, see William Julius Wilson, *The Truly Disadvantaged: The Inner City, the Underclass and Public Policy* (Chicago: University of Chicago Press, 1987), p. 150.

87

"tangle of pathology," Lee Rainwater and William L. Yancey, *The Moynihan Report and the Politics of Controversy* (Cambridge: The MIT Press, 1967), pp. 74–75.

87

Few internal government documents have been more widely discussed than the "Moynihan Report." For brief and useful histories, see Katz, pp. 23–29; Hodgson, pp. 263–68; Wilson, pp. 20–22; Moynihan's own recent work *Family and Nation* (New York: Harcourt Brace Jovanovich, 1986) is a gentle "I told you so" reprise of the entire controversy.

88

"I feel that this summer . . ." quoted in Hodgson, p. 361.

88

"a pall of black smoke . . ." Hodgson, pp. 361–62.

88

"blames everybody for the riots . . ." Nixon on the riots quoted in Stephen E. Ambrose, *Nixon: The Triumph of a Politician* (New York: Simon and Schuster, 1989), pp. 144–45.

88

Michael Novak, *The Rise of the Unmeltable Ethnics: Politics and Culture in the Seventies* (New York: Macmillan, 1971).

89

"It is all right for the blacks and . . ." Greeley, *Why Can't They Be Like Us?* p. 14.

89

"By continuing to insist . . ." Orlando Patterson, *Ethnic Chauvinism: The Reactionary Impulse*, pp. 157–58.

89

The ways in which "blue collar" and "white ethnic" came to mean the same thing is captured nicely in the title of a collection of essays that appeared in the early 1970s: Joseph A. Ryan, ed., *White Ethnics: Life in Working Class America* (Englewood Cliffs, N.J.: Prentice Hall, 1973). For a critique from the left of the tendency to lose sight of class in the ethnicity wars, see Colin Greer, "Remembering Ethnicity, Forgetting Class," *Social Policy* (November 1972/February 1973 double issue), pp. 115–18.

89

"Ethnicity is at least as much a tactic . . ." Irving Louis Horowitz, *Ideology and Utopia in the United States, 1956–1976* (New York: Oxford University Press, 1976), p. 67.

89

Ethnicity "as a strategic choice by individuals . . ." Daniel Bell, "Ethnicity and Social Change," in Nathan Glazer and Daniel P. Moynihan, *Ethnicity: Theory and Experience* (Cambridge: Harvard University Press, 1975), p. 171.

89

The phrase "vanguard of repression" is from a review that appears on the back cover of the paperback edition of Peter Binzen, *Whitetown U.S.A.* (New York: Vintage Books, 1970).

90

The formulation "imagine a hundred-yard dash" is drawn from Earl Rabb, "Quotas by Any Other Name," *Commentary* (January 1972), p. 41.

91

The Pettigrew-Riley findings on Gary, Indiana, can be found in Thomas F. Pettigrew, *Racially Separate or Together* (New York: McGraw-Hill, 1971), pp. 236–56.

91

"this average man on the street . . ." Wallace quoted by Jonathan Rieder, "The Rise of the Silent Majority," in Fraser and Gerstle, p. 249.

92

"the primal sense of community . . ." Moynihan quoted by Peter Steinfels, *The Neoconservatives* (New York: Simon and Schuster, 1979), p. 124.

92

On the "defended neighborhood," see Gerald D. Suttles, *The Social Construction of Communities* (Chicago: University of Chicago Press, 1972), pp. 245–47.

93

"No matter what the intentions . . ." Greeley, *Ethnicity: A Preliminary Reconnaissance*, pp. 201–2.

93

"The rich liberals, they look down . . ." Jonathan Rieder, *Canarsie: The Jews and Italians of Brooklyn Against Liberalism* (Cambridge: Harvard University Press, 1985), p. 200.

93–94

Connolly on the welfare state: William E. Connolly, "The Politics of Reindustrialization," *democracy* 1:3 (July 1981), pp. 9–10.

94

"as a force inimical to the working . . ." Rieder in Fraser and Gerstle, p. 258.

94–95
"these vulnerable constituencies . . ." Connolly, p. 9.

95
Charles Murray, *Losing Ground: American Social Policy, 1960–1980* (New York: Basic Books, 1984). Two excellent critiques of Murray are Robert Greenstein, "Losing Faith in Losing Ground," *New Republic* (March 25, 1985) and Christopher Jencks, "How Poor Are the Poor?" *New York Review of Books* (May 5, 1985). I am grateful to both Greenstein and Jencks, who have talked me through some of the intricacies of poverty statistics. All misinterpretations of what they told me are my responsibility. The entire Murray debate is ably summarized (from a point of view critical of Murray) in Katz, pp. 151–56.

96
"substantial job losses . . ." Wilson, p. 160.

97
the liberal perspective on the ghetto . . ." Wilson, p. 12.

97
Wilson on nonracial solutions, see pp. 149–57. For a summary of Wilson's views and proposals, see William Julius Wilson, "Race-Neutral Policies and the Democratic Coalition," *The American Prospect* (Spring 1990), pp. 74–81.

99
"We made a serious mistake . . ." Lewis quoted in Joe Klein, "Race: The Issue," *New York* (May 29, 1989), p. 34–35. Joe Klein's has been a courageous voice in the effort to create a more productive debate about race in New York City and in our country. In particular, Joe has been willing to take risks on a set of issues where most simply take cover. My views have been greatly influenced by discussions and friendly arguments with him. But since we make a point of trying to avoid agreeing on everything, he can't possibly be held accountable for the views I express here.

CHAPTER FOUR: FAMILY POLITICS

99
On conservatives applauding the new turn in feminism, see Dinesh D'Souza, "The New Feminist Revolt," in *Policy Review* 35 (Winter 1986), pp. 46–52.

99
Betty Friedan, *The Second Stage*, quoted in D'Souza, p. 47.

99
"Family, work, neighborhood and authority . . ." John Kenneth White, *The New Politics of Old Values* (Hanover: University Press of New England, 1988), p. 121.

99
"A social conservative . . ." Carlson offered his quip in a conversation with the author.

99

The *New York Times* conducted an extensive poll of American attitudes toward women and feminism. The results were reported on page A1 in the editions of August 20, 21, and 22, 1989. In 1986, a Gallup poll found that 56 percent of American women considered themselves to be "feminists." See Barbara Ehrenreich, *Fear of Falling: The Inner Life of the Middle Class* (New York: Pantheon, 1989), p. 223.

100

"I'm not really out to change . . ." Bret Easton Ellis is quoted in Sidney Blumenthal, "Reaganism and the Neokitsch Aesthetic," in Blumenthal and Thomas Byrne Edsall, eds., *The Reagan Legacy* (New York: Pantheon, 1988), p. 290.

100

"If particular care and attention . . ." Adams quoted in Seymour Martin Lipset and William Schneider, *The Confidence Gap: Business, Labor and Government in the Public Mind* (Baltimore: The Johns Hopkins University Press, 1987), pp. 1–2.

100–101

Lasch on the development of feminism: Christopher Lasch, *Haven in a Heartless World: The Family Besieged* (New York: Basic Books, 1977). The quotations and the broad thrust of Lasch's argument are drawn from pages 3–21. Although some of Lasch's ideas have drawn sharp criticisms from feminists, his broad summary of the trends is extremely insightful—and many of his arguments are quite consistent with a feminist view.

101

On female college enrollment and the growth of women's organizations and work-force participation, see Steven Mintz and Susan Kellogg, *Domestic Revolutions: A Social History of American Family Life* (New York: The Free Press, 1988), p. 111. This excellent work is exceptionally fair-minded in its analysis and full of useful information. I draw on it, and Lasch, over the next several pages. See also Lasch, p. 9.

101

On the "purity crusade," see Mintz and Kellogg, pp. 111–12.

102

"proclaimed the joys of the body . . ." Lasch, pp. 10–11.

102

"sex o'clock in America" Mintz and Kellogg, p. 111; "husbands and wives would be 'friends and lovers' . . ." Mintz and Kellogg, p. 113; "placed an unprecedented emphasis . . ." p. 115.

102

Data on 1950s' family: Mintz and Kellogg, pp. 178–79.

102

"the luxury of mutual pleasure . . ." Mintz and Kellogg, p. 186.

103
"a matriarchal society . . ." The literature criticizing the new "matriarchal" family is summarized by Mintz and Kellogg on pp. 184–86.

103
"observers of middle class life . . ." Elaine Tyler May, "Cold War, Warm Hearth: Politics and the Family in Postwar America," in Steve Fraser and Gary Gerstle, eds., *The Rise and Fall of the New Deal Order: 1930–1980* (Princeton, N.J.: Princeton University Press, 1989), p. 159.

103
"fifty-fifty deal . . ." Pat Boone is quoted by Mintz and Kellogg on p. 186.

103
"On the one hand, young women . . ." Mintz and Kellogg, p. 195.

103
"It was a strange sense of dissatisfaction . . ." Betty Friedan, *The Feminine Mystique*, 10th Anniversary Edition (New York: Dell, 1974), p. 11.

103
On the Conference on the Effective Use of Womanpower, see Allan C. Carlson, *Family Questions: Reflections on the American Social Crisis* (New Brunswick, N.J.: Transaction Books, 1988), pp. 113–14.

104
On the importance of the revolution in housework, see Carlson, pp. 112–16.

105
"the vast bulk" and "Women are now accepting . . ." James K. Galbraith, *Balancing Acts: Technology, Finance and the American Future* (New York: Basic Books, 1989), p. 101.

106
Carlson has been among the leading advocates of "the family wage." See Carlson, pp. 273–79.

106
"The point here . . ." quotation and data on taxes come from Daniel P. Moynihan, *Family and Nation* (New York: Harcourt Brace Jovanovich, 1986) pp. 159–63.

107
"It was an achievement, however . . ." Ehrenreich, p. 217. Figures on advanced degrees appear on p. 216. On the growing inequalities caused by professionals marrying professionals, see pp. 218–19.

107
"to women who are vice presidents . . ." Canellas quoted in E. J. Dionne, Jr., "Struggle for Work and Family Fueling Women's Movement," *New York Times* (August 22, 1989), p. A1. Smeal quoted in same story.

107
"Prolife women have always valued . . ." and subsequent quotations are from

Kristin Luker, *Abortion and the Politics of Motherhood* (Berkeley: University of California Press, 1984), pp. 199–200.

108
Polling data on women: Daniel Yankelovich, *New Rules* (New York: Bantam, 1982), p. 100. Yankelovich's book is filled with provocative findings such as these. The *New York Times* data were made available by Michael R. Kagay and Janet Elder of the *Times* staff. My thanks to them for much help over the years in deciphering the meaning of numbers.

109
On Reagan's "winning" despite his minority positions on ERA and abortion, see E. J. Dionne, Jr., "Even Carter's Successes Are Helping Reagan," *New York Times* (June 29, 1980), Week in Review section.

110
"a return to more traditional standards . . ." Yankelovich, p. 103.

110
"Fathers have always spent too little time . . ." Alan Wolfe, "The Day-Care Dilemma: A Scandinavian Perspective," *The Public Interest* 95 (Spring 1989), p. 21.

111
On "mediating structures," the classic text is Peter L. Berger and Richard John Neuhaus, *To Empower People: The Role of Mediating Structures in Public Policy* (Washington, D.C.: American Enterprise Institute, 1977). Michael Novak has also written widely on mediating structures. See, for example, Michael Novak, "The Communitarian Individual in America," *The Public Interest* 68 (Summer 1982), pp. 3–20, especially pp. 12–14.

112
"It was to be *asserted* . . ." Moynihan, *Family and Nation*, p. 16.

112
"Surely, the aim of the struggle . . ." Ehrenreich, p. 216.

113
"One ironic effect of these legal . . ." Mintz and Kellogg, pp. 232–33.

113
On the family and the welfare state: Steven Kellman, a professor at Harvard's John F. Kennedy School of government and an expert on Sweden, points out that the Swedish social democrats have always used the family and the household as the central symbol in their half-century campaign for collective provision. (Conversation with the author.)

114
"divorce, alcoholism, drug abuse . . ." R. Emmett Tyrrell, Jr., *The Liberal Crack-Up* (New York: Simon and Schuster, 1984), p. 51.

114
On Murray and his critics, see note for page 105.

115

On the popular response to the AIDS crisis and the queasiness of even traditionalist Americans with gay-baiting, see E. J. Dionne, Jr., "AIDS Roundtable: 12 Show Concern Over Tests, Morality and Politics," *New York Times* (July 19, 1987), p. A22.

CHAPTER FIVE: THE LOST OPPORTUNITY

116

"For one's own generation . . ." Arthur M. Schlesinger, Jr., *The Vital Center* (Boston: Houghton Mifflin, 1962), pp. xxi–xxii.

117

On the "brown scare," see Leo P. Ribuffo, *The Old Christian Right: The Protestant Far Right from the Great Depression to the Cold War* (Philadelphia: Temple University Press, 1983), especially pp. 178–224.

117

"Kennedy or Nixon: Does It Make a Difference," Godfrey Hodgson, *America in Our Time* (Garden City: Doubleday, 1976), p. 73.

120

Delegate count in Eugene J. Dionne, Jr., *Race, Community and Equality: A Study of Public Opinion in Britain and the United States* (Oxford University D.Phil. dissertation, 1981), p. 145.

121

New York Times/Time magazine polls reanalyzed by the author. Special thanks to Jack Rosenthal of the *New York Times* for making these data available and to William Schneider, Gary Orren, and Seymour Martin Lipset for their assistance and guidance in the analysis.

122

Analysis of presidential voting from Everett Carll Ladd, Jr., with Charles D. Hadley, *Transformations of the American Party System* (New York: W.W. Norton, 1975), p. 234.

123

William Schneider, "JFK's Children: The Class of '74," *The Atlantic* (March 1989), p. 35; Thomas Byrne Edsall, *The New Politics of Inequality* (New York: W.W. Norton, 1984), pp. 34–57.

124

"Without the trust thing . . ." Caddell quoted in James Wooten, *Dasher: The Roots and the Rising of Jimmy Carter* (New York: Warner Books, 1979), p. 344.

124

"He was an unknown quantity . . ." Wooten, p. 311.

125

"I see nothing wrong with ethnic purity . . ." Jules Witcover, *Marathon: The*

Pursuit of the Presidency, 1972–1976 (New York: Viking Press, 1977), p. 302. Witcover's is the definitive and complete account of the 1976 election.

126
Analysis of primary voting by the author, from the *New York Times*/CBS News poll. Most of the trends reported here were published in the *Times* during the primaries.

127
"was arguably the greatest feat . . ." Austin Ranney, "The Carter Administration," in Ranney, ed., *The American Elections of 1980* (Washington, D.C.: American Enterprise Institute, 1981), p. 4.

127
"He was clearly the most conservative . . ." Eizenstat quoted in Erwin C. Hargrove, *Jimmy Carter as President: Leadership and the Politics of the Common Good* (Baton Rouge: Louisiana State University Press, 1988), p. 34.

127
"clearly believed that the central . . ." Hargrove, p. 34.

128
Polls analyzed by author.

129
Table Three. Election results analyzed by author.

130
Analysis of 1948–76 trends from Everett Carll Ladd, "The Shifting Party Coalitions—from the 1930s to the 1970s," in Seymour Martin Lipset, ed., *Party Coalitions in the 1980s* (San Francisco: Institute for Contemporary Studies, 1981), pp. 127–49. See especially pp. 142–47.

130
Gallup Poll figures from Ranney, p. 4.

131
"the ironies of liberalism" Leo P. Ribuffo, "Jimmy Carter and the Ironies of American Liberalism," *Gettysburg Review* (Autumn 1988), pp. 738–49. I am grateful to Professor Ribuffo for making available many of his articles on Jimmy Carter, and for a series of helpful ideas on how his presidency should be analyzed.

132
The news of the Carter years was not all bad. See James K. Galbraith, *Balancing Acts: Technology, Finance and the American Future* (New York: Basic Books, 1989), pp. 27–52.

132
"Being confident of our own future . . ." Carter at Notre Dame, May 22, 1977, in *The Public Papers of Presidents of the United States: Jimmy Carter, 1977* Book 1 (Washington: U.S. Government Printing Office, 1977), p. 956. Thanks to Professor Ribuffo for finding this reference.

133
"Human rights is the soul . . ." and "Iran is an island . . ." These two quotes
are juxtaposed by Stephen Ambrose to show the contradictions inherent in
Carter's policies. See Stephen E. Ambrose, *Rise to Globalism: American Foreign Policy Since 1938*, fourth revised edition (New York: Penguin Books,
1985), p. 301.

133
James Fallows, "The Passionless Presidency," *The Atlantic* (May 1979), p. 46.

134
"The Passionless Presidency," *The Atlantic*, passim pp. 33–46.

135
On Carter's energy policy, see Hargrove, pp. 47–54.

135
On welfare reform, see Hargrove, pp. 54–60.

136
The *New York Times*/CBS News polls on welfare: Thanks to Dr. Michael R.
Kagay and Janet Elder of the *New York Times* for making these available.

136
On party-line voting, see Martin P. Wattenberg, *The Decline of American
Political Parties, 1952–1984* (Cambridge: Harvard University Press, 1986), p.
78.

137
Ribuffo on Carter's being undermined by his successes, p. 744.

138
"the most dramatic rally-'round . . ." Nelson Polsby, "The Democratic Nomination," in Ranney, ed., *The American Elections of 1980*, p. 45.

138
"If it's Carter versus Kennedy . . ." Caddell in an interview with the author.

138
Polls analyzed by author. Thanks to Dr. Michael R. Kagay for double-check-
ing past figures.

139
Anderson advertisement mention in Seymour Martin Lipset, "Party Coalitions in the 1980 Election," in *Party Coalitions in the 1980s*, p. 29.

141
On Carter's failing to deliver to working-class voters, see Ribuffo, p. 747.

141
"took refuge in a rhetoric that . . ." Robert Kuttner, *The Life of the Party:
Democratic Prospects in 1988 and Beyond* (New York: Viking, 1987), p. 12.

142
"concert of interests . . ." This analysis of special-interest politics owes much

to Arthur M. Schlesinger, Jr.'s brilliant analysis, "The Liberal Opportunity," in *The American Prospect* 1 (Spring 1990), pp. 10–18.

144

The notion that middle-class people who had gotten so much from government suddenly turned around and decided government was "the problem" is from a very funny stump speech that Sen. Ernest Hollings (D, S.C.) gave during his short-lived but in many ways inspired 1984 presidential campaign.

CHAPTER SIX: IDEAS HAVE CONSEQUENCES

147

The sense of conservative alarm over the world of 1945 is conveyed powerfully by George H. Nash at the beginning of *The Conservative Intellectual Movement in America: Since 1945* (New York: Basic Books, 1979), pp. 3–5. Nash's book has set the standard for scholarship on conservative intellectuals and was important for setting the record straight on one basic point: that the conservative intellectual movement, which was taken seriously only in the late 1970s, should have been taken seriously long before. Nash has greatly influenced my view of the history of conservatism, and I have profited especially from reading him and also from telephone interviews with him over the years.

148

"the closest thing to a real social revolution . . ." Geoffrey Perrett, *Days of Sadness, Years of Triumph: The American People, 1939–1945* (Madison: The University of Wisconsin Press, 1973), pp. 10–11.

148

"globaloney . . ." Kirk quoted in Nash, p. 71.

148

On politics during the war, see John Morton Blum, *V Was for Victory: Politics and American Culture During World War II* (New York: Harcourt Brace Jovanovich, 1977).

149

"need not involve increased state management . . ." Alan Brinkley, "The New Deal and the Idea of the State," Steve Fraser and Gary Gerstle, eds., *The Rise and Fall of the New Deal Order: 1930–1980* (Princeton, N.J.: Princeton University Press, 1989), pp. 106–7.

149

Stuart Chase quoted in Perrett, p. 355.

149

"Through the cacophonous chorus . . ." Smith quoted in Nash, p. 4.

150

"progressives, on the whole, create . . ." Arthur M. Schlesinger, Jr., *The Vital Center* (Boston: Houghton Mifflin, 1962), p. 35. The book was originally published in 1949.

150

Louis Hartz, *The Liberal Tradition in America: An Interpretation of American Liberal Thought Since the Revolution* (New York: Harcourt Brace Jovanovich, 1955).

150

Taft as a "liberal." Taft, who did not disdain the word *conservative*, either, of course maintained that the word *liberal* referred to "liberty" and opposition to state interference. In fact, Taft's legacy is a complicated one, since he was not as consistently antistatist as is now remembered. He was an ardent disciple of federal programs for housing, for example, and favored putting "a floor under essential things to give all a minimum standard of living, and all children an opportunity to get a start in life." For a balanced view of Taft's philosophy, see James T. Patterson, *Mr. Republican: A Biography of Robert A. Taft* (Boston: Houghton Mifflin, 1972), especially pp. 314–34 and 615–16. The quotation about "a minimum standard of living" appears on p. 319.

150

"Why has American conservatism . . ." Schlesinger, p. 25.

150

"They are obscure, unorganized . . ." Albert Jay Nock, "Isaiah's Job," in William F. Buckley, Jr., ed., *Did You Ever See a Dream Walking? American Conservative Thought in the Twentieth Century* (Indianapolis: Bobbs-Merrill, 1970), p. 511.

151

"You do not know . . ." Nock, p. 518.

151

"History thus gives us little reason . . ." Schlesinger, p. 26. "Terrified of change . . ." p. 31.

152

Richard Weaver, *Ideas Have Consequences* (Chicago: University of Chicago Press, 1948).

152

Friedrich A. von Hayek, *The Road to Serfdom* (Chicago: University of Chicago Press, 1944; paperback reprint, 1976). Nash on Hayek, pp. 5–9; Perrett on Hayek, pp. 296–97.

152

"the rise of fascism and Naziism . . ." Hayek, pp. 3–4.

152–53

"Economic control is not merely . . ." Hayek, p. 92.

153

Hayek devotes a chapter to "The Socialist Roots of Nazism," pp. 167–80.

153

On business interests' buying the book: "Poor Mr. Hayek," *The New Republic*

112 (April 23, 1945), p. 543. My thanks to Cecelia Stephens for helping me find this reference.

153

On the impact of Hannah Arendt on liberals, see Richard H. Pells, *The Liberal Mind in a Conservative Age* (New York: Harper and Row, 1985), pp. 96.

153

"new kind of rationally constructed society," Hayek, p. vi.

154

With the revival of libertarianism in the 1970s, there was a revival of interest in Chodorov. A collection of Chodorov's essays was published in 1980. Frank Chodorov, *Fugitive Essays*, compiled, edited, and with an introduction by Charles H. Hamilton (Indianapolis: Liberty Press, 1980).

154

"there is a source of truth . . ." Weaver, p. 3.

154

"the paradigm of essences . . ." See Buckley's introduction to *Did You Ever See a Dream Walking?* pp. xvii–xviii.

155

"objective standards for human . . ." Frank Meyer, "The Recrudescent American Conservatism," in *Did You Ever See a Dream Walking?* p. 80.

155

"For four centuries . . ." Weaver, p. 3.

155

"a propagandist . . ." quoted in Nash, p. 41.

155

"For the abstract property . . ." Weaver, p. 133.

156

Russell Kirk, *The Conservative Mind*, second revised edition (Chicago: Regnery, 1987).

156

six "canons" pp. 8–9.

156

"Conservatism is something more . . ." and "once supernatural . . ." Quoted in Nash, p. 41.

157

"the aim of the New Conservatives . . ." is from the original edition of *A Program for Conservatives*. It does not appear in the most recent editions. The fact that Kirk quoted Schlesinger giving him a compliment brought him scorn from libertarian conservatives. The reference to Schlesinger and the attack on Kirk can be found in James M. O'Connell, "The New Conservatism," *New Individualist Review* 2:1 (Spring 1962), pp. 20–21.

157
"Fascism," "a mild socialism," and "not freedom, but . . ." O'Connell, pp. 201–21.

158
"At no time did the fortunes . . ." John B. Judis, *William F. Buckley, Jr.: Patron Saint of the Conservatives* (New York: Simon and Schuster, 1988), p. 113.

158
Judis recounts the story on pages 114–31.

159
"Middle-of-the-road . . ." and "All I can say . . ." Judis, p. 133.

159
"It has been the dominating ambition . . ." William F. Buckley, Jr., *Up from Liberalism* (New York: Hillman Books, 1961), p. 114.

160
The "Eisenhower program . . ." Buckley, p. 116.

160
For an excellent summary of Meyer's thinking and his importance to the *National Review* circle, see Nash, pp. 171–81.

161
"to distinguish between . . ." in "The Recrudescent American Conservatism," in *Did You Ever See a Dream Walking?* p. 87; "*within* a basic civilizational consensus . . ." p. 85; "Nineteenth century conservatism . . ." p. 87.

162
On the distribution of Republican National Convention delegates, see Nicol C. Rae, *The Decline and Fall of Liberal Republicans: From 1952 to the Present* (New York: Oxford University Press, 1989), p. 32.

162
On *National Review*'s masthead, see Judis, pp. 121–31.

162
"In their devotion to Western . . ." Meyer, "The Recrudescent American Conservatism," p. 83.

163
"just downright idiotic" For a discussion of the Republican reaction to Korea, see William L. O'Neill, *American High: The Years of Confidence, 1945–1960* (New York: The Free Press, 1986), pp. 117–18.

164
"Joe McCarthy was the tribune of revenge." Frederick F. Siegel, *Troubled Journey: From Pearl Harbor to Ronald Reagan* (New York: Hill and Wang, 1984), p. 76. Siegel quotes Lubbell on p. 76. For Lubell's view of isolationism, see Samuel Lubell, *The Future of American Politics*, third edition (New York: Harper Colophon Books, 1965), pp. 131–55.

164
Siegel on "Asialationism," see pp. 70–77. For Viereck's view, see Peter Viereck, "The Revolt Against the Elite," in Daniel Bell, ed., *The Radical Right* (Garden City: Doubleday Anchor Books, 1964), pp. 161–83. On "Asia First," see especially pp. 171–72.

165
"yes, there are circumstances . . ." and "In the South . . ." Buckley, *Up from Liberalism*, pp. 146–47.

165
"voting qualification tests . . ." Buckley, p. 148; "The democracy of universal suffrage . . ." p. 138.

166
"Since its inception in 1955 . . ." All Hamowy quotes are from Ronald Hamowy, " 'National Review': Criticism and Reply," *New Individualist Review* 1:3 (November 1961), pp. 3–7. Liberty Press of Indianapolis has done a service to all interested in conservative and libertarian history by republishing the entire collection of issues of *New Individualist Review* in one volume (Liberty Press, 1981).

167
"Dear me . . ." Buckley's reply in William F. Buckley, Jr., " 'National Review': Criticism and Reply," *New Individualist Review* 1:3 (November 1961), pp. 7–10.

168
Nash on Viereck, Nash, pp. 65–68.

168
"lies an American synthesis . . ." Viereck, "The Revolt Against the Elite," in Daniel Bell, ed., *The Radical Right*, p. 177; "the revenge of the noses . . ." p. 162; "frustrating the will . . ." p. 169; "a synthetic substitute . . ." Peter Viereck, "The Philosophical 'New Conservatism,' " in Bell, p. 188; Viereck praises Kirk, p. 195–96.

CHAPTER SEVEN: MODERATION IS NO VIRTUE

170
"If the right wing wants . . ." Eisenhower quoted in Stephen E. Ambrose, *Eisenhower: The President* (New York: Touchstone Books, 1985), p. 220; "I'll go up and down . . ." p. 221.

171
"very conservative in fiscal affairs . . ." Gary Reichard, quoted in Nicol C. Rae, *The Decline and Fall of Liberal Republicans: From 1952 to the Present* (New York: Oxford University Press, 1989), p. 39.

171
"liberal on human issues . . ." Ambrose, p. 115; "when there was no direct . . ." p. 116.

171
Reichard on support for Eisenhower, see Rae, p. 160.

172
"forward-looking and concerned . . ." Ambrose, p. 151.

172
Arthur Larson, *A Republican Looks at His Party* (New York: Harper and Brothers, 1956; reprinted, Westport, Conn.: Greenwood Press, 1974). Larson, *What We Are For* (New York: Harpers, 1959). The first book is well-known; I learned of the existence of the second in a footnote in William F. Buckley, Jr., *Up from Liberalism* (New York: Hillman Books, 1961), p. 180.

172
"Now we have . . ." Larson, *A Republican Looks at His Party*, p. 10. Larson's goal might be seen as taking Schlesinger's Vital Center and giving it to the Republican Party. Larson's position was fiercely moderate. In the nineteenth century, he said, there was not enough government regulation, in the 1930s, too much (p. 10). Eisenhower, Larson's hero, seemed to get it exactly right. The last words of Larson's book are a paean to the existence of a "strong, confident, center-of-the-road American Consensus" (p. 204).

173
Worsthorne is quoted in William F. Buckley, Jr., *Up from Liberalism*, pp. 206–7.

173
"the era of the smooth deal," Karl E. Meyer, *The New America: Politics and Society in the Age of the Smooth Deal* (New York: Basic Books, 1961); "the Smooth Dealer is too obsessed . . ." p. 47.

174
The Lyndon Johnson/Sam Rayburn story is told in David S. Broder, *The Party's Over* (New York: Harper & Row, 1972), p. 13.

174
"verve and spirit," Buckley on Larson in *Up from Liberalism*, pp. 179–82.

175
Buckley on false teeth, p. 207.

175
"was first of all a hazy . . ." Reinhard quoted in Rae, pp. 40–41; "to win the intellectual argument . . ." Rae, pp. 79–80.

176
Broder on ticket-splitting, *The Party's Over*, pp. 12–15.

176
"was neither a moral purpose of Taft . . ." Theodore H. White, *The Making of the President, 1964* (New York: Atheneum, 1965), p. 218.

176
"a flock of little . . ." Meyer, p. 140.

177
"a masterpiece of politics," p. 132. Theodore H. White's description of the Goldwater operation can fairly be described as a masterpiece of political writing. See especially pp. 90–96 and 131–38.

177
Robert D. Novak quoted in Richard Hofstadter, *The Paranoid Style in American Politics* (New York: Vintage, 1967), p. 106. Rowland Evans and Novak were among the most astute (and sympathetic) students of the right from the very beginning. The very first Evans and Novak column, published in May 1963, predicted that Goldwater had a good chance of winning the 1964 Republican nomination—not a widespread view at the time. See Richard Kluger, *The Paper: The Life and Death of the New York Herald Tribune* (New York: Alfred A. Knopf, 1986), p. 670.

177
"the great sort of 'passionate movements' . . ." Kennedy is quoted in Samuel P. Huntington, *American Politics: The Promise of Disharmony* (Cambridge: The Belnap Press of Harvard University Press, 1981), p. 172.

178
William H. Whyte, Jr., *The Organization Man* (Garden City: Doubleday Anchor Books, 1956).

178
"complacency began to deteriorate." Huntington, p. 173. Huntington's book is one of the most brilliant commentaries on American politics that has appeared in decades—and it rewards even those who may disagree with some of Huntington's political views. The book bears rereading at a time when Americans continue to be frustrated with their politics after a brief interlude of national confidence.

178
"This Party, with its every . . ." Goldwater quoted in Theodore White, p. 216.

178
"dime-store New Deal" Hofstadter, p. 97.

179
"I would remind you . . ." Hofstadter, p. 109.

179
"Tonight, there is violence . . ." White, p. 216; "Ask yourself before . . ." White, p. 125; "I deplore those far-out . . ." White, p. 125; "There is a stir . . ." Hofstadter, p. 116; "What good is prosperity . . ." White, pp. 326–27; "when I think of the pornographic . . ." White, p. 338; "I have been speaking about man . . ." White, p. 241.

180
The story of the "Choice" documentary is told in White, pp. 332–33.

181
On California and the military-industrial complex, see Michael W. Miles, *The*

Odyssey of the American Right (New York: Oxford University Press, 1980), pp. 263–66.

181
On the shift in the composition of Republican National Convention delegates, see Rae, p. 73.

182
On Nixon and civil rights in the 1960 campaign, see Rae, pp. 41–43; Stephen E. Ambrose, *Nixon: The Education of a Politician, 1913–1962* (New York: Simon and Schuster, 1987), pp. 537–38.

182
On Goldwater and the South, see White, pp. 135–38.

183
"Throughout this land of ours . . ." White, pp. 331–32. White is best remembered as the man who got the "inside story" of campaigns. What is forgotten is that he paid close attention to what the candidates actually said in their speeches. His books are full of lengthy excerpts, such as this one, that make them invaluable resources years later.

184
The failure of the Republican moderates and liberals in 1964 is told well by White in Chapters 3, 4, 5, and 7. Robert J. Donovan, head of the *Los Angeles Times* Washington bureau and a sympathetic commentator on the Republican moderates, also wrote harshly about the failures of the anti-Goldwater Republicans. He referred to them as "a gaggle of Micawbers, waiting for something to turn up." See Robert J. Donovan, *The Future of the Republican Party* (New York: Signet Books, 1964), p. 39. His analysis of the moderates appears on pp. 38–42.

184
Among those who stayed loyal to Goldwater: In a representative comment of how the right felt betrayed by the moderates and liberals, William A. Rusher noted that while Goldwater had faithfully supported Richard Nixon in 1960, "[it] was an example that many of his liberal Republican rivals failed to follow when their turn came just four years later." William A. Rusher, *The Rise of the Right* (New York: William Morrow, 1984), p. 89.

185
Voting analysis by the author. "The Goldwater-Miller-Burch strategy . . ." quoted in Rae, p. 76. Donovan also noted the collapse of the Republican urban vote in the South, pp. 80–84.

185
Rhodes on backlash: White, p. 195.

185
Kevin Phillips was one of the few voting analysts to notice Goldwater's gains over Nixon in Catholic areas of New York City and in some other parts of the

Northeast. See Kevin P. Phillips, *The Emerging Republican Majority* (New York: Anchor Books, 1970), pp. 166–68.

185
"the right wing had its chance . . ." Donovan, p. 127.

185
"The right-wing enthusiasts . . ." Hofstadter, p. 37.

187
Jacob K. Javits *Order of Battle: A Republican's Call to Reason* (New York: Pocket Books, 1966). On "choice of ancestors" see pp. 57–108. On profit-sharing, see pp. 142–43.

188–90
On the role of the Ripon Society: In its heyday between 1964 and 1968, the society produced a slew of policy papers and books. This account comes from back issues of *The Ripon Forum* and other Society documents in the author's possession, and from interviews and conversations with Josiah Lee Auspitz, William McKenzie, George Gilder, Rep. Tim Petri, and Lee Huebner. Rae tells the Ripon story concisely on pp. 81–86. A highly literate summary of Ripon's analysis and worldview is George F. Gilder and Bruce K. Chapman, *The Party That Lost Its Head* (New York: Alfred A. Knopf, 1966). They speak of liberal Republicanism's lack of a coherent ideology on pp. 249–268 and 294–324.

190
"I can get different factions to sit down together. . . ." Stephen E. Ambrose, *Nixon: The Triumph of a Politician, 1962–1972* (New York: Simon and Schuster, 1989), p. 86.

191
"This fellow really means it . . ." Ambrose, *Nixon: The Triumph of a Politician, 1962–1972*, p. 89.

191
"the Birchers could be handled . . ." The account of Nixon's courting of the right is drawn largely from John Judis, *William F. Buckley, Jr.: Patron Saint of the Conservatives* (New York: Simon and Schuster, 1988), pp. 277–83. The Nixon and Buchanan quotes appear on p. 279; the Lasky and Freeman quotes are on p. 280.

192
"uncharacteristic but unavoidable streak . . ." and "flocked to Nixon because they liked . . ." Ambrose, *Nixon: The Triumph of a Politician*, pp. 61–62. Rusher later referred to conservative backing for Nixon as "the blunder of 1968." See Rusher, *The Rise of the Right*, pp. 209–19.

193
Percentage of delegates, Rae, p. 98.

193

On Rockefeller's telling Nixon of Reagan's Southern weakness, see Ambrose, *Nixon: The Triumph of a Politician*, p. 170.

193

"In effect, the 1968 Convention . . ." William A. Rusher, "The New Right: Past and Prospects," in Robert W. Whitaker, ed., *The New Right Papers* (New York: St. Martin's Press, 1982), p. 12.

194

For an account of the Hofstra conference on Nixon's presidency, see E. J. Dionne, Jr., "Nixon Skips Conference, but the Enigma Attends," *New York Times* (November 23, 1987), p. 14.

195

"a lion of Republicanism and reaction" and "Indeed, the philosophy . . ." Emmet John Hughes, *The Ordeal of Power: A Political Memoir of the Eisenhower Years* (New York: Atheneum, 1963), p. 317.

195

"a devastating mistake . . ." and "relegated to second . . ." Ambrose, *Nixon: The Triumph of a Politician, 1962–1972*, p. 397–98. See also Michael Barone, *Our Country: The Shaping of America from Roosevelt to Reagan* (New York: The Free Press, 1990), p. 488.

195–96

On revenue sharing, see Ambrose, *Nixon: The Triumph of a Politician, 1962–1972*, pp. 432–33.

196

The definitive, if naturally partisan, account of the Family Assistance Plan battle is Daniel P. Moynihan, *The Politics of a Guaranteed Income* (New York: Vintage Books, 1973).

197

"after his dramatic introduction . . ." Ambrose, *Nixon: The Triumph of a Politician, 1962–1972*, p. 366.

197

"Connolly's program brought . . ." Barone, p. 492.

198

"resolved to suspend . . ." Judis, p. 330. The account of Buckley's stance is drawn from Judis, pp. 330–39.

199

William Rusher, however, refused: Rusher proudly reprints an op-ed piece for the *Los Angeles Times* in 1972 in which he announced his opposition to Nixon in *The Rise of the Right*, pp. 247–50.

200

"unyoung, unpoor, and unblack" Richard M. Scammon and Ben J. Wattenberg, *The Real Majority* (New York: Coward-McCann, 1970), p. 21 and pp. 45–58.

200

"if this analysis was right . . ." Richard M. Nixon, *RN: The Memoirs of Richard Nixon* (New York: Simon and Schuster, 1990), p. 491. William Safire offered this neat summary of Nixon's view: "the best economic defense was a 'social issue' offense." William Safire, *Before the Fall: An Inside View of the Pre-Watergate White House* (Garden City: Doubleday, 1975), p. 323.

202

"us-against-them syndrome" Safire offers a brilliant analysis of the "us" against "them" syndrome on pp. 307–15.

202

Defense and nondefense spending figures come from Barone, p. 486.

203

"a politics of creedal passion" Samuel P. Huntington, *American Politics: The Promise of Disharmony* (Cambridge: The Belnap Press of Harvard University Press, 1981), p. 129.

203

"Mr. Nixon will fill the void . . ." quoted in Judis, p. 343.

204

The theory of Watergate as a coup d'état was propounded notably by Kevin P. Phillips in *Post-Conservative America* (New York: Random House, 1982), pp. 63–72.

204

"The press won in Watergate." Bradlee quoted in Huntington, p. 205.

204

"Our nation's capital . . ." Reagan quoted in Jules Witcover, *Marathon: The Pursuit of the Presidency, 1972–1976* (New York: Viking Press, 1977), p. 92.

205

"Well, I wouldn't be . . ." Betty Ford quoted in Witcover, pp. 57–58.

205

Kissinger responds to Reagan attacks: Witcover, p. 417.

206

Comparison of Nixon and Ford delegate base, Rae, pp. 98, 117.

206

"Though he was the incumbent . . ." Witcover, p. 482.

208

"it is simply purblind . . ." Rusher, "The New Right: Past and Prospects," in Whitaker, p. 17.

CHAPTER EIGHT: HELL HATH NO FURY

209

"We have few ties to this earth. . . ." Falwell himself speaks of the incongruity of his sermon in light of his later life in Jerry Falwell, *Strength for the Journey: An Autobiography* (New York: Simon and Schuster, 1987), p. 290.

210

"Respected 'evangelicals' in the 1870s . . ." Marsden quoted in Nathan Glazer, "Fundamentalism: A Defensive Offensive," in Richard John Neuhaus and Michael Cromartie, *Piety and Politics: Evangelicals and Fundamentalists Confront the World* (Washington: Ethics and Public Policy Center, 1987), p. 255–56. For those interested in an excellent sampling of scholarship and opinion on the evangelical movement, *Piety and Politics* is one of the books of choice.

211

"The real candidate for . . ." Fitch quoted in Leonard I. Sweet, "The 1960s: The Crises of Liberal Christianity and the Public Emergence of Evangelicalism," in George Marsden, ed., *Evangelicalism and Modern America* (Grand Rapids: William B. Eerdmans, 1984), p. 31.

211

"God Almighty does not . . ." Smith quoted in Flo Conway and Jim Siegelman, *Holy Terror: The Fundamentalist War on America's Freedoms in Religion, Politics and Our Private Lives* (New York: Delta Books, 1984), p. 204.

211

"We have enough votes . . ." Pat Robertson quoted in Alan Crawford, *Thunder on the Right: The "New Right" and the Politics of Resentment* (New York: Pantheon, 1980), p. 161.

211

Buckley commented on the effectiveness of Mondale's anti-Falwell commercial in conversations with the author.

212

"The great redemptive religion . . ." Harvey Cox, *Religion in the Secular City: Toward a Postmodern Theology* (New York: Simon and Schuster, 1984), p. 73. Cox's chapter on fundamentalism (pp. 72–82) was my first introduction to Machen, and Cox's treatment of Machen and the other fundamentalists— whom he disagrees with both politically and theologically—is exemplary for both scholarly fairness and Christian charity; "A separation between . . ." Cox, p. 73.

212

For Lippmann on Machen and the fundamentalists, see Walter Lippmann, *A Preface to Morals* (New York: The Macmillan Company, 1929), pp. 33–35.

213

"Fundamentalism is an offshoot . . ." Cox, p. 74.

213

"When I began to apply . . ." Rauschenbusch quoted in James Davison Hunter, "The Evangelical Worldview since 1890," in *Piety and Politics*, p. 27. The essay is reprinted from Hunter's book *American Evangelicalism: Conservative Religion and the Quandary of Modernity* (New Brunswick: Rutgers University Press, 1983).

213

Hunter on the New Christianity in Neuhaus and Cromartie, pp. 27–35.

214

"the backbone of philanthropic . . ." Dewey on Bryan quoted in Richard John Neuhaus, *The Naked Public Square: Religion and Democracy in America* (Grand Rapids: Eerdmans, 1984), p. 178.

214

"What troubled conservatives . . ." Hunter, p. 30.

214

"the inerrant . . ." p. 30.

215

"Protestantism is down with . . ." Mencken is quoted in Terry Eastland, "In Defense of Religious America," *Commentary* 71:6 (June 1981), p. 42. Eastland's article is an excellent history told from a point of view sympathetic to the evangelical rebellion. I am also grateful for many conversations with him on the subject of this chapter; many ideas in it came from those conversations.

215

"the cultural disestablishment . . ." Eastland, p. 42.

215

"The Great Depression . . ." and "personal salvation . . ." Hunter, p. 41.

215

Sunday School Times and *Kansas City Star* poll are reported on in Joel A. Carpenter, "From Fundamentalism to New Evangelical Coalition," in Marsden, ed., *Evangelicalism and Modern America*, p. 8. He mentions the popularity of "Miracles and Melodies" on p. 11.

215

For a very fair-minded treatment of the relationship between some wings of the evangelical movement and fascism, see Leo P. Ribuffo, *The Old Christian Right: The Protestant Far Right from the Great Depression to the Cold War* (Philadelphia: Temple University Press, 1983), especially pp. 3–24.

216

"no dog-in-the-manger . . ." On the ACCC and the NAE, see A. James Reichley, "The Evangelical and Fundamentalist Revolt," in *Piety and Politics*, pp. 71–72. The essay is an excerpt from Reichley's *Religion in American Public Life* (Washington: The Brookings Institution, 1985).

216
"great social achievement" Reichley, pp. 73–74.

216
"Graham was no bigot. . . ." William L. O'Neill, *American High: The Years of Confidence, 1945–1960* (New York: The Free Press, 1986), pp. 214–15.

217
"most of the early Southern . . ." Falwell, p. 338. Falwell acknowledges his change in view on p. 337.

217
Data on churchgoing in O'Neill, p. 212.

218
"is not something that makes . . ." Will Herberg, *Protestant-Catholic-Jew: An Essay in American Religious Sociology* (Garden City: Doubleday, 1955). See especially p. 285. Eisenhower's famous line is quoted by O'Neill on p. 213, and O'Neill makes the link between Herberg's theory and Eisenhower's quote proving Herberg right.

218
"officially" Catholic: Garry Wills, *Bare Ruined Choirs: Doubt, Prophecy, and Radical Religion* (Garden City: Doubleday, 1972), p. 88; the Schlesinger quote also appears on p. 88.

219
On the closeness of evangelicals and Catholics: Falwell, for one, praises the Catholic bishops for their stand on abortion on p. 335. It is almost inconceivable that a person of Falwell's religious persuasion would have been caught praising Catholic bishops thirty years ago.

219
Harvey Cox comments on the popularity of his book among Roman Catholics in the revised paperback edition, Harvey Cox, *The Secular City* (New York: Macmillan, 1966), p. xi.

220
On the resurgence of old-time religion as a revolt against modernity, see Cox, *Religion in the Secular City*, especially pp. 14–26; Peter Clecak, *America's Quest for the Ideal Self: Dissent and Fulfillment in the 60s and 70s* (New York: Oxford University Press, 1983), pp. 125–44.

220
"the counterculturalists have served . . ." Neuhaus, *The Naked Public Square*, p. 200.

220
"subjectivist search for authority" and "People began to journey . . ." See Leonard I. Sweet, "The 1960s: The Crises of Liberal Christianity and the Public Emergence of Evangelicalism," in Marsden, ed., *Evangelicalism in Modern America*, pp. 29–45; see especially pp. 37–43.

221
"The sixties cliché . . ." Sweet, p. 34.

221
"often seemed more dogmatic about doubt . . ." Sweet, p. 42. "When many churches found . . ." Sweet, p. 43.

222
"The people of Kanawha County . . ." Robert J. Hoy, "Lid on a Boiling Pot," in Robert W. Whitaker, ed., *The New Right Papers* (New York: St. Martin's Press, 1982), p. 90.

222
"What is at issue here . . ." Alice Moore quoted in Alan Crawford, *Thunder on the Right: The "New Right" and the Politics of Resentment* (New York: Pantheon, 1980), p. 156.

223
On "rednecks" and redneck religion, Cox, *Religion in the Secular City*, pp. 63–64.

223
"Put simply, those who controlled . . ." James Hitchcock, *What Is Secular Humanism? Why Humanism Became Secular and How It Is Changing Our World* (Ann Arbor: Servant Books, 1982), pp. 81–82.

224
"It is the great successes . . ." Nathan Glazer, "Fundamentalism: A Defensive Offensive," in *Piety and Politics*, pp. 250–51.

224
Falwell on *Roe*, p. 335.

224
Carter's showing in Baptist counties is reported in Albert J. Menendez, *Religion at the Polls* (Philadelphia: The Westminster Press, 1977) pp. 198–99. My thanks to Prof. Jeffrey K. Hadden for lending me his extensive collection of Menendez's very helpful analyses of elections from *Church & State* magazine.

225
"Does a Dedicated . . ." Advertisement in author's possession.

225
The best account of Jimmy Carter's faith and its impact on his electoral chances and his presidency is Leo P. Ribuffo, "God and Jimmy Carter," in Myles L. Bradbury and James B. Gilbert, *Transforming Faith: The Sacred and the Secular in Modern American History* (Westport, Conn.: Greenwood Press, 1989), pp. 141–59.

225
"It was not something specific . . ." Jules Witcover, *Marathon: The Pursuit of the Presidency, 1972–1976* (New York: Viking Press, 1977), p. 272.

225–26

"critics and journalists . . ." Clecak, p. 127.

227

On Carter's use of the White House, see Ribuffo, "God and Jimmy Carter," pp. 150–51.

228

On the *National Review* and the post-Nixon crisis, see John Judis, *William F. Buckley, Jr.: Patron Saint of the Conservatives* (New York: Simon and Schuster, 1988), pp. 367–83. See also William Rusher, *The Making of the New Majority Party* (Ottawa: Green Hill Publishers, 1975).

228

"abandoning Middle . . ." On Buckley and Phillips, see Judis, p. 377; and E. J. Dionne, Jr., "The Unlikely Populist," *Washington Post* (June 19, 1990), p. E-1.

229

"Compared to a William Buckley . . ." Paul Gottfried and Thomas Flemming, *The Conservative Movement* (Boston: Twayne Publishers, 1988), p. 78.

230

"public anger over busing . . ." Judis, p. 378.

230

"The New Right is looking for issues . . ." Reichley, p. 79.

230

"Jerry, there is in America . . ." Falwell, p. 359.

232

Harris prediction cited in Jeffrey K. Hadden, "Televangelism and Politics," in *Piety and Politics*, p. 382.

232

"ignorant democratic conservatism . . ." Russell Kirk, "The Popular Conservatives," Heritage Foundation Lecture Series (No. 168), August 4, 1988.

233

"To be lectured against the perils . . ." William F. Buckley, Jr., "Yale and the Moral Majority," in *Piety and Politics*, pp. 265–66.

233

"The truth is that . . ." Hadden, *Piety and Politics*, p. 326.

234

Polling analysis by the author.

234

Menendez, pp. 188–98; Kevin P. Phillips, *Post-Conservative America: People, Politics and Ideology in a Time of Crisis* (New York: Random House, 1982), pp. 187–88.

235
Phillips, p. 191.

235
"After 1980, they not only . . ." Haley Barbour, interview with the author.

238
"the remarkable treatment of classic . . ." Novak quoted in John Kenneth White, *The New Politics of Old Values* (Hanover: University Press of New England, 1989), p. 119.

238
"Our government needs the church . . ." and "envisioned a Federal government neutral . . ." William Bennett speech text. Thanks to Wendell Willkie for providing me with a copy.

238
"The greatness of America is departing us. . . ." From audiotape of Pat Robertson distributed by the Robertson campaign in Iowa and elsewhere.

240
"The religious person is entitled . . ." Eastland, p. 45.

CHAPTER NINE: THE DEMAND FOR SUPPLY SIDE

245
On the New York City fiscal crisis, Martin Shefter, *Political Crisis/Fiscal Crisis* (New York: Basic Books, 1985).

246
Data on California from Robert Kuttner, *Revolt of the Haves: Tax Rebellions and Hard Times* (New York: Simon and Schuster, 1980), pp. 51–55. "When inflation blended with . . ." p. 93.

246
"the Watts riot . . ." Kuttner, p. 96; data on black vote, Kuttner, p. 97.

247
"The government is cheating you." Theodore H. White, *America in Search of Itself: The Making of the President, 1956–1980* (New York: Warner Books, 1983), p. 161.

247
Jude Wanniski, *The Way the World Works* (New York: Touchstone, 1978). One of the best brief accounts of the development of supply-side ideas is in Sidney Blumenthal, *The Rise of the Counter-Establishment* (New York: Times Books, 1986), pp. 166–209. Blumenthal, no conservative, is extremely fair-minded in presenting the supply-siders, and he proves—surprisingly—that economic theorizing can be exciting to read about. Over the last decade, I have learned much from conversations with Sidney about supply-side economics and many other things.

247
The most comprehensible, simple (and sympathetic) explanation of Keynesian

economics that I have ever run across appears in Robert Kuttner, *The Economic Illusion: False Choices Between Prosperity and Social Justice* (Boston: Houghton Mifflin, 1984), pp. 1–49. I have drawn on Kuttner's explanation here. See also Wanniski, pp. 154–59, for a clear and less sympathetic view.

247
Jean Baptiste Say is explained in John Kenneth Galbraith, *Economics in Perspective* (Boston: Houghton Mifflin, 1987), pp. 74–77, and Wanniski, pp. 155–156.

248
Daniel Bell on installment buying in Bell, *The Cultural Contradictions of Capitalism* (New York: Basic Books, 1978), pp. 66–70.

249
"tight money and fiscal ease." Jude Wanniski, "The Mundell-Laffer Hypothesis—A New View of the World Economy," *The Public Interest* (Spring 1975), p. 49.

249
"The stock market crash . . ." Wanniski, *The Way the World Works*, p. 125.

249
Wanniski on the benefits of the Coolidge-Mellon tax cuts, *The Way the World Works*, pp. 117–25.

250
Wanniski on the Laffer curve: Jude Wanniski, "Taxes, Revenues and the 'Laffer Curve,' " *The Public Interest* 50 (Winter 1978), pp. 3–16.

250
"Mundell and Laffer go back to an older . . ." Wanniski, "The Mundell-Laffer Hypothesis," p. 51.

250-51
For an account of the capital-gains fight—from the point of view of one of Wanniski's opponents—see Kuttner, *Revolt of the Haves*, pp. 242–49.

251
On the Kemp conversion, see Blumenthal, pp. 184–91.

253
"Self-indulgence takes the place . . ." Wilson Carey McWilliams, "The Meaning of the Election," in Gerald M. Pomper et al., *The Election of 1980: Reports and Interpretations* (Chatham, N.J.: Chatham House, 1981), p. 183.

253
"the result is to penalize . . ." George Gilder, *Wealth and Poverty* (New York: Bantam Books, 1981), p. 16.

254
"What has been happening . . ." Gilder, p. 18; "It is the idea of economic futility . . ." Gilder, p. 305; "Capitalism begins with giving. . . ." Gilder, p. 23;

"One of the little-probed mysteries . . ." Gilder, p. 119; "How much easier . . ." Gilder, p. 122.

254
"The moral hazards . . ." Gilder, pp. 135–36.

255
"What is called . . ." Galbraith, p. 286.

256
"a supply-side microeconomics of the left" George Gilder, "A Supply-Side Economics of the Left," *The Public Interest* (Summer 1983), pp. 29–43.

257
"They didn't create wealth . . ." Hartley quoted in Steven Pearlstein, "Icon of an Era: Drexel Came to Epitomize Wall Street's 1980s Excess," *Washington Post* (February 14, 1990), p. A1.

257
"Unable to create . . ." Gilder, "A Supply-Side Economics of the Left," pp. 33–34.

258
On what he called the "collapse of the Reagan coalition," see David Stockman, *The Triumph of Politics: The Inside Story of the Reagan Revolution* (New York: Avon Books, 1987), pp. 223–47.

CHAPTER TEN: POLITICS WITHOUT GOVERNMENT

260
"the Reagan Administration has failed . . ." Edward H. Crane, "Who Will Lead?" in David Boaz, ed., *Assessing the Reagan Years* (Washington: Cato Institute, 1988), p. 423.

261
On libertarianism in the electorate, see William S. Maddox and Stuart A. Lilie, *Beyond Liberal and Conservative* (Washington: Cato Institute, 1984), p. 156–61.

262
"to the extent that it prevails . . ." Samuel Brittan, quoted in Jeff Riggenbach, "In Praise of Decadence," *The Libertarian Review* (February 1979), p. 26.

262
"the authority of previous . . ." Riggenbach, p. 27; "Like every decadent period . . ." Riggenbach, p. 29.

263
"The ruinous failing of ideologues . . ." Riggenbach takes Kirk on directly in his article. Kirk's most compact expression of his views on libertarians is "A Dispassionate Assessment of Libertarians," (Heritage Lecture 158), a speech at the Heritage Foundation given April 19, 1988.

263

The definitive account of Meyer, Kirk, and friends is, of course, George H. Nash's, *The Conservative Intellectual Movement in America* (New York: Basic, 1979). For a brief and useful account, see Paul Gottfried and Thomas Flemming, *The Conservative Movement* (Boston: Twayne Publishers, 1988). On Meyer, see pp. 15–19. On ISI, see pp. 2, 19, 24.

264

"the Randian hero is really . . ." Stephen L. Newman, *Liberalism at Wits' End: The Libertarian Revolt Against the Modern State* (Ithaca: Cornell University Press, 1984), p. 26.

265

On *New Individualist Review*: F. A. Hayek, "Freedom and Coercion: A Reply to Mr. Hamowy," *New Individualist Review* (Summer 1961), pp. 28–31; in the same issue, a review of Frank S. Meyer's *The Moulding of Communists*, pp. 31–32. Russell Kirk, "Ritualistic Liberalism," *NIR* (November 1961), pp. 12–16. In same issue, Brude Goldberg, "Ayn Rand's 'For the New Intellectual,' " pp. 17–26. "To those who are traveling . . ." quote is in Goldberg, p. 24.

265

Review of Meyer is John Weicher, "A 'Fusionist' Approach to Freedom," *NIR* (Autumn 1962), pp. 43–45; "When the American government conscripts . . ." Howard Buffett, "An Opportunity for the Republican Party," *NIR* (Summer 1962), p. 14; Murray N. Rothbard, "Herbert Clark Hoover: A Reconsideration," *NIR* (Winter 1966), pp. 3–12; M. Stanton Evans, "Raico on Liberalism and Religion," *NIR* (Winter 1966), pp. 19–25; Raico's reply, pp. 25–31.

267

The symposium on conscription occupies most of the Spring 1967 issue of *NIR*. See especially Richard Flacks, "Conscription in a Democratic Society," pp. 10–12; "rather carefully demolishes . . ." "New Books and Articles," *NIR* (Winter 1968), p. 57.

268

Hess quoted in Nash, p. 428 and p. 316.

268

Murray Rothbard, "Confessions of a Right-Wing Liberal," *Ramparts* (June 1968), pp. 48–52. My thanks to Ed Crane and David Boaz of the Cato Institute for letting me read through their excellent files of clippings on libertarianism, where I found Rothbard's famous piece—and many less well-known articles on the movement. To their credit, the libertarians save everything, and not just the flattering stuff.

269

This quick summary of libertarian history is from my own coverage of the movement, and from regular reading of *The Libertarian Review*. For other summaries of the party's history, see Joel Kotkin, "Libertarian Party: Once Obscure Fringe Group Sees 1980 as Its Year of National Appeal," *Washington Post* (March 31, 1980); and John Judis, "Libertarianism: Where the Left Meets the Right," *The Progressive* (September 1980), pp. 36–38. See also John A. Jenkins, "Free Thinkers," *TWA Ambassador* (March 1980), pp. 51–54 and 82. When a movement gets itself into an airline magazine, it has achieved a certain notoriety.

269
"the libertine impulse . . ." Nash, p. 317; "for all the sound and fury . . ." Nash, p. 318.

271–72
Robert A. Nozick, *Anarchy, the State and Utopia* (New York: Basic Books, 1974), and John Rawls, *A Theory of Justice* (Cambridge: Belnap Press, 1971). Nozick quotes in text are drawn from Nozick, pp. 30–31, ix. A brisk and informed account of the Rawls–Nozick debate is Randall Rothenberg, "Philosopher Robert Nozick *vs.* Philosopher John Rawls," *Esquire* (March 1983), pp. 201–9.

272
On Koch's role: Interviews with Ed Crane, Bob Thompson, and others; see also Judis in *The Progressive*. For an unfriendly view, see Lawrence V. Cott, "CATO Institute and the Invisible Finger," *National Review* (June 8, 1979), pp. 740–42.

274
"Conservatives believe in limited . . ." Ernest van den Haag, "Libertarians and Conservatives," *National Review* (June 8, 1979), pp. 725–39.

274
"left wing" Joseph L. Gentili, "Libertarians' Left Wing Has Captured the Party," *Human Events* (October 27, 1979), p. 14.

275
"low-tax liberal": Ed Clark, interview with author during 1980 campaign.

278
"For libertarians and populists . . ." Maddox and Lilie, p. 111; "the American public is not middle . . ." p. 116.

279
On Gary Hart, see Maddox and Lilie, pp. 79 and 97.

280
"The future of American politics . . ." David Boaz in Boaz, ed., *Left, Right and Baby Boom: America's New Politics* (Washington: Cato Institute, 1986), p. 7.

281
Rothbard quoted in Newman, p. 21.

CHAPTER ELEVEN: BALANCING ACTS

283
On Reagan's "solving" the tax and military problem, see David R. Gergen, "Following the Leaders," *Public Opinion* (June/July 1985), pp. 16, 55–57.

284
"Today, the common ground . . ." Don Devine, "Divide on the Right," *Washington Times* (June 7, 1989), p. F4.

285
"My soft-core Marxism . . ." David Stockman, *The Triumph of Politics* (New York: Avon, 1987), p. 54.

288
"At least in Vietnam . . ." The Marine made this comment to me in Lebanon, a month before the Marine barracks was blown up.

289
"In Grenada, he won . . ." This is one of the many Schneiderisms that have made Bill Schneider one of the most quoted political analysts.

290
"If you're a Republican strategist . . ." Atwater in David Boaz, ed., *Left, Right and Baby Boom* (Washington: Cato Institute, 1986), p. 49.

294
"an ostrichlike . . ." Allan C. Carlson, *Family Questions* (New Brunswick: Transaction Books, 1988), p. 111.

294
On the "family agenda," see E. J. Dionne, Jr., "Struggle for Work and Family Fueling Women's Movement," *New York Times* (August 22, 1989), p. A1.

295
Poll on 1986 available through the Democratic Leadership Council in Washington, D.C.

296
"If voters see a race . . ." Gingrich to author.

297
On diffuse "issue agenda," the first person to make this point to me was Richard Wirthlin, President Reagan's polltaker, in 1986.

298
"big spending, high taxes . . ." Reagan quoted in Jane Mayer and Doyle McManus, *Landslide: The Unmaking of the President, 1984–1988* (Boston: Houghton Mifflin, 1988), p. 292.

CHAPTER TWELVE: ONE NATION, DIVISIBLE

300
"a wide chasm": For an account of that day, see E. J. Dionne, Jr., "Republican Continues to Stress Ideology," *New York Times* (August 31, 1988), p. A1.

311
Atwater gives an account of Pinkerton and his "excellent nerds" in David Runkel, ed., *Campaign for President: The Managers Look at '88* (Dover, Mass.: Auburn House, 1989), pp. 109–10.

312
"guess what? . . ." Atwater in Runkel, p. 112.

313
Dukakis as straitlaced: Paul Taylor, "Hill Democrats Worry Party's Inferiority Complex Is Permanent," *Washington Post* (March 15, 1990), p. A1.

315
"Little kids in school . . ." Quoted in E. J. Dionne, Jr., "Despite Squeeze on the Middle Class, A Suburb's Young Voters Like Bush," *New York Times* (September 17, 1988), p. 8.

315
"Metzenbaum cast himself . . ." Quoted in E. J. Dionne, Jr., "Dukakis Camp Is Battling in Last Democratic Trench," *New York Times* (October 20, 1988), p. A1.

318
"And not seldom . . ." Kirk's speech was delivered to The Heritage Foundation in Washington, D.C., on Oct. 6, 1988. It is available from the Foundation: Russell Kirk, "The Neoconservatives: An Endangered Species," *The Heritage Lectures* no. 178, p. 5. For an excellent critical summary of the infighting on the right, see John Judis, "The Conservative Crackup," in *The American Prospect* 3 (Fall 1990), pp. 30–42.

318
Account based on interviews with Richard John Neuhaus and Alan Carlson in the fall of 1990. Judis discusses this battle in his article on pp. 33–35.

319
Patrick Buchanan, "America First—And Second and Third," *The National Interest* 19 (Spring 1990), pp. 77–82.

319
"the McGovern–Buchanan axis." Quayle quoted in David S. Broder, "Quayle Calls for Mending GOP 'Fissures' on Budget, Gulf," *Washington Post* (November 11, 1990), p. A13.

320
On the budget battle, see Thomas Byrne Edsall and E. J. Dionne, Jr., "Democracy at Work: The Tax Revolt of the Masses," *Washington Post* Outlook Section (October 14, 1990), p. K1.

321

Mandy Grunwald and others quoted on the 1990 elections in E. J. Dionne, Jr., and Dan Balz, "Democrats Find New Road Leading to the White House," *Washington Post National Weekly Edition* (November 12–18, 1990), p. 12.

322

Torricelli comment in interview with author.

322

"threw the bums back in." See Paul Taylor, "A Mood, Not a Movement," *Washington Post National Weekly Edition* (November 12–18, 1990), pp. 6–7.

323

Tom Mann made his point in an interview. I am grateful to my colleague Paul Taylor, who gave me his notes from an earlier interview with Mann.

324

On voters reelecting incumbents even when they disapproved of Congress, see Dan Balz and E. J. Dionne, Jr., "Across the Nation, Gloomy Voters Send a Mixed Message," *Washington Post* (November 7, 1990).

324

"a government whose jurisdictional reach . . ." Fred Siegel, "Dependent Individualism: A Welfare State Without an Ethical Core," *Dissent* (Fall 1988), pp. 437–44. The quotation appears on p. 443.

325–26

The Times Mirror data are available through the Times Mirror Company's Washington office. My thanks to Andrew Kohut for discussing these polls with me at length. For a summary of the first in the series of Times Mirror polls, see E. J. Dionne, Jr., "Survey of Electorate Finds Weak Political Parties and Conflicts Over Change," *New York Times* (October 1, 1987), p. D27.

326

" 'Nothing in moderation' . . ." Charles Paul Freund, "Washington Diarist," *The New Republic* (March 27, 1989). My thanks to Fred Siegel for bringing this quotation to my attention—and for six years of exceptionally enlightening political discussions. See Fred Siegel, "Nothing in Moderation," *The Atlantic* (May 1990), pp. 108–10.

CHAPTER THIRTEEN: THE POLITICS OF THE RESTIVE MAJORITY

330

"a dread and a yearning" See James A. Morone, *The Democratic Wish: Popular Participation and the Limits of American Government* (New York: Basic Books, 1990), esp. pp. 1–30 and 322–37.

332

On the declining importance of elections and the growing importance of the courts, see Martin Shefter and Benjamin Ginsberg, *Politics by Other Means* (New York: Basic Books, 1989). Fred Siegel has written often on the dangers of relying too heavily on the courts. See his May 1990 *Atlantic* article, cited above. See also E. J. Dionne, Jr., "New Court of Last Resort," *Washington Post* Outlook Section (July 29, 1990), p. K1.

333

"an overwhelming preference for smoothing over . . ." Robert Reich, *The Resurgent Liberal* (New York: Times Books/Random House, 1989), p. 283. Reich's argument about the New Deal appears on pp. 278–89.

333

"in no small part because Franklin . . ." Mark Lilla, "What Is the Civic Interest?" *The Public Interest 81* (Fall 1985), p. 76.

334

"Inability to commit oneself . . ." William M. Sullivan, *Reconstructing Public Philosophy* (Berkeley: University of California Press, 1986), p. 222. On p. 215 Sullivan makes the paradoxical but accurate point that preserving individual liberty is a cooperative enterprise.

334

I was introduced to the wonderful term "public enterprise" by Will Marshall, president of the Progressive Policy Institute in Washington.

334

"In the long run . . ." James Q. Wilson, "The Rediscovery of Character: Private Virtue and Public Policy," *The Public Interest 81* (Fall 1985), p. 16. William A. Galston elaborates on this idea brilliantly in "Liberal Virtues," *American Political Science Review* 82:4 (December 1988), esp. p. 1279. I am grateful to Bill Galston for providing me with copies of this paper and others, and for some very helpful discussions about the issues of community, obligation and virtue.

334–35

On the "new paradigm," see James P. Pinkerton, "The New Paradigm," *Ripon Forum* 26:3 (September 1990), pp. 10–11; and E. J. Dionne, Jr., "The Idea Man With a Vision Thing," *Washington Post* (December 5, 1990), p. C1. For a thoughtful book outlining the conservative approach to fighting poverty, see Stuart Butler and Anna Kondratas, *Out of the Poverty Trap: A Conservative Strategy for Welfare Reform* (New York: The Free Press, 1987).

335

On welfare and work, see Christopher Jencks and Katheryn Edin, "The Real Welfare Problem," *The American Prospect 1* (Spring 1990), pp. 31–50.

335

On the family and the "new political center," see Daniel Patrick Moynihan, *Family and Nation* (New York: Harcourt Brace Jovanovich, 1986). One of the best recent efforts to bring together policy proposals that are at once practical, egalitarian, and sensitive to both traditional and feminist views of family life is Elaine Ciulla Kamarck and William A. Galston, *Putting Children First: A Progressive Family Policy for the 1990s*, a paper published by the Progressive Policy Institute, September 1990.

336
"Past experience teaches . . ." Theda Skocpol, "Sustainable Social Policy: Fighting Poverty Without Poverty Programs," *The American Prospect* 2 (Summer 1990), pp. 58–70. Wilson expounds his views in detail in William J. Wilson, *The Truly Disadvantaged: The Inner City, the Underclass and Public Policy* (Chicago: University of Chicago Press, 1987). See also Wilson, "Race-Neutral Policies and the Democratic Coalition," *The American Prospect* (Spring 1990), pp. 74–81.

337
"in the middle of two opposing forces . . ." All of these quotations are from King's famous "Letter from Birmingham Jail," in Martin Luther King, Jr., *Why We Can't Wait* (New York: Signet Books, 1964), pp. 86–87.

337
"We can easily forget or underestimate . . ." Jerry G. Watts, "Racial Discourse in an Age of Darwinism," *Democratic Left* 18:4 (July–August 1990), p. 3.

338
On the family not being simply a "lifestyle choice" and the growing research suggesting that children from intact, two-parent families tend to be better off: Elaine Ciulla Kamarck and William A. Galston offer a useful review of the literature in *Putting Children First*, pp. 14–20. Kamarck and Galston are rightly careful to note that they are making practical judgments about policy, not moral condemnations of all who fail to adhere to traditional norms. They write: "To avoid misunderstanding, we want to make it clear that a general preference for the intact two-parent family does not mean that this is the best option in every case. Nor does it mean that all single-parent families are somehow dysfunctional; that proposition would diminish the achievements of millions of single parents who are struggling successfully against the odds to provide good homes for their children. Our point is that at the level of statistical aggregates and society-wide phenomena, significant differences do appear between one-parent and two-parent families, differences that can and should shape our understanding of social policy." (p. 2)

340
Susan Moller Okin, *Justice, Gender and the Family* (New York: Basic Books, 1989). Okin's proposals are summarized on pp. 170–189. The quotation "to the point where the standards of living . . ." appears on p. 179. On the similarities between Okin and conservatives: In its manifesto advocating "cultural conservatism," the Free Congress Research and Education argues that support payments in divorces should be structured "so as to maintain the standard of living of the partner who did not seek divorce." They also call for lump-sum payments "to a partner whose sacrifices have led to increased earning power for the other." See The Institute for Cultural Conservatism, Free Congress Research and Education Foundation, *Cultural Conservatism: Toward a New National Agenda* (Washington, 1987), p. 42.

341
On the polls and abortion, see E. J. Dionne, Jr., "Polls Find Ambivalence on Abortion Persists in U.S.," *New York Times* (August 3, 1989), p. A18. On abortion and the 1990 elections, see Maralee Schwartz and E. J. Dionne, Jr., "Abortion Showdown a Tossup," *Washington Post* (November 10, 1990).

342
"the prochoice movement has tried . . ." and subsequent quotations are drawn from Daniel Callahan, "An Ethical Challenge to Prochoice Advocates," *Commonweal* (23 November, 1990), pp. 681–87.

344
"another sign of the welcomed waning . . ." and subsequent quotations drawn from Richard Vigilante, "Prospective Friends," *National Review* (November 19, 1990), pp. 53–55.

347
On experimentation in government: David Osborne and Ted Gaebler argue in *Reinventing Government* (Reading, Mass: Addison-Wesley, 1992) that ideas like market orientation, decentralization, and competitiveness within the public sector need not necessarily be viewed as "conservative." Their point is that *liberals*, who have more of an interest than anyone else in making government work, should be prepared to borrow such ideas to improve the delivery of public services. See also David Osborne, "Ten Ways to Turn D.C. Around," *Washington Post Magazine* (December 9, 1990), pp. 19–23, 38–43.

348
Paul Kennedy makes his case in *The Rise and Fall of the Great Powers: Economic Change and Military Conflict from 1500 to 2000* (New York: Random House, 1989). For a rejoinder, see Joseph S. Nye, Jr., *Bound to Lead: The Changing Nature of American Power* (New York: Basic Books, 1990).

353
"when politics goes well. . . ." Michael J. Sandel, *Liberalism and the Limits of Justice* (New York: Cambridge University Press, 1982), p. 183.

353
"the better the constitution. . . ." J. J. Rousseau, *The Social Contract and the Discourses* translated by G. D. H. Cole (New York: E. P. Dutton, 1950), p. 93.

ACKNOWLEDGMENTS

Writing a book is a thoroughly personal matter. When you sit down to write, you're alone and the final choices are yours. That's why I bear the burden of any mistakes and misunderstandings.

Yet most books grow out of many years of conversation, discussion, and argument. Books are thus thoroughly cooperative ventures and not lonely at all. That's especially true of books about politics, and it's certainly true of this one.

I have been blessed with a most extraordinary group of friends and colleagues, people always willing to share thoughts and facts, to argue late into the evening, to do their patient best to make me see something even when I stubbornly refuse to get the obvious point. I've also been lucky to have a politically ecumenical group of friends—conservatives and neoconservatives, liberals and neoliberals, socialists and capitalists, Republicans and Democrats, and people who escape or combine these categories. If I have tried to do anything in this book, it is to give respectful attention to a great many different points of view. That's because I respect my friends. And if these acknowledgments are a bit long, I hope the reader will forgive me. It's because I have a lot of debts to pay.

To begin at the beginning: I learned to love politics from my parents, who encouraged my sister and me very early on to read, listen, argue—and then to go back to read and listen again. Politics was always on the agenda at our house. And it was every imaginable kind of politics, from what was going on in a Fall River City Council race to what was happening in Vietnam. My parents were born dissenters. In a Kennedy Democratic town in a liberal Republican state, they were Taft Republicans, which put them in a minority of the minority (and led both of them to be skeptical of the Vietnam War long before most people were). That gave me a lifelong love for contrarians. Yet my mom and dad were also exceptionally open-minded, prepared to rethink things and insistent that their children listen to points of view that they thoroughly disagreed with. They were exceptionally good citizens and great parents, too. All this is to say that this book is dedicated to them because it really is theirs.

Bert Yaffe, who would have made a great congressman, introduced me to the real world of campaigning and much else. Bill Schneider taught me that academic analysts of politics can be as shrewd as the most cunning party bosses—quite simply, he knows more about politics than just about anyone. Gary Orren is also a wise student of politics and a fine teacher. I've talked over almost every idea in this book with three spectacular friends: Jack Risko, Bud Sheppard, and Rick Weil.

The New York Times gave me much joy, and many opportunities. There are too many friends there to thank, but I will try here in rough chronological order: Thanks to Jack Rosenthal, a great friend who got me into journalism; and to Flora Lewis, Nan Robertson, Andreas Freund, Abe Rosenthal, Shelly Binn, Dave Jones, Henry Lieberman, John Vinocur, Sydney Schanberg, Craig Whitney, Bill Borders, Warren Hoge, Irv Horowitz, John Darnton, Bill Kovach, Max Frankel, Johnny Apple, and Adam Clymer. My colleagues during the 1988 campaign were always a source of pride: Rick Berke, Gerry Boyd, Maureen Dowd, Mike Kagay, Janet Elder, Andy Rosenthal, Steve Roberts, Susan Rasky, Bernie Weinraub, Janet Battaile, Mike Oreskes and Robin Toner. Rich Meislin has been a friend for two decades and a colleague in computer rooms, the state legislature and over many fine meals (some of the best of which he cooked himself). And for many particular things, warm appreciation to John Tagliabue, Tom Wicker, Tony Lewis, Bill Schmidt, Bernie Gwertzman, Mike Kaufman, Frank Lynn, Mickey Carroll, Ari Goldman, Irv Molotsky, Linda Lake, Deborah Hoffman, Anne Aghion, Cristina Fioravanti, Barbara Roffi, Giorgio Quondam, Deirdre Carmody, Marty Tolchin, Kay Shatraw, Paul Hoffman, Steve Weisman, Judy Miller, Al Siegal, Lena Williams, and Josh Barbanal. And special appreciation to Joe Lelyveld. And I ask forgiveness of so many others I should have named.

At my new professional home, *The Washington Post*, I first thank Bob Kaiser, who persuaded me it would be a good idea to come over and is a man of his word, and of lots of good ideas. Thanks, too, to my old friend Dave Ignatius, who set up the whole thing; and to Ben Bradlee and Len Downie for closing the deal with warmth and panache. Karen De Young, Fred Barbash, Boyce Rensberger and Bill Hamilton have been great and tolerant editors. And Dave Broder is an inspiration to anyone who writes about politics. For welcoming me warmly and for sharing their ideas, thanks to Michael Specter, Dale Russakoff, Paul Taylor, Dan Balz, Tom Edsall, Gwen Ifill, Maralee

Schwartz, Tom Kenwothy, Jay Mathews, T.R. Reid, Ed Walsh, Jodie Allen, Mary McGrory, Steve Mufson, John Yang, Rick Atkinson, Frank Swoboda, Haynes Johson, Ann Devroy, David Hoffman, Dan Morgan, Richard Morin, Mary Hadar, Jeff Frank, Chuck Freund, Richard Cohen, Charlie Trueheart, Lynda Richardson, Laura Sessions Stepp, Eleanor Randolph, Bill Booth, Malcolm Gladwell, Molly Moore, Bob Thompson, Steve Barr, George Lardner, Curt Suplee, Mary Jordan, Howie Kurtz, Lissa Muscatine, Jill Grisco, Joyce Murdoch, Linton Weeks, and Ruth Marcus. This list is intended as suggestive, not exhaustive.

I have many debts to the academic world. Particular thanks to Seymour Martin Lipset, Steven Lukes, Michael Hill, Sam Popkin, Todd Gitlin, Leo Ribuffo, Martin Peretz, Christopher Jencks, Jane Mansbridge, Harvey Cox, Larry Sabato, Nathan Glazer, and Martin Shefter. I am grateful to Harry Boyte of Project Public Life at the University of Minnesota for the work he and his colleagues are doing for democracy, and for letting me participate in their conferences. Thanks, too, to the late Michael Harrington, an inspiring man who always conveyed excitement about the possibilities of life and politics.

To thank everyone in the world of politics who has helped me at one point or another would overburden an already overly long list. I mention here just a few people who have shared their thoughts with me at length and on many occasions: Kelly Welsh, Tom Donilon, John Buckley, the late Lee Atwater, Mandy Grunwald, Mary Matalin, Peggy Connolly, Joan Baggett, Ann Lewis, Eddie Mahe, Stan Greenberg, Linda DiVall, Bob Shrum, Kevin Phillips, Peter Hart, Haley Barbour, Paul Maslin, Carol Darr, Roger Carrick, Al From, Bob Squier, Bob Greenstein, James K. Galbraith, Bill Harriss, Jim Shannon, Doug Schoen, Fred Martin, Frank Greer, Pat Caddell, John Sasso, Ginny Terzano, Harrison Hickman, Brad Johnson, Lance Tarrance, and Bill Carrick. Thanks, also, to Newt Gingrich, Barney Frank, Steve Solarz, Chuck Schumer, and Jim Cooper. And thanks to Sid and Jackie Blumenthal, Susan Feeney, John Judis, Jane Mayer, Bill McGurn, Jim Sleeper, Richard Sauber, Bob Tyrrell, Marty Plissner, Susan Morrison, Peggy Hamburg, Warren Mitofsky, Bob Kuttner, Paul Taylor (of Reuters), Alessandra Stanley, Peter Brown, Christopher Hitchens, David Shribman, Charlie Peters, Mickey Kauss, Jim Pinkerton, Art and Lee Beltrone, and Paula Newberg.

Washington think tanks have been generous with their help. The Cato Institute opened their extensive files on libertarianism to me; thanks to Ed Crane and David Boaz. At the Ethics and Public Policy Center, George Weigel and Michael Cromartie have been most helpful; thanks especially to Mike for sharing the Center's extensive work on evangelical Christianity. At the American Enterprise Institute, particular thanks to Karlyn Keene, Patrick Glynn, Ben Wattenberg, and Michael Novak; at the Progressive Policy Institute, special thanks to Elaine Kamarck, Rob Shapiro, Bill Galston, and Will Marshall; at the Institute for Policy Studies, thanks to Bob Borosage, Roger Wilkins and Marcus Raskin; at the Economic Policy Institute, thanks to Jeff Faux; and at the Heritage Foundation, thanks to Burt Pines, Stuart Butler, and Herb Berkowitz. Thanks to editors at *The Public Interest*, *The American Prospect* and *Policy Review* for help with sources. Thanks also to the many helpful friends in *The Washinton Post* News Research Center.

In finishing up, I leaned heavily on several friends with whom I thrashed out ideas, often to the financial benefit of AT&T: Terry Eastland, who was finishing his own book at the time; Joe Klein, who read through most of the manuscript; Peter and Peggy Steinfels, close and faithful friends; Fred Siegel and Jan Rosenberg, who understand things that most of us don't; and Jo-Ann Mort, a poet and an organizer.

There is no way to give adequate thanks to Dotty Lynch, a gifted analyst of polling and politics, but more important, as good a friend as anyone could ever have. We talked over just about every page in this book, and lots of other stuff, too. Special thanks to Dotty and Carol Darr for checking the text.

My agent, Kathy Robbins, prodded and encouraged and was helpful in every imaginable way. At Simon and Schuster, Alice Mayhew is exactly as great and gifted as everyone says she is. A writer could not ask for more care and attention, for better criticism, for a clearer sense of what works and what doesn't, for more intelligence or enthusiasm. I am deeply grateful. George Hodgman has been consistently helpful, patient, warm, and smart. And thanks to Adelle Stan, for many kindnesses and much good advice, and at Touchstone I am grateful to the gifted Heidi von Schreiner, who kept me from making false choices in the paperback edition.

At the end of this long list, the one person I find impossible to thank is Mary Boyle. I could thank her for giving the book its title, which she did. I could thank her for making me throw away parts of the book that didn't work, which she also did. I could thank her for urging me *not* to throw away other parts of the book. I could thank her for encouraging me to write most of this book in the countryside outside of Charlottesville, Va., which was one of the most blessed experiences of my life. I could thank her for introducing me to Cass Sunstein's ideas about civic republicanism. I could thank her for having all those dinners with me at Duner's.

I could come up with a better and completely different list, of course, but it still wouldn't do her justice. So instead of thanking Mary, I thank the folks who laid plans for the Washington, D.C. Metro system and decided to locate a stop at Woodley Park, which is where I met Mary Boyle one Easter Sunday afternoon. Never has anyone owed more than I do to an agency of government.

E. J. DIONNE, JR.
Keswick, Va.-Washington, D.C.

INDEX

abortion, 18, 26, 53, 200, 325, 341–43, 364, 365
    Americans' ambivalence about, 19, 341–42
    Carter's compromise on, 134, 227
    federal financing of, for poor women, 134, 139
    feminists' individualized approach to, 112
    as issue in elections of 1988, 303, 311, 312, 316
    as issue in elections of 1990, 341–42
    as issue in gubernatorial campaigns, 292
    Reagan's position on, 237, 239, 252, 289, 290
    Religious Right and, 224, 227, 230, 236, 237, 239, 289, 290
    Supreme Court decisions on, 109, 205, 230, 289–90
    and values of prolife vs. prochoice women, 107–8
Abortion and the Politics of Motherhood (Luker), 107–8
Acheson, Dean, 57
Adams, Abigail, 100
Adams, Henry, 156
Adams, John, 100, 156
"Adventures of Ozzie & Harriet, The," 223
affirmative action, 97, 99, 183, 336, 364, 373
    burden of, borne by lower-and middle-class white males, 61, 94
    for convention delegates, 49
    and metaphor of shackled runner, 90–91
    neoconservatives' critique of, 69–70, 74
Afghanistan, Soviet invasion of (1979), 132
African-Americans, *see* black Americans
Agnew, Spiro T., 186, 193, 199
Aid for Families with Dependent Children (AFDC), 95–96, 254–55
AIDS, 100, 115
alcohol, Prohibition and, 210, 214, 215, 266
Amateur Democrat, The (Wilson), 45
Ambrose, Stephen E., 133, 171, 172, 175, 190–91, 192

"America First—And Second and Third" (Buchanan), 319
American Civil Liberties Union (ACLU), 311, 314
American Council of Christian Churches (ACCC), 216
American Enterprise Institute, 229
American Jewish Committee, 240
American Prospect, 335, 344
Americans for Democratic Action, 117
America's Quest for the Ideal Self (Clecak), 41
anarchism, 36
Anarchy, State, and Utopia (Nozick), 271–72
Anderson, John, 139, 140, 207, 253, 276, 277
anti-Americanism, antiwar movement and, 51–52
anticommunism, 132, 181
    collapse of Soviet Union and, 361
    conservatism and, 67, 68, 152, 158, 160, 161–64, 165, 167, 169, 172, 176, 192, 197–98, 201, 230, 236, 262, 267, 268, 269, 274, 304, 318–19
    end-of-ideology thesis and, 58
    fundamentalism and, 209, 216–17
    fusionist consensus and, 160, 161–64, 165, 167, 169
    Kennedy's emphasis on, 42–43, 176
    liberalism associated with, 33–34, 43, 45, 47, 56, 57, 163–64
    neoconservatism and, 56, 57, 58, 71, 72
    New Left's abandonment of, 32, 33–34, 45
    Nixon's reversal and, 197–98
    of Vital Center, 117, 118
anti-Semitism, 158, 159, 165, 211, 318, 336
antistatism, *see* libertarianism, libertarians
antiwar movement, 37, 43–44, 53, 189, 198, 350
    anti-Americanism of, 51–52
    Democratic Party transformed by, 45–48, 49
    Democrats and liberals blamed for, 51–52
    neoconservatism and, 57, 64–65

428 / INDEX

Congress, U.S. (*cont.*)
  contra aid and, 287, 288
  debate on Iraq crisis in, 22
  Eisenhower's relations with, 170, 171, 174
  electoral results and, 12, 48, 123–24, 322, 324, 345
  globalism and, 362
  taxes and, 143, 250–51
  Vietnam War and, 47, 265, 284
  see also House of Representatives, U.S.; Senate, U.S.
Congress for Cultural Freedom, 58
Congress of Freedom, 158
Congress of Industrial Organizations (CIO), 47
Connally, John, 197, 202, 231, 234
Connolly, William, 52, 93–94
Conscience of a Conservative, The (Goldwater), 169
consensus politics, 36, 50
conservatism, conservatives, 24–27, 28, 44, 55, 56, 60, 61, 62, 66, 89, 100, 114–15, 118, 138, 139, 140, 144, 145–326, 344, 345–46, 347, 348, 358, 361
  anti-intellectualism of, 64
  antistatism of, 147, 148, 149–50, 152–154, 161, 163, 167; *see also* libertarianism, libertarians
  betrayed by Republican Party, 151, 162
  Bush presidency affected by conflicts in, 26, 317–21, 361
  Carter presidency and, 132, 134, 135–136, 137, 142
  and end of ideology, 371
  failure of, 11–15, 23, 363
  feminism and, 98–99, 109, 292–94, 339, 340
  flaws in world-view of, 324–25
  "Frank Capra values" and, 369
  fusionist consensus and, *see* fusionism
  impasse in (late 1980s), 283–99
  intellectual rebirth of (1940s-1950s), 24–25, 152–57
  interventionism-isolationism battle and, 161–64, 165, 167, 318–19
  judicial strategy of, 291–92
  libertarians' breakaway from, 264–69
  libertarian-traditionalist contradiction in, 25–26, 157, 159, 160–61, 241, 261–62, 263–64, 273–74, 282, 284, 286, 291
  limitations of, 26, 27
  Modern Republicanism and, 170–208; *see also* Modern Republicanism
  neoconservatism's move toward, 62, 64–65, 66–73
  neoconservative-paleoconservative conflict and, 318–19

New Left and, 24, 35–37, 50, 52–54, 64
"profamily" movement of, 106, 109–14, 339–40
racial politics and, 78–79, 81, 86, 87, 93, 94, 95–96, 97, 165–66, 336
as reactionaries lacking clear body of doctrine, 151–52
Reagan as leader in revival of, 228, 231–32
redemptive remnant theory and, 150–151, 152
Religious Right and, 209–41
as Republican Party's nominating wing, 302
Republican Party takeover attempted by (1960s), 176–86
supply-side economics and, 242–58; *see also* supply-side economics
suspicious of ethic of "public good," 332–33
and tenuousness of constituencies, 17–18
Thomas nomination and, 363–64, 365
trade policies and, 361
and transformations within communist world, 21–22, 361–62, 370
weakness of, in elections of 1988, 312, 315–16
weakness of, in postwar period, 147–52
welfare reform and, 367
and women's entry into work force, 18, 19, 106, 339
see also neoconservatism, neoconservatives; *specific topics*
Conservatism Revisited (Viereck), 168–69
Conservative Mind, The (Kirk), 156
Conservative Party, 186, 199
consumerism, 70
consumption taxes, 320, 321
Containment and Change (Oglesby), 37
contras, 287–88
Coolidge, Calvin, 176, 249, 251, 255, 286
corporations, New Left's attacks on, 37, 43
"Cosby Show, The," 238
Cost of Good Intentions, The (Morris), 245
Council for a Competitive Economy, 273
counterculture, 31, 32, 38–42, 50, 98, 116, 223, 240, 266, 334
  beats and, 38–39
  doctrines of, used by conservatives, 53–54
  drug use in, 32, 40, 53
  neoconservatives' disdain for, 39, 62, 70, 74, 75
  New Left and, 33, 38–42, 53
  religion and, 220
  rock 'n' roll and, 38, 39–40

Huntington, Samuel P., 63, 178, 203,
399n

Ideas Have Consequences (Weaver), 152,
154
ideology, end of, 371–72
If I Had a Hammer (Isserman), 33
immigrants, 366
imperialism, 43–44
In Defense of Freedom (Meyer), 160, 265
individualism, 142, 155, 165, 314, 334
family politics and, 109–13, 115
in libertarianism, 262–63, 268, 272,
275–76
industrial revolution, 101, 104, 105, 213
inflation, 131–32, 141, 243–45, 246, 247,
248–49, 253, 283
"In Praise of Decadence" (Riggenbach),
262–63
Inquiry, 273, 276
insider trading, 256
Institute for Humane Studies, 273
integration, 11, 21, 97, 125, 165
Black Power and, 85, 86
white working-class enclaves' resistance
to, 92–93
Intercollegiate Society of Individualists
(ISI), 264
interest-group politics, 68, 127
Carter and, 142–43, 144
neoconservatives' views on, 58, 69–70
interest rates, 131, 132, 227
Iran, 133
hostage crisis in, 131, 132, 137–38, 227,
287
Iran-contra scandal, 287–88, 302, 310
Iraq, Kuwait invaded by (1990), 22, 350
see also Persian Gulf War
"Isaiah's Job" (Nock), 150–51
Islam, 59
isolationism, 37, 117, 161–62
libertarians' revival of, 261, 262, 263,
265, 267, 268–69, 270
rebirth of (1990s), 318–19
Israel, 137, 318
Isserman, Maurice, 33
Italy, 59, 149
It's a Wonderful Life, 369

Jackson, Henry "Scoop," 66–67, 125, 126,
132, 195, 245
Jackson, Jesse, 49, 306–7, 308, 310
Jaffa, Harry, 178
Japan, 10, 22, 256, 313, 331, 347, 349,
351, 358, 361, 370, 372
Javits, Jacob K., 175, 187–88, 190, 195
Jefferson, Thomas, 292
Jehovah's Witnesses, 314
Jencks, Christopher, 335

Jesus movement, 220
Jews, 137, 214, 218, 219
anti-Semitism and, 158, 159, 165, 211,
318, 336
Carter's religiosity and, 225, 227
John Birch Society, 165, 191, 273
Johnson, Lyndon B., 125, 136, 186, 197,
200, 202, 251, 346
Eisenhower administration and, 174
in elections of 1964, 119, 123, 234
racial politics and, 34, 69, 81, 82, 86,
90–91
Vietnam War and, 43, 46, 198
John XXIII, Pope, 38
Jordan, Hamilton, 225
judiciary, 204, 291–92, 332
see also Supreme Court, U.S.
Judis, John B., 158–59, 191
Justice, Gender and the Family (Okin),
340–41
Justice Department, U.S., 236

Kaiser, Charles, 39–40
Kamarck, Elaine Ciulla, 418n
Kanawha County, W.Va., protests
against school textbooks in, 222–23
Kansas City Star, 215
Kaufman, Arnold, 34–35, 46, 48
Kellman, Steven, 389
Kellogg, Susan, 101, 102, 103, 113
Kemp, Jack, 27, 71, 251–52, 301, 304,
305, 362
Kemp-Roth tax bill, 251
Kennedy, Edward M., 47, 48, 137, 138,
139, 140, 237, 245
Kennedy, John F., 119, 136, 143, 197,
252, 308, 356
in elections of 1960, 117, 131, 175, 177–
178, 182, 185, 193, 218–19, 225
foreign policy of, 42–43, 71, 176
New Left and, 34, 35–37, 50
religion issue and, 218–19, 225
Religious Right and, 232–33
tax cut proposed by, 251
Kennedy, Paul, 349
Kennedy, Robert F., 46, 48, 121, 138
"Kennedy or Nixon: Does It Make a
Difference?" (Schlesinger), 117
Kerner Commission, 88
Kerouac, Jack, 38–39
Kerrey, Bob, 368
Kerry, John, 48
Keynes, John Maynard, 248
Keynesian economics, 43, 149, 150, 195,
243, 244, 247–50, 255, 258, 281
apparent failure of (1970s), 248–49
principles behind, 247–48, 249–50
Khrushchev, Nikita, 33
Kilpatrick, James Jackson, 165

Liberal Tradition in America, The
(Hartz), 150
libertarianism, libertarians, 54, 190, 230,
238, 241, 291, 292, 294, 299, 301, 326,
350
academic philosophy and, 271–72
and breakaway from conservatism,
264–69
within Democratic Party, 270–71, 276–
280
elections of 1980 and, 275–76, 277, 278
and erosion of traditional values, 262–
263
and flight from public life, 281–82
fusionist consensus and, *see* fusionism
impact of, 280–82
institutions of, 273, 276
intellectual basis for, 152–54
interventionist foreign policy opposed
by, 261, 262, 263, 265, 267, 268–69,
270, 273, 274, 319
as latent and unconscious ideology
among young voters, 261
"left-wing" deviationism of, 273–74
Maddox-Lilie electoral analysis and,
276–79
of neoconservatism, 74
of New Left, 74
Reagan and, 260, 263, 284
rebirth of (1980s), 259–82
within Republican Party, 276–80
of Stockman, 285, 286
supply-side economics and, 243
as threat to fusionism, 261
traditional conservatives' conflict with,
25–26, 157, 159, 160–61, 241, 261–62,
263–64, 273–74, 282, 284, 286, 291
welfare state and, 271–72
Libertarian Party, 260, 261, 269, 274–75
Libertarian Review, 262–63, 273, 276
liberty, 330
Libya, bombing of, 287, 308
Lieberman, Joseph, 27
Life, 103
Lilie, Stuart A., 261, 276–79, 280
Lilla, Mark, 62, 333
"Limits of Social Policy, The" (Glazer),
60
"limousine liberals," 79
Lincoln, Abraham, 187
Lindsay, John V., 79, 89, 186, 189, 191
Lippmann, Walter, 212
Lipset, Seymour Martin, 58–59
Lodge, George Cabot, 47
Lonely Crowd, The (Riesman), 178
Long, Huey, 252
Long, Russell, 196
Los Angeles Herald-Examiner, 246
Losing Ground (Murray), 95–96, 114

Lubell, Samuel, 164
Luce, Henry, 158
Lukens, Donald "Buzz," 186–87
Luker, Kristin, 107–8

MacBride, Roger, 269
McCarthy, Eugene, 46, 47, 48, 189
McCarthy, Joseph R., 64, 67, 117, 158,
164, 168, 170, 172, 201, 228
McCloskey, Paul, 199
McGovern, George, 57, 124, 125, 126,
133, 142, 201, 279, 314, 319
background of, 119
and collapse of Vital Center, 118, 119–
123
in elections of 1972, 66, 119–23, 127,
128, 129, 177, 198, 199, 224, 228, 234,
269, 278
neoconservatives and, 66–67
nominating procedures reformed by,
48–49
upper middle-class interests and, 12, 25
McGovern Commission, 48–49
Machen, J. Gresham, 212
McIntire, Carl, 216, 218
Macmillan, Harold, 172, 203
macroeconomics, 256
McWilliams, Wilson Carey, 253
Maddox, William S., 261, 276–79, 280
Madison, James, 58
Madonna, 239
Magaziner, Ira, 256
Magnuson, Warren, 142, 195
Mann, Tom, 323
Mao Zedong, 64
*Marathon: The Pursuit of the Presidency
1972–1976* (Witcover), 206–7
Marcuse, Herbert, 50, 85
marijuana, 205
Marsden, George M., 210
Marshall, George C., 170
Marshall, T. H., 353
Marshall Plan, 163
Marx, Karl, 33, 36, 50, 263, 347
Marxism, 60, 64, 151, 153, 243, 247, 285,
352
Massachusetts:
prison-furlough program in, 301, 311,
315
transformation of liberalism in, 47–48
Massachusetts Political Action for Peace
(Mass Pax), 48
mass media, 230
New Left and, 44
Religious Right and, 215–16, 223, 237–
238, 239–40
mass politics, 58
mass society, 58
materialism, 32, 154

Nader, Ralph, 51, 63, 134
Nash, George H., 61, 67, 68, 149, 152, 168, 269, 393n
Nathan, Tonie, 269
Nation, 158
National Association of Evangelicals (NAE), 216
National Association of Manufacturers, 150
National Committee for a Sane Nuclear Policy, 167–68
National Council of Churches, 213
National Endowment for the Humanities, 237
National Federation of Young Republicans, 177
National Interest, 319
nationalism, 59, 187, 195, 231–32, 361
  economic, 307–8, 310, 312–13
Nationalist Christian Crusade, 158
National Opinion Research Center, 136
National Review, 25, 35, 64, 154, 157, 172, 178, 217, 270, 318, 344
  founding of, 158–59
  fusionist consensus and, 159, 160, 161, 162, 164–65, 166–69, 241, 242, 261–262, 263, 264, 282, 301
  libertarians' conflict with, 166–69, 261–262, 263, 265, 266, 267, 269, 273–74
  New Right's challenge to dominance of, 228–30
  Nixon and, 191, 192, 228
  Religious Right and, 232–33
National Socialism, 152–53
Native Americans, 69, 89
nativism, 318
Nazism, 152–53, 163
negative campaigning, 15, 16, 17, 26, 117, 305, 317, 363
negative income tax, 188, 196
neoconservatism, neoconservatives, 23, 24, 55–76, 118, 122, 126, 144, 183, 190, 326
  angry urban whites and, 65–66
  anticommunism and, 56, 57, 58, 71, 72
  antistatist libertarianism of, 74
  capitalism advocated by, 70–71
  counterculture disdained by, 39, 62, 70, 74, 75
  defection of, from liberalism, 55–57
  drift to right of, 62, 64–65, 66–73
  end-of-ideology thesis and, 58–60
  first visible as movement in domestic politics, 57–58
  foreign policy of 1970s and, 71–73
  Goldwater as viewed by, 67–68
  interest-group pluralism as viewed by, 58, 69–70
  key terms and concepts in, 57–60

liberalism undermined by, 73–76
liberal programs critiqued by, 23, 24, 56, 60–64, 69, 73–76, 144
"new class" of reformers as elite enemy of, 63–64, 74
organizational achievements of, 73
origins of term, 55–56
paleoconservatives' conflict with, 318–319
Religious Right and, 237
roots of, 57
social policy critiqued by, 60–64, 65, 69, 73–76
Neuhaus, Richard John, 111, 220, 221, 226, 318
New American Right, The (Bell), 67
New Breed, 270
New Christianity, 213–14
"new class," 63–64, 74, 79, 122, 123
New Conservatism, 156–57, 168
New Deal, 17, 25, 27, 57, 67, 79, 91, 116, 123, 139, 151, 158, 195, 215, 246, 265, 275, 279, 285, 286, 353
  Carter and politics of, 127, 131, 141, 245
  conservatives' accommodation to, 171, 172, 173, 178
  libertarian Democrats' breakaway from, 270, 271
  national interest as perceived in, 142, 333
  party aligned with, 174, 187
  socialism and, 259–60, 261
  supply-side economics and, 247, 249, 251, 252
  World War II and, 147–49, 244
New Deal coalition, 12, 45, 141, 243, 244
New Deal liberalism, 124, 127, 164, 168, 245, 284, 314
New Democrats, 270–71
Newfield, Jack, 34
New Frontier, 35, 88
New Individualist Review, 166–68, 264–265, 266–67, 273
New Left, 31–54, 59, 85, 93, 118, 144, 159, 176, 178, 203, 268, 319, 326, 330, 361, 369
  alienated conformism combatted by, 35, 36, 40
  antiwar movement and, 43–44, 45–48, 49, 51–52, 57, 64–65
  civil rights movement and, 34, 50–51
  communitarian values of, 36, 40
  conservatives' borrowings from, 52–54
  conservatives' mistrust of, 64
  counterculture and, 33, 38–42, 53
  and Democratic Party's shift to left, 45–49
  elitism ascribed to, 49–50

Reichard, Gary W., 171
Reichley, A. James, 216
Reid, Ogden, 189
Reinhard, David, 175
Reinventing Government (Osborne and Gaebler), 369
religion, 150, 366
  cultural accommodations of, 217–18, 220–21
  freedom of, 265
  increased interest in (1950s), 217–18
  libertarianism and, 265, 266
  revival of (late 1960s-early 1970s), 221–222
  and separation of church and state, 210, 225, 227
  see also evangelicalism, evangelicals; fundamentalism, fundamentalists; Roman Catholicism, Roman Catholics
Religious Right, 25–26, 209–41, 242–43, 301, 331
  accomplishments of, 236–40
  Bush and, 236, 303, 304
  Carter and, 224–27
  elections of 1972 and, 234
  elections of 1980 and, 230–31, 232, 233–35
  elections of 1984 and, 211, 236
  fears about, 211–12, 233–34
  friendly relations between conservative Roman Catholics and, 219, 224
  goals of, 240–41
  history of, 212–24
  inflamed by liberal victories in Supreme Court, 224
  libertarianism and, 263, 282
  mass media and, 215–16, 223, 237–38, 239–40
  New Right and, 227, 230–32
  power ascribed to, 232, 233–35, 236
  Reagan and, 237, 238, 239, 240–41, 289–91, 304
  scandals in, 239–40
  school textbooks protested by, 222–223
  in shift to Republican Party, 234, 235–236
  sixties culture and, 218, 219–23
  see also evangelicalism, evangelicals; fundamentalism, fundamentalists
Religious Roundtable, 211
religious schools, government aid to, 224
republicanism, 354
Republican Looks at His Party, A (Larson), 172
Republican National Conventions:
  of 1940, 181
  of 1952, 182
  of 1964, 177, 178–79, 181
  of 1968, 193
  of 1976, 206
Republican Party, Republicans, 12, 15, 17, 25, 31, 72, 73, 104, 114, 118, 142, 162, 163, 232, 239, 241, 286–87, 289, 344–45, 361
  breakdown of, 136–37
  Bush's tax package and, 320, 321, 359
  conservatism betrayed by, 151, 162
  conservative challenge to take control of (1960s), 176–86
  Democratic Party's reform rules and, 49
  dynamics of nominating politics in, 302
  economy and, 244, 245, 251
  elections of 1968 and, 77, 78, 79–80
  elections of 1980 and, 138–39, 140, 277
  elections of 1988 and, 300–305, 310–16
  elections of 1989 and, 292–93
  elections of 1990 and, 321–23
  feminism and, 109
  libertarian tendencies within, 276–80
  loyalty tradition in, 302
  Modern Republicanism and, 170–208; *see also* Modern Republicanism
  neoconservatives' shift to, 66–73
  racial politics and, 77, 78–79, 81, 93, 94
  realignment of power in (1964), 180–83
  Religious Right and, 234, 235–36
  resurgence of (1940s), 148
  in Senate, 364, 365
  in South, 12, 166, 180–83, 184–85, 192–193, 206
"responsibility-ism," 359
revenue sharing, 188, 189, 194, 195–96
Rhodes, Jim, 185
Ribuffo, Leo P., 117, 131, 137, 227
Rieder, Jonathan, 79, 93, 94
Riesman, David, 178
Riggenbach, Jeff, 53–54, 262–63, 270
Riley, Robert T., 91
Ripon Society, 184–85, 188–90, 196, 200, 208
Rise of the Unmeltable Ethnics, The (Novak), 88
Road to Serfdom, The (Hayek), 152–53
Robertson, Rev. Pat, 211, 223, 238–39
  in elections of 1988, 241, 301, 304, 305, 312
rock 'n' roll, 38, 39–40, 53
Rockefeller, Nelson, 181, 184, 186, 191, 192, 193, 206
Rockefeller, Winthrop, 186
Rockford Institute, 318, 319
Roe v. Wade, 224, 227, 230

About the Author

E. J. Dionne, Jr., grew up in Fall River, Massachusetts. He graduated from Harvard University and received his doctorate from Oxford, where he was a Rhodes Scholar. He writes for *The Washington Post* and was previously a reporter for *The New York Times*. He has reported from all over the United States and five continents, including stints in Paris, Rome, and Beirut. He lives in Washington, D.C.